Clfr 13-Ell-

Advance Praise for
Faith in the Halls of Power:
How Evangelicals Joined the American Elite

"*Faith in the Halls of Power* is an extraordinary, definitive examination of evangelical participation in American cultural and political affairs. Lindsay brings a gift for thoughtful, clear writing to bear on an impressive amount of research, and the entire project is guided by a sincere and refreshing effort to be fair. It sparkles with insight."

> —Frederica Mathewes-Green, columnist for Beliefnet.com
> and author of *Facing East: A Pilgrim's Journey*
> *into the Mysteries of Orthodoxy*

"Who are those evangelicals? Where did they come from? And what do they intend to do with our country? Such questions asked by innumerable Americans receive in this book a response that is both sympathetic and critical. Michael Lindsay puts all of us into his debt with this thoughtful analysis of the rise of a new center of leadership in our public life."

> —The Rev. Richard John Neuhaus, Editor-in-Chief,
> *First Things*

"An outstanding book. If more proof were needed that simple stereotypes about American evangelicals, whether from Left or Right, are inadequate, this book supplies it abundantly."

> —Mark Noll, author of *America's God*

"Given the confusion and misunderstanding surrounding the evangelical movement in the U.S., Michael Lindsay has produced a work of lasting importance. A keen and disciplined researcher of the religious scene, Lindsay has drawn upon hundreds of personal interviews with evangelical leaders representing the power centers of politics, academe, entertainment, and business. He brings readers a clear and authentic account of the extent to which evangelicals are changing America."

> —George Gallup, Jr., Founding Chairman,
> The George H. Gallup International Institute

"Evangelicals are sometimes painted as complete morons; sometimes they're marginalized, sometimes demonized, sometimes ignored. Seldom are they presented as a multifaceted movement with texture, tension, depth, and even paradox. Michael Lindsay strikes the needed balance and presents 'the state of the union' for evangelicals in the U.S."

> —Brian McLaren, author of *A New Kind of Christian*

"Michael Lindsay's new book gives us a strikingly lively account of American evangelicalism at a time when an elite that was once largely closed to evangelicals now includes them in significant numbers. He makes it clear that evangelicalism is a diverse phenomenon, even in some respects an amorphous one, but in one regard, devotion to radical individualism, evangelicals are more similar to than different from other Americans. In this crucial respect they cannot be considered counter-cultural, which may be encouraging or depressing news depending on one's point of view."

—Robert Bellah, co-author of *Habits of the Heart*

"Drawing on hundreds of personal interviews, Michael Lindsay has richly captured what C. Wright Mills would have never seen a half-century ago—but has now become a potent pillar of America's 'power elite.' United by faith and friendship, evangelicals have built the networks, acquired the assets, and embraced the calling to remake American politics and culture. *Faith in the Halls of Power* is a compelling portrait of one of the most far-reaching but least appreciated social transformations of our time."

—Michael Useem, Professor of Management and Director
of the Center for Leadership and Change, Wharton School,
University of Pennsylvania

"The stereotype of evangelical Christians as uneducated, rural, and culturally marginal has been slow to break down. Yet evangelicals are prominent among political and economic power brokers, active in cultural production, and increasingly well represented among elite university students. Michael Lindsay does a large service by tracing the extent and pathways of this change. He shows an incorporation into the American 'mainstream' that is changing not only U.S. society at large but also the evangelical movement that has long seen itself as marginalized. That so many have been slow to see the pattern of change makes his book all the more welcome."

—Craig Calhoun, University Professor of the Social Sciences,
New York University

"Whether you are a disgruntled evangelical who sometimes fears that the media's caricature of evangelicals is true or a skeptic who dismisses evangelicals as members of the flat-earth society—or something in between—this is the book for you! Through D. Michael Lindsay's first-rate scholarship, we are given a fair and accurate account of who evangelicals really are and how they have influenced our culture for the good. In our age of divisiveness and distrust, this is a welcome contribution."

—Rebecca Manley Pippert, author of *Hope Has
Its Reasons* and *Out of the Salt Shaker*

FAITH IN THE HALLS OF POWER

FAITH IN THE
HALLS OF POWER

How Evangelicals

Joined the American Elite

D. MICHAEL LINDSAY

OXFORD
UNIVERSITY PRESS

2007

OXFORD
UNIVERSITY PRESS

Oxford University Press, Inc., publishes works that further
Oxford University's objective of excellence
in research, scholarship, and education.

Oxford   New York
Auckland   Cape Town   Dar es Salaam   Hong Kong   Karachi
Kuala Lumpur   Madrid   Melbourne   Mexico City   Nairobi
New Delhi   Shanghai   Taipei   Toronto

With offices in
Argentina   Austria   Brazil   Chile   Czech Republic   France   Greece
Guatemala   Hungary   Italy   Japan   Poland   Portugal   Singapore
South Korea   Switzerland   Thailand   Turkey   Ukraine   Vietnam

Copyright © 2007 by D. Michael Lindsay

Published by Oxford University Press, Inc.
198 Madison Avenue, New York, NY 10016
www.oup.com

Oxford is a registered trademark of Oxford University Press

Library of Congress Cataloging-in-Publication Data
Lindsay, D. Michael.
Faith in the halls of power : how evangelicals joined the American elite /
by D. Michael Lindsay.
p. cm.
Includes bibliographical references.
ISBN 978-0-19-532666-6
1. Evangelicalism—United States—History.
2. Elite (Social sciences)—United States—History.   I. Title.
BR1642.U5L56 2007
277.3'083—dc22   2007004790

1 3 5 7 9 8 6 4 2

Printed in the United States of America
on acid-free paper

To Rebecca and Elizabeth

CONTENTS

PREFACE

I WAS SITTING AT MY DESK at the Gallup Institute when the phone rang. "What are the figures on the rising number of evangelicals since the 1970s?" asked the journalist on the other end of the line. I had been asked the question before. Most people assumed that the number of evangelicals had grown dramatically since Jimmy Carter ran for president. Though evangelicals had been an important part of America's past, until Carter referred to himself as "born again" on the campaign trail, they were not seen as very important to America's present and even less so to its future. We have since learned otherwise, but most people assume that the rising prominence of American evangelicalism is a result of burgeoning numbers: Evangelicals are more prominent because there are more of them.

The reality, though, is that the number of evangelicals in this country has remained remarkably stable since the 1970s. In 1976, when Gallup first asked the American public if they were "born again," 35 percent of U.S. adults said yes. Twenty years later, the figure had inched up to 39 percent. In 2006, 41 percent of adults in this country described themselves on the Gallup Poll as "born again," or evangelical. If their numbers are not swelling considerably, then something else must explain the rise of evangelicalism within the nation's higher circles. That is the purpose of this book.

My interest in the role of faith in American public life began as a college student, but it was during my tenure at Gallup that I became particularly interested in the evangelical movement. For the last ten years, I have been thinking about American evangelicalism and its rising prominence in different parts of our society. I spent the last five years actively examining this subject by conducting hundreds of in-depth interviews and analyzing thousands of pages of data. This book is the culmination of that research.

The first leader I interviewed was Richard Mouw, president of Fuller Theological Seminary. He agreed to meet with me because

he knew my graduate school advisor, who wrote an e-mail introduction on my behalf. At the end of my two hours with Mouw, I
asked him to introduce me to some of his peers. Within a few
months I had interviewed thirty prominent evangelicals. Eventually,
I interviewed 157 leaders of evangelical institutions—pastors at
large churches, college and seminary presidents, and heads of organizations within the evangelical world. At the end of the interview, I would ask these interviewees to identify public leaders whose
faith was an important aspect of their life. Since these institutional
leaders headed evangelical-leaning organizations, most of their recommendations were individuals who either would identify as "evangelical" or who were very familiar with the evangelical movement.
Most even volunteered to help me secure contact details or request
an interview with the people they recommended. Because of these
personal connections, many public leaders who would not normally
grant a university researcher an hour-long interview agreed to talk
to me. This technique, which I call the "leapfrog" method, is detailed more fully in the appendix, where I also provide detailed
information on the methodology employed while researching this
book. My big break came from Daniel Vestal—the head of the Cooperative Baptist Fellowship and the father of a college friend of
mine—who is a close friend of President Jimmy Carter. I asked Vestal to put in a good word for me with President Carter's staff, and
within days someone from the Carter Center called to set up the
interview.

Over the three years I spent collecting data, I took twenty-eight
transcontinental trips and logged over three hundred thousand
miles. I traveled to seventy-two different places, from Boston to San
Diego and from Seattle to Miami. When funds ran low, family
members donated frequent flier miles and hotel points that allowed
me to keep going. I interviewed people in their offices and homes,
restaurants and coffee shops, hotel lobbies and conference centers.
Some interviews were warm and personable, with participants introducing me to family members. Others were more distant and
formal. Across all of them, I sought to learn more than just what
leaders had to say. I studied the ways they presented themselves,
their interactions with others, and the informal cues they dropped
during our time together. Some wanted to know more about me,
my background, and my interest in the topic. But most were willing
to talk even without that information, largely because they trusted
the person who introduced us. I am also convinced that some people agreed to be interviewed simply because I was willing to wait for
them. The leaders studied in this project work extremely long hours,

but I was willing to wait months, sometimes years, for an interview. Persistence and patience paid off in the end. In essence, personal connections—often helped by the kindness of mere acquaintances—were essential.

The novelty of this study also played a role. Dozens of leaders mentioned that they had never been interviewed about their faith, and many of them said they had been looking for a chance to weigh in on some of these matters. This, of course, means that some of them—probably most of them—had a point they were trying to make, an organization they wanted me to mention, or a personal legacy they wanted to help craft. Without being obsequious or overly intrusive—impulses that I felt at various moments during the project—I have attempted to convey their humanity and the complexity of their religious identities. While working on the book, I followed the "critical empathy" approach of Marie Griffith, the historian of American religion. According to her, critical empathy means communicating as accurately as possible the perspectives articulated by the people I interviewed while also applying broader analytical interpretations and the critical perspectives offered by others—both inside and outside the group—to what I studied. As she writes in *God's Daughters,* "The lived worlds of human experience, after all, are not identical to people's descriptions of these worlds." As a result, I try to recount both the content and the spirit of what various people told me, but I also reserve the right to comment on what they are *not* saying in these accounts and to point to inconsistencies and unintended consequences that flow from their actions. In the end, they may not agree with all of my conclusions, but I hope they will sense my earnest desire to present a full, balanced perspective with all of the subtlety and complexity of the lives they lead and the worlds they inhabit.

In addition to the interviews, I attended numerous meetings where evangelical leaders were in attendance. These included board meetings of large evangelical institutions, conferences for evangelical donors, retreats, and strategy sessions involving evangelical leaders. Finally, I conducted archival research on 110 evangelical organizations, programs, and initiatives. Annual statements, financial reports, correspondence with donors and external constituents, media coverage of particular groups, and internal documents provided by organizational leaders all yielded helpful information. I used these to investigate not only their missions, goals, and strategies but also the resources at their disposal and the challenges they faced.

Undertaking this kind of study on public leadership and faith required the assistance of many knowledgeable sources. I am especially grateful for the time and energy of a select group of people who particularly understand the evangelical world and helped me understand it. For being generous with their expertise and insights, I thank this special group that includes Bob Buford, Corey Cleek, Andy Crouch, Kate Harris, Peb Jackson, David Lyle Jeffrey, Gabe Lyons, Richard Mouw, Roxanne Robbins, Mark Rodgers, David Wills, and Sean Womack. A larger group offered their help to secure interviews with individuals whose participation was particularly important. I am grateful for their willingness to contact people they knew through a variety of ways—as college roommates, business associates, church friends, and others—on my behalf. More important, I appreciate the encouragement they offered in both word and deed at critical moments during the data collection process. Thanks go to Thomas G. Addington, Robert Andringa, Evan Baehr, Matt Bennett, Tom Billings, Doug Burleigh, Richard Capen, Stanley Carlson-Thies, Jennifer Chapin, Sarah Coakley, Gary Cook, Sandy Corbitt, Michael Cromartie, Shannon Sedgwick Davis, India and Ron Dennis, Dave Dias, Jenny and Peet Dickinson, Don Eberly, Abigail and Ryan Frederick, Steven French, Jacquelline Fuller, Brian and Christy Gardner, Robert George, Marcie Gold, Stephen R. Graves, Eric Gregory, Duane Grobman, Chip Hardwick, Daryl Heald, Jerry Himes, J. Douglas Holladay, Dale E. Jones, Jennifer and Dano Jukanovich, Dustin Kidd, Mary King, Fritz Kling, David Kuo, Linda Lader, Drew Ladner, Katherine Leary, Jerome Loughridge, Glenn Lucke, Jan and Scott Luley, Allan MacArthur, Mike Marker, Joe Maxwell, Matt McIlwain, Mac McQuiston, Marilee Melvin and the Wheaton College Alumni Association, Edmund C. Moy, Paul Mundey, Chuck Neder, Paul E. Nelson, David Oakley, Ryon Paton, Tim Philpot, John Porter, Paul Robbins, David Robinson, Lynn Robinson, Skip Ryan, Dorothy and Burnett Sams, Chris Seiple, Scott Sheldon, Karl Singer, James Skillen, Margaret Slusher, Kevin Small, Brad Smith, Catherine and Chris Smith, Fred Smith Jr., Janet Smith, Julie Sulc, Joshua Trent, Jonelle and Britt Tucker, Ralph Veerman, Daniel Vestal, Ken Wales, Howe Whitman, and Jeremy Wynne. I also thank the dozens of close friends and family members who helped me throughout the project. Finally, I am grateful to the 360 people who graciously shared their stories of faith and leadership with me. Without their participation, I would have nothing to say. Although they may disagree with some of my points, I hope they will sense the respect and careful attention with which I have aimed to retell their stories. For the many kind gestures they showed me, I am deeply grateful.

My research benefited from the support of several individuals and institutions. I gratefully acknowledge grants from the Earhart

Foundation, Mustard Seed Foundation, National Science Foundation, Society for the Scientific Study of Religion, and Religious Research Association. Significant financial support was also provided by the Center for the Study of Religion, Center for Arts and Cultural Policy Studies, and Department of Sociology, all of Princeton University. Friends and colleagues offered helpful feedback at various stages during the research. Many of them also helped me connect with individuals who furthered my project, either as informants or as knowledgeable sources. I especially want to thank Nancy Ammerman, Kevin Dougherty, Nicole Esparza, Jim Gibbon, Wendy Griswold, Conrad Hackett, Becky Yang Hsu, Hilary Levey, Donald Light, Rebekah Massengill, Joya Misra, Margarita Mooney, Steve Offutt, Mark Regnerus, Amy Reynolds, Gabriel Rossman, Amy Sullivan, Steven Tepper, Bradford Wilcox, and Ezra Zuckerman. Anita Kline at Princeton's Center for the Study of Religion helped me with a range of issues, including research budgets, storage space for archival materials, and sundry institutional challenges that arose during the project. I also appreciate the administrative support I received from Donna DeFrancisco, Patsy Garcia, and Valeria Gutierrez. Daisy Paul, my research associate, offered invaluable service throughout the study by conducting extensive background research, cleaning and coding interview data, and collecting supplementary research materials, as well as corresponding with study participants and maintaining the research database of three thousand contact details. Laura Hoseley did an excellent job as well, transcribing all of my interviews and research notes—about five thousand pages in all. I thank my faculty colleagues at Rice—Jenifer Bratter, Chandler Davidson, Michael Emerson, Bridget Gorman, Holly Heard, Rachel Kimbro, Stephen Klineberg, Elizabeth Long, William Martin, and Roland Smith—for their interest and feedback on my work, and I look forward to more stimulating conversations.

A few individuals read the entire manuscript, and for their very helpful feedback I thank John Bartkowski, Elaine Howard Ecklund, Michael Hamilton, Martin Ruef, John Schmalzbauer, and Viviana Zelizer. Douglas A. Hicks, Stewart M. Hoover, Mark Joseph, David Miller, Mark Noll, and Corwin Smidt offered their expertise on particular chapters of the book, which was enormously helpful. I am particularly indebted to the committee members who supervised my dissertation, out of which this book arose. I benefited from Paul DiMaggio's extensive knowledge on a range of subjects every time we met to discuss my work. Marie Griffith—through her scholarship and her professional life—has shown me how to combine intellectual rigor with interpersonal grace, which are attributes I hope will characterize my work as well. Suzanne Keller and I have forged an intellectual friendship that spans many boundaries that often exist within the academy. I was honored to be Suzanne's final doctoral student as she completed such a distinguished career, and I look forward to learning even more from her in the years ahead. Finally, I owe a special word of thanks to Robert Wuthnow. Over the last six years, Bob helped me in every conceivable way. He explored possible research questions with me, helped me draft various applications and proposals, and guided me in revising papers and securing research funds. And he did all of this with warmth, candor, and humility. Whatever its remaining flaws, this book is better thanks to the insights of all of these wonderful mentors and colleagues.

Several others have played vital roles in bringing this project to completion. I am grateful for the support and counsel provided by Bill Leigh, my agent, and his terrific colleagues. India Cooper is a superb copy editor, and it was a pleasure to work with her. In addition, the book benefited from the expertise of many talented professionals at Oxford University Press, but my greatest debt of gratitude at Oxford goes to Theo Calderara, my editor. Theo believed in this book long before most other people, which has made our collaboration on it all the more meaningful. I will always appreciate his long-standing interest in the project and the extremely careful work he did on its behalf.

Most important, my family provided never-ending encouragement throughout the years spent researching and writing this book. Having married into a wonderful family, I am particularly grateful for the interest Margaret and Bill Duff took in my research. I thank them for reading each page of the draft manuscript and for offering many helpful suggestions. I am deeply grateful to Ronnie and Anne Elizabeth Ward, who welcomed me as their son when I had the good fortune of marrying their daughter. For supporting my family with their love and presence while I traveled the nation conducting research, I will be forever indebted to them as well as to Mary Margaret Roberson and Ronald Ward. My dad and stepmom, Ken and Janet Lindsay, provided frequent flier miles and free hotel rooms several times as I worked on this project. For these tangible gifts and the moral support they represent, I am very grateful. I also thank Lucille Lindsay and Betty Ruchti for similar boosts of encouragement along the way. I thank my mom, Susan Lindsay, whose belief in my ability to complete this project was often greater than my own. A boundary-crossing leader herself, Mom embodies the deep faith and generous spirit that characterize several of the ideals I write about here. Witnessing them in her persuaded me of their empirical reality. Finally, I owe the deepest gratitude to my wife, Rebecca, and our daughter, Elizabeth. Rebecca not only reviewed every word written herein, but she also helped shape the argument when they were only disparate ideas. This project exacted a heavy toll on her personally as I was away from home many nights during Elizabeth's first three years. Her constant encouragement while I collected data and as I sought to make sense of it all buoyed my spirit in ways only a soul mate could. Elizabeth's arrival in the midst of this project provided much-needed perspective on the more important things in life. Her laugh and sweet spirit sustained my own. It is for these reasons I dedicate this work to them, the loves of my life.

FAITH IN THE HALLS OF POWER

INTRODUCTION

A TOP 30 ROCKEFELLER PLAZA in one of Manhattan's most cele-brated ballrooms, media mogul Rupert Murdoch stepped up to a microphone. It was September 2004, and gathered before him was a Who's Who of the New York publishing elite. "When an author sells a million copies of his book, we think he's a genius. When he sells twenty million, we say we're the geniuses."

Murdoch was introducing Rick Warren, a folksy Southern Baptist preacher from suburban southern California. As head of the media conglomerate that published Warren's *The Purpose-Driven Life,* Mur-doch had much to smile about. The book had become the best-selling work of nonfiction in history (other than the Bible) and had been translated into more than fifty different languages. Long be-fore this, Warren had made a name for himself in evangelical circles. An earlier book, *The Purpose-Driven Church,* had sold a million copies, and over the years thousands of pastors had attended conferences to hear Warren and his staff talk about their approach to church growth.

That evening Warren had invited several of his friends from Cali-fornia to the party, and a handful of fellow evangelicals from the East Coast were in attendance as well. This was Warren's "coming out" party—a recognition that he was now part of the nation's elite. As I spoke to Warren's wife, Kay, she casually mentioned that she had met Dan Rather's wife the night before for dinner. During the party I spotted several Fortune 500 CEOs around the room. Warren was now not just a religious leader but a public leader, endowed with responsibility and influence far beyond the evangelical world.

The mood was festive and lively, but the two groups didn't mix all that well. I was there at the invitation of a friend who knew I was doing research on America's leadership and evangelicals. I intro-duced myself to an editor from another publishing house. Upon hearing that I was from Princeton, she assumed I was part of the publishing crowd. "Do you know any of these evangelicals that are here? I'm dying to meet one," she asked.

"I do," I replied, and then introduced her to an evangelical friend who was standing nearby. Mark, a successful businessman, had lived in New York for quite some time. He, like her, had graduated from Yale, so I used that as a point of connection when introducing the two. As I turned to continue mingling, I heard her ask: "Are there many evangelicals at Yale these days?"

It's a good question. Evangelicals are the most discussed but least understood group in America today. National surveys show that their numbers have not grown dramatically in recent decades, but over that same time they have become significantly more prominent. Everything from presidential campaigns to student groups in the Ivy League has been linked to rising evangelical influence. Social groups can gain power in a variety of ways—by voting a candidate into the Oval Office, by assuming leadership of powerful corporations, or by shaping mainstream media. Evangelicals have done them all since the late 1970s, and the change has been extraordinary. But no one has explained what these developments mean—for the evangelical movement or for America.

Much of the twentieth century was spent disentangling religion from public life. Commerce and piety were once seen as complements to one another. But that connection dissolved with the rise of modern corporations, as the personal was divorced from the professional. Americans embraced pluralism in the workplace, public schools, and civic life, and these institutions worked to minimize sectarian differences among workers and citizens. In the process, religion lost some of its influence, becoming just one of many sources for individual and national identity. Gradually, religion was relegated to the private, personal sphere.

Yet even as this arrangement finally became taken for granted in many quarters of American life, opposing perspectives were emerging. In the 1970s, conservative Christians, many of whom had sequestered themselves in a distinct subculture, began returning to the cultural mainstream. Initially, they met with only limited success, and many observers ignored their entrepreneurial creativity and strong resolve to change America. Also, few connected evangelicals' activism in politics with activism in other spheres, even though evangelicals regard these as more important.

Theirs is an ambitious agenda: to bring Christian principles to bear on a range of social issues. It is a vision for moral leadership, a form of public influence that is shaped by ethics and faith while also being powerful and respected. In truth, their vision is much less—and at the same time significantly more—than skeptics and critics think. To the extent that the activities of evangelical leaders point to a cohesive vision, it is not a political or cultural agenda but one grounded in religious commitment. Fundamentally, evangelicals feel compelled to share with others what they believe is the best way to make peace with God. For them, one's relationship with the divine is primary; all other issues are secondary. This is not new, and, in fact, it is a much smaller vision for society, one that involves changing one person at a time. What is unique to the current moment is the number of high-ranking leaders who have experienced that change themselves, either before they rose to power or while in public leadership. For many of them, the evangelical imperative to bring faith into every sphere of one's life means that they cannot expunge faith from the way they lead, as some would prefer.[1] In this way, the evangelical vision is sweeping and significantly more comprehensive than outside observers realize. This is much more than a campaign to win the White House or a call for Hollywood to produce family-friendly entertainment. It is a way of life that has gripped the hearts and minds of leaders around the country, and it is not likely to go away anytime soon.

It is not every day that a media mogul throws a party for a Southern Baptist preacher, but things like that have been happening more and more. Harvard Divinity School, not always the most welcoming place for evangelicals, now has an endowed chair in evangelical theological studies. Every person who has been elected president of the United States since 1976 has been affiliated with evangelicalism in one way or another. Evangelicals have been the driving force behind debates over abortion, same-sex marriage, and foreign affairs. Indeed, they are prominent in virtually every aspect of American life today. How have evangelicals—long lodged in their own subculture and shunned by the mainstream—achieved significant power in such a short time? That is the question this book seeks to answer.

What's an Evangelical?

There are many streams of religious tradition that flow into contemporary American evangelicalism, and those who call themselves evangelicals belong to a wide variety of Protestant denominations—and many to no denomination at all.[2] Even some Catholics consider themselves evangelical. Despite these various tributaries and the different ways evangelicalism has been defined, there is a remarkable consensus among evangelicals about the Bible, God, Jesus, the Holy

Spirit, evangelism, Christian living, and the church.[3] Evangelicals are Christians who hold a particular regard for the Bible, embrace a personal relationship with God through a "conversion" to Jesus Christ, and seek to lead others on a similar spiritual journey.[4] I define an evangelical as someone who believes (1) that the Bible is the supreme authority for religious belief and practice, (2) that he or she has a personal relationship with Jesus Christ, and (3) that one should take a transforming, activist approach to faith.[5]

Evangelicalism is not just a set of beliefs; it is also a social movement and an all-encompassing identity.[6] Because evangelicals must consciously choose their faith—"accepting" Jesus, in the evangelical vernacular—they often have a stronger attachment to faith than people who simply inherit their parents' religion. Within many evangelical congregations, when a person converts, he or she is asked to make a profession of faith that refers to Jesus as "Lord of my life," and the minister often responds by challenging the new believer to dedicate every part of his or her life to God. In other words, evangelicalism is a religious identity but also much more: Evangelicals must live out their faith every moment of their lives, not just on Sunday morning.[7] Typically, this includes talking with others about one's faith—"witnessing"—but it also includes things like feeding the hungry and caring for the sick.

As America has become more religiously diverse, evangelicals have begun acting on their faith in more public ways. Evangelicals see the world largely in terms of good and evil and believe that one overcomes evil through spiritual discipline—praying, studying scripture, and the like.[8] This is what fuels their moral conviction and moves them to action. The current public activism of evangelicals is not unlike evangelicalism of previous generations. A desire to reform society spurred evangelical political involvement in the nineteenth century, and we will see several examples from the twentieth century in the chapters ahead.[9] As one senior White House staffer put it, for him it is where "you get your moral passion furnished, your depth of commitment, because you think it's true and right."

Evangelicalism also encourages spiritual improvisation and individualism. Evangelicals are urged to "work out their faith" (as stated in Philippians 2), which typically entails regular spiritual disciplines like worship, prayer, and Bible study. The individualistic component of evangelicalism is important because it allows very different ways of acting on one's faith. It is why evangelicals can, in good conscience, arrive at very different opinions about how to act on one's faith even though they may rely on the same interpretation of the Bible and share religious convictions and sensibilities. (In this book, I use "convictions" to refer to norms, reasoning, and ideology—matters of belief. "Sensibilities" refers to matters of religious practice—routines, demeanor, perceptions, and way of life.) Also, evangelicalism does not have a religious hierarchy, which permits believers the freedom to disagree with their pastors and, on occasion, church teaching.

Evangelicals further believe that they hold a responsibility to care for society. This notion of being entrusted with a mandate to work for the "common good" is seen as a covenant between God and His people. In the Bible, this covenant referred to an arrangement with the Jews, but evangelicals—along with most other Christians—believe the New Testament extended that covenant to them. This provides evangelicals with hope and encouragement to persevere in trying to overcome evil. Things may be wrong in the world, but they, working with God, can set the world aright.[10]

These beliefs have been critical to evangelicalism's success as a social movement. While evangelicals hold many different opinions, they have remained remarkably united in their campaign to interject moral convictions into American public life. They aim for their leaders to exercise "moral leadership" informed by faith and are guided by a particular moral vision of the way things ought to be.[11]

Movements depend upon more than individuals; they need resources like money and power, and these resources are usually channeled through organizations. American evangelicalism has spawned a large number of voluntary associations and organizations, ranging from publishing houses to educational institutions to social service agencies. These organizations serve as the movement's skeleton, connected by ligaments of social networks that join leaders in common cause. Through these networks evangelicals can talk about their public activism, which both mobilizes people to act and maintains momentum once their work has begun. We will look at these institutional and expressive dimensions of American evangelicalism and how they have contributed to the movement's forward momentum.[12] The goal of this movement—as in any movement—is to advance: to secure legitimacy and then to achieve shared objectives.[13]

American Evangelicalism: A Short History

In the nineteenth century, American evangelicalism was so influential that, in the words of one historian, "it was virtually a religious establishment." Conservative Protestants populated the faculties of Harvard, Yale, and Princeton. Evangelicals were also active in politics, helping to drive the temperance and women's suffrage movements as they had done decades earlier with abolitionism.[14] But forces soon began to emerge to challenge the evangelical establishment, first in the academy and then in wider society. At places like Harvard, higher biblical criticism and scientific naturalism put evangelical intellectuals to the test. At the same time, strictly nonsectarian institutions such as Johns Hopkins University were established. Evangelical dominance was also threatened demographically, as waves of new immigrants began to reach American shores. Roman Catholics and Jews emigrated from eastern and southern Europe, making America much more religiously diverse. Urbanization and industrialization posed novel challenges to the existing welfare infrastructure. Soon, religious bodies were no longer able to meet the growing need for social services, and the federal government and expanding corporations were called upon to provide them.

Nonetheless, in the early twentieth century theological conservatives fought for the continued relevance of their faith. The turning point came at the Scopes Monkey Trial in 1925. Though they won in court, "fundamentalists," as they were called by then, were ridiculed in the national media as reactionary and anti-intellectual. As a result, they set aside many of their goals for transforming society and turned their energies inward toward their own religious communities. In what has been called the "Great Reversal," they withdrew into pessimism and separatism.[15] Although they continued to generate new organizations, they separated from the cultural mainstream and maintained strong boundaries between themselves and wider society. Dancing, smoking, wearing makeup, and playing cards were deemed improper, and a legalistic attention to avoiding them became hallmarks of fundamentalism.

In 1942, the Reverend Harold J. Ockenga of Boston's Park Street Congregational Church convened a group of religious leaders for a meeting. These "neo-evangelical" leaders, including Billy Graham, wanted to enter the public square again without abandoning their religious identity.[16] They also sought to recover the tradition of rigorous intellectual inquiry wedded to a religious worldview.[17] They founded the National Association of Evangelicals (NAE), and the modern evangelical movement was born.

In 1946, Carl F. H. Henry, one of the architects of modern evangelicalism, published *Remaking the Modern Mind*. In it, he advocated a resurrection of a faith that could "do battle in the world of ideas." A year later, in *The Uneasy Conscience of Modern Fundamentalism* (1947), Henry urged fellow evangelicals to engage pressing social concerns like race, class, and war and leave aside internal debates over doctrinal minutiae. Repudiating the fundamentalist model of religious separatism, the NAE allowed denominations that were already part of the liberal Federal Council of Churches to join their association as well.[18] These evangelical leaders established institutions and networks that could sustain their lofty vision. When they founded their flagship magazine, *Christianity Today*, in 1956, they housed it not in some suburban enclave but in an office suite overlooking the White House.

While they were committed to engaging with society, evangelicals were relatively minor players among the powerful social actors of the 1960s and early 1970s. Some evangelicals became part of a loose network of political conservatives that emerged in the wake of Barry Goldwater's 1964 failed presidential bid. At the same time, a group of progressive evangelicals launched a news journal called *The Post-American*, which urged fellow believers to mobilize for social action.[19] Jane Fonda and Malcolm X grabbed headlines much more frequently than Billy Graham or his contemporaries did. Nonetheless, Graham continued to maintain strong relations with public leaders like Presidents Johnson and Nixon. Nixon, in fact, invited Graham to be the inaugural preacher at the weekly White House church service he established.

With America's bicentennial in 1976, evangelicals saw an opportunity to renew their commitment to public affairs, and as they saw it, "at age two hundred, the nation sought more than improvement; it longed to be born again."[20] That year was a turning point for American evangelicalism. First-generation leaders—like Graham and Ockenga—began to give way to new leadership.[21] It was dubbed the "year of the evangelical" as *Time* and *Newsweek* published cover stories on the emergence of a publicly oriented form of evangelicalism. Since that time, evangelicals have become even more prominent. From the White House to Wall Street, from Hollywood to Harvard, evangelicals today can be found in practically every center of elite power and influence. When *Newsweek* ran its story on evangelicals in 1976, one individual—Jimmy Carter—figured prominently. When *Time* ran a similar cover story in 2005, the magazine profiled twenty-five leaders—and, as this book will show, they could have chosen hundreds more.

Looking at Leadership

At its core, this is a book about leadership and power. It explores the subject by looking at some of the most important people in the country and examining what drives them. Though most of us know that there are growing numbers of evangelicals in leadership today, we know virtually nothing about them. Information on evangelicalism as practiced by the masses is plentiful and accessible, but the same is not true for leaders. National surveys do not interview enough of them to draw general conclusions, and most empirical studies have not examined their religious lives. When religion is considered, it is seen only as one box to be checked and has been glaringly omitted from discussions about the personal side of public leadership.[22] Is religion playing a greater role in public life?

To find out, I tried to interview as many evangelicals in leadership positions as I could find. There are two kinds of leaders who are evangelical: those who lead institutions within the evangelical movement—also referred to as movement leaders—and public leaders from government, business, and culture. Altogether, I spoke to 360 of them, making this the most comprehensive examination of faith in the lives of leaders alive today.[23]

The movement leaders I interviewed included pastors at large churches, college and seminary presidents, and heads of evangelical organizations.[24] The public leaders each held at least one leadership position of societal prominence between 1976 and 2006. They include two former presidents of the United States as well as two dozen cabinet secretaries and senior White House staffers. There are representatives from each of the five administrations in office during that time, with a significant number coming from the administration of George W. Bush. This is due, no doubt, to the prominence of evangelicals there, but it also reflects the time at which the interviews were conducted. While in office, officials are more readily available and responsive to interview requests.[25]

From the business community, there were over one hundred chairmen, chief executives, presidents, or senior executives at large firms (both public and private), from fifteen different industries, forty-two *Fortune* 500 companies, and six members of the *Forbes* 400 wealthiest families.[26] The leaders I interviewed were alumni, faculty, and administrators from 159 educational institutions, including every major university in the country. And there were leaders from television, film, journalism, and the visual and performing arts, as well as selected nonprofit organizations and professional sports.

This is a relatively homogeneous crowd. While the evangelical movement can include a variety of people, its leadership—like that of most social movements—does not reflect that diversity. Their ages ranged from thirty-two to ninety-three, with the average age being fifty-four. Practically all were married with between two and three children. White evangelicalism is still largely separate from the black church, and almost all of the leaders I interviewed are white.[27] Just

10 percent of the public leaders I interviewed are women, underscoring the dominance of men in America's elite ranks. These include women who have held senior positions in government (such as Karen Hughes), business (such as Borders president Tami Heim and Enron executive and "whistle-blower" Sherron Watkins), and culture (like Kathie Lee Gifford and actress Nancy Stafford). This percentage is not dramatically different from the percentage of women in Congress or the percentage of women who are corporate officers, but it is much lower than the percentage of women in the U.S. labor force and even those who fill MBA slots at top schools.[28]

In other words, women in elite circles are still few and far between, but there are some important differences between women in general and women within the evangelical world. Gayle Miller is a good example. The former president of Anne Klein II, Miller spent her working lifetime in the world of retail fashion. When we met for her interview in Los Angeles, she spoke at length of the challenges she faced at the start of her career in the 1950s: "No one wanted to give us credit, no one wanted to sell us fabric. [The thinking was] 'How can two dumb blondes make this on their own?'" In the end, of course, she did make it, becoming head of the country's market leader for professional women's attire. During the course of her career, she turned away from her Mormon background and became a charismatic Christian through the Vineyard Church. Over the years, she has joined the boards of evangelical organizations, often serving as the lone female director. On several occasions, she encountered an evangelical bias against women, especially as she sought to recruit more women to boards or as speakers for various programs. She told me, "When I would say something like, 'You know, women are very good organizers and speakers, and we also know how to talk to people of power,' [the men] would just laugh." Asked if evangelical women sense the exclusion at these various groups, she responded, "Sense it? They might as well have a sign out on the [door]." Several of the women I interviewed, like Miller, did not have children of their own, and they said that gave them more time for work. Among those with children, all said their husbands shared equally in family duties, something that is not true of most evangelicals or of most men in this country. In fact, many women executives said their husbands serve as primary caregivers for their children. Marjorie Dorr, president of Anthem Blue Cross and Blue Shield, whose husband stayed home for seven years with their sons, told me, "You can't do this without that [kind of support]." In similar fashion, Tami Heim's husband stayed home to take care of their daughter and her aging mother—who was suffering from Alzheimer's—while

Heim traveled the globe as president of Borders. As she began to rise within the organization, Heim's husband quit his job as a research scientist at Eli Lilly and became the family "anchor."

As much as these women appreciate the egalitarian perspectives of their husbands, all of them talked about their family situation with a tinge of regret. Marjorie Dorr hates that she doesn't get home until eight at night because it makes her feel like she is avoiding family responsibilities. Karen Hughes, counselor to President George W. Bush, shocked the political establishment when she resigned to spend more time with her teenage son. "I felt like I was . . . shirking my obligations as his mom," Hughes told me when we met. "When I worked in the Texas governor's office, I had a very busy job and a very big job. But . . . the White House is different. . . . It's pretty constant and frenetic. And it is hard to balance [work and family there]. . . . I found . . . that I was torn all the time. I felt like I wasn't really able to have time for my true priorities." She returned to Washington in 2005 after her son went away to college.

The tension between professional obligations and family expectations, grueling for all women, seems especially so for evangelical women. Some observers, especially feminists—even evangelical feminists–were "mad," Hughes said to me, when she left her powerful position in the Bush White House "because they thought that it . . . made it look as if women couldn't get to the top without leaving it all for their family." Hughes said her evangelical faith did not compel her return to Texas; if anything, she felt that it sustained her as she tried to balance work and family. Nevertheless, even though most of their own families do not exhibit the patriarchal tendencies typical of American evangelicalism, these leaders feel torn between family desires and professional ambition. From talking with many female leaders, it is obvious that the evangelical community does not support them enough in juggling these competing demands, a topic to which we will return later.[29]

The vast majority of the evangelicals I interviewed are Protestant, and most are involved in some type of faith-based small group. They are not particularly loyal to a single congregation or even a single denomination. Almost three in five have switched congregations and denominations more than once, and the figure is even higher (80 percent) among younger leaders. Surprisingly, more than half of all leaders talked about embracing the evangelical approach to faith—"deciding to follow Jesus," in evangelical parlance—after high school. Evangelicalism's most prolific pollster, George Barna, has found that "if people do not embrace Jesus Christ as their Savior before they reach their teenage years, the chance of their doing so at all is slim."[30] This suggests that American leaders' spiritual journeys are noticeably different from those of the general population. Faith is important to them, but they often embrace it later in life.

What does the typical evangelical public leader look like? Meet William Inboden. Educated at Stanford before earning a PhD in history at Yale, Inboden is like many other leaders I interviewed. He held several influential positions before assuming his current role at the National Security Council and was a primary author of the International Religious Freedom Act of 1998, legislation that reflected growing evangelical activism in foreign affairs. As Inboden has worked into the upper echelons of government, he has not jettisoned his evangelical convictions; in fact, he regards them as deeply enmeshed in his work. He told me, "My work and [professional] gifts are a stewardship from God to be used for his glory. . . . [It requires] me to act with honor and integrity and to love those whom I work with as [ones] created in the image of God." Like others I interviewed, Inboden embraces an irenic, ecumenical spirit that has emerged in recent years among Protestants and Catholics, and he believes there is an "imperative" that he share his faith with others. Inboden has also been involved with various networks of influential evangelicals, groups that have helped advance his own career. To support his studies at Yale, he received a Harvey Fellowship, which is a scholarship for talented evangelical graduate students. And while in Washington he has participated in evangelical groups like Faith and Law and Civitas. Inboden's vision is shared by many I interviewed: an evangelical engagement with the political, intellectual, and cultural currents of the day in such a way that people of faith not only "follow the culture [but actually] shape it." That, in brief, is a snapshot of evangelical leaders today and what they hope to accomplish from within the halls of power.

Since 1976, hundreds of evangelicals like Inboden have risen to positions of public influence. But they have not done so by chance. The rise of evangelicalism is the result of the efforts of a select group of leaders seeking to implement their vision of moral leadership. They have founded organizations, formed social networks, exercised what I call "convening power," and drawn upon formal and informal positions of authority to advance the movement. Sociologist Randall Collins has argued that recognition and acclaim are bestowed upon leaders and ideas through structured, status-oriented networks.[31] Over the last three decades, the legitimacy that has come to the evangelical movement has come through the political, corporate, and cultural leaders who were willing to publicly associate with it. Evangelicalism, with its history of spanning denominational boundaries, is well suited to help evangelicals build connections with important leaders and prestigious institutions. They have formed alliances with diverse groups, giving the movement additional cachet and power in surprising ways. Leaders are often at the vanguard of a movement, and this book shows how evangelicals endowed with public responsibility have been at the forefront of social change over the last thirty years. By building networks of powerful people, they have introduced evangelicalism into the higher circles of American life. The moral leadership they practice certainly grows out of their evangelical convictions, but it also reflects the privileges they enjoy and the power they wield. Indeed, their leadership is an extension of—not a departure from—the elite social worlds they inhabit.

As I left the News Corp party that Rupert Murdoch threw back in 2004, I was handed a gift package with a note from Rick Warren inside. It read:

> Thank you for honoring me with your presence this evening. No one is more amazed than I am with the Purpose Driven Life phenomenon. Who could have predicted it would make publishing history? It's both astonishing and humbling. Because you are a leader that has expressed some interest in living with purpose, I'd like to invite you to be part of a very exclusive group. Each Thursday morning I lead an international study by conference call for influential leaders. It is a by invitation only group that has included some of the best known leaders in entertainment, business, politics, education, sports, media and the military. It is quite a mix of people, with the only common denominator being people of influence who have a desire to live with more purpose in their lives. If you are interested in listening in on one of these calls, just email [me] and I'll send you the details.

Around the country, leaders have joined groups like these: exclusive, regular gatherings where participants discuss matters of faith. They are occurring not only in the Bible Belt, but in places like Manhattan and Hollywood. I responded to Warren's invitation to join his weekly conference call, and though I never received a reply, my interviews were a gateway into this rarefied world. This book provides an inside look at American evangelicalism's rise to power and the leaders who have made it happen.

PART I

CAMPAIGNS, COALITIONS,

AND THE OVAL OFFICE

1

Presidents and Politics

Tucked off to the side of the Oval Office, opposite the doors that open onto the Rose Garden, is a small private study. At times of crisis, Jimmy Carter would often take refuge there. "I would kneel," he told me, "and ask God to give me wisdom and strength." Carter felt these times of prayer gave him a sense of "equanimity."

This was exactly what American evangelicals had longed for: one of their own praying in the inner chamber of political power. Indeed, perhaps no factor influences evangelical voters more than the personal faith of a candidate: It is how presidential hopefuls forge personal connections with the faithful. On the campaign trail, presidential candidates talk about shared ideals, experiences, and priorities. For voters, casting a ballot is not just a choice of one set of policies over another; it is an expression of identity and a way of making their values heard in the public square.[1] Indeed, voting in presidential elections entails an expressive component of political action. Voters don't just send a candidate to Washington; they send a message about what's important to them. When you identify with a candidate in a fundamental way, voting for the candidate is, in a sense, voting for yourself.

Evangelicals have long felt distant from centers of power. That is why movement leaders often speak as if they were part of a persecuted minority even as evangelicals sit in the White House and Congress. By supporting evangelical candidates, evangelical voters are asserting their right to a place at the table. When they are successful on Election Day, it reinforces their commitment, which further strengthens the movement. That explains why some evangelicals have voted for candidates when it was clearly against their economic interests.[2] They're not simply choosing morals over money; they're asserting their identity and boosting their own sense of values and belief. And when they see one of their own in a position of power, they feel validated.

In recent years, there has been a flood of books on evangelical involvement in politics—some thoughtful and scholarly, many sloppy and hysterical.[3] Almost none of these writers has spoken to the actual political leaders they write about. How do presidents and politicians account for the rise of evangelical influence in Washington? How do they see faith influencing their politics? To find out, I spoke to fifty people who served in the White House between 1976 and 2006. What they told me shows how leaders marshaled the resources and built the organizations that have thrust evangelicals into the halls of power.

From public speeches to presidential appointments, evangelical politicians have drawn upon their faith as a way of signaling their allegiances, which in turn has won the support of fellow evangelicals. These appeals to shared values are not simply political pandering, although they clearly have helped politicians get elected. They have also motivated evangelicals to become more active citizens and stimulated their involvement in civic life. With every president since Carter, evangelicals have tapped into politics as a way of expressing their faith, bringing evangelicalism into the public sphere. Evangelicalism is a faith buttressed by a spirit of activism, and while for many years evangelicals shied away from such a publicly engaged faith, more recently they have returned to their activist roots. This activism includes local issues, such as school board debates, but it also reaches to the nation's highest office. From Billy Graham's tacit endorsement of Richard Nixon in 1968 to Bill Hybels' close relationship with Bill Clinton throughout the 1990s, evangelical leaders have been frequent confidants of U.S. presidents. In fact, not a single president in recent history has *not* had a close personal relationship with at least one evangelical leader. By forging personal relationships with presidents, the evangelical movement has built its strength from the top down, not simply from the bottom up. The fact that evangelicalism is broad and diverse enough to include segments close to both Republican and Democratic presidents has enabled it to maintain significant influence regardless of which party is in power.

The Oval Office

It all started, really, with Jimmy Carter. Carter was the first major candidate to refer to himself as "born again," and he spoke the language of evangelicalism. Movement leaders like Billy Graham, who, like Carter, was a Southern Baptist, refused to endorse Carter outright, but that did not keep others from backing him and, in the process, reigniting evangelicals' long-dormant political activism.[4]

Pat Robertson is now one of the most recognizable figures on the "Religious Right," but back then he had mixed political allegiances. Robertson's father had been a long-serving Democratic congressman from Virginia, and he is a distant relative of the ninth U.S. president, William Henry Harrison, and his grandson, the twenty-third president, Benjamin Harrison. A Phi Beta Kappa graduate of Washington and Lee University, Robertson also earned a law degree from Yale before establishing the Christian Broadcasting Network in 1960.[5] When I interviewed him, we met for lunch in his office overlooking the manicured lawns of CBN headquarters in Virginia Beach. Robertson, like other evangelical leaders I met, had visible security surrounding him; the building is flanked with barricades, and security personnel escort visitors to his third-floor office suite. We ate in a boardroom decorated in the Federalist style, complete with wood paneling and elaborate dental molding along the ceiling. The setting—which effused patriotic and patrician sensibilities, both of which Robertson embodies—reminded me of nearby Colonial Williamsburg.

Though he is now a staunch conservative, it was Jimmy Carter's candidacy, Robertson told me, that really got him involved in politics. "Carter was the one who activated me and a lot of others. We had great hopes.... [He was] like our champion." He and other leaders of the evangelical movement saw in Carter a candidate of great promise, the answer to their political prayers. Carter spoke in evangelical tones: "I believe God wants me to be the best politician I can be."[6] And his promise never to lie to the American people appealed to evangelicals who, after Watergate, hoped to inject some morality into politics.

Every new president has the opportunity to name hundreds to Senate-confirmed appointments and thousands to lesser advisory boards and political jobs within the administration. Presidential appointments are symbolically significant, for they signal the importance of a particular group by bringing its members into circles of power. When a constituency throws its weight behind a presidential candidate, it invariably hopes to enjoy the spoils of victory in the form of such appointments, so evangelicals were keen to see some of their own in the Carter administration. But practically none of Carter's senior advisors were evangelicals. Most of his top appointees were associated with the Trilateral Commission and the Council on Foreign Relations, neither of which included many evangelicals.[7] Alonzo McDonald, who served President Carter in a role that is equivalent to today's deputy White House chief of staff, acknowledged to me that he didn't "know of anybody" in the White House except the president and his liaison to the religious community—not appointed by Carter until 1979—who spoke much about their faith.

Two events during the Carter administration were particularly disconcerting to his fellow evangelicals. The first involved a threat by the Internal Revenue Service to strip Christian schools of their tax-exempt status because of de facto racial segregation at these schools. Evangelicals perceived this not merely as advocating a liberal agenda with which they disagreed but as an alarming infringement on their own institutions and ideals. They regarded it as a hostile act against their entire faith.[8] Eventually, the IRS abandoned its plan, through an arrangement negotiated by members of Congress, but evangelical leaders were outraged that President Carter had not intervened on their behalf. If a fellow evangelical in the White House would not stand up for their faith, who would? Two years later, in 1980, the president convened a White House Conference on Families, fulfilling a campaign pledge from 1976. When he refused to exclude homosexuals, evangelicals were outraged.[9] In the end, the conference was unable to agree on a definition of the "family," and many believed the event merely increased the stature of the gay and lesbian movement—much to the dismay of evangelicals. In sum, many in the evangelical world did not feel President Carter stood with them. The rift between Carter's type of evangelicalism, which was less sectarian and more in line with the social gospel, and a more conservative brand of American evangelicalism continued to widen.

By 1980, Carter had lost significant support among evangelical leaders, and Ronald Reagan seized the moment. At a nonpartisan event sponsored by the Religious Roundtable in Dallas that year, Reagan told the crowd, "I know you cannot endorse me, but I endorse you."[10] With that, the evangelical audience leapt to its feet and erupted in applause. By courting evangelicals, Reagan brought many of them officially into the GOP for the first time, and his overt endorsement of evangelicals on the campaign trail and more subtly while in office gave the evangelical movement much more visibility and political clout than ever.[11]

Reagan's election heralded a new era for the evangelical movement. The coalitions formed by conservative evangelicals during the 1970s played a key role in aligning the movement behind his candidacy.[12] As a result, movement leaders hoped that President Reagan would appoint a few evangelicals to key positions, including at least a couple of cabinet-level posts. They got their wish. Two of the most prominent were James G. Watt and C. Everett Koop. Watt, a former vice-chairman of the Federal Power Commission, was Reagan's choice—as well as the choice of several senators from western states—for secretary of the interior. An adult convert to evangelical Christianity, Watt viewed his governmental service as an opportunity to leave what he called a "footprint in the pages of history." This type of bold, proactive stance was exactly what leaders of the evangelical movement hoped for in a presidential appointment. From the outset, Watt's public comments attracted attention for their occasional religious references. While testifying before the House Interior Committee in 1981, Watt said, "I do not know how many future generations we can count on before the Lord returns; whatever it is, we have to manage with a skill to leave the resources needed for future generations." This raised hackles inside the Beltway, as critics pegged Watt to be a fundamentalist yearning for the apocalypse. Watt's political career ended a few years later after another controversial remark. Asked about the diversity of his appointments to an oversight committee, Watt answered: "I have a black, a woman, two Jews and a cripple. And we have talent."[13] Republicans and Democrats alike excoriated Watt for the comment. Among his harshest critics was Senator Robert Dole, who lost use of his right arm during World War II. When I spoke to Watt in his Arizona home, he told me, "I'll never forget the conversation I had with Bob Dole. . . . He looked me straight in the eye and he said, 'You know, it's unforgivable that you'd use the word "cripple." ' " Watt resigned in November 1983 after thirty months on the job. But evangelical influence within the Department of Interior did not end there. Watt's undersecretary Donald Hodel, whom Reagan had named secretary of energy in 1982, eventually succeeded him.[14]

President Reagan named Dr. C. Everett Koop surgeon general in 1981. At the time, Koop was an eminent pediatric surgeon at Children's Hospital of Philadelphia (CHOP). A graduate of Dartmouth and Cornell Medical School, Koop had converted to Christianity as an adult while attending Tenth Presbyterian Church in Philadelphia. While at CHOP, he established the nation's first neonatal unit and performed one of the first successful separations of conjoined twins. Despite his credentials, many in Congress opposed Koop's appointment, largely because of his outspoken opposition to abortion. At the time, evangelicals were less active than Catholics in the pro-life movement, but Koop had been talking about abortion for decades.[15] As Koop acknowledges, "I was the most outspoken anti-abortion physician in this country from about 1971 until 1980." Decades earlier, over dinner at his home, Koop had persuaded Carl Henry, one of the architects of the modern evangelical movement, to oppose abortion. Both Billy Graham and Reagan's pastor in California, Dr. Donn Moomaw, encouraged the president-elect to nominate Koop. As governor of California, Reagan had actually liberalized the state's abortion policy. However, he understood the power of symbols, and he made abortion central to the surgeon general's nomination.

Reagan also appointed a number of federal judges who were sympathetic to evangelical concerns. Insiders attest that many Reagan White House staffers were Christians. As James Watt told me, some of them "didn't have big titles—you don't know about them—but they were there." These appointments were not only symbols of the movement's political influence; they also facilitated closer relations between leaders within the movement and decision-makers in government. After the 1980 election, James Dobson, head of a newly formed evangelical organization called Focus on the Family, found that he had several personal connections with President Reagan's inner circle.[16] Most notable among these was Susan Baker, wife of Chief of Staff James Baker and a member of Focus on the Family's board. Dobson exerted significant sway in the Reagan administration. He was appointed to the National Advisory Commission to the Office of Juvenile Justice and Delinquency Prevention in 1982, and in Reagan's second term he was frequently consulted on policy issues.[17] This almost certainly reflected the influence of fellow evangelical Gary Bauer, who served as Reagan's top domestic policy advisor. Connections like these served evangelical leaders well. With evangelicals in top administration positions, movement leaders were given access to the White House. This had a snowball effect: As evangelicals began to be seen as a political force, they attracted more support, which made the movement even more powerful.

President George H. W. Bush, who described to me his own personal faith as "quiet," did not appoint many evangelicals to senior positions, but he had warm relations with the broader evangelical movement.[18] Bush has been a faithful churchgoer throughout his life. "My faith gave me a lot of strength in my life as a public official. Prayer and Bible reading have been part of my life, . . . [and] Dr. Billy Graham is a spiritual mentor and counselor to me and to other members of my family," he told me. Administration officials admit that evangelicals in the George H. W. Bush White House "were few and far between," although in many ways he basked in the afterglow of evangelicals' relationship with Ronald Reagan.

But even politicians without close ties to the evangelicals' world know that their support can be important and that to win that support they have to talk the talk. During the 1992 campaign, Bush sought to present himself as the candidate with a "pro-family" agenda. At the Republican convention in Houston, he blasted the Democrats for removing references to God from their platform. Pat Robertson addressed convention delegates, as did Bush's primary-season opponent Pat Buchanan.[19] Buchanan spoke of a "religious war going on in our country for the soul of America," a message that resonated with conservative evangelicals who believed they were engaged in an all-out "culture war."[20] With a sluggish economy plaguing Bush in the waning months of his campaign, appealing to voters on social issues made sense. Mainline Protestants, a tradition that included Bush himself, were growing increasingly critical of Bush because of the sagging economy, and though they had voted for him in 1988, they appeared to be defecting to Clinton and third-party renegade Ross Perot.[21] The overtly religious tone of Bush's campaign helped him win the votes of white evangelicals. On Election Day, they were his strongest supporters; 63 percent of them voted for the Episcopalian Bush over the ticket composed of two Southern Baptist evangelicals, Bill Clinton and Al Gore.[22] Roughly speaking, white evangelicals who attended church regularly were as important to Bush as black Protestants were to Clinton.

During the 1992 campaign and throughout his presidency, Bill Clinton relied on religious symbols to win support for his domestic policies. His "New Covenant" platform, which appealed to religious voters, employed biblical references to advocate a closer relationship between the federal government and the American people.[23] During the 1992 campaign, he highlighted his faithful participation in the choir at Little Rock's Immanuel Baptist Church. And while in the White House, Clinton and his family regularly attended the 11:00 A.M. service at Foundry United Methodist Church, a fact that appeared regularly in news reports.[24] Clinton also used evangelical rhetoric more frequently than other recent presidents. For example, he cited Jesus, Jesus Christ, or Christ on average 5.1 times per year during his administration, which was more often than even George W. Bush (4.7).[25] Moreover, in the reelection year of 1996, President Clinton spoke of Christ in nine different statements. "No politician in modern times mixed politics and religion with complete impunity to the extent Bill Clinton did," writes Paul Kengor.[26] Indeed, President Clinton demonstrated that appealing to evangelical sensibilities in public speech and action was not the exclusive purview of Republicans.

The Clinton administration was similar to Carter's, with an evangelical at the top but not many other levels. In fact, during the last six years of President Clinton's administration, White House staffers disbanded the in-house Bible study that had met continuously since the Eisenhower administration.[27] Insiders even say that some Clinton administration officials were downright hostile toward people of faith. Several senior officials saw a significant divide between secular rationality and evangelical belief. Robert Reich, who served as secretary of labor from 1993 to 1997, later wrote about an "underlying battle" between "those who believe in the primacy of the individual and those who believe that human beings owe blind allegiance to a higher authority," between "those who believe that truth is revealed solely through scripture and religious dogma, and those who rely primarily on science, reason and logic."[28] In a White House where reactions to evangelical faith ranged from general indifference to blatant animosity, evangelicals did not feel welcome.[29]

Evangelicals were actively involved on both sides of partisan skirmishes during the Clinton administration. Beginning in 1994 there was a great deal of tension between the White House and Capitol Hill. Republicans, flush with power after gaining a majority in the House for the first time in forty years, issued a platform called the Contract with America. The Christian Coalition, under Ralph Reed's leadership, followed shortly thereafter with its own Contract with the American Family. Some people I interviewed called this the era of "triumphalistic evangelicalism," a time when conservative evangelicals strongly opposed the president and the policies of his administration under the banner of faith. Numerous evangelical leaders I talked with mentioned rumors and admissions regarding the president's extramarital sexual activity with Paula Jones, Gennifer Flowers, Kathleen Willey, and, most notably, Monica Lewinsky. Rumors of scandal had dogged the Clinton White House from its earliest months, and in 1994 Congress reauthorized the Office of Independent Counsel to investigate the death of Deputy White House Counsel Vince Foster and the president's involvement in the Whitewater land transactions in Arkansas. Kenneth Starr, a talented lawyer who had clerked for Chief Justice Warren Burger, was appointed as independent counsel. At the time, he was held in high regard by both Democrats and Republicans. A former U.S. solicitor general (1989–93) and a federal judge on the D.C. Circuit Court of Appeals (1983–89), Starr was regarded as a moderate conservative and had been widely mentioned as a likely nominee to the U.S. Supreme Court. The son of a Church of Christ minister, Starr is also an active evangelical.

I interviewed Starr at his office on the campus of Pepperdine University. Perched above the Pacific coastline in Malibu, California,

Pepperdine has strong ties to its affiliated denomination, the Churches of Christ, and its stock is rising among evangelicals. Starr came to Pepperdine in 2004 as dean of its school of law. When we met, he was clothed in the traditional conservative attire of navy suit and red tie, and the late afternoon sun was beginning to set.

Starr told me that when he was appointed independent counsel he expected to complete his task within a few months, but he was given very broad powers in the role and soon expanded the investigation. Critics began complaining about Starr's aggressive tactics, charging him with trying to hound the president from office with an evangelist's zeal. Clinton and Starr were actually close to many of the same evangelical leaders. One evangelical businessman, for instance, considers them both good friends and wrote a book that featured promotional blurbs from both men. In Washington, Clinton and Starr sometimes ran in similar circles. When I interviewed governmental leaders about their evangelical faith and the Whitewater investigation, several of them acknowledged that it was "one of those issues [on which] people of faith can [arrive at] a different conclusion." I asked Starr about the Lewinsky phase of his investigation, when more than one pundit claimed his investigation was born out of repressed sexual energy because of his evangelical faith. He replied, "I constantly prayed for wisdom.... We weren't particularly happy with doing it. [During that time] I would steep myself in particular in books such as Psalms, Proverbs, the Acts of the Apostles, and the book of James, and then I would lighten it up with a bit of British comedy."

While several conservative evangelicals, including Starr, were prominent in the investigation and then the impeachment of the president, other evangelical leaders were huddling with him in spiritual solidarity. Bill Hybels, the pastor of the nation's largest megachurch at the time, Willow Creek Community Church in suburban Chicago, was a close friend and pastoral advisor to President Clinton throughout his term in office. Other evangelical leaders like Tony Campolo and Gordon McDonald advised the president, and in the months following the Lewinsky scandal, the three of them met regularly with him for spiritual counsel.[30] In 2000, while emceeing a session of Willow Creek's Leadership Summit for several thousand evangelical pastors, Hybels interviewed President Clinton about a range of topics. To the ire of some in attendance and many others in the evangelical world, Hybels did not confront the president about the tension between his self-identification as a Christian and his lying under oath about the relationship with Lewinsky. But Robert Seiple, another evangelical leader who served in the Clinton administration, could relate to Hybels' predicament. He first met the president at a prayer meeting in 1993 that Hybels organized.[31] After the meeting, Seiple told me, those in attendance "got the dickens beat out of us by the rest of the evangelical community because we did not raise the issue of sanctity of life and abortion." They had not, Seiple said, because "all of us were taken aback" when the president opened the meeting by asking them to tell him "things that would help [his] spirituality." Seiple continued, "Say what you want about the guy, [but] this is a guy that's reaching out. So that's what we talked about." President Clinton and his wife, Hillary Rodham Clinton, have also had a long relationship with evangelical icon Billy Graham.[32]

Though Clinton talked often about his faith, the presidency of George W. Bush strikes many observers as the most evangelical in recent memory.[33] Unlike that of other recent presidents, George W. Bush's spirituality bears the typical markers of evangelical faith. Whereas Presidents Carter, Reagan, and George H. W. Bush were more reticent to speak about their personal beliefs, George W. Bush alludes publicly and frequently to his faith.[34] At the encouragement of Douglas Wead, an advisor to both Bushes, the younger Bush signaled his evangelical credentials to the faithful early and often. He told the story of how a talk with Billy Graham on a beach in Maine led to his born-again experience, and he called Jesus Christ his favorite political philosopher.[35] In turn, evangelical voters— representing about a quarter of the adult population—strongly supported Bush in his race for the White House. He received 72 percent of the evangelical vote in 2000 and 87 percent in 2004. Additionally, aides let it be known that he regularly reads the classic evangelical devotional text, *My Utmost for His Highest* by Oswald Chambers, and he is sometimes seen at the 8:00 A.M. service at St. John's Episcopal Church in Lafayette Square, though not every week.[36]

One of the keys to Bush's support among evangelicals was the work of his speechwriter—and fellow evangelical—Michael Gerson. Affectionately referred to as "the scribe" by the president, Gerson started writing speeches for Bush during the 2000 presidential campaign, preferring to draft them in a bustling Starbucks rather than in his quiet office. Their shared faith allowed Gerson to deftly insert biblical and cultural allusions that would resonate with the president's evangelical constituents. Gerson told me:

> There are several appropriate cases for the use of religious language in public rhetoric.... When people are presented with entirely unfair and unreasonable suffering, the president of the United States has to assure them ... that the universe has meaning, and that the universe is not an

emptying, echoing void.... I've had, sometimes, complaints about that [type of rhetoric], but never at the time. People know intuitively that when the space shuttle blows up or thousands of people die in a terrible terrorist act, you have to say the universe has meaning.

At such moments, he said, there is a "great emotional, national need that only the president could fulfill, to begin a process of understanding and healing. Without the ability to do that, a president couldn't be a leader, and American rhetoric would be just sterile and unequal to the task."

A graduate of Wheaton College, a school regarded by many as the "Harvard of American evangelicalism," Gerson supported Jimmy Carter when he ran for president in 1976. Even speaking from his West Wing office in 2005, the devout evangelical said, "I've always liked Jimmy Carter and still do." Indeed, Carter's religious rhetoric resonated with him, even though such language has its detractors. Gerson—whose office was just steps away from the Oval Office— acknowledged that religious elements in some presidential rhetoric, such as Reagan's description of the Soviet Union as an "evil empire" and Bush's identification of a global "axis of evil," can be offensive. President Bush often speaks of the so-called war on terror as a Manichean struggle between forces of "light" and forces of "darkness."[37] The apocalyptic overtones in these speeches are hard to miss, and on several occasions President Bush has referred to U.S. military action in Afghanistan and Iraq as bringing a divinely sanctioned "gift of liberty" to people around the world. When I interviewed Jim Wallis, editor of the left-leaning evangelical journal *Sojourners,* he told me, "President Bush has used the language of [spiritual] salvation [that] evangelicals believe is found [only] in Jesus Christ. President Bush crafts it to fit his international policy, something dangerous for both Christian belief and American foreign policy." Indeed, some evangelicals I spoke to worry that the president endorses a theology of empire that confuses national interests with the will of God. When Bush talks about shining light into the darkness, they claim, it is not God's light but rather the light of the United States. This, some feel, is a misuse of biblical language. Defenders, though, claim that Bush's religious rhetoric falls within a long tradition of presidents referring to divine purpose and providence. The Reverend Richard John Neuhaus, editor of the conservative journal *First Things,* says, "There is nothing Bush has said . . . that Abraham Lincoln did not say."[38] Interestingly, although he is widely regarded as the political favorite of American evangelicals, Bush does not describe himself that way. He prefers to call himself a "mere

Christian" instead of "evangelical" or even "born again," as interviews with several of his aides confirm. That phrase, which alludes to a book by the English writer C. S. Lewis, shows how a political leader can use religious language to appeal to voters in a nonsectarian way.[39]

In talking to people within the administration, I found that it is not evangelical movement leaders, like Richard Land or D. James Kennedy, who exert the greatest influence on the politicians they help elect. When it comes to actual policy decisions, the most powerful evangelical voices come from those working inside an administration. This is the difference a presidential appointment can make and explains, in part, why the Carter administration had a much less evangelical tenor than that of George W. Bush.

Bush has surrounded himself with more evangelicals than any other U.S. president in the last fifty years.[40] Even among nonevangelicals, there is a general affinity for religious faith; for example, former White House chief of staff Andrew Card is married to a mainline Methodist minister. And many who have been the president's top advisors are evangelicals: Claude Allen (assistant to the president), John Ashcroft (attorney general), John Danforth (U.S. representative to the United Nations), John DiIulio (assistant to the president), Donald Evans (secretary of commerce), Michael Gerson (assistant to the president), Glenn Hubbard (chairman of the White House Council of Economic Advisors), Karen Hughes (counselor to the president), Stephen Johnson (EPA administrator), Kay James (Office of Personnel Management director), David Leitch (deputy White House counsel), Mel Martinez (secretary of housing and urban development), Harriet Miers (White House counsel), Donald Powell (FDIC chairman), and Condoleezza Rice (national security advisor and secretary of state).[41] Additionally, I found dozens of appointees at slightly lower levels who share the president's style of evangelical faith. And whereas in previous administrations six to ten White House staffers would regularly attend Bible study, today's White House Christian Fellowship is attended by fifteen to a hundred people. Similar Bible study groups honeycomb the administration, across numerous federal departments and agencies. Some non-evangelicals, like speechwriter David Frum, were surprised at how evangelical the Bush White House was. After leaving the administration, Frum wrote that this was a "White House where attendance at Bible study was, if not compulsory, not quite uncompulsory, either," a fact he says "was disconcerting to a non-Christian like me." Others, like Jay Lefkowitz, an observant Jew who served as Bush's chief domestic policy advisor, have said it was never a problem for them.[42] The sheer number of evangelicals in top positions is a novelty, yet the Bush administration can hardly be described as an "evangelical administration." Evangelicals are still a minority on the senior staff.[43] When I asked him about the perception that evangelicals dominate the administration, David Leitch, who served as Deputy White House counsel, responded, "I think there are a lot of evangelicals in the administration . . . but I certainly don't view it as an evangelical administration. . . . It's not a religious organization; it's [the federal] government." Still, the Bush White House has consulted with evangelical leaders more regularly and forged closer relations with the evangelical movement than any other administration in recent history. This is new ground for evangelicals.

In the Bush years, tensions between evangelicals and the Democratic leadership have grown. Bush's outspoken identification with evangelicals has helped strengthen the boundaries between Democrats and Republicans on matters of religious conviction. To complicate matters, many evangelical Democrats have grown increasingly frustrated with their own party. In interviews, Democrats expressed disappointment, calling the party "fouled up" because of the party leadership's reluctance to talk about faith "publicly." Tony Campolo, a Democrat and evangelical leader who has been close to Bill and Hillary Clinton for many years, told me his party is "ashamed of Jesus," which he believes continues to cost them votes. While speaking to thirty-seven of the forty-four Democratic senators at a 2006 meeting organized by Hillary Clinton, Campolo asked the group, "In your speeches . . . do you ever quote Socrates? . . . Jefferson? . . . Aside from the fact that I'm saying He's the Son of God . . . you would have to admit that [Jesus] has to stand among the greatest moral teachers of all time. Why wouldn't you quote the greatest moral teacher of all time?" The senators had no response, and Campolo believes it shows just how "ashamed" the Democratic Party can be on matters of religion. At a recent Renaissance Weekend, Beliefnet.com editor Steve Waldman related a story from the 2004 campaign. Waldman had invited the various presidential candidates to talk about their spiritual lives in an online column early in the primary season. While staffers for one Democratic candidate debated whether their candidate should participate, part of their e-mail correspondence was sent to Waldman by mistake. In response to Waldman's request, a senior campaign strategist had asked his colleagues, "Do we talk about that stuff?"

Despite these developments, evangelicals have not altogether abandoned the political left. In fact, there remains a vibrant constituency of liberal or progressive evangelicals that has been around for decades.[44] During the presidency of George W. Bush, this camp has grown increasingly vocal under the leadership of outspoken evangelicals like Jim Wallis, Tony Campolo, and Ron Sider. They have strongly criticized parts of Bush's domestic agenda—from tax cuts that came at the expense of welfare for the poor to environmental policies that favored big business. And when the president gave the 2005 commencement address at Calvin College, a strong evangelical institution in the heart of conservative western Michigan, one-third of the faculty signed a full-page ad protesting his policy on Iraq.[45] Indeed, around the country, leaders expressed frustration with the Bush administration during their interviews with me. One business leader, Timothy Collins of Manhattan, said he wouldn't vote for George W. Bush for "dog-catcher." Others voiced concern that programs like faith-based initiatives eroded the wall separating church and state, saying, "It takes only one or two generations to lose the religious liberty that we have known as Americans." Bruce Kennedy, former CEO of Alaska Airlines, said, "I never dreamed I'd be anything but a Republican," yet in 2004 he became what he called an "ABB" voter, "anybody but Bush." Even stronger opposition can be found among Hollywood evangelicals who not only refused to support Bush but actively supported and campaigned for Al Gore in 2000 and then again for John Kerry in 2004.

All of these individuals are part of a larger group of the electorate, dubbed "freestyle evangelicals."[46] These are evangelicals who, for the most part, are social conservatives but who are also concerned about the environment and fiscal policies that hurt the poor. Among these, some have supported liberal or progressive evangelical activism like the grassroots movement Call to Renewal. Established in 1995 by Tony Campolo and Jim Wallis, Call to Renewal is an advocacy group aimed at eradicating poverty in the United States. A similar group, also headed by Wallis, is Sojourners, which is an evangelical ministry that publishes a magazine of the same name, convenes gatherings for left-leaning evangelicals interested in social justice, and sponsors an annual internship program. Although Wallis and his work have been present in Washington since 1975, only about two hundred thousand people are on their mailing list; by comparison, the conservative group Focus on the Family has a mailing list of more than two million. Nonetheless, these groups bear witness to the "kaleidoscopic diversity" of American evangelicalism. Fully 70 percent of evangelicals in America do not identify with the Religious Right.[47]

Recently, the Democratic leadership has undertaken several steps to reach out to faith communities. Burns Strider, a self-identified born-again evangelical who grew up as a Southern Baptist in Mississippi, was hired in 2004 to lead the Democratic Faith Working Group with the goal of trying to help congressional Democrats connect their faith to the party's agenda. Focused more on the personal connection between faith and policy, as opposed to strategy and communicating with the media, the Faith Working Group, Strider told me, is for members with "authentic faith" from a variety of religious traditions, including evangelicalism.[48] He has since signed on to work for Senator Hillary Clinton's campaign. There is also now a consulting firm for Democrats focused on helping their candidates connect with faith communities and an online Christian community called Faithful Democrats.[49] And throughout the Democratic Party, leaders have begun referring to themselves as the party of "religious progressives," echoing the language of evangelical leaders like Campolo, Sider, and Wallis. However, in their zeal to portray certain policies as born of religious conviction, some observers think these Democrats are "making the same mistakes that the folk on the right made," attaching religious labels to partisan positions in ways that strike some as disingenuous. Consider, for example, the recent assertion by evangelical progressives that tax policies and the federal budget are just as much "moral issues" as abortion or human sexuality.[50] These fiscal concerns are important and certainly affect the lives of more voters directly than some of the "moral values" that traditionally inspire religious conservatives. But issues surrounding the human body invariably hit people in a visceral way and are particularly salient to people whose primary concern is public morality.[51] Because of this, it is doubtful that many evangelicals will regard taxes and abortion as issues of equal moral weight. Democrats and progressive evangelicals are certainly seeking ways to reach out to religiously motivated voters, but simply calling certain matters "moral issues" will not win them widespread evangelical support.

Public Faith

How do political leaders connect their evangelical faith to their duties? The answer varies tremendously, but nearly all the people I spoke with said their faith provided them with a larger sense of meaning and purpose.[52] One of the defining characteristics of American evangelicalism is its emphasis on evangelism—that is, talking with others about faith. During his presidency, Jimmy Carter sometimes talked about his faith with other world leaders. In this regard, President Carter is clearly the most evangelical occupant of the White House in modern history. No other recent president, including

George W. Bush, has talked so directly about his faith with foreign leaders. Typically, Carter would do this away from Washington when foreign heads of state would ask him questions about his faith. This allowed him to maintain his allegiance to the separation of church and state, which, he says, he learned as a boy, while also being true to his evangelical faith. Carter told me two stories:

> Once I was in South Korea and met with President Park. . . . I was there to condemn his abuse of human rights and his warlike attitude toward other people. And I was very frank in putting my view forward about human rights, like I did with every leader. [Then] he asked me to, in effect, witness to him. So I shared with him my Christian faith at his request, and he expressed a deep interest in becoming a Christian. . . . I had to leave . . . but I got [the Reverend] Billy Kim, who was a prominent Christian in South Korea, . . . to get together [with him] after I left.
>
> [Also], when I normalized relations with China, Deng Xiaoping came over . . . and brought the subject up of Christianity. . . . He knew that the heritage of the Christian faith in China had, in one way, a profound and beneficial impact on health and education. But he was very aggravated with and averse to the role of missionaries because they came to China and attempted to change their culture and live like kings and queens. . . . [That] was his position. I said, "When I grew up, as a five-year-old boy, I would give a nickel a week to China for hospitals and schools, and the most famous people in my town were not [people like] the president of the United States. They were missionaries who came back from China and would travel around on their vacation time and come to our church, and they were exalted like saints." And he thought for a few minutes, [and then] he said, "I'll permit Bibles to come back. I'll try to change the constitution to guarantee freedom of religion." [Carter had requested both earlier in the conversation. Regarding Carter's request to permit the return of missionaries to China, though, he said,] "I will never permit missionaries to come." As soon as he got back . . . he issued an edict to permit Bibles. . . . He wouldn't let . . . missionaries . . . come back, [but] they changed the constitution to guarantee the freedom of religion.

President Carter also sees his commitment to peace as coming from his evangelical faith. It spurred his desire to reconcile Israel with the Arab world in the late 1970s, and it influenced some of the proceedings at the Camp David Peace Accords.[53] Insiders familiar with the negotiations say Carter's respectful and informed approach to the religious convictions of both Israeli prime minister Menachem Begin and Egyptian president Anwar Sadat bonded the three leaders as personal friends. For all three men, faith was personally important.

As Carter told me, "When I got to Camp David with Begin and Sadat, Doug Coe [leader of the Fellowship in Washington] suggested that the three of us should issue a worldwide call for prayer that we would be successful.... That was the first thing we did at Camp David."

Though Carter acted on his faith, he felt quite uncomfortable mixing matters of church and state.[54] Despite his own evangelical convictions, he never prayed with his advisors while in the White House. He says, "President Nixon had regular religious services in the White House, [but] I thought that was outside my purview as an elected public official." President Carter told me he did, however, spend a great deal of time praying. "When I was president I was more deeply committed to prayer than ever before or since. Just praying each day that I would do God's will, that the words of my mouth and the meditation of my heart would be acceptable in God's eyes, and that I could make the decisions in a political realm that were compatible with the teachings of Christ." Carter says the centrality of human rights to his foreign policy was born of faith convictions, as was his strong desire to avoid military conflict. Alonzo McDonald, a senior White House official at the time, told me about the day the president learned about the death of the first member of the armed forces during his administration. "President Carter was, even though a military man by reputation and training, ... crushed because he had hoped to go through four years without a single member of the military who died in combat."

By contrast, President Reagan rarely spoke of his faith in the context of international policy or military action. Officials close to him, though, say it was important to him. James Baker, who served as chief of staff during Reagan's first term, says President Reagan was a man of faith who "didn't talk about [his faith] much ... [and] did not profess his Christianity, to the extent that Carter did." Like Carter, President Reagan rarely prayed with close advisors, and he never permitted the press to photograph him praying. Edwin Meese, a senior advisor who worked with him for many years, told me that he and the president prayed together "on a couple of occasions," but most of the time the president prayed "privately." When asked about the president's spiritual practices, James Baker offered the following example. Before the only debate between Carter and Reagan during the 1980 campaign, Baker was waiting in the greenroom. As the two men sat alone, Reagan turned to Baker and said, "Jim, would you give me a moment, please, with the Man upstairs," and Baker complied. Others close to President Reagan agree that his faith was genuine but discreet. According to Robert "Bud" McFarlane, who was national security advisor, President Reagan "didn't have his faith on his sleeve, but it was passionately a part of his governance.... It was a personal connection with Christ, and that was private. But it was undeniable." Others, of course, disagree. Critics argue that his massive military spending and fiscal policies, which widened the gap between rich and poor, were at odds with a Christian approach to public policy. The sharpest public critic of the divide between Reagan's policies and his faith was Archbishop Desmond Tutu of South Africa. Tutu, who won the Nobel Peace Prize in 1984, called Reagan's support of apartheid in that country "immoral, evil, and totally un-Christian."[55]

When I interviewed James Baker at his office on the campus of Rice University, he acknowledged, "I'm far more comfortable talking about foreign policy or things like that than about expressing my personal faith." Yet the speech that garnered "more comments... around the world" than any other was not an address he delivered on American foreign policy or the nation's fiscal health; it was his talk at the 1990 National Prayer Breakfast, shortly after becoming secretary of state. In that speech, he noted, "Living in the centrifuge of power and politics encouraged, even demanded, spiritual growth." He continued:

> Back in the early 1980s, when I was President Reagan's White House Chief of Staff, I saw a man walking down Pennsylvania Avenue. He was someone many of you would have recognized—a Chief of Staff in a previous Administration. There he was, alone—no reporters, no security, no adoring public, no trappings of power—just one solitary man alone with his thoughts. That mental picture continually served to remind me of the impermanence of power and place. That man had it all—but only for a time.

Baker concluded by saying, "There are few things more difficult to exercise than real leadership. But I am convinced that understanding it is not power, but faith and friendship, that are meaningful and lasting, help us succeed at leadership." Baker's willingness to speak openly about his evangelical faith while serving in a senior government post is representative of the public expressions of evangelical faith that have become increasingly common.[56]

Given the demands of governmental leadership, it is not surprising that public leaders find ways to connect their daily activities to a larger sense of purpose. Religious practices like praying are not the exclusive purview of evangelicals. However, evangelicalism is unique in two ways. Unlike some other religious traditions, it makes claims on all aspects of the adherent's life. As a result, evangelicals are encouraged to pray about important as well as mundane parts of their lives. This includes interactions and activities at work. Second, evangelicalism emerged from a stream of Protestantism that stresses personal experience and emotional affect.[57] This is why many evangelicals are so ardent in their political positions. The evangelical faith provides a moral passion for governmental service. Within the political maelstrom, evangelicalism bestows upon adherents what Michael Gerson called a "depth of commitment [that compels them to action] because you think it's true and right."

Members of both parties spoke about the discouragement that comes from political defeat, whether in an election or a legislative battle. Nearly all said their evangelical faith helped them overcome disappointment and find some other arena of public service. Asa Hutchinson, who lost bids for U.S. senator as well as governor and attorney general of Arkansas, says he felt these races were "door[s] of opportunity the Lord had opened up, . . . [but] for various reasons, God didn't want me to win. I accept that [because] even in losing a number of races, my career progressed and other doors were opened up." Former Arkansas governor Mike Huckabee, who was an evangelical pastor before beginning his political career, says, "It's wrong for us to assume that God is going to cast a vote in an election, that he's for this guy, he's against that guy. I think that's presumptuous on our part." Nonetheless, many evangelicals said they felt God wanted them to run for office. Several people told me they heard a "spiritual calling," not unlike people who enter the ordained ministry. For some evangelicals, therefore, running for political office is a spiritual decision. I found the following quote from German theologian Martin Luther on one political leader's desk: "The very ablest youth should be reserved and educated not for the office of preaching, but for government, because in preaching, the Holy Spirit does it all, whereas, in government one must exercise reason in the shadowy realms where ambiguity and uncertainty are the order of the day." There are undoubtedly some evangelical politicians who believe God is on their side and will lead them to victory on Election Day, but most of those I interviewed were less confident. They express a deep ambivalence about the relationship between elections and divine providence. They identify with Luther's description of the "shadowy realms" of ambiguity and uncertainty that exist within the corridors of power.

For several people I spoke with, public leadership led them to existential crises. They talked about the initial exhilaration of working in government, but as the years progressed they found the whole experience anticlimactic. Alonzo McDonald, a top official in Carter's

White House, said, "I had spent much of my life just climbing the ladder, and . . . even though I was not at the top, I could pretty well see it from my office, next door to the Oval Office. And I didn't see much beyond that was that satisfying. In fact, it looked like a big abyss." He began reflecting on larger questions about the meaning of his work and its cosmic significance, and eventually McDonald experienced what he called a "spiritual renewal." Others told me how the demands of working in places like the White House invariably led them to ask questions for which evangelical spirituality provided answers. Certainly, there are some who feign a religious conversion for political purposes, but many spoke of the "clarifying" role that positions of power played in their own assessments of identity and purpose. Evangelical faith, with the totalizing claims it makes on an adherent's whole life—whether at church, in the office, or at home—appealed to these leaders. And in almost every case, they spoke of a colleague who introduced them to a group of other evangelical leaders who were similarly stationed and had found answers in the faith. Their faith was formed in the crucible of power, which also partly explains why evangelicalism has persisted among America's leadership despite an increasingly pluralistic public square.

Many of the political leaders I spoke with had spiritual epiphanies in the face of political challenges. "Bud" McFarlane served as President Reagan's national security advisor from 1983 to 1985 and was a central figure in the Iran-Contra affair. On the day he was to testify before Congress about his involvement, McFarlane attempted suicide by overdosing on Valium. He became even more depressed when he awoke from the failed suicide attempt, but that afternoon he received a call from former president Richard Nixon. Their conversation led McFarlane to a spiritual epiphany.

The next day [President Nixon] got on an airplane by himself . . . and walked into the hospital room in Bethesda. In the course of an hour, he recounted his own depression after leaving office . . . and the very dark time of despair he went through trying to determine what could possibly lay ahead for a disgraced individual. . . . [Nixon] recounted how the Lord had lifted him up [convincing the ex-president that he was] blessed with intellect and opportunity . . . and to ignore it was to sin. And then he was quite stern. He said, "You are similarly blessed. . . . Get your butt out of bed, get back into mainstream life, and find a way to do something worthwhile." . . . It motivated me to get out of bed and begin to pray and to seek guidance about how I could be a positive influence in the world again. . . . [We] didn't read any scripture, [but] we did pray, at his insistence.

Soon thereafter McFarlane got involved in an evangelical fellowship group, which has been "a strong foundation ever since."[58]

One group has been particularly important to the spiritual lives of political leaders: an entity known as "the Fellowship." In 1944, Abraham Vereide started an organization called International Christian Leadership that hosted prayer breakfast groups for business and government leaders. This group eventually became the Fellowship. Vereide organized the first annual National Prayer Breakfast in 1953.[59] President Eisenhower attended that year, as has every U.S. president since. Vereide died in 1969 and passed the reins to Douglas Coe. Coe, who avoids the limelight, has been closer to more U.S. presidents than any other religious leader, including Billy Graham. Indeed, he has been called a "stealth Billy Graham."[60] Coe has befriended a succession of world leaders. Jimmy Carter called him a "dear friend," and President George H. W. Bush praised Coe for his "quiet diplomacy" and said to me, "I have great respect for Doug Coe. I have known him for many years. He is widely respected abroad. . . . The best evidence of this is when one sees people from countries abroad attending the National Prayer Breakfast and paying tribute to Doug Coe."[61] The late Reverend Dr. Richard Halverson, chaplain to the U.S. Senate and pastor of Fourth Presbyterian Church in Bethesda, Maryland, served alongside Vereide and Coe for many years. Observers referred to him as the "theological gravitas" of the movement.

Of the leaders I interviewed, one in three mentioned Coe or the Fellowship as an important influence. Indeed, there is no other organization like the Fellowship, especially among religious groups, in terms of its access or clout among the country's leadership.[62] For example, while serving as counselor to the president, Edwin Meese and several other senior leaders in the federal government, including General John W. Vessey, then chairman of the Joint Chiefs of Staff, would meet every Tuesday in a small fellowship group for prayer and Bible study. Reagan's chief of staff James Baker attended a similar fellowship group (which Coe helped facilitate) on Capitol Hill. Baker, who told me his faith is "very important," says he gained a great deal of spiritual nourishment from this group. Fellow attendees included Republicans Pete Domenici and Mark Hatfield as well as Democrats Al Gore and Lawton Chiles. Indeed, the Fellowship is able to bring together public leaders from across the political spectrum. "We would share our personal concerns, . . . trials and tribulations with children and family," Baker told me, "but we never did any business in those meetings, even though we had an awful lot of business with each other. . . . Some of us were allies and some of us were adversaries." With the ongoing support of the Fellowship and the prayer breakfast movement, meetings like these have been occurring throughout Washington for decades. Informed observers estimate that several hundred fellowship groups meet around Washington on a regular basis. According to C. Everett Koop, when he lived in Washington during the 1980s there was a Bible study "in every conceivable group of people in government . . . for the staff of the Supreme Court, for the Senate, the staff of the Senate, for the House, for the staff of the House," along with many others. What difference do they make in the world of politics?

First, these groups support a network of interpersonal relations at the highest levels. For instance, when Secretary Baker became one of the first Western diplomats to visit Albania as it emerged from communist rule, he was greeted on the tarmac by Albanian foreign minister Muhamet Kapllani. As Baker extended his hand, Kapllani warmly said to the secretary of state, "I greet you in the name of Doug Coe." Several people I interviewed referred to the Fellowship as an "underground State Department," and the Fellowship has been particularly effective at reaching areas of the world where the State Department is constrained in one way or another. People associated with the Fellowship have been involved in brokering the peace agreement between the Democratic Republic of the Congo and Rwanda and, more recently, in the 2005 peace talks in the Sudan. At least on the international front, this is a very powerful group.[63]

Beyond its occasional diplomatic efforts, the Fellowship provides much-needed social lubrication for an increasingly partisan Washington. Informal get-togethers for elected officials and their spouses used to foster goodwill that contributed to collaborations across the aisle. Now, with many members of Congress returning to their districts every weekend, many families and spouses do not move to Washington, and longtime insiders I interviewed report that this has contributed a great deal to the deepening divisions along partisan lines.[64] Fellowship gatherings are an antidote to this trend. Of course, individuals maintain their partisan allegiances at Fellowship venues, but the group is not organized by party. The Fellowship provides "neutral space" where leaders gather more as people than as governmental officials or business executives. This is very important to public leaders, who see these gatherings as "a haven for people in public life" where they can establish and maintain a sense of "intimacy with other people." The religious component of the Fellowship provides a bond that distinguishes it from other groups. The esteem in which many political leaders hold the Fellowship has enabled the group to expand its influence over the years and across administrations.[65] The long tenure of its ministry, along with the group's aversion to taking positions on contentious issues like abortion, has given the Fellowship unrivaled access to governmental leaders. Its low-key attitude allowed it to attract people of various religious traditions, both inside and outside the evangelical world— a subtle, "quieter" form of evangelical outreach that appeals to religious traditionalists like James Baker and George H. W. Bush.[66] The Fellowship represents a different kind of evangelicalism, one that is less fanatical and extreme, an evangelicalism of the establishment. This, in turn, has been extremely important to building a sense of cohesion among political leaders, a cohesion that crosses party lines and sectors of governmental life. As we shall see, these kinds of strong personal connections, grounded in faith, have been essential to evangelicals' rise to power.

2

Allies and Enemies

ONE EVENING, the entertainer Kathie Lee Gifford, a self-identified evangelical, sat at a dinner party beside New York governor George Pataki. She told me:

> We were having dinner one time in the Hamptons, at a friend's home, and we [a charity for children with AIDS that Gifford supports] were suing the State of New York because they had blinded HIV testing for pregnant women [meaning that the women could not learn the results]. And as a result, babies were coming into the world with the HIV virus and sometimes full-blown AIDS. [If those same babies had received] a cocktail of AZT and some other [drugs while in utero], it would go from over 40 percent to less than an 8 percent chance that [these women] would have an AIDS baby.... All they [the State of New York] were doing was tracking pregnant women, testing them, and sending the blinded test results to the CDC to track the disease.
>
> Here's where I say my ministry is, if I have one. If I were off in Africa as a missionary, I wouldn't be sitting in the Hamptons having dinner with George Pataki.[1] ... I'm his dinner partner and I've got him for two hours, and I can sit with him and tell him why it's immoral that pregnant women are not told the test results so that they could get a very simple cocktail and, as a result, bring a child into this world that will probably not have the AIDS virus. He listened to me intently, and because I was knowledgeable...he said, "We're on the wrong side of this lawsuit.... This is wrong and...I'm going to do something about it." ... Within one month, he mandated that all of HIV testing in New York State be unblinded so that the woman would know the results and...could get the in utero protection. That's the first year that the death rates of AIDS went down in New York State.

Evangelicals have brought their faith convictions to bear on a variety of public issues in recent decades, including AIDS, poverty, and human trafficking. Celebrities and business leaders have used their connections to influence other parties, and for many, this is a way they act on religious convictions. This, in turn, has contributed to wider evangelical influence in American political life.

Faith and Public Policy

So what role does faith play in shaping public policy? Just as evangelicals express their identity by voting, many of the leaders I interviewed said that the chance to implement policies grounded in their faith was what drove their political ambitions. In what follows, I show how evangelicals framed particular issues in moral and/or religious terms and what difference that makes. As we proceed, we should attend not only to the messages but also to the messengers. Many of the same White House officials who were appointed to reward the evangelical movement were the driving forces behind their favored policies. The people I spoke with said three policy areas were particularly important to evangelicals. We begin with the most contentious political issue of the last thirty years: abortion.

The Conscience of a Nation

Francis Schaeffer was one of the first evangelical leaders to frame abortion as a moral issue. In the 1950s, the American pastor relocated his family to Switzerland to establish a quasi-commune called L'Abri in the Alps. Schaeffer influenced many young evangelicals who visited L'Abri from the 1950s to the 1970s, urging them to think deeply about the claims their Christian faith made on issues of public relevance. Schaeffer believed evangelicals should be at the forefront of politics, the arts, and the academy. Indeed, many people who went on to hold positions of societal influence in these areas—including many of those I interviewed—were spurred on by Schaeffer. One of the boldest moves Schaeffer undertook, according to evangelical leader Tony Campolo, was his "frontal attack" against existentialism, the prevailing philosophy of his time. Although few Christian philosophers agree with Schaeffer's argument today, at the time his willingness to challenge such a widely held position buoyed the spirits of many within the fold.

Dr. C. Everett Koop and Dr. Harold O. J. Brown, an evangelical theologian and ethicist, were also key figures in the pro-life movement. Brown believed at least part of the reticence among evangelicals to embrace a pro-life position stemmed from latent anti-Catholic bias, since the Roman Catholics were then leading the attack against abortion. Koop and Brown first met in February 1975 at a Christian men's conference in New Orleans. Later that year, they joined Billy Graham and Schaeffer in forming the Christian Action Council, a group focused on lobbying Congress for legislation that would tighten restrictions on abortions. In 1977, Koop, Schaeffer, and Schaeffer's son Franky produced a five-segment film series and companion book entitled *Whatever Happened to the Human Race?* The film, which featured a memorable scene of Koop standing along the shore of Israel's Dead Sea surrounded by thousands of baby dolls, argued that abortion was both the cause and the end result of society's eroding commitment to the sanctity of human life. The film also suggested that Koop was standing on the site of the biblical city of Sodom, which was destroyed because of its moral depravity. It was impossible to miss the implied message for America. Koop and Schaeffer traveled the nation, promoting their film and spurring the faithful to action. Soon thereafter, what began as a Roman Catholic concern became a passionate issue for evangelicals as well.

President Reagan's nomination of Koop to be surgeon general was therefore an important symbolic act. Not only was it a way of shoring up Reagan's credentials as a pro-life president, but it also demonstrated to evangelicals that he would nominate a few of their own to high office.[2] During the 1980s, as the Supreme Court muddled its way through the particulars of abortion laws, the debate was increasingly framed in moral terms.[3] In 1983, Reagan authored the only book to be released by a U.S. president while in office, *Abortion and the Conscience of a Nation.*[4] Citing the tenth anniversary of *Roe v. Wade* as the occasion for his comments, Reagan argued that legalized abortion diminished the value of "all human life." He then touted efforts he and his political allies had undertaken to "reverse the tide of abortion," admonishing them to "not lose heart." On June 17, 1984, the Reagan administration announced a significant policy change relating to abortion funding. The Mexico City Policy, as it was called, required nongovernmental organizations to agree they would not perform or promote abortion.[5] If they refused, they would receive no federal funds. The policy became a political hot potato. In 1990, a federal court dismissed Planned Parenthood's lawsuit challenging the Mexico City Policy, but on his first day in office, President Clinton issued an executive order repealing it, only to have the policy reinstated by George W. Bush on *his* first day in office.[6]

Despite Reagan's rhetoric, many evangelical leaders felt that he did not deliver on abortion. No constitutional amendment banning abortion was passed, and two of his nominees to the U.S. Supreme Court—as the country would eventually learn with 1992's *Planned Parenthood v. Casey*—were unwilling to reverse *Roe v. Wade*.[7] In the final weeks of his presidency, Reagan and his evangelical surgeon general, Dr. Koop, came under considerable fire from evangelical leaders. President Reagan, persuaded by several of his pro-life staffers, had commissioned the surgeon general to study the health effects of abortion on women. These staffers were convinced the results would be so conclusive against abortion that *Roe v. Wade* would be rendered ineffective. Koop conducted the study at the president's request and submitted a letter in January 1989 detailing the results. The letter concluded, "I regret, Mr. President, in spite of a diligent review on the part of many in the Public Health System and in the private sector, the scientific studies do not provide conclusive data about the health effects of abortion on women." Once the letter was leaked to the press, the pro-choice camp claimed a victory, and Reagan's pro-life constituents howled with outrage. The involvement of Koop—who was originally selected for his pro-life credentials—astounded evangelical leaders. How could he have made such claims, they reasoned, especially since he had spent years talking about the psychological damage abortion did to women? Koop insists to this day that he had much anecdotal evidence along these lines but not enough scientific data to draw firm conclusions. Despite this, he remains a seminal figure in the abortion debate, and like other evangelicals, Koop continues to frame the abortion issue as a religious matter.

Even some Democrats I interviewed frame abortion in religious terms. President Carter told me, "I never have felt that Christ would approve abortion." Ohio congressman Tony Hall agreed with Carter and spoke of the issue this way: "God wants to save these children; He doesn't want these children killed." Hall told me that his position on abortion, which he switched after becoming an evangelical while in office, has "caused me a lot of trouble. . . . You can mention my name [among the Democratic Party leadership] and they spit. . . . [They] even . . . walk across the street not to talk to me because they hated the fact that I . . . was a Democrat and yet pro-life." The alliance between Democrats and pro-choice advocates, which has become more entrenched since the 1970s, is something that leaders I spoke to mentioned repeatedly when asked why they were Republicans. In fact, among those leaders who mentioned they were Republicans, the top reason given for their political affiliation was the party's pro-life position.[8]

Sexuality is also of paramount importance to evangelicals. Recently, they have turned their attention to policies that relate to the gay and lesbian community. After the Defense of Marriage Act was passed by Congress in 1996, most political activity on same-sex unions shifted to the state level.[9] In states around the country, evangelicals have been at the forefront of legislative efforts to bar homosexuals from marrying. Results have been mixed, as many states have recognized domestic partnerships and civil unions for gay couples, even if they do not call them "marriages." But in 2004, evangelicals were successful in passing amendments to state constitutions that banned same-sex marriage in thirteen states. Many political observers link this political victory to high voter turnout among evangelicals that year—especially in battleground states like Ohio and Missouri—which also helped reelect George W. Bush. In 2006, seven additional states did the same, but the proposition's rejection by Arizona voters that year points to ongoing differences of opinion among the American electorate. Court decisions such as *Lawrence v. Texas,* which overturned Texas state law criminalizing sodomy, have recently reinvigorated evangelical political activism, just as *Roe v. Wade* did in the 1970s.

Faith, Justice, and Foreign Affairs

As evangelicals became politically engaged in the 1960s and 1970s, most of their political ambitions revolved around domestic issues like abortion and public schooling. By the mid-1990s, evangelicals had started to frame foreign policy issues in religious terms, and in a span of ten years, they have become the foreign policy conscience of political conservatives, championing issues like religious freedom, human rights, the abolition of human trafficking, and increased foreign aid. Their interest in foreign affairs begins, of course, with their long involvement in the missionary movement. Evangelicals were the prime movers during the flowering of foreign missions agencies in the nineteenth century, spreading the message of their faith to far corners of the world. Through correspondence with missionaries abroad and extended conversations when missionaries returned home, rank-and-file evangelicals remained informed about regional conflicts, natural disasters, and personal tribulations. Tales about the persecution of missionaries became part of evangelical lore, but as technology made communication faster and more reliable, evangelicals began to learn of episodes like these within hours or days instead of weeks or months. Under the influence of a few key individuals, the evangelical community mobilized around concerns over religious persecution.[10] Michael Horowitz, a lawyer in the Reagan administration, was one example. In the 1980s, he helped maintain White House pressure on the Soviet Union so that persecuted Jews could emigrate, and by the 1990s, he was concerned about the plight of persecuted Christians as well. Using connections he had forged with evangelicals through the Reagan White House, Horowitz rallied evangelical leaders to action, faxing and calling them constantly. In January 1996, Horowitz's lobbying efforts paid off: The National Association of Evangelicals approved a Statement of Conscience that detailed the steps necessary to secure religious liberty around the world. With this statement, the concept of "religious liberty" became a key driver for evangelical political activism.[11] In many ways, the rhetoric around religious liberty not only reflected changes within American evangelicalism but also helped bring evangelicalism into the mainstream. Instead of talking about converting others, evangelicals framed their involvement in foreign affairs around issues of human rights. This has been a key part of the movement's maturation.

With the NAE's support, in 1996 evangelical leaders began lobbying Congress for action. The result was the passage of the International Religious Freedom Act (IRFA), signed into law by President Clinton in October 1998. This legislation, the most sweeping of its kind ever passed, made freedom of religion a core objective of U.S. foreign policy, created an independent Commission on International Religious Freedom and an ambassador-at-large for international religious freedom, and required an annual report from the State Department on the status of religious freedom in every country of the world.[12] John V. Hanford, the current ambassador-at-large for international religious freedom, was one of the main drafters of the legislation that became known as IRFA. Hanford's background includes work in both the religious and political spheres: He holds a graduate theological degree and spent many years serving as the executive director of the Congressional Fellows program. Today, he is regarded as among the most knowledgeable in his field, and he embodies the nuanced approach to foreign affairs that many evangelicals have embraced in recent years. Evangelical involvement in international religious freedom began, in part, out of concern for evangelical missionaries abroad, particularly in places where their safety and well-being were not guaranteed by foreign governments. Gradually, however, it grew to include the protection of religious liberty for people of all faiths and to the extension of other basic human rights.

In addition to their lobbying efforts on Capitol Hill, evangelicals actively courted the White House. To the surprise of some, the Clinton administration was quite receptive. In 2004, Ted Haggard, then president of the NAE, told me that the media may say "there's more [evangelical] influence [with the Bush White House] than ever before, but it's not true. We were concerned about the state of believers in communist China, [and] the Clinton White House was very receptive to those types of things."

Historian Gary Scott Smith argues it is usually in foreign policy that a president shows his true philosophical commitments. Domestic politics, and especially relations with Congress, can constrain the president, but in foreign affairs, the president has much greater latitude to act.[13] Indeed, on the international front, President Clinton appointed evangelicals to very prominent posts.[14] One of these was Brady Anderson, a former missionary in Africa for Wycliffe Bible Translators. Anderson served as U.S. ambassador to Tanzania during President Clinton's first term and then as administrator for the United States Agency for International Development (USAID) during his second. Also, when Clinton named the first ambassador-at-large for international religious freedom, he chose Robert Seiple, the then-CEO of the massive evangelical aid agency World Vision.[15] When I interviewed them, these leaders stressed the importance of not giving preferential treatment to fellow evangelicals. Referring to federal grants from USAID, Anderson said to me, "As the head of the organization, I never awarded anybody anything. I may have signed things, but decisions were made [by others]. I was careful not to give the appearance of some sort of bias because I was a Christian. [However,] in terms of foreign aid, the U.S. government has long used Christian organizations . . . big-time." Out of a sense of spiritual concern, evangelicals have become active in a variety of governmental structures, including the U.S. State Department and USAID. Through unique channels, such as connections with missionaries, evangelicals have maintained their interest in issues abroad. More recently, they have acted using governmental resources, not simply religious ones. Lobbying the U.S. government on foreign affairs is a new form of evangelical activism, but it falls within a longer stream of evangelical concern for developments abroad. At the same time, evangelicals have established some new nongovernmental organizations directed toward providing international aid and development.

Consider two examples: the International Justice Mission (IJM) and Rick Warren's PEACE plan. Both were formed in recent years, and both rely on the language of evangelical activism and Christian compassion. In 1997, Gary Haugen, a civil rights attorney at the

Department of Justice, launched IJM, which is focused on helping the poor and suffering abroad by providing them with legal protection. Haugen told me that he founded IJM with the goal of "rescuing people who suffer from injustice," whether they are children trapped in sex slavery or migrant workers abused by a corrupt police force. Working through indigenous attorneys and law enforcement professionals, IJM receives case referrals from and works with other nongovernmental organizations around the world. Haugen, whose vision for the ministry arose from an evangelical Bible study meeting he regularly attended with other lawyers, said, "Twenty-five years ago, IJM couldn't have made this kind of progress. Previous generations [of evangelicals] thought the social gospel was a distraction to spiritual concerns." Yet today, IJM is pursuing an evangelical social gospel.[16] Geared more toward case work than policy advocacy, IJM aims to "motivate the evangelical community...to care about what's going on in the world beyond [U.S.] borders and to pay attention to the sin of injustice." This concern for social justice overseas reflects a broadening of evangelicals' political ambition. No longer satisfied with focusing on domestic issues, they have formed an ambitious agenda born out of religious conviction.

Not all matters of foreign policy are of interest to evangelicals. They show substantially less interest in trade policy or military alliances, even though these are central to U.S. foreign policy. Instead, evangelicals are focused on humanitarian issues and, generally speaking, the same kinds of issues that have concerned them at home. For example, their activism against sex slavery and prostitution is driven by their strong beliefs about sex. Those I spoke to suggested that sex slavery represents an arena where contemporary evangelicals see themselves as heirs to nineteenth-century abolitionists.[17] For forty-five years, evangelical politician William Wilberforce lobbied for the abolition of the slave trade in England, and many of the leaders I spoke to cited Wilberforce as a role model in their fight against human trafficking.[18] Evangelicals have also actively lobbied the Bush administration for an increase in foreign aid to Africa. The evangelical missionary movement long relied on an image of "savage" Africa to motivate people for evangelism. But in more recent years, things have changed. For instance, after the incredible success of *The Purpose-Driven Life,* evangelical pastor Rick Warren launched his PEACE plan, aimed at enlisting four hundred thousand churches in forty-seven nations to nurse, feed, and educate the poor. His long-term goal is to make Africa more entrepreneurial and self-sustaining. Through a personal friendship with Rwandan president Paul Kagame, Warren and his southern California congregation have launched an unprecedented effort to create a "purpose-driven nation" that they hope will make the country a leader on the African continent. Warren's PEACE plan, funded in part by the royalties from his best-selling book, is an ambitious project to link congregations, evangelical organizations, other nongovernmental organizations, and foreign governments in a shared vision for addressing poverty in Africa.[19] This trend, of combining evangelistic projects with concerns such as famine and disease, represents an important shift, both substantively and rhetorically, within the evangelical movement. Of course, these efforts have their detractors. Some experts in foreign aid and development see Warren's plan as naïve and claim that he underestimates challenges like the West's restrictive agricultural trade policies: Even if Rwanda is able to produce enough agricultural goods for foreign export, Western markets will be closed to them under current policy. Some also raise concerns about Warren's coziness with Kagame. In 1994, Kagame led the Tutsi forces that ended his country's genocide, and for that he is praised. But his forces still occupy parts of the Democratic Republic of Congo, and human rights observers have accused these troops of raping and murdering innocent civilians.

Other evangelical entities, like World Vision, have brought issues such as AIDS and famine on the African continent to the attention of American evangelicals. With an annual budget over $1.3 billion, World Vision International was the largest handler of food in 2005, and nearly all of that food was donated by the U.S. government. Indeed, the synergy between evangelical groups like World Vision and the U.S. government has helped increase evangelical involvement in foreign affairs. And while evangelism—converting others— may have been their original motive, groups like World Vision are far less evangelistic than many might assume. In fact, it is World Vision's policy to hire workers from the countries where it operates, which in certain countries means employing Muslims. One evangelical philanthropist talked with me about this; in a disapproving tone, he noted, "World Vision is the largest Christian employer of Muslims around the world."

How did this alliance between the U.S. government and the evangelical community come about? One key element has been the placement of committed evangelicals in senior governmental positions. Like President Clinton, President Bush has placed numerous evangelicals in important advisory roles. When asked, current administration officials minimize the place of religious sentiment in shaping public policy. Dan Bartlett, counselor to the president, said in a 2003 interview, "George W. Bush is not making decisions based on his personal faith,"[20] and when I asked Karen Hughes, one of President Bush's closest advisors and a fellow evangelical, about the president's faith, she described it as "a foundation . . . a set of beliefs on which we try to live and try to base decisions. [Faith] shapes our view of the world." But, she said, it does not usually come up in "decision-making conversations in the Oval Office"; it recedes to the background. Despite these statements, I found that presidential appointments are not only symbolically important. Certain policies have been heavily shaped by evangelical staffers. This was clearly the case when Gary Bauer served as President Reagan's domestic policy advisor, and it has been the case with one of President Bush's chief advisors, Michael Gerson.

Echoing a message expressed by several other evangelicals who work in the Bush White House, Gerson talked about the tension between his own faith-based convictions on certain positions and the need for a president to make "publicly accessible arguments." He told me, "That means appealing to moral and philosophic principles that are often arrived at by faith, but *not always* arrived at by faith. . . . Clearly my own . . . views are influenced by my faith, but I think it's possible for people to come to those views by other routes." In addition to Gerson's critical role in shaping Bush's speeches, he served as the in-house guardian of the president's agenda of "compassionate conservatism." When I interviewed Gerson, gnawed pen caps littering his desk, he declared, "Christianity is not just a statement about personal piety; it's a statement about social justice." That commitment to social justice, which drew him to Jimmy Carter thirty years ago, compelled him to act once inside the Bush White House.

Soon after his arrival, Gerson and Joshua Bolten, then the deputy White House chief of staff (he would later become White House chief of staff), began gathering data on the global AIDS pandemic, what the U.S. government was doing, and what else could be done. Gerson's concern about AIDS demonstrates a significant shift in opinion within the evangelical world. When C. Everett Koop took up the issue, most evangelical leaders denounced him. To them, the disease was God's scourge for sinful behavior, and government intervention would be thwarting divine judgment. By 2003, though, the tide had turned. Evangelicals in the White House were actively involved in changing the federal government's position. When President Bush announced his intention to dedicate $15 billion to fight the spread of AIDS, evangelical leaders praised it as a bold act. Some of these were the same people who had excoriated Koop for giving the disease national attention back in 1986. Bush's announcement transformed what was a glaring omission from the public agenda of conservative evangelicals into a cause célèbre. Gerson and Bolten, insiders attest, were critical to getting AIDS on the president's agenda.[21]

Evangelicals' involvement in foreign affairs has resulted in unlikely alliances with liberal Jews, Tibetan Buddhists, and various feminist groups, all of whom regard human rights as moral concerns. By 2000, evangelicals had joined forces with Gloria Steinem and every major feminist organization to lobby for the Victims of Trafficking and Protection Act, legislation aimed at curbing the spread of sex slavery and human trafficking. Demonstrating commitment to their political allies, evangelicals successfully lobbied the Bush White House to name John Miller, a former Republican congressman from Seattle and a Jew, to be the first head of the State Department's Trafficking in Persons Office. Of course, evangelical activism abroad is not without controversy. One of the more contentious issues has been the nexus between evangelical involvement in foreign affairs and economic globalization. In particular, groups like World Relief, originally sponsored by the National Association of Evangelicals, provide assistance in poor countries through micro enterprise development and financial assistance. Former NAE president Ted Haggard told me that he sees globalization as "the greatest friend of the Bible-believing Christian. . . . We need globalization to communicate the gospel message." Globalization, he claimed, benefits the poor. "The resources in the first world didn't become the resources of the first world because we stole them from the third world. The resources of the first world became the resources of the first world because we discovered the miracle of the creation of wealth, and that's what's happening in Africa today."

Not all Americans, and indeed not all evangelicals, agree with Haggard. At a recent conference for evangelical philanthropists, a representative from John Stott Ministries (JSM) spoke of the relationship between globalization and the poor. Stott's group, founded by the man many regard as "evangelicalism's pope," is an important foil to free-trade advocates within the evangelical community.[22] The JSM speaker argued that economic globalization worsens the condition of the poor worldwide. Even as he praised the cultural benefits of globalization, he condemned evangelicals for "baptizing" the economic imperialism of the West. So even as evangelicals have pushed the Bush administration in certain directions, strong differences of opinion can be found within the movement. From speaking to leaders, I get the sense that they are pleased by things like the tripling of the amount of American aid to Africa. Conservative evangelicals are particularly pleased that this support has not gone through groups like the U.N. Population Fund, whose policies on abortion and contraception are anathema to evangelicals. Perhaps the most intriguing development is that many evangelical leaders now embrace what they rejected during the Carter presidency—namely, a rhetoric that makes human rights the bedrock of American foreign policy.

The Armies of Compassion

On his ninth day in office, George W. Bush announced the Faith-Based and Community Initiative, which he argued was designed to end a "legacy of discrimination against faith-based charities."[23] Immediately, detractors raised concerns about the separation of church and state. Political critics also charged that Bush was simply pandering to the African American community. And indeed, many African American religious leaders responded favorably to the prospect of federal money for inner-city programs. Bush chose John DiIulio, a Harvard-trained political scientist, to head up the Office of Faith-Based and Community Initiatives (OFBCI). DiIulio, whom the president called "Big John" because of his formidable intellect and stocky build, shared the president's born-again faith. Each of them had embraced his faith as an adult, and each subsequently garnered public attention for the transformation. DiIulio now runs a research center at the University of Pennsylvania where he also serves as Fox Leadership Professor. I sat down with DiIulio on Election Day in 2004—an unusually warm day made worse by the fact that the building's air conditioner never works. The center had spearheaded a get-out-the-vote initiative among Penn undergrads, and the conference room where we met was strewn with candy wrappers and empty Coke cans left over from the all-nighter pulled by students working with DiIulio. Although he was a Democrat voting for Bush, DiIulio was primarily interested in motivating Penn students to civic activism, regardless of their preferred candidate.

During our time together, DiIulio talked about his faith awakening. It occurred when he was thirty-eight. "Some people have a quiet faith experience. I had to tell the world and create a White House office. . . . I broke a lot of china along the way." DiIulio was also a lifelong Democrat and a self-described "born-again *Catholic*," making him different from both the secular advisors surrounding Bush and the evangelical Protestants in the president's inner circle. Yet the two men believed strongly in the effectiveness of faith-based programs, with Bush's support based in part on the role of faith in his battle against alcoholism. Early on, they were about the only ones who liked the idea. As DiIulio told me, "Some people thought the president needed a warm and fuzzy. This warm and fuzzy had all kinds of thorns.... [In fact] there was only one person in the White House who consistently loved the idea, and his name is George W. Bush."[24] As governor of Texas, Bush had invited faith-based groups like Prison Fellowship to take an active role in the state's penal system, so he had some experience with government support of faith-based programs.

The president hoped DiIulio's credentials as an academic and a Democrat would sway liberal detractors in favor of the fledgling program. To signal the program's importance, President Bush issued two executive orders, one establishing the office and appointing DiIulio, who would answer directly to the president, and the other commissioning a six-month study on what should be done. DiIulio told me that from the beginning, the office was not intended to resemble "1-800-Dial-a-Prayer," but it was a priority for the president, born in part out of his own evangelical faith. When the Senate failed to pass a bill that hewed to the administration's initiative in 2001, the president proceeded by using his executive powers. Such action allowed the president to bypass Congress on more contentious issues like federal grants for religious organizations. However, a future president can rescind Bush's orders easily, whereas federal legislation, if it had passed, would have been more difficult to change. In addition to the White House OFBCI, suboffices were created within five cabinet agencies. With the president's backing, evangelicals working at these various agencies introduced their colleagues to evangelical organizations that might produce worthy grant applications.[25] I spoke to Steven Law when he was deputy secretary of labor. He explained it this way:

> One of the things that I did early on was bring in someone from World Vision to meet with our career-level people. We have a little entity here called the International Labor Affairs Bureau.... It administers a lot of grants, and it has a big footprint on trade issues. Previous to that time, I think...most of our career professionals...had never heard of World Vision.... [When they met with some of them, though,] they were just blown away,....completely impressed.... Then we also brought in International Justice Mission. International Justice Mission submitted what the career people said was the highest quality grant solicitation they'd ever seen.

Though then–Vice President Gore and then–Governor Bush both supported some form of faith-based initiatives during the 2000 campaign, Bush's program was clearly the more comprehensive. Recognizing that Washington is home to, in his words, "the Super Bowl of high-contact, high-impact political conflict," DiIulio and others realized relatively quickly that there was no chance of legislation that might maintain the policy after Bush's presidency. That is why the executive orders have been so critical. Even without legislative sanction, as one critic, speaking off the record, said to me, "Now, with eight years of Bush policy in place, that train has left the station, and it's not coming back." Evangelical language has been key to selling faith-based initiatives. In his 2003 State of the Union Address, Bush, alluding to a well-known evangelical hymn, referred to the "power, wonder-working power" in the compassionate acts performed by Americans every day.[26] He continued, "These good works deserve our praise ... and when appropriate, they deserve the assistance of the federal government."

Each of these policy areas—abortion and human sexuality, foreign aid, and government funding of faith-based groups—is important. However, compared to the staggering range of issues every administration faces, they are relatively small. Evangelicals have rarely framed economic, health care, or energy policies as religious issues. In terms of actual policies, therefore, religious faith has played a relatively small role in governance, even when outspoken evangelicals have occupied the White House. Practically no political leader—of either party—that I interviewed could identify legislation or executive action that was born entirely out of faith conviction, including officials in the present administration. Some claim that Bush's evangelicalism strongly influences the administration's relations with Israel and Arab nations. This assertion links the apocalyptic eschatology of a fragment of American evangelicals to a much larger constituency.[27] However, such assertions assume a cohesive theology and ideology within the movement that simply does not exist. Like many other evangelicals, President Bush appears to draw from a theological and ideological mosaic instead of a cohesive, systematic theology.[28] For example, when Bush became the first U.S. president to publicly support a separate state for Palestinians, he defied conservative theologians who believe the United States should favor Israel because of biblical prophecy. Indeed, conservative biblical prophecy on the Middle East is completely foreign to Bush and his approach toward Israel and Palestine, based on the interviews I conducted. Not even Bush's critics that I talked with could cite an example of this being part of a policy discussion within the administration. Tony Campolo, a leader among liberal evangelicals, says the president's groundbreaking position on Palestine has elicited scorn and derision among many of his fellow evangelicals.

Religion does play an important role in policymaking by providing a shared language for framing particular policies. But the actual number of policies affected is relatively small.[29]

Building a Movement

As evangelicals have become more politically involved, they have formed strategic coalitions with all kinds of groups. These coalitions have helped mightily in bringing evangelicalism to the forefront of American political life. Sociologist J. P. Nettl has pointed out that grassroots and elite mobilization are two forms of the same phenomenon, just as stalagmite and stalactite mineral formations converge toward a common end.[30] American evangelicalism has gained political momentum as its leaders have built coalitions with others who are interested in similar objectives. This has happened largely at the leadership level, but rank-and-file support has soon followed. Grassroots support within a movement is easier to mobilize when clear boundaries are drawn between allies and adversaries, and evangelicals have excelled at this.

Common Enemies

Eric Hoffer has argued that social movements may not need a "God," but they must have a "devil."[31] If only for rhetorical purposes, social movements require a nemesis as a rallying point. According to several observers from within the movement, American evangelicalism has a history of opposing particular devils, and many movement leaders are keenly aware of this. Tony Campolo once organized a meeting between President Clinton and several moderate evangelical leaders. At that meeting, Campolo told me, Clinton wanted to know why evangelicals were opposing him and other Democrats. Mark Noll, a celebrated evangelical historian, told the president that evangelicals often rally around a common enemy, and the Clintons were that enemy during the 1990s. But the Democratic Party was just the latest in a succession of evangelical devils. In the 1920s, the devil was Darwin. From the 1930s to the 1960s, it was communism. Partly as a result of their opposition to "godless communism," evangelicals rallied around the American flag and a sense of America as a distinctively "Christian" nation.[32] This was particularly the case among the Youth for Christ leaders in the 1940s, many of whom, like Billy Graham and Ted Engstrom, would later take the helm of large evangelical organizations.[33] Opposition, of course, is not the only reason evangelicals began working together. American evangelicals first united out of a common sense of mission—namely, to share their religious vision with those outside the movement. But how did American evangelicalism become wedded to conservative politics?[34]

The answer can be found in the 1960s. Changing views of gender roles, the success of the civil rights movement, and the emergence of mass mobilization eroded the powerful—some would say dominating—influence of just a few American institutions like the church, school, and family. The civil rights movement demonstrated that prominent private citizens working outside established institutions could bring about seismic change. Historian George Marsden suggests that once the major battles over civil rights had ended, Southerners turned their attention away from race and toward religion.[35] Indeed, many evangelical leaders interested in politics—such as Jerry Falwell, Pat Robertson, and James Robison—came from the South. These leaders were socially conservative but often registered as Democrats. Their uneasy alliance with the Democratic Party finally came apart when Lyndon Johnson signed the Civil Rights Act of 1965. At the same time, supporters of conservative Republican Barry Goldwater, who lost in a landslide to Johnson in 1964, began marshaling forces to establish the broad-based coalitions that would revive American conservatism. In 1965, they founded the American Conservative Union. Phyllis Schlafly, a Harvard graduate and Goldwater supporter, founded her own political newsletter, *The Phyllis Schlafly Report*, and by 1972 she had established a formidable women's group to oppose the Equal Rights Amendment. That organization, now called the Eagle Forum, is a critical part of the conservative infrastructure. Another Goldwater supporter, Paul Weyrich, had been impressed by the way disparate liberal groups coordinated strategy and communication in the 1960s. With the financial sponsorship of Joseph Coors, head of the Colorado brewing family, he pushed conservatives to do the same. Two entities birthed by Weyrich's leadership, the Heritage Foundation and the Committee for the Survival of a Free Congress, were major players in bringing evangelicals into conservative politics.[36] Ironically, neither Weyrich nor Schlafly came from the evangelical world of Billy Graham and Bill Bright; both grew up Catholic. But conservative politicians knew

Graham and his world quite well. President Nixon was very close to the evangelical leader, and Nixon's political team actively courted him.[37] During the 1968 campaign, Graham arranged for the candidate to be seated in the VIP section at his Pittsburgh crusade. Months later, in the run-up to the November election, the evangelist let it slip that he had cast an early vote for Nixon on his absentee ballot, and Graham's tacit endorsement solidified Nixon's standing with evangelicals. The Sunday following his inauguration, the president instituted the first regular religious service in the history of the White House, and Billy Graham was the inaugural preacher. Nixon also appointed a liaison to the religious community, a position that has existed ever since.[38]

Watergate threatened the emerging evangelical–Republican alliance. Billy Graham and others were shocked by President Nixon's involvement. Accompanying this erosion of public trust was a feeling among evangelicals that America was abandoning traditional values. Jimmy Carter's candidacy gave evangelicals the chance to renew their commitment by electing the nation's first modern-day evangelical. But once he was elected, many of these same leaders grew frustrated with his inability to enact policies they favored or to appoint fellow evangelicals to prominent positions. As he would soon learn, Carter was being associated with the next "devil" to which evangelicals were mounting opposition: secular humanism.

The term "secular humanism" comes from Francis Schaeffer's *How Should We Then Live?* (1976). It became a catch-all phrase for the ideology evangelicals believed was driving religion from the public square. Schaeffer distinguished secular humanism from Christian humanism. Christian humanism, an idea that flourished during the Renaissance, advocated a high view of humanity and the advancement of human culture. It did so not by rejecting God but by embracing the conviction that humans, even though born sinful, were created in God's image and therefore of great worth. Secular humanism, in Schaeffer's formulation, flowed from the *Humanist Manifesto*, written in 1933, which argued that "religions that place revelation, God, ritual or creed above human needs and experience do a disservice to the human species." In fact, Schaeffer's last work, *The Christian Manifesto* (1982), was a direct response to this 1933 publication. In it, the pastor-theologian argued that Christians should actively resist state-sponsored forms of secularism.[39]

President Carter first encountered the term "secular humanism" during a 1979 Oval Office conversation with Adrian Rogers, the newly elected president of Carter's own denomination, the Southern

Baptist Convention.[40] The meeting, Carter told me, is one he has never forgotten.

> We had a very pleasant discussion about different aspects of life, not unpleasant at all. And then as he was leaving the Oval Office, I remember exactly where I was standing. He said, "Mr. President I hope that you will abandon your commitment as a secular humanist." . . . I was taken aback. I had no idea what he was talking about. I didn't know what a secular humanist was, . . . so when I . . . got back to eat lunch with Rosalyn, I asked her if she ever heard of the phrase "secular humanist." And she said, "No, I don't know what it means."

It is strange that a Baptist Sunday school teacher would be accused of being a secular humanist by the leader of his own denomination, but Rogers' charge was leveled more at his administration. As one cabinet secretary from the Reagan administration said to me, Carter "brought people with him who had a humanist worldview" who "went out of their way to undercut Jimmy Carter anytime he came up with an initiative that didn't suit them."[41] Conservative evangelical leaders also charged Carter with permitting the spread of communism in far-flung places like Angola and Mozambique and allowing the rise of the Sandinistas in Nicaragua. Conservatives further resented the sense of despair that had enveloped the nation, to which Carter alluded in his famous "Crisis of Confidence" speech. In it, the president referred to "a crisis that strikes at the very heart and soul and spirit of our national will. We can see this crisis in the growing doubt about the meaning of our own lives and in the loss of a unity of purpose for our nation." In the days that followed, pundits thought the speech made Carter sound more like a doomsday prophet than a savior. Conservative evangelicals thought the administration was completely adrift. Pat Robertson told me "millions of evangelicals were frankly disgusted" with Carter, his policies, and his sense of despair. In a last-ditch effort to repair relations, the president hosted a breakfast meeting with several evangelical leaders, including D. James Kennedy, Charles Stanley, and Jerry Falwell. During their conversation, the leaders became increasingly dissatisfied with the president's comments about abortion, equal rights for women, and various appointments he had made over the course of his administration. This, they have since claimed, was the final straw. After that meeting, several of them turned their back on Carter and organized in support of a clearly conservative political and social agenda.

Many of the same movement leaders who walked away frustrated from that meeting with President Carter became important figures in the formation of the Moral Majority. Founded in 1979, the Moral Majority campaigned for issues that conservative evangelicals cared about: outlawing abortion, suppressing gay rights, and advancing their vision for family life. The Moral Majority and other groups like it rely on Francis Schaeffer's concept of *co-belligerency*: the idea that there were many groups who shared evangelicals' convictions and that they could achieve more by working together. Evangelicals had seen the political benefits of joining with conservative Catholics in the pro-life coalition of the 1970s. The Moral Majority similarly reached out to these like-minded groups. They joined forces to fight the encroachment of secularism in the public sphere and on matters like abortion, prayer in schools, and homosexuality. Over time, the evangelical community became the driving force behind these political alliances. In April 1980, movement leaders Bill Bright and Pat Robertson sponsored an event called "Washington for Jesus." This was a turning point in evangelical political activism. Through television programs, mailing lists, and personal outreach, movement leaders gathered half a million evangelicals in Washington, D.C., on April 29, the anniversary of the first settlers landing at Jamestown in 1607. The event linked evangelical fervor with patriotic sentiment, and the movement's conservative leanings reappeared—with a clear preference for Ronald Reagan's candidacy. The Religious Right was more sophisticated and organized than it had ever been.[42]

Even though the Moral Majority succeeded in galvanizing evangelicals in the 1980s, as early as 1985 leaders within the group were growing uneasy about the alliance between religion and politics. Moral Majority vice president Cal Thomas resigned from the organization to pursue a career as a columnist. When I interviewed Thomas, he told me that evangelical political action at the time was—and according to him still is—"operating in the flesh and attaching God's name to it.... It's doomed to futility." In 1996, Thomas and evangelical pastor Ed Dobson (no relation to Focus on the Family's James Dobson) wrote *Blinded by Might,* in which they asked, "How can [evangelicals] impose a morality on people that you can't impose on yourself?" Citing rampant materialism, sexual promiscuity, and evangelical hubris, Thomas and Dobson renounced their involvement with the Religious Right. Despite these differences of opinion, much of American evangelicalism continued to mobilize behind conservative politics.

The next major milestone was Pat Robertson's 1988 bid for the White House. During the primary season, for the first time in U.S.

history two clergymen decided to run for the presidency: Jesse Jackson and Pat Robertson.[43] In the end, neither minister prevailed, but their involvement—especially Robertson's—mobilized evangelicals in new, important ways. Robertson's strategy had centered upon support at the local caucus level, especially in places like Iowa and Michigan, where caucuses happen early in the primary season. When the evangelical entrepreneur folded his campaign, thousands of evangelicals were ready to do something with their political muscle. They were trained and mobilized but had nowhere to go. Ralph Reed, a young, energetic evangelical who had been the executive director of the College Republican National Committee, was hired by Robertson to transform the remnants of his campaign into a political machine. The result was the Christian Coalition. Through this group, evangelicals became the backbone of local Republican politics in pockets around the country. Robertson credits their diligence. "They worked hard. They walked the blocks. They licked the stamps...and the next thing you know they found themselves in positions of authority in these party structures." By the 2004 election, the Coalition had begun to ramp down operations. Its main legacy will be as the organization through which evangelicals have channeled their political energy into the Republican Party.

The coalitions built by American evangelicals point to an elasticity in their faith that is at odds with conventional wisdom. In fact, this is one of the keys to evangelical influence. Just as the civil rights, peace, and women's movements of the 1960s succeeded by forming political alliances, so also has evangelicalism. Today, conservative evangelicals—and particularly movement leaders like James Dobson and D. James Kennedy—use these political alliances to maintain close relations with government leaders. For several years, they have convened weekly meetings with leaders from Congress and the administration to discuss issues, strategy, and communication. These strictly closed-door meetings include the Values Action Team and the Arlington Group, both of which are attended by officials like Senator Sam Brownback (R-KS) and Timothy Goeglein from the White House. Groups like these have existed for many years, but the prominence of conservative evangelicals in Washington has pushed these strategy-shaping meetings into the limelight.[44] While groups like these are important, we must be careful not to overstate the political impact of individual attendees. For example, James Dobson, the head of Focus on the Family, was much more influential in the Reagan White House than in that of George W. Bush. I interviewed more than twenty senior officials in the Bush White House, and not a single person mentioned Dobson as one of the "most influential" evangelical leaders they or the White House listened to. Instead, they referred to Dobson's "lack of political finesse," "ineptitude in politics," and "inability to focus on the family because he's always focusing on someone else's business." Of course, the Bush White House clearly wants to maintain good relations with him and his constituents. Although nearly every description of Dobson's political activism by informants was negative in tone, no one was willing to speak about him on the record. Several expressed appreciation for the parenting and family advice he and his organization provide, and nearly all recognized his tremendous influence in this arena. Indeed, Dobson's organization has grown into a massive, worldwide operation that today offers free counseling and resources for parents and families in need of help. The organization receives so much correspondence that it has its own zip code, and when mobilized, Dobson's audience can be a formidable political force.[45]

The movement leader who seems to have the greatest influence is Charles Colson, the former Nixon administration official who founded Prison Fellowship. Colson, a graduate of Brown University, served as special counsel to President Nixon and was known as the administration's "hatchet man." During his rise to power, Colson had become friends with Thomas Phillips, CEO of the defense contractor Raytheon. As Colson faced arrest for his involvement with Watergate, Phillips gave him a copy of C. S. Lewis' *Mere Christianity* and began talking more directly about his own spiritual pilgrimage that led to a born-again faith. One evening after they met, Colson says, he prayed to "receive Christ" while sitting in his car parked in Phillips' driveway. As news of Colson's conversion became public, political cartoons lampooned it as a ploy to reduce his jail sentence. In 1976, after serving seven months in prison, Colson published *Born Again,* an international best-seller detailing his spiritual transformation. In the thirty years since, Colson has become one of evangelicalism's most significant leaders. Not only does his organization reach many of the evangelical rank and file, but Colson has been particularly close to many public leaders who share his evangelical faith.

It was Colson who suggested Michael Gerson to George W. Bush when he was looking for a speechwriter, and dozens of leaders that I interviewed spoke positively of Colson. They cite his experience in the White House as giving him the chance to understand what is and isn't possible in politics in a way few other movement leaders do. Moreover, his reputation as a ruthless conservative operative wins him points with Republicans in Washington. Yet his organization, which helps prisoners during and after their incarceration, has a social gospel element that many Democrats find attractive. In fact, more than a quarter of the people I interviewed mentioned Colson by name when asked about important evangelical leaders. To the extent that Colson has more influence than other leaders like Richard Land of the Southern Baptist Convention or Tony Perkins of the Family Research Council, it arises not from additional strategy sessions or political advising. The alliance between the evangelical movement and elite political actors is built primarily on personal relationships.[46] Long before running for office or working at the White House, these leaders served on the boards of evangelical organizations, attended meetings for evangelical donors, and interacted with movement leaders over dinner or on vacation. Evangelicals' place in the corridors of power is the result of connections formed outside Washington. Indeed, evangelical identity has become an important source of unity among a significant portion of the nation's leadership.

Building Networks

Starting in the early 1980s, three new organizations were formed that would become important political players in the years ahead. In 1981, a band of conservatives founded the Council for National Policy (CNP), an exclusive group that included Phyllis Schlafly and Paul Weyrich. According to the group's website, "Members are united in their belief in a free enterprise system, a strong national defense, and support for traditional western values."[47] The organization was started as a conservative Christian alternative to the Council on Foreign Relations. Evangelical pastor and writer Tim LaHaye, of *Left Behind* fame, co-founded the group, and evangelical leaders can be found throughout the group today. Members include Pat Robertson, Donald Wildmon of the American Family Association, Tony Perkins of the Family Research Council, James Dobson, Ted Baehr of the Christian Film and Television Commission, Robert Reccord of the North American Mission Board, and Sam Moore of Thomas-Nelson, an evangelical publishing house. CNP holds multiday conferences three times a year at exclusive hotels and resorts. Just before the 2004 Republican convention, the group met at New York's Plaza Hotel. Meetings often include discussions about taxes and economic issues, marriage policy, national defense, and a host of other issues. Then, at the end of the evening, time is set aside for prayer for anyone who wishes to attend. Several Reagan-era officials, including Edwin Meese and Don Hodel, have held leadership positions within the group; in fact, Hodel served as the group's president from 2004 to 2006. Council meetings are closed to the media and the general public, and organizational documents state, "The media should not know when or where or who takes part in our programs, before or after a meeting." Special guests may attend only with advance unanimous approval of the executive committee, and detailed biographies of speakers, members, guests, and spouses are all provided in briefing packets. All nonmembers wear special name tags so members can easily spot outsiders. The few hundred members pay at least $1,750 annually for membership, and Gold Circle members pay up to $10,000. Peb Jackson, a seasoned fundraiser and executive with evangelical organizations ranging from Focus on the Family to Young Life to Rick Warren's PurposeDriven, has been involved with CNP for many years. Recently, Jackson helped launch a new group called Legacy that joins evangelical faith to conservative politics by seeking to sustain the "legacy" of a compassionate conservative agenda and, in the words of one participant, "building [that into] the DNA of the political culture." Like CNP's, Legacy's meetings include briefings on political, economic, and social issues of interest to conservative Christians and meetings are by-invitation-only. Legacy, though, reaches a much younger crowd; most members are in their thirties and forties. Also, Legacy does not exhibit the same degree of secrecy or exclusivity as CNP. It has nonetheless gained a reputation as "one of the most eagerly courted screening committees for the next G.O.P. presidential nominee."[48] Groups like Legacy and CNP facilitate interaction between evangelical leaders and conservative political leaders who are also evangelical. This is important for building an elite network.

In the same year CNP was formed, South Carolina entrepreneur Phil Lader and his wife, Linda LeSourd Lader, founded Renaissance Weekend. Renaissance, which began as an extended family retreat over Thanksgiving in 1981, has grown to include five annual gatherings around the country, the largest being held over New Year's weekend in Charleston, South Carolina. Renaissance Weekends seek to build bridges "among innovative leaders from diverse fields" and feature an array of panel sessions on subjects ranging from the Asian economy to zoology.[49] Like CNP meetings, Renaissance Weekends are private, by-invitation-only gatherings that include a wide spectrum of leaders from government, business, and other fields. And as in CNP, evangelicals can be found throughout the organization. Both groups allow evangelical leaders to network informally and off the record. They also provide forums for evangelicals to discuss policy issues with actual policymakers away from the glare of the media spotlight. As one Congressional staffer told me, these gatherings "facilitate friendships among unlikely allies [across party lines]. . . . People can become friends, not just acquaintances. . . . I can easily call up any person I met in [this context] and ask them for information. . . . Friendships formed in these contexts facilitate that."

Although described as "nonpartisan" gatherings, Renaissance Weekends have included a Who's Who of the Democratic Party. Bill and Hillary Clinton were early participants. Left-of-center evangelicals like Tony Campolo, Ron Sider, and Jim Wallis have attended meetings, as have a host of other evangelical leaders including Leighton Ford and former *Christianity Today* editor Mickey Maudlin. However, even at gatherings like these, evangelicals remain a small minority.[50]

In 1995, a group called Faith and Law—composed mostly of senior staffers on Capitol Hill—began meeting regularly to discuss articles and books that brought faith into conversation with public life. Over the years, the bipartisan group has discussed works such as *The Abolition of Man* by C. S. Lewis and *Christ and Culture* by H. Richard Niebuhr. Mark Rodgers, a veteran Hill staffer, organized the group—most of whom self-identify as evangelical—out of a desire to help participants "think through" the implications of a faith-informed public policy. Curiously, from the outset, Rodgers and other participants have been pessimistic about the lasting impact they could have through politics. Rodgers told me, "Politics cannot renew the culture. Sure, politics has a role to play, but a much smaller role than many people think. . . . The real change-agent comes not from the political realm but from the cultural [realm]. The culture is upstream from politics."

This idea—that culture is more fundamental to societal transformation than politics—reveals differences in political orientation, as the late Senator Daniel Patrick Moynihan summarized: "The central conservative truth is that it is culture, not politics, that determines the success of a society. The central liberal truth is that politics can change a culture and save it from itself."[51] Faith and Law has embraced a statement first attributed to Damon of Athens: "Give me the songs of a nation and it doesn't matter who writes its laws." In other words, they feel, poets and songwriters, intellectuals and artists are more important than politicians in shaping cultural mores. They have actively sought to work with cultural icons like entertainers and producers. In part, this reflects a chastening of political ambitions among conservative evangelicals. Bill Wichterman, another founder of Faith and Law, argued, "Cultural conservatives, concerned about moral erosion, spent much of their energy working for change in the political sphere, but too little energy working in the cultural sphere. . . . Political life, while it may appear to be at the vanguard of a society, is more like the infantry. . . . [For evangelicals] politics is not enough." Indeed, the openness with which the Faith and Law group has approached influential leaders in film and music shows that shared religious identity is increasingly bringing leaders together. When I observed Faith and Law—made up entirely of people working in government—during one of its weekend gatherings, several cultural leaders, including academics and Hollywood executives, were in attendance. Rodgers, Wichterman, and others have played a key role in connecting stars like U2's Bono with political leaders to work for everything from forgiving foreign debt owed by African nations, as has been Bono's passion, to promoting positive values for children through mainstream media.[52]

Evangelicalism is a salient identity for many within the political elite, and through informal fellowship groups or more organized groups like CNP, these leaders have the opportunity to interact with others who share their religious identity. This has contributed to dense, overlapping social networks among some sectors of the nation's leadership. Bible studies involving White House officials and Pentagon leaders, in and of themselves, are not necessarily important to political action, but they contribute to a shared sense of identity among leaders who, without that common faith, probably would not have worked together at all.[53] This cohesion has contributed greatly to the rise of American evangelicalism.

A House Divided

Remarkably, at the same time that evangelicalism has provided a source of unity among certain segments of America's leadership, the movement has also been the site of deep divisions, several of which have political consequences. Not only are there differences of opinion between evangelicals in the two major parties, but there have been divisions among evangelicals in the same White House. It is no surprise, then, that not all evangelicals supported Pat Robertson in his 1988 bid for the White House.[54] As we shall see, American evangelicalism is far from monolithic.

Party Insiders and Outsiders

Even within Republican ranks, there are sharp divisions among evangelicals. In the course of my interviews, several people expressed frustration at what they perceived as inaccurate reporting that collapsed diverse parts of the evangelical movement—like radical Christian Reconstructionists and apocalyptic premillennialists—into a monolithic whole.[55] While there is certainly theological diversity within the movement, more important is another kind of division: that between movement leaders and the political leaders they help elect. Evangelicalism is an entrepreneurial religion, and the movement is dominated by big personalities and large-scale projects. As leaders like the late Jerry Falwell, D. James Kennedy, James Dobson, and Pat Robertson began to mobilize evangelicals for political action in the 1970s and 1980s, some of their preferred candidates were elected or appointed to high office, and movement leaders hoped they would implement an evangelical agenda. But when those political leaders did not deliver, movement leaders became some of their worst enemies.

When he was nominated by President Reagan to be surgeon general, C. Everett Koop had widespread support among the evangelical community. Others, however, did not hold such sanguine views. Planned Parenthood and the National Organization for Women called him an anti-abortion extremist. Others resisted Koop's nomination because of his inexperience in public health. The *New York Times* ran an editorial on him under the title "Dr. Unqualified," and the Washington press corps began referring to him as "Dr. Kook." Even the American Public Health Association opposed his nomination, with their executive director saying, "We'd be better off with no surgeon general than with Koop."[56] Nine months after his nomination, Koop was finally approved by Congress.[57] For Reagan's first term, Koop remained popular with most evangelical leaders, but the tide turned in 1986. That year, President Reagan asked the surgeon general to prepare a report on AIDS as the United States confirmed its ten-thousandth case. Leaders of the evangelical movement did not want Koop to write the report, nor did senior White House staffers who shared Koop's evangelical convictions. As Dr. Koop related to me, "Gary Bauer [Reagan's chief advisor on domestic policy] . . . was my nemesis in Washington because he kept me from the president. He kept me from the cabinet and he set up a wall of enmity between me and most of the people that surrounded Reagan because he believed that anybody who had AIDS ought to die with it. . . . That was God's punishment for them." Despite this opposition, Koop persisted, conducting in-depth interviews with dozens of groups, including evangelical organizations and groups from the gay community. After finishing twenty-seven different drafts, which he wrote personally, the surgeon general issued his report. It was a bombshell. With graphic detail, the report discussed anal sex, intravenous drug use, and a host of other topics heretofore never mentioned by such a high-ranking public official. Saying in the report that "we are fighting a disease, not people," Koop urged the federal government to recommend condoms for those involved in homosexual activity as well as nonmonogamous heterosexual activity. He also advocated early sex education, starting as early as the third grade. "In one day . . . I changed my whole constituency. . . . The conservatives . . . dropped me cold, and the liberals joined me."

Fellow evangelicals mobilized against Koop with tremendous force. Several movement leaders urged a boycott of a dinner being held in his honor, characterizing Koop as a turncoat whose "proposals for stopping AIDS represent the homosexuals' views, *not* those of the pro-family movement."[58] For them, advocating the use of condoms and sterile needles was tantamount to condoning homosexuality and recreational drug use. No Republican candidate in the 1988 primary season attended, although Vice President Bush sent Koop a warm personal letter. Among the conservative Republicans who had originally agreed to participate in the tribute, only Senator Orrin Hatch showed up. As fellow evangelicals organized public opposition, Bauer, the president's domestic policy advisor, challenged Koop from within the White House. Originally, Bauer asked the surgeon general to remove all references to condoms in the report, but Koop refused. Then Bauer argued against teaching sex education in elementary schools, saying he did not want his own daughters exposed to such material. While Koop felt the same way, he argued that such information could save the lives of thousands, if not millions, of American children. He also reminded Bauer that the report strongly recommended against sex outside monogamous relationships and opposed the use of illicit drugs. Nonetheless, Bauer and others fiercely opposed the surgeon general. What outsiders perceive to be a monolithic movement may actually be many mini-movements, each with its own allies and opponents. According to Koop, his fiercest political battle was waged not with liberals or so-called secularists but rather with other evangelicals, and the rift between Koop and his fellow evangelicals still persists twenty-five years later. Speaking of Bauer, Koop said, "I don't bear any animosity to him. . . . I've forgiven him for all the stinky, rotten things he did to me,... [but still today] I don't have any desire to be in his company."

Ten years after Koop left government, leaders within the evangelical community mobilized against another fellow evangelical, House Majority Leader Richard Armey. At a contentious 1998 meeting between Armey and several movement leaders—including Charles Colson, James Dobson, and Gary Bauer—Armey disagreed with them:

> I said to him [Dobson], "You don't know how the legislative process works....All you want to do is come up whining and complaining about the failures we've experienced and you ought to mind your own business." You know, there's a song by the Pointer Sisters, "Mr. Big Shot, who do you think you are?" It wasn't his business to come up here and tell us that we weren't serving the Lord because we didn't succeed....I was so deeply offended by his audacity....[Also, there was] this little wimpy guy...that ran for president, Gary Bauer,...and he's one of these arrogant guys that was telling me about how he made me the majority. As Shania Twain says, "That don't impress me much."...In effect they're saying, you know, "Look at me, I'm bigger than the Lord. I put you where you are, and I can take you out." Who do they think they are?

After the confrontational meeting, Dobson and others launched a campaign to remove Armey from the leadership position. In the end, Armey prevailed, but still today he says of the experience, "I am not tough enough to have Christians for friends....I was never so wrongfully and viciously attacked in all my eighteen years in Washington as I was by the Christian leaders."

The Racial Divide

The evangelical movement is also divided along racial lines. Whereas most white evangelicals today vote Republican, black Protestants continue to be loyal Democrats.[59] Drawing on national surveys and extensive interview data, Michael Emerson and Christian Smith have argued that "white evangelicalism likely does more to perpetuate the racialized society than to reduce it."[60] Evangelicals tend to minimize concerns about racism and treat it as an individual-level problem, not a structural one. They also assign blame for racial inequality to blacks themselves. While Emerson and Smith acknowledge that white evangelicals have recently expressed interest in improving black-white relations, they find that there are structural barriers that evangelical good intentions have little chance of over-coming. Additionally, they found, evangelical congregations—which are almost entirely homogeneous with regard to race—actually *facilitate* racial inequality. It seems, therefore, that the evangelical movement today is not doing much to end racial divisions.

Yet evangelicals have recently made efforts to undo some of this country's racial inequality.[61] Most of these have been at the level of individual interactions, small group efforts, and congregational ex-periments in racial reconciliation. Such efforts must not be over-looked, for personal relations, especially within elite circles, are the bedrock of elite power, and individual efforts by public leaders can spark social change. In 1953, Billy Graham personally removed the ropes marking the section reserved for blacks at his Chattanooga Crusade. After that heroic stance in Chattanooga, Graham moder-ated his position for a few months, but within a year, all of his cru-sades were racially integrated. In 1957, he invited Dr. Martin Luther King Jr. to his New York Crusade in Madison Square Garden, and when President Eisenhower called him that same year to tell him he intended to send federal troops to force the racial integration of Central High School in Little Rock, Arkansas, the evangelist told the president it was "the only thing you can do."[62] While the history of the evangelical movement is replete with racism, dozens of evan-gelical public leaders I interviewed have close friendships across the racial divide. In nearly every case, they said their shared faith is what brought them together.

Consider Kay Coles James, who is black, and Donald Powell, who is white. James, who directed the U.S. Office of Personnel Manage-ment (OPM) during the first term of George W. Bush's adminis-tration, met Powell when he first moved to Washington. A lifelong banker from West Texas, Powell had known the Bush family for many years, and in 2001 he was appointed chairman of the Federal Deposit Insurance Corporation (FDIC). Although born into a blue-collar family, Powell rose to a position of community leadership. Over dinner one evening, Powell admitted to me that prior to moving to Washington, he had never had a close black friend. He said, "In Amarillo, Texas, . . . it was not part of the culture." While the District of Columbia is not known for being especially amenable to bridging racial divides, James—who was widely known in Wa-shington for her evangelical faith—reached out to Powell.[63] Soon, they began meeting regularly to pray together and their spouses became friends as well. "It's not every day that a white man from Texas . . . has that kind of spiritual kinship" with an African Ameri-can, Powell told me, but their shared evangelical faith helped them form a deep friendship. As we have seen, personal friendships can play a key role in public policy. In 2005, Powell stepped down from his position at FDIC to serve as the federal coordinator of Gulf Coast rebuilding in the wake of Hurricanes Katrina, Rita, and Wilma. In his new position he sought to repair what many regard as contentious racial divisions in places like New Orleans, and he says his friendship with James spurred him. He acknowledges that race relations in this country are not good but concludes, "I'm hopeful." Certainly, good intentions are not enough, and structural changes are needed. However, the relationship between Powell and James is just one of many friendships across racial lines that leaders mentioned to me. In every case they said their shared faith was either the reason they became friends or the reason they remained close.[64]

Evangelicals have shown themselves to be innovative builders of strategic political alliances, and while my research says little about the long-term chance of racial reconciliation, it does point to the possibility of a political coalition between black Protestants and white evangelicals. For evangelical political power, nothing could be more formidable than an alliance between the white evangelical and African American communities. Already, movement leaders I interviewed claim civil rights activists like Martin Luther King Jr. as one of their own. One said to me, "There's no evangelical since Dr. Martin Luther King Jr. that's been as influential as Dr. Martin Luther King Jr. He got those bills through Congress; he was able to rally the Washington Mall crowd, and he was authentic. . . . He was a man of God." Of course, such an alliance would represent a significant shift in contemporary political alignments. However, it would be a mistake to underestimate the extent to which evangelicalism's coalition-building impulse could make this a reality. Already, conservative coalitions like the Arlington Group and the Council for National Policy include several prominent African Americans. For now, though, these kinds of alliances and interactions are the exception, not the rule. American evangelicals remain divided by race.

Looking to the Future

What lies ahead for evangelicals in politics? Will they be able to establish a long-term political presence? Over the last thirty years, they have built an impressive infrastructure. In particular, evangelicals have underwritten think tanks and programs for the movement's next generation of leadership, which bodes well for their long-term political success.[65] In addition, it has given them tremendous access to cable news programs, which rely heavily on Washington think tanks for guests. At the same time, evangelicals have sponsored a number of organizations and initiatives that train future evangelical leaders. These include new universities like Patrick Henry College in Virginia and year-long educational and internship programs sponsored by the Trinity Forum Academy and the Falls Church Fellows program, both based in the Washington area. Outside the capital, evangelicals have built local infrastructures for everything from school board decisions to mayoral and congressional races to presidential campaigns.

Though they are now firmly entrenched within the Republican Party, there are indications that Democrats, too, want to bring evangelicals into the fold, and the evangelical movement is showing signs of getting out of the Republicans' pockets. In 2004, the National Association of Evangelicals released a statement called "For the Health of the Nation: An Evangelical Call to Civic Responsibility." The twelve-page document, originally drafted by *Christianity Today* editor David Neff, called on the evangelical community to support governmental initiatives that upheld traditional notions of marriage and opposed what the NAE believes are "social evils" like gambling, drugs, abortion, and the use of human embryos for stem-cell research. But it also called for government protections for the poor, sick, and disabled through fair wages, health care, and education, among other things. The statement points to an emerging appreciation for both liberal and conservative political priorities. Richard Mouw, the president of Fuller Theological Seminary, has referred to this development as "a maturing of the evangelical public mind."

The committee that drafted the document was co-chaired by two evangelical leaders, the late Diane Knippers of the Institute on Religion and Democracy and Ron Sider of Evangelicals for Social Action (ESA).[66] Sider, who has not endorsed a presidential candidate since McGovern in 1972, told me he voted for George W. Bush in 2000 because he was drawn to the president's agenda for compassionate conservatism. Sider later published a book, *The Scandal of the Evangelical Conscience*, in which he expressed disappointment with Bush's inability to enact a comprehensive agenda of governmental compassion. Sider has for quite some time been bringing together evangelicals from across the political divide. Time and again, the people I interviewed spoke positively of Sider's bridging ability. Indeed, he is seen by some to be at the forefront of a wider shift within American evangelicalism that recognizes that neither political party hews closely to an evangelical vision for public policy.

Popular Manhattan pastor Tim Keller says that neither Democrats nor Republicans attend to the "breadth, balance, or basis of biblical ethical concerns."[67]

Still, evangelicals have, for the most part, aligned themselves with conservative Republicanism, perhaps to their political disadvantage. The courtship began in the Goldwater campaign, and the union has been consummated in the presidency of George W. Bush. Murmurs within the movement by liberal progressives suggest the marriage may not last forever, but research shows the remarkable ways in which President Bush has connected with all kinds of evangelicals.[68] Indeed, the Christian Right, which used to exist as an independent political structure in the 1970s and 1980s, has now become integrated into the Republican Party. As Hanna Rosin wrote in the *Washington Post* in March 2005, "Evangelicals in public office have finally become so numerous that they've blended in to the permanent Washington backdrop, a new establishment that has absorbed the local habits and mores. . . . In Washington, the evangelicals are the new Episcopalians—established, connected, respectable." As they have become integrated into the Republican establishment, evangelicals have certainly become more sophisticated politically. Gone is the bombast of placard-bearing protests, and in its place are Capitol Hill meetings and West Wing strategy sessions. But this dulling of the edges of the evangelical movement comes at a cost. A growing number of movement leaders fear that evangelicalism has, in the words of Pat MacMillan, become "marginalized or pigeonholed" because of its close ties to the Republican Party. In the process, they fear, evangelicalism is being co-opted by the party, diminishing the movement's ability to speak independently. Peter Wehner, who runs the Office of Strategic Initiatives at the White House, told me:

> It's just very easy, when you get involved in political movements, to let them overtake you. . . . It's easy for people who are Christians and feel like they have a calling and an obligation to make a difference to feel like they are indispensable or that the Lord's will can't be done unless they're doing it. . . . And so you lose the sense that history is driven by God; that you do the best you can, but at the end you hold lightly to the things of the world and trust that His will will be done. [Also,] it can create an attitude, a certain rigidity, a certain anger toward people who are critics and who have positions different than yours. . . . On some level it can hurt in terms of the public witness of Christianity, if our faith gets identified with a political ideology. Obviously people who don't hold that particular political ideology can be driven away from it.

So even as evangelicals have gained attention because of their political success in working with conservative Republicans, they risk erasing the line between evangelicalism as a religious movement and conservative politics. This boundary was critical to their ascent in the 1970s and 1980s and facilitated their influence in both parties across several administrations. Many of the people I spoke to expressed concerns that elements of the movement seem to have become enamored with political power. Charles Colson, the evangelical leader and former White House staffer, wrote about this:

> When I served under President Nixon, one of my jobs was to work with special-interest groups, including religious leaders. We would invite them to the White House, wine and dine them, take them on cruises aboard the presidential yacht.... Ironically, few were more easily impressed than religious leaders. The very people who should have been immune to the worldly pomp seemed most vulnerable.[69]

According to other observers, like Les Csorba, an evangelical who worked in presidential personnel at the White House, these evangelical leaders "get invited...and see the president and become enamored.... There's a lot of power and a lot of prestige and recognition that goes with that...[that is] unhealthy." An unintended consequence of evangelicals' success is that they are likely to be taken for granted by Republican strategists.

Also, evangelical political activists have long appealed to the group's "majority" status among the American electorate. Yet, using the broadest definition of the term "evangelical," they are less than half of the U.S. adult population, and more likely they number between one-quarter and one-third.[70] Regardless of their numbers, evangelicals participate in a pluralist democracy where, as the Constitution's framers intended, tolerance and protection of minority rights are guaranteed, especially on matters relating to the public expression of religion. However, evangelical leaders have not devoted enough attention to how they can achieve their political ambitions without imposing, or giving the impression of imposing, their beliefs on the rest of the populace. Persuasion and tolerance are the keys to securing a lasting public influence. Trying to impose their views on the country through a triumphalistic majoritarianism— what Tocqueville called the "tyranny of the majority"—will not work. If history is any indication, evangelicals have little chance of rolling back the liberal advances of previous generations. The American public responds more favorably to appeals that expand, rather than restrict, liberty and freedom. Along these lines, evangelicals more than once have portrayed themselves as having a monopoly on patriotic sentiment and questioned the patriotism of their opponents. Movement leaders would be wise to listen carefully to how rank-and-file evangelicals define a "Christian America." According to them, it has less to do with restoring the past and more to do with a vibrant religious sphere where personal choice and individual freedom prevail.[71]

There are also several internal factions that pose threats to the movement. An organized minority always triumphs over a less organized majority. Reaching across party lines may indeed represent a maturing of evangelical political activism, but it also points to issues around which the movement could easily fracture. There remains significant disagreement on matters like the environment and welfare, and as the number of issues with which evangelicals are concerned grows, the movement could lose its political cohesion, which has been critical to its success.[72] As evangelicals secure more influence in Congress, the White House, and the Pentagon, the fabric that once held the diverse movement together may begin ripping at the seams.

Evangelicals are still a long way from being a majority in politics. They remain a minority voice even within the appointed inner circle of the Bush administration, one of the most evangelical-friendly administrations in modern U.S. history. And their involvement has not yielded sweeping new legislation, executive action, or judicial appointments. The number of acrimonious meetings between movement leaders and Republican politicians points to on-going challenges evangelicals will face in pursuing their political agenda.[73]

PART II

INTELLECTUALS AND THE GROVES

OF ACADEME

3

Knowledge to Change the World

WITH THE YEAR 1899 DRAWING TO A CLOSE and a new century on the horizon, leaders around the country began offering their hopes and visions for the future. William Rainey Harper, president of the University of Chicago (and a Baptist Sunday school superintendent) argued that the university should undertake a messianic mission. Even though his institution was explicitly nonsectarian, Harper—and to a lesser degree his university—possessed an underlying Protestant sensibility that permeated most elite universities at the time. Yet his was a progressive vision. Harper favored an institution free of church interference, an institution that would provide an arena in which "the universal brotherhood of man [could be] understood and accepted by all."[1] According to him, the university—not the church—would be the prophet, priest, and sage of modern society. In many ways, Harper's prediction has come true. For many, this has liberated intellectual life and expanded scholarly horizons; freed from religious constraint, scholars can advance knowledge without fear of running afoul of religious authorities. For others, though, the old religious authority has simply been replaced by something just as inflexible: secularism.[2]

For centuries, higher education was under the control of the church, and many American colleges and universities remain affiliated with some body of organized religion. American evangelicals have been particularly active within the world of higher education, launching new institutions and spawning religious outreach programs for college students, faculty, and administrators.[3] In recent decades, they have made a strong push to secure academic respectability: funding the research agendas of promising evangelical scholars, introducing faith-friendly programs on the campuses of major universities, supporting intellectual friendships among evangelical students and scholars, and forming alliances with Roman Catholics. The evangelical movement has also launched a number of educational initiatives, directed at both secular leaders and rank-and-file adherents, including several aimed at America's most prestigious universities. In the process, they have transformed both American higher education and the evangelical movement itself.

Religion and the University

The purpose of higher education has always been to train young leaders to assume the mantle of public responsibility. For most of history, that training was done by the churches. In the United States, the earliest colleges (including most of the Ivy League) were established for clergy formation. In the latter decades of the nineteenth century, theological conservatives wedded rigorous academic scholarship to a religious view of the world.[4] They did so not at second-rate institutions but at places like Harvard and Princeton. But the tide was turning. An alternative vision for higher education—one that emphasized academic freedom, skepticism, and the importance of independent learning—began to take root. Out of such convictions, the modern research university was born. Gradually, the research model for higher education became more deeply entrenched at America's top institutions and at new universities like Stanford, Johns Hopkins, and the University of Chicago. Theological conservatives—then called "fundamentalists"—became increasingly uneasy. They began to mobilize against the rise of biblical criticism at places like Princeton Seminary and the teaching of evolution in public schools. They were not, however, inherently anti-intellectual. In fact, even today, fundamentalism relies on a form of tight logic; much of the genre of Christian apologetics depends on reason. But its notion of truth had become so fixed that its proponents began to resent anything that appeared to be counter-evidence. Hence, fundamentalist anti-intellectualism is really an opposition to and resentment of *academic intellectualism,* especially as practiced in the modern research university. It is grounded in the fear that scholarship will chip away at the fundamentalist edifice that has become increasingly calcified and brittle. Fundamentalist anti-intellectualism came to a head at the Scopes Monkey Trial of 1925, and the tensions have never been resolved. As a result, many conservative Christians keep their distance from academic life.[5]

While American fundamentalists stood defiantly outside the academic establishment, another group of theological conservatives began to engage it. These self-described "neo-evangelicals" opposed modern fundamentalism and its academic anti-intellectualism.[6]

Early movement leaders like Carl Henry were highly educated and advocated an intellectual and cultural renaissance among theological conservatives, one that would be characterized by an irenic, hopeful spirit.[7] Henry and his colleagues recognized that evangelicals would have to produce scholarship on their own. He also realized, however, that because of their fundamentalist heritage and the biases against it, it would be difficult for them to succeed in traditional academia. Accordingly, they established separate journals, publishing houses, and conferences for evangelical scholars. Though they sought to transform the whole society, much of their energy was devoted to this parallel universe that existed outside the wider culture. This subculture allowed evangelical scholarship to mature away from the limelight, only later to emerge into the mainstream. Indeed, this separate subculture may very well have been necessary to lift evangelical intellectual activity out of the academic ghetto.[8]

At the same time, evangelicals were establishing campus outreach groups. Some, such as the Princeton Evangelical Fellowship, had been present on elite campuses for a couple of decades. The Crusader Club—later renamed the Ambassadors—began as a group of evangelical students from Princeton's Class of 1912. Their influence is remarkable. One of its founders, for example, was Samuel Shoemaker, who later helped establish Alcoholics Anonymous. Shoemaker's twelve-step program for overcoming addiction was formulated in this campus group. Evangelicals established other campus ministries like InterVarsity Christian Fellowship (1941), the Navigators (1943), and Campus Crusade for Christ (1950), many of them modeled on the Inter-Collegiate Christian Unions of Oxford and Cambridge and the Youth for Christ movement in the United States. Despite these efforts, though, neo-evangelicals did not have a major impact on American university life in the 1940s and 1950s, especially at elite institutions. To the extent that religious sentiment existed at these institutions, it was a remnant of the mainline Protestant establishment of earlier generations. Since then, some argue, we have seen the secularization of American higher education.[9] They argue that the differentiation of knowledge into compartmentalized areas, reliance on rationalization at the expense of religion, and the privatization of religion have contributed to the widespread decline of religion's influence. This has led some to conclude that today

religion in most universities is about as important as the baseball team. Not only has religion become peripheral, but also there is a definite bias against any perceptible religiously informed perspectives getting a hearing in the university classroom.[10]

Not all of the evidence, though, points in this direction. Though America's universities have moved away from their denominational sponsors and most universities are no longer led by clergy, this does not mean that religion has been completely marginalized. In fact, developments in recent decades show American religion is more resilient than some people think. The story of religion's relation to the university is more one of gradual change than of outright decline. Indeed, some claim that whatever "secularist stage" may have existed earlier has now been replaced with a "hermeneutic stage" in which religious conviction has a seat at the academic table. In fact, many believe we are in an era of increasingly de-privatized religion, and trends in higher education reflect this.[11]

New Faces on Campus

Every year more and more evangelicals can be found at America's top universities. One likely reason is demographics. Over the last thirty years, the percentage of evangelicals earning at least a college degree has increased by 133 percent, which is much more than any other religious tradition.[12] And many of those degrees are from elite institutions. This increase has occurred primarily at the undergraduate level, yet evangelicals remain below the national average in terms of educational attainment. This trend does, however, point to a narrowing of the gap between evangelicals and the rest of the country.

The Reverend Peter Gomes, Harvard's longest-serving Plummer Professor of Christian Morals as well as minister of Memorial Church, says, "There are probably more evangelicals [on Harvard's campus today] than at any time since the seventeenth century."[13] The Ivy League's desire for diversity has opened new doors for religiously committed students. These institutions now recruit in the South and Midwest—regions populated with deeply religious high school students—as vigorously as they do on the East and West Coasts. Ethnic diversity plays an important role as well. Whereas Asian Americans account for only 4 percent of the U.S. population, they are 15 percent of the student body in the Ivy League, and many are involved in evangelical campus groups. In fact, Asian Americans have come to dominate such groups on the campuses of selective universities.[14] At Yale, 90 percent of the Campus Crusade members are Asian American; in the 1980s, the same chapter was 100 percent white.[15] Asian American students are among the most disciplined and regular participants in evangelical Bible studies at places like Yale and Harvard, where I interviewed ministry leaders and observed evangelical gatherings. In stark contrast to most Ivy League students, many are fervent about their faith. Indeed, the growing presence of Asian Americans on these campuses may be the single largest demographic variable in explaining evangelicalism's ascent within the ranks of America's top universities. These trends are even more pronounced at West Coast institutions. For Asian American students, and evangelicals more generally, elite education is a path to better jobs and greater financial security. Religious conviction and the American Dream often go hand in hand.[16]

Another important factor is that evangelical young adults tend to become evangelical adults: They are much less likely than others to abandon their faith.[17] Hence, evangelical children attending selective universities become alumni and donors. This development may be at the crux of the evangelical intellectual renaissance. Many students are coming to places like Harvard, Yale, and Princeton and bringing a strong religious identity that they "refuse to check at [Princeton's] Fitz-Randolph Gate," in the words of one professor. This is a different kind of diversity, an unintended consequence of elite schools' efforts to transform their student bodies over the last fifty years. As Peter Gomes says, "People tend to think of affirmative action as only affecting racial minorities, but the change in Harvard demographics in the late seventies and early eighties meant that a lot of Midwestern white-bread Protestant Christian evangelicals at whom Harvard would never have looked in the past, and who would have never looked at Harvard, suddenly became members of the university."[18]

As important as these demographic shifts have undoubtedly been, there are other factors at work. As the movement has shed its cultural insularity, it has become more engaged in the world of ideas. More and more evangelical scholars are being recognized for academic excellence, and evangelical institutions have grown in prestige.[19] Why are evangelicals so interested in higher education? Principally, they see it as an arena they once "held" and no longer occupy. I asked Paul Klaassen, an evangelical CEO who graduated from Georgetown University and is actively involved with several evangelical educational initiatives, about this. He told me:

> [Evangelicals are] not in the belief-shaping sectors ... [that is,] entertainment and arts and music and law, advertising and politics and the academy.... We've allowed ourselves to become compartmentalized....

> We lost the universities. We lost the cities and thought centers. We lost the media. We lost certain belief-shaping forces over the last century, and that's cost people of faith a lot in terms of the kind of world we now live in.

As Klaassen's statement suggests, evangelicals feel a sense of loss because they no longer occupy influential roles in society. Currently, however, the evangelical movement appears to be undergoing what some are calling a "clarifying moment." Today's evangelicals seek to shed their reputation as "largely poor, uneducated, and easy to command." Their historic connection with fundamentalism, which shunned academic inquiry, contributed to what some have called an "intellectual disaster." The effects of this anti-intellectualism were felt for decades, causing one observer to conclude that twentieth century evangelicalism ranks "dead last in intellectual stature" among all religious traditions in the United States.[20] Yet, there has appeared in recent decades an "opening" of the evangelical mind. How has it happened?

Fellowship and Fellowships

Dennis Bakke is the former CEO of energy giant AES. In 1992, he and his family launched an initiative that, he told me, aimed to bring evangelicals into the "ivory tower and the corridors of power." The Harvey Fellows Program, which Bakke and his wife, Eileen, modeled in part on the White House Fellows Program, provides financial support for graduate study in a top academic program. By requiring applicants to sign a statement of faith, Bakke sees to it that the funds only support evangelical-leaning graduate students.[21] By asking applicants to demonstrate the top ranking of their academic department, the program ensures that only elite students are selected. Like these students, both Bakkes have earned degrees from major universities: Dennis at Harvard Business School and Eileen at Princeton. Each summer, new fellows participate in a week-long seminar in Washington, D.C. From being hosted at the Supreme Court by an associate justice to interacting with the librarian of Congress, Harvey Fellows are offered educational experiences that rival those of Rhodes, Marshall, and Gates scholars. Indeed, this initiative, among others, points to "an expanding beachhead of evangelicals in the American elite."[22] The Bakkes' patronage, now a multimillion-dollar venture, is designed to lead to long-term cultural change—in Bakke's words, "to redeem the structures that shape society, as well as the people in it." To date, the program has supported approximately 250 fellows worldwide in everything from the arts, humanities, and social sciences to law, medicine, business, science, and engineering. The impact of this group's influence remains to be seen, but the program has enabled a sizable group of evangelical graduate students to enter highly competitive programs.

Two private foundations have played particularly significant roles as patrons of evangelical academic activity over the last three decades: the Pew Charitable Trusts, founded by evangelical oil magnate J. Howard Pew, and the Lilly Endowment, established by the family behind the Eli Lilly pharmaceutical company. Colonel Eli Lilly started a pharmaceutical lab in 1876, and within two generations his family became the wealthiest people in town. In 1937, the founder's grandson, also named Eli, created the Lilly Endowment. One of his philanthropic interests was religion, particularly how faith could inform character development. With exclusive marketing rights to penicillin, later insulin, and today, most notably, Prozac, Lilly's fortunes have grown exponentially, making it one of the world's largest private foundations.

In the 1970s, Timothy Smith, a respected historian at Johns Hopkins and an evangelical pastor, introduced Robert Lynn, then head of Lilly's religion program, to a group of young evangelical historians, most of whom studied American religious history. These rising scholars demonstrated to Lynn that they could draw on their faith to produce fair, nuanced history. The more he got to know them, he told me, the more he was impressed. Among these younger scholars were Mark Noll and Nathan Hatch. In 1979, Lynn arranged for Wheaton College to receive a grant of $15,000 to support a conference on the Bible.[23] Lynn followed that up with a $200,000 grant to launch the Institute for the Study of American Evangelicals (ISAE) at Wheaton. It was the first of several grants given to evangelical academics and institutions. Noll and Hatch headed the board, and another historian, Joel Carpenter, became its director. Carpenter had been a graduate student of Timothy Smith's at Johns Hopkins; indeed, there were many personal ties among the key players at this stage.

Perhaps one of Lilly's most important contributions over the years has been its efforts to facilitate conversations among evangelical scholars. For example, in 1995 Lilly launched the Rhodes Consultation on the Future of the Church-Related College. To date, ninety religious institutions, some of them evangelical, have participated. The Rhodes Consultation has funded many other conferences and seminars specifically directed at junior faculty to examine the "nature of church relatedness on their campuses" and to ensure that this relationship is a "meaningful aspect of campus life in the future."[24] Additionally, Lilly has invested more than $171 million in religious institutions since 2001 through its Theological Exploration of Vocation initiative. This program, which reaches nearly one hundred colleges and universities, seeks to examine the relationship between work and calling for people of faith who serve in all sectors of society. In turn, Lilly aims to raise a generation of future leaders for the church—among both clergy and lay leadership—whose work is endowed with significance and "lasting meaning."[25] By far, Lilly has contributed the most of any private foundation to religious causes. The dollar value of Lilly's religious grants, many of which go to evangelicals, is greater than the total amounts given to religion by the next four foundations *combined*.[26] Notably, four of the top five foundation givers to religion have been staunch supporters of evangelical causes: Lilly, the DeMoss Foundation, Pew, and the DeVos Foundation.

The Pew Charitable Trusts has also been a vital supporter of evangelical academic life, and its support of evangelical projects stretches back to the early days of the modern evangelical movement. J. Howard Pew put forward a significant sum to launch *Christianity Today* in 1956 and Gordon-Conwell Theological Seminary in 1969. After his death in 1971, the foundation staff was not nearly as enthusiastic about funding evangelicalism, but they were looking to raise Pew's stature in the world of philanthropy while still fulfilling the founder's mission.[27] Robert Lynn of Lilly introduced Martin Trimble, a junior program associate in religion at Pew, to the evangelical academics he had been funding. Trimble, the son of an Episcopal priest with a theology degree from Harvard himself, was impressed—and surprised—by what he saw.

Trimble convened a group of evangelical scholars, along with their families, for a meeting on Cape Cod in 1985. The participants were hand-picked for their scholarly potential and their decidedly nonfundamentalist faith. They included historians Harry Stout of Yale, Timothy Smith of Johns Hopkins, Grant Wacker of the University of North Carolina at Chapel Hill, Joel Carpenter of Wheaton, George Marsden of Calvin, Nathan Hatch of Notre Dame, and George Rawlyk of Queen's, along with sociologists Robert Wuthnow of Princeton and James Davison Hunter of the University of Virginia. Trimble wanted to learn more about these rising evangelical scholars, their research ambitions, and how Pew might help them. A few months later they met again, this time in Hilton Head, South

Carolina. By that time, Trimble had persuaded his colleagues at Pew that funding evangelical scholars would be a way to allow them to maintain their benefactor's wishes while gaining respectability in the cosmopolitan world of philanthropy. At Hilton Head, they decided to launch an Evangelical Scholars Program. Several participants joined the board of this new venture, including historian Nathan Hatch, who had just assumed an administrative post at Notre Dame. Pew elevated the religion division to stand-alone status within the organization. Joel Carpenter, an evangelical himself, was hired to run it. Carpenter had established a reputation within the evangelical world for being a consummate diplomat. Those skills would be required at Pew, because no outspoken evangelical had worked there for quite some time, and many people within the organization were not pleased with the move.

In the 1990s, the money flowed freely from Pew to the Evangelical Scholars Program. Over the course of the decade, Pew put more than $15 million toward invigorating evangelical intellectual life, including conferences, research, scholarly publications, graduate student mentoring, and campus lectures.[28] Pew has also funded "Centers of Excellence" for the academic study of religion, including evangelicalism, at several major universities—including Yale, Emory, and NYU—helping legitimate religion as a field of study even in thoroughly secular settings. Under the leadership of Carpenter, who later became provost at evangelical Calvin College, Pew established programs and networks for evangelical academics. Like Lilly, Pew believed that achieving any long-term goal required relationship-building and strategically placed social networks. Pew sought to improve evangelical scholarship and to get it noticed. The record suggests it did both. In 1990, 33 percent of the work of Pew-funded scholars was published in secular outlets. By 2001, that figure was 80 percent. Moreover, observers referred to "a visible evangelical presence" in the academy and a general "opening of the evangelical mind" as a result of Pew's philanthropy.[29]

Another key to the success of evangelicals in the academy has been the growth of evangelical institutions of higher learning. Enrollment at these institutions, all of which depend heavily on tuition dollars, is growing exponentially. At the hundred-plus member institutions of the Council for Christian Colleges and Universities, enrollment grew 60 percent between 1990 and 2002, while the general college student population has barely changed over the same time.[30] Evangelical institutions have also improved their fundraising. For example, Fuller Theological Seminary has recently raised more than $125 million—its largest financial campaign ever—and appears poised to raise an additional $20 million in the next two years.

However, the most intriguing element of evangelicals' patronage of higher education today is their investment in the nation's most selective universities. Consider the story of Marc Belton. A senior executive with General Mills, Belton has launched a program at his alma mater, Dartmouth, called Spiritual Vistas. Although he was not an active evangelical in his undergraduate days, Belton told me that he aims to "create opportunities for kids . . . who may have a heart for God and want to put their faith into real life for a semester." Through the program, Belton funds students who wish to spend a portion of their undergraduate careers working with the underprivileged or in some other kind of service. Service can take place during term or while on break; it can occur close to campus or halfway around the world. The goal, says Belton, is to provide Dartmouth students with a chance to "make their faith a real, tangible thing."

> There are tremendous pulls for [evangelicals at Dartmouth] to work on Wall Street and all the same things I experienced, and they may still end up working on Wall Street. But I want them to experience Beat Street before they experience Wall Street. I want them to have a tangible, viable, integrated faith-life experience before they [graduate and move on].

Similar efforts are being made by other evangelical Ivy League graduates, many of whom want their alma maters to be more hospitable to evangelicals. Twin brothers Matt and Monty Bennett are Cornell University alumni, and over the last fifteen years they have developed what they call a "heart for ministry" to the eight Ivy League campuses. In 2002, they launched an evangelical organization called Christian Union with the stated purpose of "transforming the Ivy League Universities for Christ." Through Bible studies, conferences, and social outreach, Christian Union seeks to serve the entire university community. They also support existing ministry groups on those eight campuses, including Campus Crusade for Christ, InterVarsity Christian Fellowship, and the Navigators. Although the Bennetts would not tell me their total financial contributions to this program, conservative estimates extend to six figures annually. The Bennetts are deeply committed to the program's long-term success. Monty told me:

> Graduates from the eight Ivy League institutions have a disproportionate influence on our society. In politics, in business, academia, journalism,

[and in] all of the centers of power in this country... there is a heavy overrepresentation of Ivy League graduates. On those same campuses, there is a general hostility towards people [of faith as well as toward]... God. So we thought that to change the world and to influence it for better, [we would create a presence] on these campuses where students could learn about the claims of Jesus Christ and learn about scripture.

Evangelicals' support is geared not only to the Ivy League but also to a variety of selective, nonsectarian institutions. For example, one of the CEOs I spoke to gives scholarship money to his undergraduate institution, Amherst College. The funds are primarily awarded to active student volunteers in such a way that "the scholarships have [typically] been given to Christians." Several people told me that they prefer not to give money to what they call the "crappy schools" that populate the evangelical subculture but instead prefer to contribute funds to "serious" places like Harvard and Yale, while targeting particular scholars or programs that welcome and engage evangelicals.

God on the Quad

In 1951, William F. Buckley published *God and Man at Yale*. Buckley claimed that his alma mater practiced a superstitious form of "academic freedom" in which only modernist liberalism was tolerated and religious conviction was mocked. The book attracted widespread attention, but it did little to change the tone on campus. At the time, George Bennett was serving as Harvard's deputy treasurer, working directly alongside treasurer Paul Cabot. Bennett, Harvard Class of 1933, insists that he was hand-picked by Cabot because his evangelical leanings reminded Cabot of his own mother's faith. Bennett succeeded Cabot as treasurer at Harvard, thereby becoming part of the seven-member governing body of the school, the Harvard Corporation.[31] If anyone was in a position to change Harvard, it was George Bennett. He and a number of other evangelicals wanted to return Harvard to its Christian roots. But Bennett told me that he did not have much of a spiritual impact on the campus. "Harvard being what it is now,... religion takes a backseat.... Being an evangelical, I couldn't feel that way."

Bennett's experience was a common one among the people I spoke to. Many who attended elite universities between the 1950s and the 1980s reported feeling like outcasts. Mark Berner, an evangelical businessman, described Yale in the early 1970s as a place where Christians were "running scared intellectually. There was no real, credible, intellectual Christian [on campus] at the time." As a result, campus evangelical groups engaged only a small fraction of the student body. C. Everett Koop attended Dartmouth as an undergraduate. He described the academic world in Ivy League circles as a "very cruel, competitive world [with] an unbelievable and undeserved arrogance.... These people [faculty members on Ivy League campuses] aren't that good to be that arrogant." Kenneth Elzinga, now a senior professor of economics at the University of Virginia, says that when he arrived on campus in the 1960s, evangelical student groups were not even permitted to meet on the grounds of the university.[32] That restriction has since been lifted, but for many years evangelicals did not feel welcome at certain schools. How, then, did evangelicals return to places like Stanford, Duke, and Virginia?

First, evangelicals have increasingly supported alternative programs on the campuses of major universities. From the Institute for Advanced Studies in Culture at Virginia to the Yale Center for Faith and Culture, evangelicals have poured thousands of dollars into academic programs where their perspective is at least accepted as valid, if not preferred. At public institutions where such arrangements are not possible, independent programs have grown up alongside the universities. Institutions like these enable evangelical scholars to maintain their academic credentials but also to have outlets for their faith. As I observed some of these institutions around the country, I saw that they provide a sense of community for evangelical academics—students and scholars alike—many of whom feel marginalized at both their churches and their colleges. These programs have also linked evangelicals with conservative Catholics in common cause. The best example of this is Princeton's James Madison Program in American Ideals and Institutions. Founded in 2000 by Robert George, Princeton's McCormick Professor of Jurisprudence, the Madison Program has given voice to evangelical scholars sponsoring conferences on "Faith and the Challenges of Secularism" and "The Conservative Movement: Its Past, Present, and Future." A Roman Catholic himself, George has been at the vanguard of the rapprochement between evangelicals and Catholics in recent decades.[33]

Evangelicals have also endowed privately funded professorships at elite universities. This is not altogether new, and evangelicals have simply followed the lead of others. Harvard Divinity School, for instance, inaugurated the Charles Chauncey Stillman Chair in Roman Catholic Theological Studies in the late 1950s—a progressive idea at the time. Endowed chairs in Jewish studies began emerging in higher education in the 1970s, and in the early 1980s Harvard added the Albert A. List Professorship in Jewish Studies.[34] But the school's first chair in evangelical theological studies was endowed only recently by Alonzo McDonald, a Harvard alumnus who also served in the Carter White House and as worldwide managing partner for McKinsey & Company. The McDonald Family Professorship in Evangelical Theological Studies represents an intriguing opportunity for an evangelical to occupy a tenured position on the Divinity School faculty.[35] Some report that this has caused concern—particularly the prospect of a self-identified evangelical voting on tenure—while others report that everyone on the faculty has been "favorable to the position." McDonald's passion, he told me, is "to create more space for evangelicals in places like Emory and Harvard."

Carl Henry once envisioned a "great metropolitan Christian university" in New York City, one that could rival schools like Columbia.[36] Henry, like many of the evangelicals I interviewed, firmly believed that the evangelical movement could not secure academic respectability until its institutional base was located at the cultural center. Manhattan is about as central as Henry could have imagined. At the time, he was unable to persuade evangelical donors to launch such an expensive, risky venture. In the decades since, a segment of the movement's leadership has persisted in trying to launch a respected institution of higher learning in Manhattan.

Recently, The King's College, an evangelical college in Manhattan, was offered the opportunity to purchase the campus of Union Theological Seminary, located on the Upper West Side and across the street from Columbia University. Evangelicals could not have hoped for a better strategic location in New York. The chance for students at The King's College to attend classes at Columbia, Teachers College, or the Manhattan School of Music was a remarkable "lucky break" for the school's leaders. Of course, evangelicals have not always had a very good relationship with Union Seminary. A bastion of liberal Protestantism, the seminary was home to theological superstars like Paul Tillich and Reinhold Niebuhr. Were they alive, they would be shocked to learn that Union's recent financial hardships had brought the institution to a point where its property was up for sale, especially to a group of evangelicals. In the end, though, it was the evangelicals who walked away. Despite the pleas of King's president Stan Oakes, evangelical donors decided that the Upper West Side and the area surrounding Riverside Park was "too unsafe" a neighborhood, particularly for the school's young women. This was the closest evangelicals have gotten to realizing Henry's dream.[37]

For many years, faculty members at schools such as Wheaton and
Calvin have received national attention for their scholarship, particularly in history and philosophy. While these institutions may lack
the resources to support cutting-edge research in genomics or nano-
technology, they have successfully created a niche for themselves
where talented scholars in certain fields can thrive intellectually in an
evangelical community. Of the leaders I interviewed, more attended
Wheaton than any other school except Harvard. Second to Wheaton
among evangelical schools is Baylor University, and recently Baylor
has also been seeking to make a name for itself.

Founded in 1845 by the Republic of Texas, Baylor has a long-
standing relationship with the Baptist General Convention of Texas
(BGCT) and for decades was referred to by many as the "crown jewel"
institution of Texas Baptists. In 1990, amid a power struggle within
the denomination, Baylor amended its charter, giving the BGCT less
power. Yet the university did not jettison its religious identity, as some
had predicted it would. In late 2001, Baylor launched an ambitious
plan for the next ten years (called Baylor 2012) to strengthen its
academic and religious commitments. Initiatives include reducing
the student-faculty ratio from 19:1 to 13:1, establishing an Honors
College, increasing the number of PhD programs from fourteen to
more than twenty, thereby increasing the number of doctoral students by 30 percent, and constructing numerous new facilities, including a $103 million Life Sciences Building. Exact figures are
difficult to obtain, but conservative cost estimates are in the hundreds of millions of dollars—beyond the additional funds provided
by tuition increases. The plan also calls for nearly tripling the university endowment to $2 billion.[38] Baylor supporters have contributed
more than $500 million toward the 2012 vision. Indeed, this may
represent the largest investment by evangelicals in a single institution
over the last thirty years. Of course, whether these Texas-sized ambitions will actually come to fruition remains to be seen.[39] One of
Baylor's early goals was to advance to the top-tier class of research
institutions as labeled by the Carnegie Foundation for the Advancement of Teaching. In 2006, Carnegie released its most recent assessment, and Baylor advanced to the category of "high research"
institution, placing it among a group of schools that includes Boston
College and Georgetown. While Baylor has not yet reached the top
designation of "very high research activity," the improved rating has
bolstered the school's image and validated, in some measure, initiatives already undertaken in Baylor 2012.

At the same time, evangelicals have also launched a few institutions of higher education specifically geared toward preparing

students for leadership positions. The King's College, for example, says in its promotional materials, "We are focused on what we call the ruling disciplines—those areas where you should be prepared for leadership—if you want to make a difference in the world." These include undergraduate programs in government, business, media, law, education, and religion. Regent University—located in Virginia Beach, next to Pat Robertson's CBN television network—offers programs in similar fields at the graduate level. Patrick Henry College, a small Christian school located on the outskirts of Washington, D.C., was founded in 2000 and has made news for the number of its students who have secured coveted White House internships.[40] Jerry Falwell's Liberty University, founded in 1971, has garnered attention in recent years for its top-ranked debate team.

These efforts alone will not result in significant social change, but evangelicals are committing major resources to building institutions where faith-related intellectual engagement can take place. The fact that these proceedings are occurring in a variety of settings—from small Christian schools to major universities, in public and private institutions, and in every region of the nation—suggests that evangelical leaders, while not necessarily coordinating their activities, are pursuing parallel paths. When I asked leaders why they expend such resources, especially on campuses where they are not welcomed at first, academic respectability was the answer they gave. This is part of a larger effort to secure much-needed legitimacy and respect in the wider society. As one leader stated, "I don't mind standing up for the gospel at all, but I don't feel like standing up for [it] in a place where I don't think I'll be successful." Establishing places where evangelicals can be successful is indispensable to evangelicalism's success as a social movement.

Gathering the Faithful

Networks of evangelical students and scholars have been vital to their resurgence in the academy. Networks are fundamental to the rise of movements within the academy because they determine the standards and conventions of scholarship and bestow prestige on a select few.[41] They also provide the energy—most often through face-to-face encounters—that spurs scholarly creativity and productivity. Chains of influence are formed and prestige is passed from one generation to the next.

The extent of evangelical social networks is remarkable. Evangelicals have several different types of networks that have helped bring the movement into the mainstream, and my research suggests that they are the direct result of planning by evangelical leaders. These networks, which include professors, alumni, and donors, span university campuses and cross the country. The inclusion of students and scholars at highly selective institutions has been particularly critical since elites confer legitimacy on the networks of which they are a part.

David Grizzle, a senior executive with Continental Airlines, and his wife, Anne, graduated from Harvard in the late 1970s. After finishing his undergraduate thesis, Grizzle told me, he proceeded to explore "the claims of Jesus Christ to determine if they were more likely than not to be correct." Before making a faith decision, he wanted to satisfy his intellectual objections. Josh McDowell's *Evidence That Demands a Verdict* persuaded him that the evangelical faith was a viable option for someone like him, who approached the subject with an open yet critical mind. He made a decision to respond, in his words, "intellectually to the work that God had been doing in my heart previously."

This kind of intellectual exploration of Christianity is not uncommon among the leaders I interviewed, especially those who attended secular universities. Typically, these explorations begin with private reflection and individual reading, often books by evangelical authors seeking to offer a defense of Christian convictions. The most popular of these writers is C. S. Lewis, who was an Oxford tutor and Cambridge professor of medieval literature. Lewis, who died in 1963, wrote dozens of scholarly and popular books, but perhaps his most famous is *Mere Christianity,* a slim volume published in 1952. The book is based on a series of fifteen-minute radio talks he delivered on the BBC in the 1940s. Nearly one in four of the people I interviewed mentioned Lewis' influence on their own spiritual journey, and many have read his works multiple times. One CEO told me, "I've read *Mere Christianity* six times. . . . I almost have it memorized."

While these faith investigations usually begin in private, most of the people I spoke to said a campus group helped solidify their faith. These groups are the backbone of evangelical networks. In the 1970s, there were not many evangelical groups on Harvard's campus. In fact, in the words of George Bennett, "there wasn't much encouragement for Christians at all." From the university's chapel, Memorial Church, to the academic classroom, he said, "nobody took a straight, strong stand" about his or her evangelical convictions, and several people who were students at the time told me they felt as if they were under, in one student's words, a "constant drumfire of attack." More recently, however, campus ministry groups have become more prominent and have engaged more students. Though some of these groups dated from the 1930s and 1940s, by the late 1990s many other groups could also be found on Ivy League campuses. Collectively, they reached a sizable number of undergraduates. At Princeton alone, for example, I found approximately four hundred undergraduate students—close to 10 percent of the student body—regularly involved in one or more evangelical groups on campus.[42] And the number of students involved with the Harvard chapter of Campus Crusade has increased fivefold over the last two decades.[43] These findings mirror wider trends within the Ivy League. They still do not reach large segments of the student body (except perhaps at Princeton), but these and other evangelical groups like InterVarsity Christian Fellowship and campus ministries for particular ethnic groups have seen similar growth. Taken together, these point to a significant shift on the campuses of America's top universities. Groups like these have sponsored conferences, working groups, and informal alliances across campuses, bringing evangelicals from places like Harvard into contact with co-religionists from other elite schools. At the same time, such venues have introduced students to leaders from the wider evangelical world. A prime example is the Veritas Forum, named in part for Harvard's motto, *Veritas,* or Truth.

The Veritas Forum sponsors events that bring students and professors together to discuss "life's hardest questions and the relevance of Jesus Christ." The Forum began at Harvard in 1992 and quickly became well known throughout the evangelical world when it published *Finding God at Harvard,* a book that chronicled the faith stories of prominent Harvard alumni and was edited by Veritas' founder, Kelly Monroe. In 1996, evangelical groups at Yale hosted their first Veritas Forum, and these forums have since spread to over fifty campuses. Designed to encourage faith exploration at America's top universities, Veritas Forums have brought evangelical thought leaders like Dallas Willard, Os Guinness, and N. T. Wright to address groups of students and faculty on campuses across the country.[44] These and other conferences, such as the biennial "Following Christ" conferences sponsored by InterVarsity Christian Fellowship, allow evangelical academics to meet and discuss ongoing research interests. The Ivy League Congress on Faith and Action is another good example. Sponsored by Christian Union, this weekend-long conference has included members of the U.S. Congress and the British House of Lords, corporate leaders, and faculty members from major universities, all of whom speak about their faith commitments and their professional lives. Undergraduate and graduate students can meet with successful alumni and discuss not only spiritual concerns but also professional ambitions, interests, and opportunities. While attending this, I overheard several participants expressing surprise at the number of highly placed evangelical alumni from these institutions. The long-term effect of these emerging networks remains to be seen, but they represent a novel form of social organization within the evangelical movement.

Evangelicals have also formed important networks at the institutional level. Funding agencies like the Lilly Endowment have brought together representatives from institutions that have received funding through programs like the Lilly Fellows Program and the Rhodes Consultations. Additionally, the Council for Christian Colleges and Universities (CCCU) sponsors numerous joint initiatives that bring scholars, students, and administrators into conversation with one another. Through programs like CCCU's study abroad initiatives, these institutions pool resources to offer better programs than they could independently. These, in turn, have enabled academics from smaller institutions with fewer resources to study and conduct research at places like Oxford. Finally, a number of institutional partnerships and dialogues have begun in recent years between evangelical and secular institutions. In 2001, for instance, an eight-person delegation of administrators, professors, and students from Baylor University accepted an invitation to visit the Harvard Divinity School "in a spirit of overcoming traditions of institutional suspicion and stereotype." Harvey Cox, the Thomas Professor of Divinity at Harvard Divinity School, noted that the visit was important not only for the individuals involved but also for its symbolism: "It was another way to enlarge [Harvard's] conversation with evangelicals."[45] Each of these incremental efforts has enabled evangelical students and scholars to interact with interlocutors outside the evangelical subculture. In the process, the evangelical movement has been introduced to a wider constituency.

Cohesive networks of talented students and scholars have helped broaden the intellectual horizons of American evangelicalism, resulting in an "upsurge of well-educated born-again Christians."[46] But the people I spoke to are reluctant to call these networks at all. For most of them, they are professional friendships or collegial relations with fellow Christians designed to build community. Networking, according to one person I interviewed, "takes this most human of experiences and diminishes it into a mere sharing of Rolodexes." Though evangelicals have made strides in recent decades, many challenges remain. As recently as 2004, an evangelical professor at Harvard reported a colleague saying, "You know, I think you're the first

Christian I've ever met who isn't stupid."[47] This is far from an isolated incident. Even though most leaders I interviewed over the last several years do not feel inferior or derided for their evangelical identities, a recent national survey reveals that 47 percent of American evangelicals believe that other Americans look down on them.[48] America's intellectual circles may be more open to evangelicals today, yet the impression of prejudice still lingers. Despite such feelings, evangelicals are undaunted in their quest to garner academic respectability, for it is vital to their larger objective of changing the world.

4

Life of the Mind

ROBERTA AND HOWARD AHMANSON have been patrons of the evangelical mind for more than twenty years. Howard, heir to the Home Savings of America fortune, and his wife have given away over $100 million to various causes, including the *Ancient Christian Commentary on Scripture* and a Seattle-based think tank called the Discovery Institute. Roberta Ahmanson told me that the commentary series is "one arrow in the quiver" in their efforts to revive intellectual engagement with classical Christianity. The Discovery Institute, on the other hand, supports intelligent design research. Instead of getting involved in local school board disputes, the Discovery Institute focuses on elite actors. Philip Johnson, a professor of law emeritus at the University of California, Berkeley, is at the vanguard of this element of the movement: "I am waging the war at the university level and the national science organization, the scholarly journals and the elite educational community level.... I believe the point has to be made there."[1] The Ahmansons are cultural entrepreneurs, seeking to use their financial clout to reshape cultural mores and institutionalized ways of thinking. They seek to reinvigorate the life of the mind within American evangelicalism. Such an objective requires deep pockets and a commitment that is larger than any single project.

By the time I sat down with the Ahmansons, I had passed through a long vetting process. They have been portrayed as eccentric—and, at times, dangerous—for their support of conservative causes. As a result, they have tended to avoid academics and journalists. Prior to our time together, I was screened by one of their associates and they inquired about me through various mutual contacts. Eventually, though, they agreed to my interview request. But as we talked, they made their own tape recording of our conversation. We talked for several hours at their unassuming southern California home that overlooks the Pacific. For people who rarely grant interviews, they had much to say, especially on matters of faith and the mind.

The Ahmansons are voracious readers—they say they sometimes read for as many as forty hours per week—and they have underwritten many academic projects in recent decades. For example, they have funded Donald Miller's research on Pentecostalism even though Miller, a professor of religion at the University of Southern California, is not an evangelical himself. The Ahmansons have been particularly supportive of James Davison Hunter, a sociologist at the University of Virginia and the author of several books on the relationship between faith and culture. Hunter also serves as a member of the National Council of the National Endowment for the Humanities and directs a broad-ranging research center at Virginia.[2] The Ahmansons fund the work of Hunter and others because they regard it, in their words, as "a light in the academy." For them, the fact that Hunter does research that addresses issues that are important to people of faith and does it at a secular institution like Virginia is important to evangelicalism's academic respectability. Several other evangelical philanthropists told me that the Ahmansons are the "most strategic, forward-thinking" evangelical donors. Indeed, their strategic philanthropy, along with a few others', has been critical to evangelicalism's rise in the academy. Much of this philanthropy has involved bringing evangelical academics together to share ideas, critique one another, and build community.

Evangelical scholars have been very active in scholarly and professional societies. The Society of Christian Philosophers, founded in 1978, is the largest single-interest group in American philosophy.[3] Even older is the Conference on Christianity and Literature, which has been meeting since 1956 and has a membership of over 1,300. These groups have grown so much over the last three decades that there is now an umbrella organization, the Council of Christian Scholarly Societies, that coordinates their activities. There are also scholarly bodies in fields where religion has become a subdisciplinary area of study.[4] At these gatherings, evangelical scholars exchange ideas and interact both formally and informally. These, and similar venues for senior scholars who are evangelicals, have extended evangelicalism's reach in the academy.[5] According to several people I spoke to, these meetings and gatherings have been "very important" for those Christians "interested in doing excellent work" because of the encouragement and accountability they provide.

The Catholic Alliance

In their rise to new intellectual heights, evangelicals have been helped along by some unlikely allies: Roman Catholics. Their reconciliation has been a boon to both traditions.[6] Catholics benefit from evangelicals' entrepreneurial creativity and ability to connect with popular audiences, while evangelicals have gained new bases of support. Evangelicals now draw on a vast array of source material that is rooted in the Catholic tradition. They also reach entirely new scholarly audiences. And Catholics have shown them new ways of wedding religious identity to intellectually rigorous scholarship.

The détente between American evangelicals and Catholics is a recent development. For centuries, Protestants referred to the Roman pontiff as "that antichrist," a "man of sin, and son of perdition."[7] As recently as 1949 an American evangelical leader could write, "Catholicism is among the arch enemies of America and our way of life and of the true faith."[8] In the 1960s, however, evangelicals and Catholics both began to perceive Christianity as being "under assault," and they joined together to fight secularism under the banner of Francis Schaeffer's co-belligerency. While they were joining forces in the political realm, similar movements were afoot in the world of ideas. Not only did they coalesce around their views of sexuality and the body, but they jointly opposed the loosening of mores with liberal modernity. After the Catholic Church weeded out modernist clerics in the 1950s, a significant theological bridge was built between the two camps.[9] In fact, liberal Protestantism, which embraced modernism, posed a challenge for evangelicals and Catholics alike. As early as 1923, evangelical leader J. Gresham Machen discussed the "profound" gulf between Roman Catholics and evangelicals but then concluded that "it seems almost trifling compared to the abyss" between evangelicalism and liberal Protestantism.[10]

Charles Colson had never shared fundamentalism's vitriolic opposition to the Catholic Church. He is, in fact, married to a practicing Roman Catholic. Colson says he has grave concerns about the growing materialism and what he perceives to be the "moral chaos" of American culture. When I interviewed Colson, he said the struggle became "no longer Protestantism versus Catholicism so much as orthodoxy against modernism." Colson found an ally in Father Richard John Neuhaus, a U.S. Catholic leader and founder of the journal *First Things*. Neuhaus, who converted to Catholicism as an adult, invited a group of Catholics to join him in a meeting with Colson and other evangelicals in July 1993. That consultation resulted in the joint statement "Evangelicals and Catholics Together: The Christian Mission in the Third Millennium" (ECT). The document outlined areas of theological unity and joint mission as well as some areas of disagreement between Catholic and evangelical teachings. A large portion of the document was devoted to concerns like abortion, public education, pornography, the family, and the grow-ing coarseness of popular culture. In effect, they were joining forces in the culture wars.[11]

Most of the people I interviewed spoke positively about the rec-onciliation emerging from initiatives like ECT, though they recog-nize that tensions remain. Even some who signed the document acknowledged the continuation of "mutual suspicion and inflam-matory talk," and some evangelicals thought ECT was "a tacit be-trayal of the gospel."[12] Despite these objections, hostility toward Catholics diminished, and the group that helped draft ECT con-tinues to meet to this day.

This emerging consensus is not a continuation of the liberal Protestant ecumenical movement, which endorsed a lowest-common-denominator model for religious unity. Those involved in ECT told me they prefer to maintain their sectarian differences on certain issues. Yet the ECT initiative does represent a softening of some of those differences. For instance, at the end of Billy Graham's first meeting with Pope John Paul II in 1981, the pontiff reached over, clutched the evangelist's hand, and said, "We are brothers." These and other gestures of reconciliation have generated an overall "less-ening of suspicion on both sides of the evangelical–Catholic gulf and a growing awareness of the possibilities for working together."[13] Several evangelical leaders spoke about the rediscovery of common Christian convictions on a core set of beliefs about God and Jesus. In *Mere Christianity* (1960), C. S. Lewis likened the common ground shared by all Christians to a central hallway, with different rooms off the hallway representing different traditions. As comfortable as these individual rooms may be, Lewis argued, Christians must pre-sent a united front to the rest of the world, which requires supporting that symbolic central hallway. Lewis' influence can be seen in the fact that about two dozen of the people I interviewed referred to themselves as "mere Christians."

Harmony between evangelicals and Catholics has now reached the point where some observers wonder if the Protestant Reforma-tion is over.[14] While that probably goes too far, this ongoing dialogue with Catholics has dramatically influenced modern evangelicalism.

Rapprochement and University Life

Most significantly, the reconciliation with Catholics has provided an institutional base that encourages evangelical scholarship. Ironically, this base was the most Catholic of American institutions, the

University of Notre Dame. Two key players, Joel Carpenter and Nathan Hatch, made this happen. Carpenter, who now serves as provost of Calvin College, once directed the religious portfolio of philanthropic activities sponsored by the Pew Charitable Trusts. Hatch, now the president of Wake Forest University, served for many years as Notre Dame's provost and is described by others as "the most strategic thinker among evangelicals" when it comes to raising the movement's intellectual horizons. Together they crafted a series of programs, housed at Notre Dame and sponsored by Pew, that enabled senior evangelical scholars to collaborate. Through fellowships for sabbatical research, sponsored lecture series and conferences, as well as access to research materials, the Notre Dame–Pew partnership provided new opportunities for evangelical scholars. It also provided an environment where scholars from secular institutions could freely discuss the relevance of faith to their scholarship—the kind of discussion that, they told me, was not encouraged at their own institutions. Hatch, himself an evangelical, witnessed firsthand the institutional support Notre Dame could provide for serious intellectual engagement among devout Christians. He and Carpenter helped launch the Evangelical Scholarship Initiative in 1988 with the goal of "stimulating and supporting Christian scholarly activity and productivity by creating sustainable networks and programs." They knew that an institutional base was needed to nurture a critical mass of students and scholars who could produce long-term change in the academy—a goal both shared. Hatch, as a new administrator at Notre Dame, had written a proposal that Pew wanted to fund, contingent on Hatch's overseeing the project; Hatch hired one of his graduate students, Michael Hamilton, also an evangelical historian, to help manage the program's day-to-day operations. The original grant was for two programs: The first offered multiyear grants of $100,000 each to a few senior evangelical scholars; the second gave grants of $25,000 each to evangelical scholars to spend a year writing a scholarly book. Two years later, the program expanded to include a portable fellowship for evangelical students to attend a selective graduate program. Through a summer seminar program for rising undergraduate seniors, Pew hoped to encourage some of evangelicalism's best students to pursue advanced degrees in the humanities and social sciences at major universities. These promising students developed relationships with distinguished experts, many of whom became students' advisors in top graduate programs. The Pew Younger Scholars Program was the most strategic initiative evangelicals undertook over the last thirty years. It enabled more evangelicals to attend select graduate programs and establish a foothold for evangelicals at some of the world's most prestigious universities. Unlike in politics, where mobilized citizens can vote their representative into office, advancement in the world of ideas requires the approval of academic gatekeepers. Pew's philanthropy secured academic respectability for evangelicals and produced a revolution in evangelical scholarship.[15]

The establishment of the Evangelical Scholars Initiative came at a key moment when other developments were bringing evangelical and Catholic academics together. For example, evangelicals were beginning to explore more deeply the idea of "cultural engagement"— first articulated for them by Carl Henry in 1947. According to Henry, the Bible taught that believers should be active in society, not retreat from it. Evangelical scholars were drawn to the example of Roman Catholics, who, unlike evangelicals, have never isolated themselves from the culture. Many of those I spoke to noted that in the 1980s, evangelical colleges and universities began hiring more Catholics, and many of those new professors had attended graduate school at Notre Dame.[16] So when the Pew programs were established at Notre Dame, evangelical academics did not scoff as their forebears might have. Moreover, many saw new funding—over $2 million initially—become available to them, and, as one person told me, "we didn't care where it was based."

Evangelicals continue to look to Notre Dame as a model institution. A former president of Baylor told me that Notre Dame is the "industry leader." The data support that assertion. Notre Dame has consistently been ranked among the top twenty research universities by *U.S. News & World Report*. In addition, it has received more research fellowships from the National Endowment for the Humanities than any other university in the nation over the last five years. These institutional strengths, coupled with the number of Notre Dame departments that sponsor doctoral programs, create an environment where evangelical scholars can interact with colleagues who share their vision for first-rate scholarship conducted by practicing Christians. Notre Dame has raised the bar for evangelical scholarship substantially.

Religious Ways of Knowing

Most baby boomer–era evangelical academics did not have role models.[17] Devout evangelicals who were also intellectual giants were few and far between. As a result, many came to base their confidence as academics "on things like having a [doctoral] degree from Ohio State," as one leader told me, rather than on being able to offer a unique scholarly contribution as a person of faith. More recently, evangelicals have discovered a model for intellectual engagement, one that does not eschew nuance but also is not afraid to speak up for its religious convictions. This "religious way of knowing" seeks to uncover affinities between religious convictions and theoretical and empirical insights in various fields.[18] Catholic scholars have provided the model.

Conservative Catholic Robert George has been a key figure in bringing together evangelical and Catholic scholars. Through Princeton's Madison Program, George has helped evangelical students and scholars establish new networks and renew existing ones by inviting evangelical leaders to campus and hosting conferences and events.[19] These kinds of collaboration have spurred confidence in evangelical intellectualism. From presidents of evangelical institutions like Richard Mouw to academic leaders like David Lyle Jeffrey, many scholars told me that "faithful" Christian scholarship, as practiced by many evangelicals and Catholics, is able to see "blind spots" in scholarship. Believing Christians bring new perspectives to old questions, evangelical and Catholic academics alike have argued that all knowledge is filtered through a particular viewpoint. From the 1960s through the 1980s, Roman Catholic scholars demonstrated a self-consciously "Catholic way of thinking," and from them evangelicals learned to create a distinct intellectual framework for their own fields of study.[20] In 1991, Yale historian Jon Butler referred to the "evangelical paradigm" as the "single most powerful explanatory device adopted by academic historians to account for the distinctive features of American society, culture, and identity." And large-scale investigations of the secularization of higher education have captured the attention of both evangelicals and Catholics. They are united in their resistance to the secularization of the academy and have proposed similar solutions, including publicizing scholarship by outspoken people of faith.[21]

Catholic scholarship offers a particularly useful model for evangelicalism because both groups have in the past been charged with anti-intellectualism. Richard Hofstadter's landmark 1967 book, *Anti-Intellectualism in American Life,* concluded that American Catholicism was "intellectually impoverished" and had failed to create a distinctive intellectual culture of its own. Using survey data, Andrew Greeley has shown that Hofstadter's claims of Catholic anti-intellectualism were obsolete even at the time he was writing.[22] By the 1990s, observers affirmed the "impressive educational strides [made by Catholics] in recent decades, leading [to expectations of] a stronger and more visible Catholic presence in national intellectual life in the coming century."[23] Evangelicals believe they can emulate the Catholic way of bringing faith into conversation with scholarship.

This alliance has been especially productive because it has spurred evangelicals to address questions of wider interest and to publish outside the evangelical subculture. In the process, evangelical scholarship has experienced a "de-ghettoization" that permits scholars to "translate their convictions into terms that are comprehensible to those outside their religious communities."[24] An independent evaluation of the Pew Evangelical Scholars Initiative found that it attracted "excellent project proposals, stronger than those funded by comparable programs of the National Endowment for the Humanities."[25] As more evangelical scholars have gained a reputation for excellence in fields such as literary scholarship, psychology, and history, a visible evangelical presence has emerged in the academy. Moreover, as evangelicals have joined Catholic scholars, both groups have exerted a greater influence on the academy as a whole. Indeed, many evangelical and Catholic scholars are working together to "reintroduce faith" into American intellectual life.[26]

Strategic Initiatives

Evangelicals have created a constellation of intellectually oriented organizations, programs, and publications. While these have not necessarily targeted evangelical scholars or thought leaders, they further evangelicalism's intellectual ambitions. The people I interviewed mentioned many different groups and initiatives, each with its own goals and intended audiences. Among these, three distinct types stand out.

Witnessing to the Secular Elite

For many, evangelicalism's rising intellectual tide offers opportunities to communicate with, and perhaps persuade, secular critics. Luder Whitlock, head of two evangelical educational initiatives, told me evangelicals have tended to emphasize conversion and evangelism and have not been as concerned "about reaching the minds of people. This has been a major error because it has left most evangelicals without the benefit of an intellectual orientation or Christian worldview." In an attempt to change this, evangelicals have launched a series of programs over the last three decades directed toward the "type of people who listen to NPR and read the *Atlantic*," according to one leader I spoke to. This more "cerebral" form of religious outreach is well suited to the sensibilities of the leaders I talked with, who themselves hold Ivy League degrees and are patrons of the arts. Several of them cite literature or poetry to distinguish themselves as "thinking" Christians. Status markers like these and the posh locations where these programs take place are rarely discussed directly. No one asks whether they are in line with Christian teachings on stewardship, humility, or care for the poor. Rather, a subtle reference here or there is a way of building a connection with a perceived peer or distinguishing oneself from certain segments of American evangelicalism.[27] Status is an important part of evangelical efforts to open up "the spiritual component" in the lives of public leaders through intellectual engagement.

The Trinity Forum, founded in 1991, was established "to contribute to the transformation and renewal of society through the transformation and renewal of leaders."[28] With its by-invitation-only Leader Forums, it has been particularly effective at reaching some of the nation's top government and corporate figures. Os Guinness, who was one of the organization's early leaders, is an Oxford-trained sociologist who speaks authoritatively on a host of subjects. Those I spoke to cite the Trinity Forum as one of the movement's "best examples of how to mainstream evangelicalism at high levels," and they hold Guinness in high regard. Nearly one in three mentioned him or the Trinity Forum as being important to their own spiritual journeys. According to a board member of the Trinity Forum, the program is designed to strengthen "the spiritual balance and the lives of our society's leadership ... [and] to expand the number and importance of examples and voices among Christ's followers who might be seen, heard, respected, and ultimately followed by the general public." At Trinity Forum gatherings, public leaders discuss matters of faith and spiritual significance with their peers. They engage in personal reflection and discuss classical Christian texts. As part of the initiative, the group publishes selections of works by "thoughtful" Christians like Leo Tolstoy and Blaise Pascal, many of which include introductions written by Alonzo McDonald, the forum's founding chair. Mark Berner, a Manhattan-based Trinity Forum board member, told me, "The [Trinity Forum] Study Series shows how some of the classical literature of Western civilization and [the literature of] the Christian faith can work together in addressing the problems we face today." This initiative was designed to create "nonthreatening" environments, in upscale resorts and hotels, where "the gatekeepers of power, intellectual thought, economic leverage and influence in our society" meet and share their thoughts and personal stories in confidence. A Christian facilitator leads the discussion and elicits both questions and answers from participants. From its founding, the Trinity Forum has been modeled after such successful elite gatherings as the Aspen Institute.

Socrates in the City takes to heart the philosopher's maxim that "the unexamined life is not worth living." Founded by a group of upwardly mobile New Yorkers, it appeals to "urban, savvy, bright" professionals who are "open to thinking about the bigger questions in life," said Eric Metaxas, the group's founder. These forums have created a new species of evangelicals: the Christian public intellectual. Among the most frequently mentioned are Guinness, Yale Law professor Stephen Carter, and University of Southern California philosopher Dallas Willard. Monthly gatherings of Socrates in the City, comprised largely of New York professionals in their twenties, thirties, and forties, are held at upscale venues like the University Club on Fifth Avenue or the Colony Club on the Upper East Side. Following hors d'oeuvres and drinks, 150 to 250 people gather in a large room to hear an hour-long lecture. [29] Topics range from "Can Atheists Be Good Citizens?" to "Can a Smart Person Believe in God?" Metaxas, who hosts the program, peppers his humorous introductory comments with allusions to American evangelicalism, but the references are never overt. In this way, evangelical attendees recognize the program and Metaxas as one of their own, but hopefully, say Socrates supporters, the target audience—New York's secular elite—will not perceive them as "a crowd of Bible-bashers." The main goal of the program, said Metaxas, is to "present the Christian perspective on various topics in an intellectually-respectable, honest, and, . . . hopefully, attractive way." Programs like these endeavor to lay "an intellectual foundation" in the minds of secular critics whereby "the gospel can be more plausible," said Andy Crouch, another evangelical intellectual. This method does not yield the quick, measurable results of a Billy Graham Mission, but as one leader acknowledged, "This is a new day. . . . In large part, that type of outreach no longer works, and especially not with this type of crowd."

In 1967, Armand Nicholi, an associate clinical professor of psychiatry at Harvard Medical School, began offering a course on the philosophical writings of Freud. "The students found Freud's works very interesting but unbalanced," says Nicholi, who has taught the course without interruption every year since. Nicholi remembered a book by C. S. Lewis entitled *The Problem of Pain* and decided to pose Lewis against Freud in his seminar the following year. By the 1980s, it was one of the most popular courses at Harvard. In 1987, a member of the Kennedy family who participated in the seminar called Douglas Holladay, an evangelical entrepreneur and friend, and suggested that the course be made into a PBS documentary. Nothing happened for several years, but in September 2004, *The Question of God* finally ran as a four-hour documentary. The show, based on Nicholi's book of the same title, aired on every PBS station nationwide for two weeks in a row. Nicholi told me that he uses the philosophical writings of Freud to represent a secular viewpoint and the works of Lewis as illustrative of a "thoroughly spiritual perspective." Although in the course Nicholi never chooses sides in this manufactured Freud–Lewis debate (Lewis and Freud never met), he more directly supports Lewis in the book and in interviews.

This is an excellent example of evangelicalism's intellectually oriented outreach. It highlights the work of a popular, longtime professor of psychiatry who is among the most recognized evangelicals on Harvard's campus. Evangelical backers of the documentary wanted a "subtle, evenhanded" account of the differences between Freud and Lewis and insisted that the program "not preach" so that viewers could decide which perspective was truer to their experience. As a result, the program featured interviews with experts like Freud archivist Harold Blum and Lewis specialist Peter Kreeft and presented seven different perspectives including those of *Skeptic* publisher Michael Shermer and Jungian analyst Margaret Klenck. By raising all of the necessary funds for production, distribution, and promotion before approaching PBS, Holladay and others wanted to virtually guarantee that PBS would agree to the idea. "PBS was critical for this type of project," says Holladay, because "their audience was our direct target." Indeed, the PBS audience, with its higher level of education and its reputation for being more cosmopolitan and refined than the general public, is precisely the group evangelicals hope to persuade with initiatives like these. And they hope that evangelicalism will emerge as a legitimate—indeed desirable—way of life for educated people. They are pleased with the results. The review for the Skeptics Society concluded, "On balance... *The Question of God* serves well as an introduction to these complex issues. In the current media climate of news-bites, humiliating reality TV, and shrill oppositional politics, the real *miracle* is that an intelligent show about God was made at all."[30]

Educating the Faithful

Evangelicals have created a number of outlets in which they can address a broad range of topics within the context of their faith. For previous generations of evangelicals, the Bible served as the single authority on a wide range of subjects; it remains authoritative for the movement as a whole, but elites have begun discussing these issues more broadly.[31] *Books & Culture,* a "bimonthly review that engages the contemporary world from a Christian perspective," is modeled on the *New York Review of Books.*[32] Even though it loses money, Christianity Today International continues to publish the journal because, in the words of its publisher, it "represents who we want to be and what we want to do . . . [help evangelicalism] become intellectually grounded." Similarly, the *Mars Hill Audio Journal* seeks "to advance the plausibility of Christian claims in light of the messages advanced by dominant cultural institutions." The *Journal*'s founder, Ken Myers (a former NPR editor and producer) calls this "cultural apologetics," seeking to help listeners integrate media fare into a "Christian way of thinking." Other publications that seek to stimulate evangelicals' thinking include *First Things, Touchstone,* and *Image.*[33] Although written primarily for religious audiences, these publications have gained wider attention. For example, material first published in *Image* has appeared in the *Pushcart Prize* anthology, *Best American Essays, New Stories from the South,* and *Best American Movie Writing,* among others. These publications introduce evangelical readers to everything from current debates over bioethics to the latest novel by John Updike, exposing the evangelical community to contemporary intellectual debates.

Evangelical organizations have also initiated conferences, retreats, and intensive study programs to help the evangelical laity engage more deeply with a wide array of subjects relevant to their faith. For example, the C. S. Lewis Institute, based in Washington, D.C., sponsors year-long study groups in a demanding program of readings and training in theology, apologetics, and spirituality. The program aims to "fortify the intellectual capital" of professionals in Washington.[34] One senior White House staffer calls the program "the single greatest intellectual and spiritual exercise of my life." The Centurions Program, led by Charles Colson and his Wilberforce Forum, is another example. Its goal is to spawn more Christian public intellectuals, all "steeped in a biblical worldview" and conversant with debates in politics, law, science, technology, and other topics, who will become forceful advocates in the public arena.[35] Although program participants are selected through an application process, Colson hopes to reach the evangelical masses, not a select elite: "I don't believe societies are moved as much by the societal elites as they are by changes in the habits of the heart. I think that you have to give people, the masses of people, a different vision to live by.... [John] Nesbitt said that fads start from the top down, movements from the bottom up." A growing number of evangelicals disagree with Colson. James Davison Hunter has said Colson's strategy suffers from "fatal naïveté."[36] Hunter argues that culture only changes when individuals and ideas infiltrate elite networks and the organizations they control. The leaders I spoke to prefer Hunter's approach—probably because they are part of those elite networks already.

The Next Generation

Evangelicals are also trying to raise the intellectual stature of the next generation of leaders: students and recent college graduates. The best example of this is the L'Abri Fellowship. L'Abri was established by Francis Schaeffer as a place where students could contemplate existential questions in an intellectually and spiritually "safe place" as well as practice Christian living in the company of other believers. Since its founding in 1955, L'Abri has expanded into multiple study centers in Europe, North America, and Asia. Many of the leaders I interviewed spent time at L'Abri; Os Guinness describes it as having a "profound influence" on his life. For decades, American evangelicals have supported fulfilling the Great Commission, a passage at the end of Matthew's gospel in which Jesus asks his followers to "go and make disciples among all nations." L'Abri is dedicated to helping fulfill what they call the "cultural commission." Schaeffer encouraged younger evangelicals to move into centers of elite cultural production and to engage secular society. From political activism to scholarly research, Schaeffer argued for evangelical involvement in all areas of social significance.[37] As evangelical executive Mark Berner put it, "Schaeffer gave us permission to think and more than that, to integrate.... He broke the ice like a Coast Guard cutter breaking up the ice so that other boats could come along behind it."

The popularity of L'Abri, especially among evangelicals who came of age in the 1960s and 1970s, has spawned an array of programs for students and recent college graduates. The Council for Christian Colleges and Universities, for instance, sponsors intensive study programs for students at member institutions around the globe; from Kampala to Oxford, from Washington to Los Angeles, its study programs expose college students to Christian leaders in different sectors of society while also expanding their vocational and intellectual horizons. The World Journalism Institute in New York holds summer seminars for young evangelicals pursuing careers in media. The Falls Church, an evangelical Episcopal church in suburban Washington, D.C., sponsors a year-long program for recent college graduates that combines a rigorous graduate-level education in theology with workplace experience in fields like law, government, business, and medicine. And in 2001, the Trinity Forum launched a program for recent college graduates called the Trinity Forum Academy. During this nine-month residential program held at a picturesque resort on Maryland's Eastern Shore, young evangelicals read great works of literature, philosophy, and theology and attend cultural events like the ballet and the symphony. The entire program is designed to prepare young people for public leadership while nurturing the formation of a Christian mind.

Of course, youthful exuberance can generate criticism as well. In September 2005, Dartmouth's student body president, Noah Riner, delivered a speech to welcome incoming freshmen. An outspoken evangelical, Riner used the opportunity to talk about how his own faith had shaped his understanding of personal character. At the speech's conclusion, Riner spoke explicitly about "Jesus' message of redemption." Fellow evangelicals both applauded and criticized him.[38] A critical editorial appeared in the *Boston Globe*, while William F. Buckley praised Riner in the *National Review*. The student assembly vice president for student life resigned in protest, calling the speech "reprehensible and an abuse of power," according to press accounts. The incident demonstrates the tension young evangelical leaders face as they try to determine where and when to share their evangelical faith. Despite the remarkable gains that evangelicals have made in recent decades, Ivy League campuses are not as interested in a religious revival as some evangelicals may hope.

The Future of the Evangelical Mind

The visibility of evangelical intellectualism has grown remarkably in a relatively short time. Not surprisingly, within the evangelical movement many vestiges of fundamentalism's disdain for the academic world persist. One of the most contentious issues with which evangelical academics continue to grapple is academic freedom. Wheaton, Calvin, and many other evangelical colleges require faculty members to sign and regularly reaffirm statements of faith, which organizations such as the American Association of University Professors (AAUP) regard as antithetical to academic freedom. Such faith statements, they argue, inhibit the range of intellectual questions that can be asked and impose a limitation on the kinds of answers that can be offered. An AAUP committee stated as recently as 1988 that these types of institutions forfeit "the moral right to proclaim themselves as authentic seats of learning." Based on the same concerns, Phi Beta Kappa has denied membership to even the best liberal arts colleges within the Council for Christian Colleges and Universities.[39] And differing opinions on the subject of academic freedom can be found on many evangelical campuses. For example, at Baylor University, the provost and a law school professor publicly debated the subject in the fall of 2004. The provost suggested that the academic freedom of the Baylor professor should not override the freedom of the academic community to establish boundaries for scholarly pursuits. In this notion of academic freedom, institutions have the right to establish limits to the questions and answers addressed by scholars within their communities. In essence, the institution enjoys a form of "academic freedom" that allows it to differ from prevailing norms in higher education today. This position seeks to ensure that none of the research agendas pursued by individual faculty members violate institution-wide norms and shared convictions. Taken to the extreme, this policy could require professors to abandon entire research interests if they were determined, by some source of authority, to contradict the core beliefs shared by members of the institution. While I did not find a single example of such an extreme situation, the prospect of it concerns many.

Many argue that elevating the idea of academic freedom to the institutional level nullifies the entire purpose of academic freedom: to protect individual scholars from their institutions. This argument draws on evangelicalism's high regard for the individual: the idea that there is no mediator between humans and God. It is not surprising, therefore, that individual freedom of conscience is invoked in these disputes. Moreover, this preference for individual freedom is in line with the modern academy's concern for protecting the intellectual pursuits of individual scholars. Academic freedom remains a hotly contested topic within the world of evangelical colleges and universities and influences wider perceptions of the evangelical academy. Barring unforeseen changes among credential-granting organizations like the AAUP and Phi Beta Kappa, evangelical scholars will either have to persuade their institutions to change their policies or remain content without this form of external validation—and the status that comes with it. This poses a considerable obstacle to evangelical scholars who seek to gain entrée at top institutions.

A related concern is that most academics keep their distance from American evangelicalism. In her study of natural and social scientists at twenty-one of the nation's top universities, Elaine Howard Ecklund discovered that university professors maintain strong boundaries between "good" and "bad" religion as it relates to science.[40] "Good" religion was adaptable, based on moral "principles," encouraged a plurality of beliefs, and remained within the domain of religion. "Bad" religion, on the other hand, was rigid, based on moral "commands," imposed uniform belief structures, and intruded into other domains, such as science. Ecklund found that "the religion that this group of respondents most often described in positive terms was Buddhism and the religion that they most often described in negative terms was evangelicalism/fundamentalism (which respondents generally lumped together in the same category)." Of course, this is not altogether surprising, for this and previous studies have shown that only 1.5 percent of elite scientists identify as evangelical, compared to anywhere from 25 to 47 percent of the general population.[41] Moreover, this study shows that 52 percent of scientists at major universities have no religious affiliation, compared to 14 percent of the general population.[42] Evangelicals' interest in intelligent design is particularly troubling to elite scientists. During the course of my research, one scientist at a major university referred to religious conservatives' zeal for intelligent design as "the thing that makes their faith the most unattractive" to her. In sum, elite scientists are not likely to be evangelical, and most of them present themselves and their work as being in opposition to evangelicalism and its belief system. They are not likely allies.

Perhaps the greatest challenges to evangelicalism's intellectual stature is the movement's distinctive subculture. While evangelical scholarship has moved beyond the subculture, nearly everyone I spoke to acknowledged the persistence of what some call "a cheesy Christian subculture," with its own journals, conferences, and publishing outlets that do not appeal to mainstream audiences. When evangelical scholars use these avenues to disseminate their research, their works have little chance of persuading the wider academic community of their scholarship's rigor or value. Prestige remains the main currency among academics, and evangelical publishing houses lack the cachet of major university presses.[43] It is conceivable that such perceptions could change over time, but they will likely only do so as authors published in evangelical outlets also publish in prestigious secular outlets. Such a trend has begun, but a large segment of the evangelical academic world has not yet caught up.

Then there is the most recognized element of American evangelicalism, the megachurch. These are large congregations, some of which have more than twenty thousand members, that have emerged on the religious landscape during the same time that there has been an "opening of the evangelical mind."[44] However, the two developments are pulling evangelicalism in opposite directions. Megachurch pastors favor pragmatic topics and dramatic presentations over intellectual sophistication or nuance.[45] As one evangelical seminary president told me, the pressure for these pastors to produce entertaining worship services and engaging sermons "sometimes comes at the cost of... [having] no theological [or intellectual] basis." The elites I spoke to generally had a distaste for the "dumbing down of Christianity" that they observe in parts of the evangelical subculture. The *Left Behind* series and contemporary Christian music have few elite followers.

This is the public face of evangelicalism, and it may very well limit evangelicalism's intellectual horizons. Unless evangelical scholarship becomes commercially viable, it will never penetrate the mass evangelical audience. But to the extent that evangelicalism gains popular support, it risks losing the approval it seeks in academic circles. Numerous people told me that they were concerned that evangelicalism would become "triumphalistic," which for academics is, in the words of one college president, an "immediate turn-off." The evangelical preference for an all-encompassing "Christian worldview" is a "scary prospect" for leaders in elite cultural centers, according to one senior governmental advisor, "because the other side, those who are trained and deeply wedded to an ideal of nuance and secular sophistication, [are] fearful of a system that embraces absolutes." Evangelicalism is, after all, a tradition that has a history of stifling academic inquiry and banning books from public libraries.[46] For evangelicalism's intellectual strides to "stick," says another evangelical public leader, the movement must "address the secularists' fear of both us [evangelicals] and what we might do if we were to 'win the day.' " These leaders claim that critics will not accept them as peers—in the academy and in other sectors of influence—until they like them as colleagues. Changing outsiders' perception of evangelicalism is one of the main concerns of the leaders I interviewed. In elite circles, social networks are critical to prestige.

The greatest challenge facing American evangelicalism is the persistence of its subculture of lower educational attainment. Though the percentage of evangelicals attaining a bachelor's degree has increased dramatically, the percentage of evangelicals who dropped out of high school is still greater than it is among the general population: 16 percent compared to 13 percent. They also are less likely to have a college degree (15 percent compared to 18 percent) or a graduate degree (6 percent compared to 10 percent).[47] Evangelicals have narrowed the educational gap with the general U.S. population since 1976, but differences remain. Of course, this is not simply a result of religious identity. Social class and family background play important roles. Even controlling for this variation, though, evangelicals do not attain the levels of education found among Jews or mainline Protestants.[48] Evangelical academics stand far apart from the rest of the evangelical community, which will make it difficult to advance the movement's intellectual horizons.

There are, however, reasons for optimism among evangelicals. Chief among these is the movement's flexible structure and entrepreneurial creativity. Modern evangelicalism lacks an established hierarchy with clearly defined boundaries, and this engenders cooperation (and also competition) across sectors, institutions, and regions of the country. The landscape of higher education has moved from being discipline- and institution-based to a more fluid, network-oriented structure. Contemporary higher education is in an era of fuzzy boundaries between disciplines. Just as specialization led to secularization within the academy, the interdisciplinary enterprise currently under way could help reverse the effect. The flowering of interdisciplinary centers and cooperative agreements across institutions reflects this new form of academic organization.[49] As a decentralized movement, evangelicalism possesses a nimble structure that is particularly well positioned to embrace these emerging models for academic organization. In particular, evangelicalism's moral perspective could be useful for scholars as questions about human nature come to the forefront of intellectual discourse across the disciplines. Clark Kerr, former president of the University of California system, has said recently that universities lack "great visions to lure them on."[50] It is possible that the moral framework underlying evangelicalism could unite some disparate constituents, providing a moral vocabulary for the communitarian project that academics have urged their colleagues and institutions to pursue.[51]

Christian anti-intellectualism is an anomaly of the twentieth century. Fundamentalist distrust of academic inquiry is not representative of Christian history. In fact, history is on the side of evangelical intellectual strivings. For most of Christianity's history, learning and piety have been closely wedded. The church, in both the Roman Catholic and Protestant traditions, has supported a range of intellectual activity, from the scientific research of Newton to the literary contributions of Chesterton.

Evangelical scholars who have been at the vanguard of the movement's rise have removed some of the prejudicial barriers for younger evangelicals. One historian I interviewed, for example, mentioned that he has received requests for book proposals from "every major university press in America" over the last two years. At this moment in the movement's history, there are very few barriers preventing evangelical scholars from publishing in major outlets. It remains to be seen how many scholars will take advantage of this opportunity, but evangelicals are showing a strong commitment to scholarly endeavors. Many told me they feel "called" to their work, and academics were among them. The philanthropists, institutional leaders, and evangelical pastors I interviewed see the pursuit of knowledge and the production of new scholarship as an important Christian endeavor. In this way, evangelicalism endows intellectual life with seriousness and significance. Serving others is part of their faith, and education, they feel, is one form of preparation for service. As I talked with various leaders, this calling to service included everything from discovering the cure for terminal illnesses to explaining references to the Bible in Shakespeare. Unlike previous generations of evangelicals, who prized the work of missionaries and preachers, for many of the evangelicals I met the professoriate is as much a holy calling as the priesthood.

Finally, religion has come to the forefront of intellectual discourse in recent years. In his January 2005 column for the *Chronicle of Higher Education*, Stanley Fish, America's leading proponent of postmodern literary criticism, wrote, "When Jacques Derrida died I was called by a reporter who wanted to know what would succeed high theory and the triumvirate of race, gender, and class as the center of intellectual energy in the academy. I answered like a shot: religion." In the same piece, he contends that religion must not be simply studied at arm's length but must be considered as a viable "candidate for the truth."[52] American evangelicalism has, in the words of Tony Campolo, "developed intellectual capabilities" over the last thirty years. In the process, it has established institutional bases and developed a measure of academic cachet that has furthered the movement's agenda for wider society. Evangelicalism's activities in the realm of education are as much about cultural legitimacy as they are about imposing an intellectual agenda. While some have argued that universities do not need more Christianity, a religious way of approaching scholarship can add new perspectives to academic conversations.[53] This, of course, is not unique to evangelicalism, but in fields like history, philosophy, and sociology, many scholars are pursuing their work from an evangelical perspective.

Mark Noll, a recognized scholar of American history and professor at the University of Notre Dame, published *The Scandal of the Evangelical Mind* in 1994, when he was on the faculty of Wheaton College. In it Noll bemoaned evangelicalism's poor record of achievement in academic circles and urged fellow evangelicals to pursue a more intellectually rigorous approach to faith and academic pursuits. Many of the people I spoke to said the book was key to the intellectual renaissance of the last decade. And although the process of lifting evangelicalism out of the academic ghetto was well under way when Noll's book appeared, he now acknowledges that "were I to [write] *The Scandal of the Evangelical Mind* today, it would have a different tone—more hopeful than despairing, more attuned to possibilities than to problems, more concerned with theological resources than theological deficiencies."[54] Academic prestige and educational credentials can enable a group to move from the social margins to the intellectual mainstream, and evangelicals are well on their way.

PART III

ARTISTS, CELEBRITIES,

AND THE PUBLIC STAGE

5

From Protest to Patronage

IN 1988, American evangelicals led the fight against Martin Scorsese's *The Last Temptation of Christ*. Though Scorsese had hired two evangelical leaders to serve as consultants, his portrayal of Jesus ignited a firestorm of evangelical fury. The film, based on Nikos Kazantzakis' 1955 novel, presents Jesus Christ as a tormented figure struggling with his identity and his place in human history.[1] At one point, he watches Mary Magdalene, a prostitute, as she meets a client. Later, as Jesus is being crucified, Satan tempts him to leave the cross for an ordinary life, complete with the joys of sex, marriage, and family. In the end, more than twenty-five thousand people protested outside Universal Studios in Hollywood, and opposition was so strong that Blockbuster Video refused to carry *The Last Temptation of Christ* in its stores, making it the most protested film in the history of cinema.[2]

When it comes to arts and entertainment, this is the public face of evangelicalism. Indeed, this has been the stance of conservative Christians for much of the latter half of the twentieth century, and the church's complex relationship to the arts dates much further back. Early Christians refused to patronize the Roman theater.[3] After Constantine established Christianity as Rome's recognized religion, the church became a patron of the arts. By the fifteenth century, the Vatican was commissioning works by Michelangelo, Rafael, and Leonardo da Vinci. Yet Protestant Reformers such as Martin Luther and John Calvin advocated a return to an earlier model for church life, part of which was the preference for a doctrine based solely on scripture (*sola scriptura*) with less interest in aesthetics. Ornate stained glass windows and intricate masonry were replaced with simple, unadorned church buildings. The minister's sermon became the centerpiece of community worship, and while instrumental music and congregational singing remained, all artistic expressions in worship were secondary to the spoken word.

At the start of the twentieth century, conservative Protestants maintained the primacy of the Bible. Artistic expression within the church was deemed acceptable, but new forms of entertainment such as the nickelodeon were viewed as potentially harmful to one's spiritual development. In the 1920s, fundamentalists felt increasingly out of step with American society. Through entities like the National Board of Film Review, established in 1909, theological conservatives sought to influence the content of new forms of entertainment. By 1922, the nascent entertainment industry had elected to self-regulate films under the aegis of the Motion Picture Producers and Distributors of America (MPPDA). Will Hays, a former postmaster general, headed the office, and in 1930, MPPDA issued a formal production code, called the Hays Code, outlining acceptable content for major studio productions.[4]

From 1930 into the 1960s, the National Council of Churches (NCC) oversaw the Protestant Film Commission, reviewing every script made into a motion picture by each of the major studios. Studio executives relied on this office and its Catholic counterpart to ensure that the film industry produced movies that would be well received by religious believers. Starting in the 1950s, though, a series of Supreme Court decisions called into question the legality of review commissions like these.[5] In 1966, the NCC closed the Protestant Film Commission, deeming the office's $35,000 annual cost too high for ongoing support. According to several informed sources, studio executives were troubled by this decision, fearing that the creative community would lose touch with its audience. In 1968, the film rating system was instituted, thereby shifting the decision-making power from the producer to the consumer. This greatly expanded the creative possibilities for filmmakers. If they could persuade the studio that a film would be acceptable to a large enough customer base, they were given the artistic license to create it. The marketplace, not censors, would determine film content. That operating principle has remained, and the studios' reliance on profitability as a barometer for film content is why evangelicals have occasionally resorted to protests and boycotts as ways to influence the entertainment sector.

And protesting is certainly a big part of the movement. Echoing political groups like the Moral Majority, movement leaders like Donald Wildmon have launched important organizations within the evangelical world. Wildmon's American Family Association currently claims a membership of more than four hundred thousand with over five hundred local branches.[6] Groups like this claim to be defending "traditional morality" against secularists—or, to use the term earlier leveled against President Carter, "secular humanists"—and they frame these battles as "us versus them." They use mass mobilizations and acts of protest to communicate their disdain for violence on television, sexuality in film, and explicit lyrics in music. Presenting themselves as "outsiders," they have increased the distance between the evangelical world and centers of elite cultural production like New York and Los Angeles.[7]

Distance

Syndicated columnist Cal Thomas told me about being invited by a publicist to attend an advance screening of *Saved,* a 2004 movie set in an evangelical high school:

> I got called by one of the studios [to preview the film *Saved*]. . . . They had seen the column I'd written about *The Passion*. . . .
>
> So the publicist calls me the next day: "Listen, I understand you walked out [of the screening]. . . . You didn't like it?"
>
> I said, "Are you old enough to remember . . . a television show . . . called *Amos 'n' Andy*?" She replied, "Oh, yes." . . .
>
> "Would you have shown any of those films to an NAACP convention? [The publicist does not answer.] You have taken the message of Christ and turned it into a joke. All of the kids in this Christian school are hypocrites . . . and then the one straitlaced [character] is a hyper Bible-quoting perfectionist-type. . . . There's not a genuine believer in there."

Others told me of similar incidents that incensed them. Several perceive mainstream media outlets as hostile to people of faith. Many of those I interviewed mentioned hearing snide remarks and snickering about evangelicalism. Some producers describe studio executives as "anti-Christian" and the broader entertainment world as suspicious of "religion in general and of Christianity in particular."[8] Even successful producers contend that evangelicals are "blackballed" in Hollywood and that being recognized as an evangelical can make it harder for an actor, writer, or director to find work. Popular entertainers like Pat Boone believe the Hollywood establishment exhibits a "visceral rejection" of the evangelical lifestyle, which translates into a "visceral rejection" of people like him. Hollywood insiders suggest, though, that the studio executives or artists who hold these positions have limited interaction with actual evangelicals. As one successful producer said, "Their interaction with Christians is . . . primarily people boycotting or sending nasty mail and then getting in the headlines the next day for going to a prostitute."

More often, evangelicals feel that their secular peers aren't really hostile but do show prejudice. These subtle slights foster feelings of alienation that persist even years after the incident. A few people shared with me stories of being embarrassed in social situations where someone made a derogatory remark about evangelicals to which they were called on to respond. One person told me about a party hosted by a friend of his, an aide to Senator Ted Kennedy, who had invited several members of the media to a backyard barbecue. A *New York Times* reporter, recognizing this person as an evangelical and seeing that a storm was approaching, shouted to him, "Hey, can you do anything about the weather?" The person responded, "No,...I only raise the dead." After relating this, he turned to me and said, "Now, can you imagine saying that? If I were black, [can you imagine him saying,] 'Hey,...can you do your Amos and Andy impression?'...So you get that a lot [as an evangelical running in these circles]. It goes with the territory." Of course, such incidents may not be intended to demean or embarrass, and at face value, they seem harmless enough. But as they pile up, people sense that their faith is belittled. As one person put it, insulting evangelicals is "the dirty little secret still tolerated in today's [politically correct] environment."

Still others argue that Hollywood elites are simply uninformed about matters of faith. Jody Hassett Sanchez, a former producer for ABC's *World News Tonight*, believes this happens because there is "no intellectual shame attached to not knowing about religion. So you can still be taken seriously as a journalist but not know the difference between a Pentecostal or Presbyterian, whereas you would never dare make that mistake, if you went to the Pentagon, between an A-4 and an A-14." Evangelicals up and down the eastern seaboard and across the country bemoan this situation. For example, in early 2006 *Newsweek* discussed Jerry Falwell's Liberty University and the surprising fact that Liberty's debate team was ranked number one in the nation at that time while Harvard was number fourteen. In the original version of the report, *Newsweek* misquoted Falwell as referring to the debate team as "assault ministry," affirming the media image of evangelicals as militant culture warriors. In fact, Falwell spoke of the program as "a salt ministry"—a reference to Matthew 5, where Jesus admonishes his disciples to be the "salt of the earth." *Newsweek* later acknowledged the error, but evangelicals saw it as the latest example of journalistic ignorance on matters of faith.[9]

By the same token, evangelicals are suspicious of mainstream culture and the cultural elite. Studies show that American evangelicals are more disapproving than other Christians of artists and the broader artistic world. For example, evangelicals are more likely than mainline Protestants or Roman Catholics to think that artists are materialistic and to claim that artists dishonor God. They are also more likely than other religious groups to say that they have seen art that disgusts them and to have heard a sermon on the dangers of contemporary art and music.[10] Theologically conservative ministers report lower levels of exposure to the arts (such as visiting an art gallery or museum) and lower levels of interest in the arts and are much more likely to say that "contemporary art and music are leading us away from the Bible." Compared to theological moderates or liberals, these ministers are more likely to suggest that religious leaders should speak out against contemporary art and that churches should promote only "Christian" art or music. In sum, there are sizable segments of American evangelicalism that oppose the culture-producing industries.

Evangelical forays in Hollywood have not often been successful. Veteran television producer Michael Warren told me, "I have a meeting about once a year with somebody that says, 'You know, George has made $100 million in the rug business, and he's decided to do some great thing [in the media world].' [But] it's coming from a person that [has no understanding of the] media [business] at all." Others cite the example of Dallas businessman Norm Miller of Interstate Batteries, who "entered Hollywood with a big plan but accomplished practically nothing." His media ventures included bankrolling *Extreme Days* (2001) and *The Joyriders* (1999). Miller told me his work in Hollywood was "the biggest mess I've ever gotten into." After a series of "fiascos" he closed down his entertainment company and now says he has "no more passion" for making films.

Many of the public leaders I interviewed expressed frustration over the distance between the entertainment industry and evangelicalism. American evangelicalism is dependent on cultural production. Evangelicals see television, movies, and music as tools they can use to spread their message as well as ways to channel believers' creative energies in service to the movement.[11] And they have been early adopters of new media technology from the earliest days of the modern movement. From Paul Rader's *Breakfast Brigade* to Charles Fuller's *Old-Fashioned Revival Hour*, evangelicals, and their fundamentalist forebears, were at the forefront of commercial radio programming in the twentieth century.[12] At the height of his radio career, Charles Fuller was as recognized a voice as Bing Crosby.

Forty years later, evangelicals were at the vanguard of using satellite technology in broadcast television. In 1977, Pat Robertson's CBN joined HBO and Ted Turner's WTBS as the first cable satellite networks. This bodes positively for evangelicals today as the digital revolution takes root. Evangelicals clearly hope to be part of "making culture," but the transition from protest to patronage has made waves both inside and outside the evangelical movement.

Evangelical Subculture

Modern American evangelicalism still retains elements of separatism from its fundamentalist past, including homeschooling and Christian colleges as well as Christian bookstores, radio stations, and even clothing. The subculture can include political ventures or missions activities, but typically it relates to media. Nearly everyone I spoke to used it as a shorthand for the constellation of organizations and individuals that produce cultural goods—books, magazines, music, and artwork—for the evangelical consumer.[13] Today, the evangelical subculture is vast, with an enormous distribution network. For example, Focus on the Family's weekly commentary reaches thirty million people through radio and television. In 1996, Focus on the Family launched *Plugged In,* one of the first broadly circulated evangelical magazines dedicated to reviewing music, movies, television, and other media. Others, including *Christianity Today,* the flagship magazine of American evangelicalism, have followed suit. Evangelicals are an important demographic. The market for religious products is expected to top $8.6 billion in annual sales by 2008, and evangelicals are estimated to be anywhere from 25 percent to 40 percent of the U.S. population. As such, they represent a huge market for both religious and secular entertainment.[14] Indeed, evangelical support for *The Passion of the Christ* and *The Chronicles of Narnia* catapulted both films onto the list of the twenty-five all-time top-grossing movies in the United States.[15] For both, evangelical church leaders previewed the films, endorsed them through media campaigns, and then reserved thousands of seats for their opening weekends in theaters across the nation.

Sociologist Christian Smith has argued that evangelicalism thrives as a movement because its distinctive subculture offers adherents a sense of personal meaning and belonging. The evangelical subculture flourishes because it is both *distinct from* and *engaged with* wider society, without being genuinely countercultural. Smith proposes that groups that differ from prevailing norms and mores—without being so opposed that they disengage entirely from society—foster a strong sense of identity, which leads to greater loyalty and commitment. That identity is strongest when members cast themselves as "embattled," and evangelical leaders present the group as being persecuted, yet not so persecuted that they are completely removed from wider society. Smith concludes that this distinction-with-engagement is the most effective way to maintain religious vitality.

Baggage

The evangelical subculture is highly visible at the grassroots level, but many of the leaders I interviewed do not identify with it.[16] In fact, they actively seek to distance themselves from the movement's subculture. Not a single artist or entertainer referred to the evangelical subculture in positive terms. Derision was more likely. They used terms like "gross," "cheesy," and "anemic." They regularly referred to the evangelical subculture as "baggage" weighing them down on their way up the social ladder. Yet, upon closer investigation, I found that many of them depended upon that "baggage" as they and their movement rose in prominence and prestige. Perhaps the evangelical subculture did keep them from climbing faster, but many would not have climbed as far without it.

Evangelicals place a premium on "safe" entertainment: music that does not contain offensive lyrics, films that do not feature sex or drugs, and video games that avoid graphic violence. Christian radio stations tout programming as "safe and fun for the whole family."[17] While movement leaders like James Dobson demonize secular entertainment and often allude to a "culture war," the products their organizations produce are far from potent. Instead, they are promoted as safe, innocuous, and on occasion beneficial.

Doubtless, the appeal of "safe" entertainment to many evangelicals spurred their support for cultural goods like the television series *Touched by an Angel.* Yet evangelicals also patronize graphic movies like *The Passion of the Christ* (2004) and *The End of the Spear* (2006). This is where tension within the evangelical movement is most apparent. Making a fetish of safety is one of the defining characteristics of the evangelical subculture, and Hollywood evangelicals want little to do with it. Barbara Nicolosi, a screenwriter, told me that the evangelical subculture sees faith as providing a "place of rest," whereas she thinks it should do the opposite: Faith, in her words, should "energize you so that you can go and bring more people home."

Many of the people I interviewed see the subculture as a distraction from the movement's primary goal of reaching others and expanding evangelicalism's influence. They argue that it depletes creative energies and drains support and resources from mainstream outlets. The evangelical subculture generates sizable profits, and many of the leaders I spoke with said they would like to see those resources directed toward mainstream projects, not ones relegated to the "subcultural ghetto." For instance, the contemporary Christian music genre sold $700 million worth of albums and singles in 2004. This represents more than 6 percent of all music sales in the United States, a figure that has doubled in ten years.[18] The people I talked with would like to tap into this market even more for mainstream cultural production. Without the legitimacy provided by these successful mainstream artists and entertainers, the local subculture would not be able to survive.

But many feel that the subculture distracts mainstream leaders with small concerns when their focus should be elsewhere. Take Howard Kazanjian. The producer of the blockbusters *Raiders of the Lost Ark* and *Return of the Jedi*, Kazanjian wields considerable clout in the entertainment world. Over the years, a handful of evangelicals have completed the University of Southern California's highly selective film program, giving them a big leg up in a competitive field. For years, Kazanjian had a policy of meeting USC graduates. Today, though, he invests his time in students at a nearby school, Azusa Pacific University, not USC. At Azusa Pacific, he helped establish a new program in cinema and broadcast arts, and he continues to devote significant time and energy to the program and its students. He describes his shifted loyalties: "It used to be that I would only talk to USC graduates. . . . Now I rarely will meet with a USC graduate, but I'll meet with any Azusa Pacific student."[19] Many evangelicals feel this is a waste of talent.

One of the biggest problems for the evangelical subculture is that it discourages creative freedom for the artist. Erik Lokkesmoe, founder of Brewing Culture, a faith-based organization that supports the artistic world, refers to this as "soggy" material. He writes, "Do we really want art that never challenges our convictions, wrestles with our beliefs, or questions our faith? Let's not forget: beauty is hardly safe, truth is never tame, goodness is anything but trite." Because the evangelical subculture values "safe" content, anything deemed "unsafe" gets little support, even if it is produced by evangelicals. Kenneth Morefield, a professor at Campbell University, reviewed *The Exorcism of Emily Rose* for Christian Spotlight on Entertainment. In a subsequent interview, Morefield noted the irony that, although the film was directed by an evangelical, the "ambiguity [*Emily Rose*] tries to promote, so as not to put off secular audiences, will be one that Christian audiences won't be very quick to embrace."[20] Although none of them wanted to speak on the record, several people said that the evangelical subculture "stifles" creativity. Ted Baehr, chairman of the Christian Film & Television Commission, publishes film reviews in *Movieguide,* primarily for fellow evangelicals. His reviews are known for counting the number of curse words, sexually suggestive scenes, and other elements evangelical constituents might consider offensive. "It is stuff like this," said one Hollywood director, "that trivializes the artistic works we are seeking to produce. Am I going to censor my work for Ted Baehr's 'wholesome' rating? Some would say I should.... [But] as an artist, I'm disgusted by that.... Where's the commendation for making an authentic movie, one that points to truth—no matter how bloody or dirty the truth may be?" I asked if Baehr's *Movieguide* would endorse his next film, which dealt with a graphic subject. He replied, "I hope not. If he does, I've probably failed."[21]

In fact, a number of people told me that, ironically, nonevangelical artists have done a better job than evangelicals communicating evangelical truths. *Chariots of Fire* (1981) is the classic example, a movie that points to evangelical ideals such as a sense of religious "calling" to secular endeavors but was directed by someone religiously indifferent. Other films frequently mentioned include *Places in the Heart* (1984), *Hoosiers* (1986), and *Magnolia* (1999). Of course, none of these movies contain an explicitly Christian message—film communicates through metaphor, not text messaging. But across the artistic and entertainment sectors, leading evangelicals refer to these works as "models" for future filmmakers who want to use cinema to convey elements of their faith and a sense of the transcendent.

The evangelical subculture also produces works that are embarrassing to mainstream artists and entertainers, and they fear that their own projects may have been tainted by association with other evangelicals. Reputation plays a large role in deciding whether a new show gets produced, so any "excess baggage" could hurt their chances of success. People I interviewed call movies like *Left Behind* "pathetic" and representative of a movie genre Scott Derrickson has dubbed "Godsploitation" that is more like "junk food for the soul" than good filmmaking.[22]

The differences between the mainstream and the subculture are most apparent with someone like Thomas Kinkade, an evangelical painter whose work is enormously popular. Kinkade has sold more canvases than any other painter in history, so he is not just popular among subcultural audiences; his work has mass appeal, and for that he receives accolades.[23] But many do not see its artistic value. Makoto Fujimura, a visual artist, told me, "The fact that every person in middle America knows Thomas Kinkade is a tribute to Thomas Kinkade's enormous capacity as a businessman. He's an amazing entrepreneur...but at the same time you are concerned about the lack of content in his work that is ultimately very superficial." The self-described "Painter of Light," Kinkade told *Christianity Today*: "My whole ministry [as a painter] is an expression of Matthew 5:16: 'Let your light so shine before men, that they may see your good works, and glorify your Father which is in heaven.' "[24] The sentimentalism of Kinkade's paintings resonates with the populist strain of American evangelicalism whose adherents scorn the cultural elite, but there is another element of the evangelical movement that seeks to distance itself from artists like Kinkade. For example, although Kinkade has made overtures toward offering financial support to groups like Christians in the Visual Arts (CIVA), they have never had a close relationship. Sandra Bowden, CIVA's longtime president, says CIVA does not encourage its members to follow Kinkade's example, although they applaud the sincerity of his faith. At her home on Cape Cod, Bowden and I talked about Kinkade: "Number one, it's not good art. Technically, it's been done a million times.... I think some people have been inspired by his work, and that's why we [CIVA] can't condemn him, but that would not be the kind of work that we would be pushing toward." Other artists expressed similar feelings about parts of the subculture from intellectually shallow best-selling books to worship choruses that are musically simplistic. Differences of opinion on taste, especially regarding what is considered "good" art, are central to the divide between the cosmopolitanism of many leaders and the parochialism they perceive within the evangelical subculture.[25]

Despite their complaints, I found that many artists and entertainers benefited from involvement with the subculture that they disdained. Institutions within the evangelical subculture—such as Christian colleges and universities—provide training that is essential to young evangelicals who hope to move into mainstream positions of influence. For many, the desire to pursue careers in the arts, entertainment, and media was first instilled on an evangelical campus. More importantly, several of those institutions have invested millions of dollars in programs and personnel that have helped translate those desires into cutting-edge training. Act One, a month-long training program for aspiring screenwriters in Hollywood, draws most of its students from the ranks of recent graduates of Christian colleges and universities. Evangelical megachurches provide volunteers the opportunity to master technical aspects of production with sound, lighting, and recording equipment that rivals what's found at some of the country's best training facilities. Several Hollywood insiders also mentioned state-of-the-art studios and facilities at evangelical schools like Regent University and Biola University, where students are being trained using the very latest technology. More broadly, these institutions offer students not only the chance to hone their skills but also the theological justification for their work.[26] This is critical because evangelical churches seldom offer that kind of support. Without it, evangelical young people might have to choose between their religious identity and their professional interests. Hence the evangelical subculture provides many evangelicals a path to the cultural mainstream.

For example, Terry Botwick served as senior vice president for programming at CBS in the late 1990s, overseeing all of CBS' decisions regarding scheduling and new shows. Prior to that, though, Botwick rose through the ranks at the Family Channel.[27] He told me this experience was critical to his performance at CBS. "I could not have succeeded at CBS without first having had the chance to make some mistakes at the Family Channel, away from the glare of such an intense spotlight." Similarly, several successful Hollywood careers began at the Billy Graham Evangelistic Association.[28] The evangelical subculture provides a "safe," supportive environment in which aspiring writers and artists can test out their talents and receive encouraging feedback while learning their craft. Veteran Hollywood producer Ralph Winter told me, "the church is a perfect [place] . . . because we're so forgiving. . . . We'll take anything you put up there, and it's a forgiving audience that will pat you on the back, no matter what." Indeed, several of the people I interviewed acknowledged the church as the first place where others affirmed their creative talent. And the evangelical subculture is not just an intermediary stop from cultural marginalization to mainstream. Many leaders go back and forth throughout their careers.[29]

Some successful entertainers and artists have even turned to the subculture when they disagreed with the editorial demands of mainstream executives. Warner Brothers, for example, agreed to produce the entire series of *Left Behind* movies, based on the late-1990s best-selling book series, but demanded final editorial oversight. The evangelicals who had the movie rights did not want to give up that power—fearing that the studio would demand edits that did not match evangelicals' convictions. In the end, the deal with Warner Brothers disintegrated, and the series' initial film was distributed largely through churches and on home video, bypassing the mainstream studios. While tactics like these do not always enhance a project's prospects of mainstream success, they can, on occasion, serve such purposes. Rick Warren's best-seller, *The Purpose-Driven Life*, was written for an evangelical audience and originally marketed only to evangelicals. After millions of evangelicals purchased the book in its first few months, it gained a wider reputation and gradually became a mainstream success. Warren's publisher told me the book would never have succeeded in the mainstream market if it had not first sold widely within the evangelical subculture.

What nearly everyone I spoke to appreciated most about the subculture is that it's not all about money. In Hollywood, "TV is just a delivery system for ads," says television executive Dean Batali. While the subculture is not above financial considerations, ideological purity is as important as, if not more important than, profit. This is critical, because evangelicals have yet to make a big impact in Hollywood. Granted, they have made important strides, and all accounts from informed sources say that Hollywood has more outspoken evangelicals than ever. But evangelicals still comprise a slim minority there, and even with more evangelicals than have been present in the past, there has not been a significant change in the content coming out of Hollywood.[30] In fact, the actual cultural goods recently produced by evangelicals show few signs of evangelical influence. *That '70s Show, Elf,* and *Planet of the Apes*—all produced by Hollywood evangelicals—do not immediately suggest spiritual themes. Although there have been television programs—including *Touched by an Angel, Joan of Arcadia,* and *Highway to Heaven*—that communicated more explicit religious messages, all of them have been canceled by the networks. Indeed, in light of the number of films and television programs produced, evangelicals' contributions seem quite small.

Evangelical public leaders are like immigrant children who long to dissociate from the cultural contexts of their parents. The subculture was fundamental to their ascent to the top, but now they want to move beyond it. Certainly, there are some costs associated with producing cultural goods only within the evangelical subculture—including limits on artistic freedom, narrower distribution channels, and an association with lesser-quality products. But along with these costs, the subculture affords artists and entertainers several important benefits like professional training, career mobility, and the chance to do work connected to their personal convictions. On balance, most people I interviewed expressed a desire not to "marginalize" their message by producing goods exclusively for evangelicals. As movie producer John Shepherd told me, "We need to be out there mixing it up and working at the highest levels. . . . I certainly want to do things that point toward God, but not everything has to be labeled evangelical or pro-God." In an attempt to move to the cultural center, evangelicals in the arts and media help and encourage one another. Veteran journalist David Aikman formed a fellowship of Christians working for mainstream media organizations called Gegrapha, from a Greek term that connotes "testifying to truth." The group's stated vision is "to transform journalism into a profession that is regularly associated with the qualities of high integrity, character, and skill in truth telling." Groups like these have cropped up across the evangelical landscape to encourage people to work in the secular media while remaining true to their faith. A sense of community and accountability is critical to maintaining evangelical identity outside the subculture.

It is difficult to assess the influence of the subculture on wider society. Evangelical icons like Billy Graham and Rick Warren have received widespread attention in the news media. Evangelical singers like Amy Grant have "crossed over." And sometimes the line between religious and secular is quite thin. From major motion pictures to the National Council on the Arts, evangelicals are involved in mainstream culture. I encountered them at the highest levels of television, film, graphic and video arts, music, publishing, poetry, short and long fiction, theater and the performing arts, visual arts, fashion, modeling, professional athletics, journalism, broadcasting, advertising, architecture, interior design, and urban planning. As they have moved into areas of cultural influence, they have been forced to renegotiate their relationships with the evangelical subculture. At times, tensions flare. One person told me of a film review he had written that was widely distributed. A few weeks after its publication, a friend forwarded him an e-mail written by a leader in the evangelical subculture, plagiarizing entire paragraphs of his review. When confronted, she apologized profusely and said the e-mail had been forwarded to a much larger audience than she originally intended. When he asked her to retract the review and admit that she had plagiarized it, her response was, "Oh, I couldn't do that. . . . It would hurt my ministry." "That is what is wrong with the evangelical subculture," the writer told me. Such conflicts show the ongoing tension between the subculture and the mainstream.

Alan Wolfe has argued that "American faith has met American culture—and American culture has triumphed."[31] Wolfe describes what he calls "toothless evangelicalism": the triumph of market forces and American individualism over doctrine and values. In many ways, Wolfe is correct about the loss of a distinctive evangelical lifestyle.

As I found, evangelicals in Hollywood differ little from others in the entertainment industry. They drive luxury cars, live in exclusive communities, and worry that their fame and talent will evaporate overnight. And the evangelical movement does look more like mainstream society. Megachurches track attendance and donor figures with the precision of a Fortune 500 company. Ministry leaders resemble corporate executives, calling themselves "chairman and chief executive officer" rather than "pastor" or "chaplain." Indeed, American evangelicalism contributes to a cult of personality with movement leaders elevated to iconic status, despite biblical injunctions for modesty and humility. I once sat backstage at a large meeting for evangelicals, where the various entourages—and their sycophantic behavior—seemed more appropriate for a rock concert or political rally than a meeting of church people. The evangelical publishing world and contemporary Christian music have fed this hero worship, with armies of publicists and personal assistants surrounding a select few leaders whose names garner media attention. Personality-driven book sales have catapulted evangelical leaders into the cultural mainstream even though industry insiders say some have not even written the books themselves, relying instead on ghostwriters. Indeed, the very existence of such a thing as a "Christian celebrity" shows how evangelicals have adopted the practices of secular society.

Yet religious fervor is as strong as ever. There is a divide between those with cosmopolitan sensibilities and those of a more populist bent. Evangelical populism dominates the movement's subculture, and leaders like Joel Osteen and Jerry Falwell can mobilize millions for collective action. But the movement's cosmopolitan figures— including many of those I interviewed—take a more nuanced approach to the goals that they share with their more populist brothers and sisters. These evangelicals have higher levels of education and cultural capital and occupy positions of mainstream influence, but they still retain ties with the subculture.[32]

Take, for instance, evangelical pastor Tim Keller of Redeemer Presbyterian Church in New York City. Keller is one of the most influential pastors among cosmopolitan evangelicals. He has a high regard for the Bible and believes followers of Jesus Christ should have distinctive ways of life. But this countercultural attitude, he contends, must not oppose the mainstream by becoming insular and forming a separate subculture. Instead, the evangelical counterculture ought to exist for a *common good,* for all people and not just fellow believers. In place of cultural goods and services produced almost entirely for fellow evangelicals, Keller told me he favors "a

Christian community that actually engages the city, works for the common good, shows itself to be ... the very best residents of New York City and love the city and still are shaped in their [life and] practices by the gospel.... That's what I think will actually change the culture." More and more evangelicals are embracing Keller's vision.[33] This is no "toothless" evangelicalism, but it is a different evangelicalism altogether.

Embracing the Mainstream

In 2004, Mel Gibson's *The Passion of the Christ* demonstrated to Hollywood skeptics what many evangelicals have been claiming for years: Faith-friendly films can be extremely profitable. *The Passion* is among the highest-grossing motion pictures in Hollywood history. To date, it has made Gibson and his investors hundreds of millions of dollars in profit. Six months after *The Passion*'s release, I sat down with Steve McEveety, who produced the film with Gibson. McEveety and Gibson have been close for many years, and McEveety has produced nearly every Gibson film since he founded Icon Productions in 1989. Born and raised in southern California, McEveety shares a conservative Catholic faith with Gibson as well, and neither of them was surprised at *The Passion*'s box office success. "If you look at what's made the money [in film]," McEveety told me, "the majority have pretty good values in them." The commercial success of *The Passion* is due, in large measure, to the mobilization of the Christian community. The filmmakers' personal commitment to conservative Christianity validated the project for many. Steve Largent, the NFL wide receiver–turned–congressman, told me he has "tremendous respect" for their "courage ... to go totally against the Hollywood culture." When *The Passion* producers ran into difficulty finding a distributor, they realized grassroots support for the film would be critical. In a move that has been copied several times since, Gibson's company hired Paul Lauer to promote the film to Christians. Lauer employed a wide range of tactics: from advance screenings of the film for pastors and evangelical leaders to granting the Christian media in-depth interviews with Gibson and star Jim Caviezel. Megachurch pastors, heads of parachurch organizations, and evangelical media personalities praised the project. Many also thanked Gibson for undertaking it, reflecting the increased affinity between evangelicals and conservative Roman Catholics. Today, there is an entire cottage industry of consultants and publicists in Hollywood dedicated to promoting projects within the evangelical community. Grace Hill Media, led by Jonathan Bock, is representative of this group. His firm's mission is to highlight "entertainment for the faith community which shares in their beliefs, that explores their values, and that enhances and elevates their view of the world."[34]

One evangelical leader, George Barna, has transformed his organization from one focused primarily on survey research into one that promotes films. In 2004 he—along with Hollywood insider Mark Joseph and Barna's pastor, Thom Black—launched Barna-Films Preview Night. This is a quarterly event at theaters around the country where evangelicals can preview upcoming films that are deemed "significant" and "outstanding" by the group while also affirming "the truths [evangelicals] believe can change lives." As promoters of faith-friendly entertainment, these ministry leaders have brought Hollywood and the evangelical community closer together.

This is a significant change for evangelicalism. Previous generations of evangelicals viewed the works of "secular" artists with distrust if not outright disdain. Evangelist Charles Finney once said that he could not believe that "a person who has ever known the love of God [could] relish a secular novel."[35] But today, evangelical artists and writers speak of there being "a lot of truth" in "godless culture." As screenwriter Brian Godawa said to me, this is "truth that comes from the *via negativa*. . . . Showing man without God . . . can be just as powerful a truth as trying to communicate what man with God is like." Makoto Fujimura argues that secularists' "suppression of the truth is a point of contact to speak about the Gospel to [a] nonbelieving world."

To be sure, much of the movement's interest in mainstream culture has involved an evangelistic purpose. Through films, television programs, religious artwork, and dramatic presentations, evangelicals have channeled their creative impulses to communicate the messages of the Christian gospel. Mainstream cultural production also channels believers' creative energies in service to the movement. These evangelistic efforts have been happening for some time. Many of the early leaders of the neo-evangelical movement, including Billy Graham and Bill Bright, reached out to artists. In his 1957 New York Crusade, Graham sought out the New York Christian Arts Fellowship. Since the 1950s, the Billy Graham Evangelistic Association has produced over fifty motion pictures and short-run films through its media affiliate, World Wide Pictures. Among them is *The Hiding Place* (1975), the true story of Corrie ten Boom and her family, who hid a Jewish family in the attic of their home to help them escape the Nazis. Graham and Bright launched outreach efforts using media organizations, and Campus Crusade for Christ distributed *The Jesus Film,* which the organization claims has been viewed by 5.4 billion people since 1979.[36] The goal of artistic creations like these is to elicit a spiritual response from the audience, to encourage them to convert to Christianity. While these efforts are alive and well in some quarters of the movement, many evangelicals are moving away from using art for purely instrumental purposes. Ken Myers, an evangelical who edits the *Mars Hill Audio Journal,* told me, "These efforts...are trying to produce cultural goods primarily as a way of finding a point of contact with unbelievers. It's a means of evangelism.... Much of the megachurches' use of media is borne out of a desire to be relevant and winsome.... [But] the problem is that PowerPoint presentations eliminate the need for poetic expression."[37] Myers and others have been trying to persuade fellow evangelicals that evangelical creativity can be directed toward aesthetic and artistic aims—to inspire and elicit questions without providing "easy, quick" answers. This, in turn, has spawned an interest in channeling evangelical creativity into mainstream outlets.

Ralph Winter, a veteran Hollywood producer whose credits include the X-Men films and *Fantastic Four,* says that over the last thirty years evangelical churches have gradually become "more open-minded about [film and television] instead of [seeing them as primarily] the work of the devil." Today, Winter remains active in his home church, Glendale Presbyterian, and feels supported and encouraged for the work he does.[38] Movement leaders like Charles Colson and Richard Mouw have popularized the idea of a "cultural commission" that compels evangelicals to engage with society, giving religious sanction to evangelical forays into mainstream culture, even ones that are not explicitly religious. These include "creating, commissioning, and celebrating transcendent works of art and media" and providing a "catalyst for cultural renewal" by supporting individual artists and the wider arts community.[39] Across the country, evangelical congregations have increasingly incorporated the arts into worship, sometimes using contemporary musical instruments like drums and electric guitars to accompany congregational singing. Weekly worship services have also included video clips from popular movies, celebrity testimonials, as well as drama and liturgical dance. Entrepreneurial church leaders have been at the forefront of these developments, and in many cases they have been driven by their personal appreciation for popular culture and the arts.

Jack Hayford's evangelical congregation, Church on the Way in Van Nuys, California, is the home church for many Hollywood celebrities and professionals, and the church has used media in worship for a long time.[40] "I was never raised to be prudish toward the culture around me while growing up," Hayford told me. He says that his church didn't go on a "crusade for Hollywood, but we just wanted to penetrate the local community with the love of God. . . . Our local community happened to include Hollywood, so we did what we could to help more people of light move into realms that had been dark." This reference to "light" and "darkness" was something that emerged often as I spoke to creative people. Several said they did not want to be known as ones who "curse the darkness" by simply denouncing popular entertainment. Instead, they want to "light a candle."[41]

Scott Derrickson, an evangelical who directed *The Exorcism of Emily Rose,* told me these changing attitudes reflect generational differences. Today, he thinks younger evangelicals show an "openness and passion for aesthetics." He considers the evangelical film students he now teaches as being in a "different league altogether" than the evangelicals he went to school with in the late 1980s.

No other evangelical active in Hollywood has garnered more attention among insiders than Denver billionaire Phil Anschutz. He is at the vanguard of evangelicalism's embrace of the mainstream. Anschutz, who has made his fortune in multiple industries, is currently the largest single operator of U.S. movie theaters. He owns or holds major interests in two newspapers, four professional soccer teams, the Staples Center in Los Angeles, the London Arena, and a variety of other entertainment venues. Yet it is his two production companies, Walden Media and Bristol Bay Productions, that have caught the eye of Hollywood.

Anschutz is the only evangelical with the financial clout and production infrastructure to "green-light" a major film. As a result, many aspiring screenwriters and producers who share Anschutz's faith seek to work for him. A devout and conservative Presbyterian, Anschutz hired his former pastor, the Reverend Bob Beltz, to help him manage faith-friendly projects out of the Denver office. He and Walden Media's president, Micheal Flaherty, are the public faces of Anschutz's Hollywood projects. Anschutz prefers a lower profile. For nearly thirty years, he has not granted an on-the-record interview to a journalist or a researcher, making him one of the most elusive figures I encountered. I had the opportunity to hear Anschutz and his associates speak on the relationship between faith and the entertainment world at a small gathering at the Four Seasons Hotel in Beverly Hills in the fall of 2004.[42] At that time, they were gearing up for the release of their most successful project, *The Chronicles of Narnia,* which hit theaters in December 2005. Adapted from the classic tale by evangelical literary icon C. S. Lewis, *Narnia* was a stunning financial success. The total production budget for the film was $180 million, and as of this writing it has earned $738 million worldwide. Not all of Anschutz's media investments have succeeded; his Hollywood flops include *Joshua* and *Around the World in 80 Days.* But with another six tales left in Lewis' *Narnia* series, over which Walden has the production rights, the Anschutz Film Group appears poised for further success.

Anschutz's model is unique, and evangelicals in Hollywood have two responses to his "fund-it-yourself filmmaking": hopeful and skeptical. Many writers, producers, and entertainers hope that Anschutz succeeds because they see Hollywood, in the words of one insider, as "a small community [where] . . . a lot of what happens [occurs] . . . before contracts are signed." If Anschutz thrives, evangelicals throughout the industry hope to benefit from the close-knit ties among key Hollywood decision-makers. Several people told me they hope that the Film Group will select their projects because of the faith they and Anschutz share. Indeed, Ken Wales, a Hollywood producer whose work has been overlooked by many because he was viewed as too religious, was hired by Anschutz to produce his latest big release, *Amazing Grace,* the story of Victorian-era reformer William Wilberforce, the evangelical member of Parliament who worked nearly forty years to abolish the English slave trade. Many see Wales as an evangelical pioneer in the field, and with Anschutz's blessing, he is finally producing a major motion picture.[43] Others are less sanguine about Anschutz's plans, regarding him as yet another successful "outsider" pouring money into Hollywood without a chance of long-term success. With Anschutz's roots in Denver and Boston— outside typical media channels—he, like others before him, may fail in the long term, but he is already the most successful Hollywood "outsider" in the industry.

Despite the attention Anschutz and Mel Gibson have received, conservative Christians still represent only a fraction of creative people in Hollywood. The Screen Actors Guild, the premier union representing actors, includes more than one hundred thousand members; by even the most liberal counts, publicly identified evangelicals comprise less than 1 percent of that figure. There are more evangelical writers, directors, and producers, but even they constitute only a small segment of the industry. This, however, has not dissuaded evangelical activity in Hollywood.

For most of the twentieth century, evangelicals kept their distance from Hollywood, pursuing a strategy of intimidation and protest on the few occasions they engaged mainstream entertainment for anything other than evangelistic purposes. During that time, the evangelical subculture provided important channels for distributing the cultural production of writers, artists, and entertainers within the movement. Recently, some evangelicals have moved beyond that and sought mainstream audiences. Subcultural leaders and leaders in elite centers of culture are grappling over the future of evangelical culture. To what extent should they endorse and patronize mainstream media? The distance between Colorado Springs and Hollywood has never been greater.[44] Today, this is where the battle lines are drawn, not between those who embrace art and those who denounce it but between those who think evangelicals should look inward and those who think they should reach out.

6

A Cultural Revolution

THE JAPANESE-AMERICAN PAINTER MAKOTO "MAKO" FUJIMURA is an acclaimed visual artist and was the youngest artist ever to have a piece acquired by the Museum of Contemporary Art in Tokyo. Born in Boston but reared in Japan, Fujimura was appointed to the National Council on the Arts in 2003. His works have gained both popular and critical acclaim. His largest work to date fills the lobby of CNN Asia's headquarters in Hong Kong, and in 2005 Vice President Cheney selected one of his paintings for the family's Christmas card. Despite his youth, his artistic talent caught the attention of the faculty at Tokyo National University, and he was the first outsider to be invited into its doctoral program—a major accomplishment in Japan's highly structured academic meritocracy.

As an artistic Christian, a term he prefers to "Christian artist," Fujimura has juggled multiple—and sometimes competing—identities for quite some time. I sat down with him at a neighborhood coffee shop in TriBeCa. His thin frame and casual appearance blended well with our surroundings. Fujimura speaks in complete paragraphs, dense with allusions. Only after reviewing the transcript of our conversation did I realize how carefully he spoke. Fujimura told me that many elements of his work as a painter, from the images he selects to the method he uses, are shaped by his commitments as an artistic Christian. He framed it this way: "God gave us this gift to create, and every artwork speaks of this reality." For him there is an underlying unity between art and its motivation, and for him and many other artists creativity is a way of communing with God.[1]

After graduating from Bucknell University, Fujimura returned to Japan to learn the traditional Japanese art of Nihonga, a kind of watercolor painting that utilizes mineral pigments. Today, his works combine abstract expressionism with Nihonga. For most of his paintings, Fujimura pulverizes minerals like azurite and malachite, mixes the pigment with water and glue, and then applies it to handmade paper. The results are brilliant colors—created literally by hand from semiprecious stones—melded into paintings that reflect the influence of artists like Mark Rothko and Arshile Gorky. In a talk coinciding with a recent exhibition of his work, *Water Flames,* Fujimura spoke about the influence of Dante and T. S. Eliot on his art, saying he shares with them spiritual sources of inspiration. Sara Tecchia, a gallery curator, observed of Fujimura: "He is a profound believer and I am totally secular. But he is like a professor to me. Fujimura's paintings allow for skeptics [such] as myself to do the one thing that secularism has labeled as a sign of weakness: to hope."[2]

Evangelical spirituality has been important to Fujimura in perfecting his craft. Through spiritual practices, he and other artists told me they experience moments of transcendence, which become flashes of artistic inspiration. Doug TenNapel, a successful Hollywood animator, said to me, "When I create, I feel direct empathy with God, as the creator." This is not explicitly an evangelical spirituality, but it does demonstrate the marrying of transcendent experience to a personal connection with the divine, which is an evangelical touchstone.

The "religious imagination," as it is often called, is a process by which creators seek to imagine what God, heaven, or other spiritual entities are like.[3] Through this they commune with God and deepen their spirituality. Often, religious practices like prayer and meditation become part of the "imagining" process. Todd Komarnicki, a seasoned Hollywood writer, told me, "Prayer is the spine of what I do in writing. . . . I seek to tell the truth, and our Savior is the truth. . . . I pray before [I write], I pray while [writing, and] I pray after [I write]. I pray all the time." For him, prayer offers a chance to reflect and to gain insight for the stories he writes. During college Komarnicki explored other religions but gradually returned to the Christian faith of his childhood, believing it to be more "authentic." Like other writers I interviewed, Komarnicki prizes authenticity in his writing and in his worldview. Ultimate truth, for these evangelical writers, is grounded in selflessness: "Even though [Buddhism, which he explored] was about ridding yourself of all desire, . . . ultimately it struck me as being selfish. . . . The point was, by getting rid of all these things, you were [ultimately] benefiting yourself." Christianity, he decided, offered an alternative approach. Komarnicki says faith keeps him grounded and enables him to handle ongoing disappointment. Despite success in Hollywood, writing, he says, is "brutally discouraging, . . . indescribably discouraging. [But] that's part of the active grace of being alive and doing what I do. . . . I have a wonderful life . . . but ninety-eight percent of my life is 'No.'"

Others also spoke of the importance of prayer in their lives. For artists, entertainers, athletes, and writers alike, as for other leaders I interviewed, prayer is a valued professional resource. Evangelical practices—and the social networks within the evangelical world—provide them with advantages. When Richard Capen was named publisher of the *Miami Herald,* his first act was to call a group of fellow Christians into his office for prayer. Among professional athletes, prayer spurs evangelicals on while minimizing their fears about the risks involved. A few, like David Robinson, say that God speaks to them through their prayers or at night in their dreams. But nearly all of them use prayer to voice their concerns about upcoming games and to ask God to enable them to play their best. Tennis legend Stan Smith told me, "I pray that I am really able to perform well and handle the situation . . . knowing that the results are totally in God's hands." Through prayer, the athletes say, they are freed from fear or anxiety about their performance. It allows them to relinquish control, and many believe the "centering" that comes from that process enables them to perform better. Paul Wylie, the Olympic medalist and professional skater, sought the help of a sports psychologist before the 1992 Olympics. He wanted help with visualization, a mental technique used by many athletes to enhance their performance. The psychologist was Armand Nicholi, one of Wylie's undergraduate professors at Harvard. He told the skater that "praying is sort of the original visualization." Not all athletes interviewed feel comfortable praying for victory.[4] On one end of the spectrum is Hall of Fame golfer Nancy Lopez. She never prays to win, fearing "I would get punished if I asked for that." Olympic swimmer John Naber considers praying to win "selfish," but when competing he did pray to "glorify [God] in the results of my performance [and] prayed to leave nothing undone . . . so that I could walk away from the pool . . . saying, 'I did as well as I could have done.'" On the other end of the spectrum are athletes like NFL quarterback Kurt Warner. He says, "I think every aspect of my life is important to God, and so I'm going to pray about it. Does that mean I have to win every game? No. But I pray to be successful in everything that I do, and that includes praying to win the big game."

Particularly important to evangelical spirituality and the creative process is the idea of "calling." Brian Bird was a television writer for several years, but he eventually left the business to work for World Vision, the evangelical aid agency. During the first part of his Hollywood career, his greatest accomplishment was writing the complete script for a single episode of *Fantasy Island.* While in Addis Ababa, Ethiopia, filming an infomercial for World Vision, Bird turned on the television in his hotel. He instantly recognized his show. He referred to that as "a crystal moment.... I got down on my hands and knees and... said, 'God, if something that trivial is being exported all over the world, then the... converse has to be true. The opportunity for life- and faith-affirming media is wide open.' I just said, 'Put me back in the game.' " In similar fashion, Stephen Clapp, dean at the Juilliard School, told me his work at the renowned music school is like being "on assignment.... I think all the places I've been, I've been put there by God." Not all the people I spoke to said that they sensed a divine calling at the outset of their careers, but many described feeling "a gradual sense of confirmation" from God.

Evangelicals in the pews also link the arts to their personal spirituality. They are more likely than other religious groups to report feeling close to God through music or art, and they are more likely to report music or poetry as being important in their spiritual lives.[5] Evangelical public leaders have begun offering theological rationales for artistic creativity and evangelicalism's burgeoning interest in culture is shifting the boundaries between "sacred" and "secular." Leading evangelicals are engaging with mainstream culture, opening the wider evangelical movement to outside influence. This has contributed to the movement's emergence on the public stage, but it has also revitalized evangelicals' connection with the divine. When framed as a spiritual "calling," artistry becomes transcendent. It is this quest for transcendence and creative inspiration that draws many evangelicals to the arts and entertainment. Religious practices and beliefs also ground their ambition for greater cultural influence.

Change from Within

"Being There," an essay by poet and journalist Steve Turner, has become a manifesto for expanding the evangelical presence in mainstream culture. Turner urges evangelicals to create professional and personal communities in cultural centers so that they can reach general audiences. This is sometimes referred to as a "ministry of presence." Increasingly evangelicals have recognized the value of "being present" in centers of elite cultural production. The strategic location of Hollywood Presbyterian Church, for example, is not lost on evangelicals. Its website features a picture of the church that shows the cross in the steeple aligned with the iconic Hollywood sign in the background.[6] No longer is evangelicalism confined to "middle America," if it ever was. Much of the movement's institution-building since the 1980s has taken place in areas where evangelicals have not always exerted influence, such as the Northeast Corridor between Boston and Washington. Evangelical congregations have planted dozens of new churches there, and evangelicals in places like Hollywood and Manhattan often gravitate to particular churches where they can meet one another.[7] Across the evangelical landscape a "theology of the city" has emerged. Several people I spoke to said they were inspired by a passage in Jeremiah 29 where the prophet admonished the exiled Jews to seek the peace and prosperity of their cities, even though they were in areas populated, and ruled, by Babylonian pagans. I was struck by the number of people—all of whom were working in places of elite cultural production—who referred to this passage. Evangelicals living and working in these cosmopolitan centers identify with the exiled Jews, for many of them feel a great deal of tension between the worlds of their faith and their profession. They referred to urban centers as "flashpoints" on the "battle lines" between people of faith and their secular opponents and pointed to missionary activities of the early church that centered along trade routes. These are justifications evangelicals offer for their involvement—not necessarily explanations they give to outsiders, but ways they legitimate their involvement to fellow believers.

Evangelical philanthropists have been trying for quite some time to establish a bigger presence in strategic locations. Nancy DeMoss, whose family foundation gives away tens of millions of dollars annually to evangelical causes, owned a residence on the Upper East Side of Manhattan for several years in the 1980s. From here, Campus Crusade hosted ministry outreach programs for New York professionals, and a group of people who used to hang out regularly at DeMoss House eventually formed the core of a new congregation, Redeemer Presbyterian Church. Tim Keller, Redeemer's pastor, says that DeMoss House was "fundamental" to establishing a Christian community among young, up-and-coming professionals in the city. By being explicit about their faith, these accomplished artists, writers, and entertainers demonstrate their bona fide evangelical commitments, but more important, they pull part of American evangelicalism closer to the cosmopolitan worlds in which they dwell.

Some evangelicals pursue Hollywood because it is a "bully pulpit," and others are motivated by the vast "mission field" it represents. But most insiders I interviewed simply hope to "make a difference" through their daily responsibilities on the job. They seek to change the entertainment industry from the inside. They all feel that the onus is on them as *individuals*. Nearly all spoke about the task of "changing the world," "renewing society," or "transforming the culture" in light of individual actions they take.[8]

Michael Warren is a good example. Warren produced several successful situation comedies, but he talked to me at length about his vision for *Happy Days*. He sought to make episodes on the show like "little morality plays." Often, he says, the television networks would want the show to advance a particular cause: "The network was usually driven by people who were politically very liberal and very secular." In one episode, Tom Hanks was scheduled for a guest appearance, and the network wanted him to be cast as a middle school friend of Fonzie, Potsie, and Richie who returns to Milwaukee years later and reveals that he's gay. Warren did not want to write a script that would advance a pro-gay message but, rather than say that, he simply argued that the story line was inappropriate for the tone of the show. Warren says that he and his team did not broach the issue with ABC "from the standpoint of... 'we've got this [evangelical] agenda that we want to do.'... My approach was always to say, 'But don't ask us to do something that we really can't do.... It's your show, [so] if you want to hire somebody else to do it, that's fine, but [I won't].'" Warren sees this as an example of bringing his faith to bear on professional responsibilities. In the end, his lobbying effort succeeded.

Several leaders I interviewed believe that they are more "in touch" with their audiences because of their evangelical faith. Others in the industry, they say, are not necessarily attempting to indoctrinate the audience—although they claim that it has happened in a few cases. More often, they say, it is simply a matter of inattention. Dean Batali, who served as co-executive producer of *That '70s Show*, told me most writers do not consider the implicit messages being communicated by the lifestyles of their characters. He says, "I can look at the *Cheers* writers, who I think are...very moral people... committed to their kids, but I don't think they ever gave any thought to Sam Malone [the protagonist on *Cheers*].... [They do not consider the question of] 'Are we influencing the culture with Sam Malone's behavior?'" Likewise in the movie industry, Steve McEveety said to me, "There are many, many people that are in the film business and in television that, though they may be very good people, they leave their consciences at home." The implication is that evangelicals do not.

Building a Structure for Change

Evangelicals have invested tens of millions of dollars in various initiatives aimed at enlivening and expanding their influence in the arts, media, and entertainment worlds. I encountered approximately one hundred such programs, organizations, and initiatives that were founded at some time between 1976 and 2006, most of which have grown in size and scope since the time of their founding.[9] These include church-based support groups, media outlets, professional development programs, and groups dedicated to training future artists and entertainers. With the backing of flagship evangelical institutions like Fuller Theological Seminary, these new programs likely will survive and thrive, especially those located in centers like New York, Chicago, and Los Angeles. Whereas evangelicals in the political domain are splintering, there seems to be much greater unity on the cultural front. This may be the result of the success evangelicals have enjoyed in politics. Their continuing minority status in the worlds of entertainment and the arts fosters unity and focus. Moreover, the sustaining role of the evangelical subculture—with its own modes of production, distribution, and consumption—provides backing for their efforts in the mainstream.

At the forefront of this activity is a former nun named Barbara Nicolosi. She directs Act One, a faith-based nonprofit whose office stands in the shadow of the famed Hollywood sign. Act One principally directs two programs, one for aspiring film and television writers and one for aspiring entertainment executives, both of which focus on preparing young people of faith for careers in mainstream film and television. A screenwriter herself, Nicolosi regards the program as a Christian calling, one that will produce future generations of successful, faithful writers and executives. The highly selective program—it admits about 12 percent of all applicants—was founded in 1999, and its centerpiece is a month-long workshop where accomplished professionals in television and film, all of whom are evangelicals or conservative Catholics, teach and mentor approximately thirty promising young people. The program costs over $10,000 per participant, but students—most of whom are under thirty—only pay $1,200. The rest is subsidized by donations to Act One. In addition to proving their potential as future entertainment professionals, applicants must provide essay-length responses to questions like "What is the role of the arts in the church and the world?" and "How does your faith play into your everyday life?" Believing that long-term change in Hollywood requires an active network of professionals, Act One sponsors a variety of initiatives for its alumni, including the chance for graduates to receive ongoing feedback on their projects from industry executives who share their faith. Although nearly every Hollywood evangelical I met speaks very highly of the program, segments of the evangelical world remain unsupportive. One Focus on the Family staff member met Nicolosi at a writers' conference in North Carolina and remarked, "We don't need Hollywood because we have Focus on the Family.... We provide enough for any family to raise their children with." Incredulous, Nicolosi says, "I was like, 'What, are you smoking, crack?'" Many Christians in Hollywood share this view.

Evangelicals in both the subculture and the mainstream share a concern over the coarsening of American culture and lessening of moral strictures. As Les Csorba, a Houston executive, said to me, "Our culture is just sinking and becoming more vile and coarse." Wayne Huizenga Jr., whose family owns the Miami Dolphins football team, told me, "It's scary to me as I look at the population and what's become acceptable. It's gone from doing what is acceptable . . . to 'I have the right to do whatever I want and live my life however I want.' . . . There are no boundaries. . . . Everything goes."

Despite these observations, only about one in five leaders I interviewed say they are pessimistic about America's declining moral state. Instead, many of them are hopeful about the prospect for change because of the number of initiatives people of faith have undertaken in media centers like New York and Los Angeles.

Makoto Fujimura says he established the International Arts Movement (IAM) as a means for "renewing culture and the arts by . . . translating heavenly existence to the earthly, . . . translating the 'substance of things hoped for' with words, paint and other materials into both the content and form of art." Founded in 1990 and still directed by Fujimura, the group seeks to reconcile people of faith with artists, and to introduce artists to people of faith. Because both religious and artistic communities are drawn to Fujimura and his work, IAM serves as a point of contact for networks of contemporary artists and believers. The group hosts weekly discussions as well as special lectures, symposia, and exhibitions aimed at uniting these two groups.[10] *Image: A Journal of the Arts and Religion* is a literary and arts quarterly founded in 1989 that also seeks to link artistic and religious expression. Featuring essays, poetry, artwork, and interviews with prominent artists, the journal has garnered mainstream attention. According to *Image* editor Gregory Wolfe, the quarterly faces in two directions: "One side faces the church; . . . the other side . . . faces . . . the mainstream literary artistic culture of America." Common to these initiatives is a sense of appreciation for the contributions of artists from outside the evangelical tradition.

Indeed, many of these evangelical organizations have brought people of faith much closer to secular society. They have also eroded the boundaries that existed between evangelicals and secularists.

Contrary to the idea—common among movement leaders—that evangelicals are still embattled by a secular elite, most of the people I spoke to think differently. In fact, Don Holt, who once edited *Fortune* and *Newsweek*, referred to this sense of being embattled as a "manufactured thing" that is felt more often by evangelicals in "middle America" than by those working among the secular elite.[11] As one person expressed the consensus, cultural leaders are "not antagonistic toward Christianity. They're apathetic toward Christianity.... They just don't want to deal with it....They don't care." In response to this indifference, evangelicals are training future cultural leaders and providing feedback loops for those already in the field. This, they believe, will contribute to evangelicalism's "success" by helping individuals who will produce faith-friendly, though not explicitly religious, entertainment.

New programs in places like Hollywood address a range of needs. They help newcomers learn everything from where to find a bank to where to find a church, sponsor programs that provide venues where Christian professionals can perform their works, and offer opportunities for Christians to meet other Christians. They also have launched film festivals and centers for theological reflection.[12] Of course, there has been an evangelical presence in Hollywood for decades. One of the matriarchs of modern American evangelicalism is Henrietta Mears, the director of Christian education at First Presbyterian Church of Hollywood. In the living room of her home, the church began a "Hollywood Christian Group" which included Roy Rogers and Dale Evans. Ever since, the church has supported a ministry to the entertainment community. However, it was not until the 1990s that programs like Inter-Mission and Act One—all of them originally housed in a single office building across from the church—began to take root. Soon, other churches in the area began specialized ministries to Hollywood.[13]

There are also support groups for Christian executives in Hollywood and New York sponsored by evangelical nonprofit organizations MasterMedia and Media Fellowship International, neither of which is connected to a local congregation. In fact, Hollywood insiders often prefer ministries that are not connected to a particular denomination or congregation. In 1993, a group of artists and actors began meeting quarterly as the Renaissance Group to discuss how they could take their evangelical convictions into the mainstream. Approximately forty people would be in attendance at any given meeting, and out of this grew a regular e-mail list that now includes about 750 individuals. And for several years, the pastor of St. Louis Family Church, Jeff Perry, has flown to Hollywood once a month at the invitation of several Hollywood insiders. They meet on the third Tuesday of every month for Bible study and worship at the Writers Guild Theater. These programs, though, are by-invitation-only and are designed for industry professionals. Insiders insist this has become essential as more evangelicals migrate to Hollywood. Actress Nancy Stafford told me the evangelical attraction to Hollywood "brings slews of other people into this industry who are not necessarily [interested] in the industry themselves, but they want to be close to people who are. . . . They want to rub shoulders with famous people." Other groups, like Hollywood Writers, Premise, and support groups sponsored by MasterMedia, have found it necessary to exclude those not in the industry from their gatherings as a way of preserving the personal vulnerability that is expected of group members. Echoing comments from business executives and political leaders, accomplished evangelicals in the entertainment field do not like the fact that some evangelicals view Hollywood as a place populated by nonbelievers in need of conversion. Stafford, whose acting credits include *Matlock* and *St. Elsewhere*, said during our interview, "I think what bothers me [most] about the language is that it almost becomes us versus them, . . . something [they] have to conquer." Despite these occasional experiences of feeling "targeted" by evangelists, most Hollywood evangelicals I interviewed are pleased with the flowering of recent programs dedicated to the entertainment world. A larger evangelical community in Hollywood has provided them with a greater base of personal support for their work: more industry-specific ministry programs, more opportunities to network, and wider circles of friendship.

Women, on the other hand, have received less support. Leading ladies in Hollywood have commanded large paychecks for decades, and book publishing and media have provided roads to the top for many women. Indeed, the cultural arena has the highest representation of women (17 percent) of any sector in this study. Among governmental leaders I interviewed, they represent 9 percent and among the business leaders, 6 percent.[14] Men dominate as writers, producers, and directors, but women are better represented in acting and television journalism. And in areas like modeling and high fashion, women command much higher salaries and receive far greater attention. But succeeding because of your looks is problematic. One actress said to me, "My heart breaks for young women in the industry now. . . . I wouldn't be twenty-five and beautiful in the industry anymore for anything because it's very, very, very difficult to navigate." Men in Hollywood agree; Joel McHale said, "I think actresses have to deal with way more than actors. They have to deal with nudity; they have to deal with body issues; they have to deal with their age...with all of these things constantly." Hollywood icon Art Linkletter told me, "I think that the hardest thing...in Hollywood is to be[come] successful and famous as a woman star.... Hollywood has always been a place where young girls come—willing, anxious, eager to do anything—to get into the TV, radio or a movie career.... They find out that there are a certain number of guys who are looking for the opportunity to maybe give them a walk-on part and in return [receive] sexual favors." Blatant sexism, widely acknowledged by those I interviewed, is not a new phenomenon. In 1938, Linkletter got his first acting job. When we met in his Beverly Hills office, here is how he recounted his first experience on the studio lot:

> The assistant director showed me around this great big studio....He says, "You'll find out, Mr. Linkletter, that making movies, we get about a minute and a half of film a day, which means that most of the time you're sitting around....You'll have plenty of time....I have three [coarse term for women] who got walk-on parts that are available [for you]."
>
> I said, "You mean, right here?"
>
> He said, "Yeah, nobody will bother you, just give me the word."
>
> So, I'm looking up, and there are guys up there [in the lighting rafters]....I said, "What about those guys up there?"
>
> He says, "They've seen it all."

People I interviewed confirm that although sexist attitudes in Hollywood are expressed in subtler terms today, they persist. The evangelical women I interviewed feel further alienated by Hollywood's permissive sexual culture, and they fear that will keep them from achieving stardom. No one expressed a desire to jettison her convictions about sexuality, but more than one referred to their faith as "binding" on this matter. During various conversations with women in entertainment, their use of this term connoted two meanings. It compelled them not to use sex to get ahead, but this, in turn, put them at a disadvantage when competing with women who would. Ironically, though, the very mechanisms that have permitted mobility for women undercut their prospects of wielding long-term influence. This, along with evangelical convictions regarding human sexuality and the body, creates a double bind for evangelical women in Hollywood.[15] Evangelical theology about relations between men and women further confounds the challenges facing women within the movement. With some notable exceptions, the evangelical movement has not supported women in their rise to leadership. The few women who have made it say they have done so *in spite of*, not *because of*, evangelical culture. Hence, even in an arena that is amenable to female advancement, evangelical women have a difficult time.[16]

Changing Wider Culture

Evangelicals have discovered that Hollywood is an outstanding stage from which to carry out their mission to change the world. Enticed by the prospect of transforming society through the media, evangelical activism has multiplied in recent decades. In the early 1980s, only three evangelical ministries were operating in Hollywood, all of them focused on traditional forms of one-on-one evangelism.[17] Then some evangelical patrons expressed concern that Christians had lost their public influence, especially among "belief-shaping forces" like the university and the media. Evangelicals stirred into action. From large-scale events in global cities like New York and London to glitzy media campaigns, evangelicals see the media as the most critical arena for evangelism. As one business executive in Cincinnati noted, "This vehicle [the Hollywood film industry] is so powerful that people are willing to pay...someone else to lead them [on] how they should live their life." That kind of influence in people's lives is especially attractive to evangelicals. In response, the evangelical movement has spawned a number of organizations and programs to expand evangelical influence in the culture-producing industries. Often, as in other fields, this includes working with like-minded Catholics either on specific projects such as *The Passion of the Christ* or on joint ventures like training the next generation of Hollywood professionals.

The leaders I spoke to express high hopes for Hollywood's potential to be a positive influence through films and television. They hold similarly optimistic outlooks for the arts, celebrities, and the media. In evangelical parlance, they are acting on the biblical exhortation (Philippians 4) to reflect on "the good, the true, and the beautiful." One evangelical film executive acknowledged, "We're still in our infant stages as Christians in terms of the good, the true, and the beautiful when it comes to film," but the desire to influence society compels them to action. Screenwriter Brian Godawa told me, "The Bible is...eighty percent story and visual....God communicates more through story than he does through propositional truth....The [evangelical] church for all these years has focused [on] propositional truth and logic [but] ... story changes the world."

Image Makeover

When evangelicalism was establishing itself as a distinct religious tradition after World War II, movement leaders like Billy Graham and Bill Bright sought—through large-scale stadium events unabashedly called "crusades" and face-to-face conversations—to change American society one soul at a time. Dedicated followers used evangelical tracts like "The Four Spiritual Laws" to try to convert friends, neighbors, colleagues, and even strangers. "Accepting Jesus Christ into your heart" was the expression in the evangelical vernacular, and being able to identify a time and place when that happened became a mark of evangelical identity. Evangelism was the *raison d'être* of American evangelicalism—what distinguished it from mainline and liberal Protestantism and Roman Catholicism.

Evangelicals continue along this path today, seeking to reform American society by encouraging others to embrace the faith, but their methods are more varied. Evangelicals in the culture-producing industries argue that the movement's strategy must not be focused on providing concrete answers but rather on posing compelling questions. Terry Mattingly, a mainstream journalist who also directs the Washington Journalism Center at the Council for Christian Colleges and Universities, says, "I think media makes lousy evangelism. There's not some sort of magic bullet that you shoot someone with and they go, 'Oh, I've got faith.' That's not how media works. Media changes people over time."[18] This face of evangelism—softer, more dependent upon metaphor, and less direct—matches well with what film and television can offer, and evangelicals believe the culture-producing industries can contribute to their vision for society. Only 5 percent of American adults think movies and television do a "good job" of raising the ethical and moral standards of the nation, but 60 percent believe that movies could have "a great deal of influence" in the future, and 78 percent say the same of television.[19] Evangelicals have tried to harness the power of mainstream media and entertainment to achieve the level of influence they desire.

The evangelicals I interviewed want to change the public impression of their movement, and they feel that media management and public relations can be critical to their success. Cal Thomas says he was motivated to enter journalism by the media's portrayal of evangelicals. According to him, the media would present "all these professors from Princeton or wherever on *Good Morning America* [representing secular perspectives], and then they'd have this West Virginia hick with a missing couple of teeth [representing the evangelical perspective], . . . and they'd all laugh it up because all those religious nuts are . . . religious nuts." Similarly, public relations experts for the evangelical movement actively seek media interviews and television specials for more moderate evangelical leaders. Mark DeMoss, who runs the DeMoss Group, an Atlanta-based public relations firm, said to me, "I cannot tell you how hard we try to get certain [moderate] evangelical voices on *Larry King Live,* but the show's producers won't have it. They want to prop up the stereotypical image of the red-faced evangelical who is mad and ready to pronounce judgment on the world." People I interviewed hope someone like Rick Warren will become the "public face" of American evangelicalism, one less known for conservative politics and public denunciations. According to one evangelical leader, "Rick Warren will come across very, very differently than a Jerry Falwell, although [they] are very good friends and . . . share [similar] ideology. . . . Rick will communicate to the American public very differently than Jerry Falwell did." Warren is a very popular figure among evangelicals; in fact, a number of those I interviewed offered unsolicited praise for Warren and his leadership, and others agree. In 2005, the Center for Public Leadership at Harvard's John F. Kennedy School of Government and *U.S. News & World Report* convened a national panel to identify "America's Best Leaders." Among the twenty-four leaders selected by the committee were Oprah Winfrey, Bill and Melinda Gates, Colin Powell, Condoleezza Rice, and two evangelicals: Francis Collins, director of the National Human Genome Research Institute, and Rick Warren.[20]

As evangelicals seek to improve their image, celebrities can be powerful forces for change. For decades evangelical professional athletes have been identified for their religious commitments. One notable example involved an evangelical book called *Power for Living.* First published in 1983 by the DeMoss Foundation, the book includes profiles of several prominent Christians including then-popular Dallas Cowboys quarterback Roger Staubach.

Evangelical athletes are also known to take advantage of media attention to talk about their faith. Several professional athletes I spoke to mentioned this as the primary way in which they seek to "change the world" or "influence society." One of the most-repeated stories among evangelical sports fans is Kurt Warner's response to a reporter's question after his MVP performance in the St. Louis Rams' victory in Super Bowl XXXIV. The interviewer began, "Kurt, first things first—tell me about the final touchdown pass." Warner responded, "Well, first things first, I've got to thank my Lord and Savior up above—thank you, Jesus." Warner now plays for the Arizona Cardinals, and I talked to him after practice one afternoon in June 2005 at the Cardinals' training facility in Tempe. Warner leaned forward as I asked him about the reporter's query. He said his response was not preplanned, but like others I interviewed he cited the biblical injunction to give an answer for his faith when the question is raised; for him, the moment seemed right. He said, "To me, it's just about loving Jesus.... When you love something, all you want to do is talk about it, ... and that's just how I feel about my faith."

John Naber won a gold medal in swimming in the 1976 Olympics. On the awards stand in Montreal, he bowed his head for prayer and then looked up toward the sky. "I knew the camera was on me as I bowed and prayed. I cannot say that I was unaware of that, but [I did not necessarily plan] it. I just wanted to say thank you [to God, so] instead of looking out, I looked up."

Evangelical celebrities also talk about their faith with other players or performers. David Robinson, the former San Antonio Spurs' center and an NBA Rookie of the Year and MVP—nicknamed "the Admiral" because he attended the Naval Academy—was the Spurs' team leader. In that role, he felt that he had an obligation to be identified with his evangelical faith. He would lead the team in prayer before games—a practice that is common in high school and collegiate sports but not as common in professional athletics. As he told me, he was motivated by the Old Testament story of David: "David said, ... 'As long as I'm king, we're going to serve the Lord.' And that was what I said when I went into the locker room, 'As long as this is my team, we're going to pray together.'" Some observers are concerned about evangelical activism within professional sports, regarding it as the introduction of "an exclusive form of Christianity laden with a divisive worldview and considerable political baggage."[21] Certainly, not all of Robinson's teammates agreed with his actions, but no one, including a Muslim player, actively resisted. For Robinson, bringing his faith to the locker room was incumbent upon him as an evangelical Christian and a leader.

Since the famous hold this kind of potential, it is not surprising that leaders in the evangelical movement seek out celebrities for support. But some ministry leaders take advantage. More than one person I interviewed told me about a particular ministry leader in Hollywood who had a reputation for "rubbernecking" at a dinner held each year before the National Prayer Breakfast. As he talked with an individual, he would turn toward the door to see if someone else entered the room and would sometimes end the conversation so that he could greet someone more powerful. According to people I interviewed, this ministry leader also distributed two types of business cards at the annual gathering. One contained his standard contact details, complete with name, organization, mailing address, phone number, and e-mail address. The other simply contained his name and organization. This may be common in other realms, but everyone who raised this issue felt that the evangelical world ought to be different. As it turns out, Hollywood evangelicals often feel used by leaders of the evangelical subculture. One Hollywood couple put it this way: "We have been invited to parties where we'd go to the party and [then] realize: They didn't want *us* here, they just wanted to be able *to say* we were here."

Signals

Evangelicals in the mainstream often use "signaling" to communicate with other believers without alerting a secular audience. This type of signaling activity depends upon implicit, subtle, and often disguised messages. I found numerous examples of this behavior, including VeggieTales. Phil Vischer, who described himself to me as a "contrarian" evangelical, created VeggieTales in the spare bedroom of his family's home in suburban Chicago.[22] Originally, Vischer says, he thought about using candy bars as animated characters, but his wife convinced him that mothers would prefer their kids to fall in love with vegetables. Using vegetable-shaped characters like Bob the Tomato, VeggieTales aimed to communicate Christian ideals through computer-animated films. The first VeggieTales video was released in 1993, and by 2006—when NBC purchased the rights to feature VeggieTales on Saturday morning—more than 50 million copies of its videos had been sold. Although the series has benefited from sales at Wal-Mart and other mainstream outlets, Vischer says every episode "winks" at evangelicals, who are the primary audience. "We wink when we talk about God. . . . It's a way for us to say [to the evangelical audience] 'We know you're still with us, and thanks.'"

Sometimes evangelicals signal without direct reference to God. For example, at the exclusive Renaissance Weekend gatherings, evangelicals in attendance often made references to particular evangelical writers or leaders. When a speaker cites Francis Schaeffer, members who do not recognize the name miss it, but for those in the know, it signals the speaker's evangelical allegiances. The message is subtle, but strong for those who can hear it.

U2, the popular rock band from Ireland, excels at signaling. With a record twenty-two Grammy awards, the musicians have used their public platform to advocate for various Christian concerns, including the Make Poverty History campaign and lead singer Bono's DATA campaign, focused on debt, AIDS, and trade in Africa. In 1987, U2 released *The Joshua Tree,* which featured the No. 1 hit single "I Still Haven't Found What I'm Looking For." In both Hebrew and Aramaic, "joshua" and "jesus" are closely related, and the album title directly alludes to the cross of Jesus Christ. The cover for the 2000 album *All That You Can't Leave Behind* features an airport sign with "j33-3→," which alludes to Jeremiah 33:3. As Bono explains, "That's Jeremiah 33:3. The Scripture is 'Call unto me, and I will answer you.' It's celestial telephony."[23]

If an entertainer is trying to mobilize fellow evangelicals to watch his movie or listen to her song, signaling can be an effective way to indicate their shared identity without potentially turning off non-evangelicals. In 2004, Jim Caviezel, a devout Catholic, played Jesus in *The Passion of the Christ.* In media interviews Caviezel was quoted as saying, "I don't want people to see me. All I want them to see is Jesus Christ."[24] While obviously an appropriate thing for an actor playing Jesus Christ to say, it meant something more to evangelicals, for whom the phrase describes their desire to bear witness to Jesus through their lives. From evangelical music ("Do They See Jesus in Me?" and "I Can See Jesus in You") to expressions in evangelical youth culture ("You're the only Jesus some will ever see") the phrase is a powerful one for evangelicals.[25] Thus, Caviezel signaled to an entire segment of the American population that he was "one of them." Signaling is usually not premeditated and often may not even be deliberate, but in an era of media consultants and public relations experts, in this instance it surely was.

Learning from Others

Evangelicals have shown a remarkable willingness to learn from other social movements. This was one of the most surprising aspects of the movement I encountered, not so much that evangelicals were open to learning from others but who some of those others were. Evangelical leaders see elements of themselves in other groups that are regarded as different. Several people told me how impressed they have been with the success of gays and lesbians in gaining acceptance in the culture. In particular, they applaud the movement's effective use of media. As Dean Batali says, "I think a case could be made, in terms of homosexuals on television and in films, that it became okay for people to go, "Well, I've seen them here, here, and here. I see that gay character on *Dawson's Creek*, ... [so] maybe it's okay for me to go this way." Though they often battle the homosexual community, evangelical leaders have seen the results of gay and lesbian activism in the culture-producing industries. Evangelical leaders have been particularly impressed with the number of sympathetic gay characters that have been incorporated in mainstream movies and television programs. From *Philadelphia* (1993) to *Brokeback Mountain* (2005), they believe movies have softened public opposition to homosexuality. They also mentioned to me the number of celebrities who identify as gay or lesbian, hoping that similar things might happen for evangelicals. "If we could get an Ellen DeGeneres figure who is likable and popular to 'come out' as an evangelical," says one ministry executive, "many more people would have positive impressions of the movement as a whole."[26]

Leaders I interviewed also admire the media savvy of the gay and lesbian movement. Says one successful producer, "They exert a lot of pressure. I remember when I used to go to the Emmys, [I would wonder] why people are always wearing those red ribbons. [I discovered that] they have people outside that are actually giving [the red ribbons] to you and pinning them on you. ... It's not like people went down and paid a buck for this ribbon and put it on because they really believe in it. It's because there are people outside the doors, standing there, waiting, handing them out. And I remember having to go, 'No, [I don't want to wear a ribbon].' ... That's how organized it is." Others admire the way the gay and lesbian community supports the arts, museums, and high culture.

When pressed about the irony of evangelical leaders admiring the gay and lesbian movement, evangelical public leaders would not comment any further than to say that both groups have a vision for changing society. The gay and lesbian community appears to have succeeded. In a 2006 Gallup poll, 31 percent of American adults said that they would like to see homosexuality be more widely accepted in this nation. This is a major shift. In 1977, for example, 56 percent of Americans told Gallup that homosexuals should have equal rights in hiring. By 2005, that figure had jumped to 87 percent, and the percentage who did not favor equal rights had dropped from 33 percent to 11 percent. To a person, all the evangelical leaders who mentioned gays and lesbians in this context mentioned that they would like to see similar acceptance of their own movement in the years ahead. It also appears that certain quarters of the evangelical movement are more accepting of homosexuality today. I surmise that the openness of some to learn from the gay and lesbian movement—even though none wanted to be quoted on the record as acknowledging that—points to a lessening of strictures around homosexuality. Evangelical leader Tony Campolo, a sociologist and frequent speaker, told me when we met, "Even Jim Dobson [who has been quite vocal about his opposition to homosexuality] knows that people cannot change their orientation.... Anyone with a PhD from a secular university who examines the data knows that you cannot change that." Campolo advocates that Christians who have a homosexual orientation practice celibacy. Another leader, the president of a prominent evangelical seminary, shared with me the story of a student who came to talk to him about her lesbian identity and his subsequent handling of the issue. Episodes like these, while isolated, emerged across interviews I conducted.[27]

To the extent that gays and lesbians have succeeded in Hollywood, how has it happened? First, gays and lesbians tried to get mainstream media outlets to feature more gay and lesbian characters, and for more than ten years the Gay and Lesbian Alliance Against Defamation (GLAAD) has published an annual survey detailing how successful those efforts have been. Gay characters made occasional appearances on TV in the 1970s and 1980s, but not until 1992 did a recurring gay character appear for an extended series of shows on network television. Shortly thereafter, though, popular cable television shows like *The Real World* (MTV) and later *Queer as Folk* (Showtime) regularly spotlighted gay characters. Other hit television programs like *Friends* (NBC), *Ellen* (ABC), *Survivor* (CBS), and *Spin City* (ABC) followed suit, featuring gay and lesbian characters in both leading and supporting roles. Indeed, in the 1996–97 season Ellen DeGeneres attracted worldwide attention as she portrayed the first openly homosexual title character in U.S. primetime television history.[28]

I found no Christian version of GLAAD's annual survey, and—excepting a few shows like *Touched by an Angel, Seventh Heaven,* and *The Simpsons*—evangelicals bemoan the dearth of openly Christian characters. Dean Batali captures the sentiment of many I interviewed: "I would like to see as many Christian characters on television as there are gay characters.... If we can just point out to people that they're not freaks, that they're intellectuals, that they're your neighbors, maybe more people would consider, 'Maybe it [Christianity] is not such a bad way to go.'" When asked why there are not more Christians on television shows or in movies, almost everyone said it was because of the executives who approve new shows. Batali continues:

> The reality is, if you're going in and pitching a show with a gay character,... there's going to be [at least one] gay executive in one of the rooms, and they're going to say, "I can relate to that," and they're going to put it on the air. Well, I can't find... an evangelical Christian [in those decision-making circles] who can say, "I can relate to that [evangelical character]."

Research confirms Batali's intuition. One of the largest studies of the entertainment elite was conducted by Robert Lichter, Linda Lichter, and Stanley Rothman; they showed that the "collective worldview" of Hollywood's creative community invariably influences the content of their shows.[29] For instance, in 1982 only 5 percent of television executives strongly felt that homosexuality was wrong. Among the general public, that figure was 76 percent. So it is hardly surprising to find positive portrayals of the gay and lesbian community on primetime television.[30]

The same researchers found a correspondence between the personal background of Hollywood's creative community and the relative obscurity of pro-religious themes in primetime television. Of course, programs like *Highway to Heaven* and *Touched by an Angel* portray spiritual themes in a positive light, but on balance they found that "traditional religious messages [have been] replaced by television's social gospel and cautionary tales about the need to question religious authority." They cited an episode from the then-popular sitcom *WKRP in Cincinnati* in which the radio station fought, and eventually won, a censorship battle with a fundamentalist minister. Evangelicals are often shown opposing social progress, favoring censorship, and being generally out of step with the rest of society. Fully 93 percent of participants in the study conducted by Lichter and his colleagues said they seldom or never attend religious services, a figure double the national average at that time. In essence, issues appear in mainstream media because creators and decision-makers think they're important.[31] To date, evangelicals have not found support in Hollywood's inner circle.

In addition to altering the public face of American evangelicalism, movement leaders are developing the next generation of artists and entertainers. They have devoted significant resources, including their own time and energy, to help future leaders in the arts and entertainment. One Hollywood insider expresses the sentiment of many: "I really want to be available to the next generation. I take the blessing God has given me very seriously, and I want to be available to [help] the people coming behind me." This is not mere charity; people I interviewed spoke repeatedly of their desire to transform the culture and change society, born out of a sense of mission and purpose. Barbara Nicolosi told me, "Right now, there simply aren't enough talented Christians who have paid their dues, but within five to ten years, we will see Christians in Hollywood with real power."

In recent years, she claims, there has been "a trend where you had to have a gay character in every TV show; you had to have a gay theme." Given recent shifts in the entertainment world, Nicolosi believes that this "same sensitivity may be shown to Christians as well." She and other evangelicals I interviewed would applaud such a development: "I'd rather have them pandering to us for a change, instead of ignoring us," she said. In 2005, Nicolosi was invited to appear on the tabloid television show *Inside Edition*. She was there to talk about Act One and Christians' rising prominence in Hollywood. So when she said to one of the show's staffers, "I never thought in my wildest dreams I would be on *Inside Edition*," his response did not completely surprise her. "Didn't you know?" he retorted, "Christian is the new gay."[32]

PART IV

CORPORATE TITANS

AND THE CORNER OFFICE

7

Faith-Friendly Firms

Douglas Holladay first began thinking about the relationship between faith and work while working with a Washington-based ministry for political and business leaders. He says that he entered ministry just after college because "I really wanted to make a difference, and [at the time the people whom I regarded as] the most alive to God and making an impact were people in the full-time ministry. I had never met a lawyer or a doctor or an investment banker that said, 'I love what I'm doing, and this is where God's placed me.'" But Holladay gradually became convinced that his impact was limited. He was interested in helping connect the world of piety with the world of action, but he sensed that the ministry was the last place where this would happen. Workers, managers, and professionals in "secular" business settings had the greatest influence. Surprisingly, though, these individuals rarely recognized what Holladay thought was so obvious: They, not ministers, were on the "front lines" of faith—around the conference table and in the corner offices. Holladay continues:

I was having dinner with the head of a large oil company...at the Key Bridge Marriot. We were up top in the dining room, looking down the Potomac. It was a lovely, inspiring sight....This guy was telling me how great I was, affirming the fact that God is really using me [in ministry]....Finally, I decided maybe I should ask him about what he does, and I said, "Well, how's it going with you? Why are you in D.C.?" He said he had dinner with Henry Kissinger last night [and later] met with the president, but he kept changing the subject. Then he looked me in the eye and said, "Doug, someday I want to really make a difference and do what you're doing." It was jarring to me because I realized that I was part of the problem. There's a religious caste system, and if somebody will...fund people in the full-time realm, then they get a pass in their own life. They don't have to really wrestle with questions [of vocation.

Christian ministers say to business leaders,] 'If you will fund our ministry, we'll never ask you any questions again about what you're doing.' . . . Basically we don't want business people to be engaged in ministry.

Holladay decided to switch to what he calls the "other side of the table." He has since held senior positions in the White House, the State Department, and Goldman Sachs and today runs Park Avenue Equity Partners, yet he still views his work as a form of "ministry."[1]

Faith and Work

In 1924, Bruce Barton, a successful advertising executive, wrote *The Man Nobody Knows*. In it, he described Jesus as "the founder of the modern business." Barton believed that Jesus' ability to select twelve disciples who later "conquered" the world demonstrates His leadership ability—an example other business leaders should follow. Twenty-five years later, Elton Trueblood criticized the distinction between ordained ministry—"full-time Christian work"—and the laity, and 1960s Protestants and Catholics alike began to speak of a "theology of the laity" that encouraged believers to integrate their religious convictions into professional life. Starting in the 1970s, a "faith at work" movement began to spread across the commercial sector, and evangelicals were at the forefront.[2] Since then, the faith-at-work movement has grown dramatically, comprising more than two thousand groups, institutions, and organizations—the vast majority of which were founded since 1976. Though the 1980s and 1990s were generally good years for American commerce, many business leaders I talked with said that their lives needed "balance" or spiritual "grounding," now more than ever. Spiritual seekers were trying to integrate different parts of their life, renegotiating boundaries between personal faith and the workplace.[3]

In 1997, President Clinton issued a White House directive allowing federal employees to engage in religious expression to the same extent that they were permitted to engage in comparable nonreligious private expression in the federal workplace.[4] It was the most sweeping sanction of religious expression in the federal workplace ever issued. This order meant that workers could discuss their religious views in hallways and cafeterias, just as they would discuss a football game or an upcoming vacation. It also meant they could display religious messages such as "What Would Jesus Do?" just as they were permitted to display comparable messages like cartoons. Perhaps most relevant to evangelicals, the guidelines stated, "Some

religions encourage adherents to spread the faith at every opportunity, a duty that can encompass the adherent's workplace. As a
general matter, proselytizing is as entitled to constitutional protection as any other form of speech." For the first time, bringing one's
faith to work was government-sanctioned; the American workplace
has not been the same since.[5]

The borders between the religious and the economic realms have
become increasingly porous: Faith is not only influencing business,
but business is influencing faith.[6] To some, this has been alarming,
but the commercialization of religion is hard to overlook, as evangelicals have established robust publishing and music industries, to
name just two. And recent decades have witnessed a professionalization of the evangelical ministry. Not only are preachers talking like
corporate managers, but business and movement leaders move
back and forth between sectors a great deal these days. Entrepreneurs like Bob Buford and Richard Stearns have gone from executive
positions in secular businesses to leadership positions at evangelical
ministries. Jim Mellado, head of the Willow Creek Association, and
Stephen Douglass, head of Campus Crusade for Christ, have MBAs
from Harvard Business School.[7] The Maclellan Foundation has
provided significant funding to help evangelical groups become
more efficient and effective. Bob Buford's Leadership Network has
brought an entrepreneurial edge to the nation's largest and fastest
growing megachurches. There are now striking similarities between
the evangelical world and American corporate life. How has this
happened?

Business as a Moral Activity

While I interviewed Les Csorba, a business leader in Houston, he
cited Peter Drucker, America's management guru, as saying that the
purpose of business is to create a customer. Csorba then concluded,
"If that's the purpose of business, then you have to develop contacts,
relationships. Everything is based on mutual trust and a ... bond.
It's a moral activity. [Through work] we are contributing to that
moral enterprise, ... so in those ways, I see [my work as highly]
valuable." Evangelicals in business have embraced the idea that they
are "called" to a particular line of work for the glory of God.[8] Dozens
of business leaders talked about using their position as a "platform"
for bearing witness to their faith, helping the poor, and encouraging
fellow believers. For evangelicals at both the elite and rank-and-file
levels, career choice is heavily influenced by spiritual convictions.

Forty percent of American evangelicals say that their spiritual beliefs had a "large" effect on the work that they chose to pursue, and another 30 percent say it had "some" effect. These figures are significantly different from the general U.S. population, where only 54 percent said their faith had a "large" or "some" effect on their choice.[9]

Among the hundred business leaders I interviewed, many said they had a strong sense of being called to their profession, and six executives applied to or strongly considered attending seminary before going into business. As John Brandon, a technology executive, said to me, "I had grown up in a slice of Christianity that taught that if you want to fulfill God's highest calling in your life, that had to be full-time Christian work, ... [but really I felt] called to the business world." While working as a consultant at Starbucks after a successful career at Microsoft, John Sage applied to seminary, although he says he did so "begrudgingly. ... [I didn't] feel like that was where I was called [because] I liked business too much." His solution was to start a coffee company that would donate its profits to children and families in coffee-growing countries. Allen Morris, an entrepreneur in Miami, attributes his calling to a conversation with Francis Schaeffer. Schaeffer, knowing Morris could soon take over the family business, told him not to go to seminary, saying that he had "a unique platform in the business community to influence people." And Wal-Mart vice-chairman Michael Duke says he has always felt "God's plan for my life was in business. ... We have 1.2 million associates in the U.S. [with] about 130 million people that visit our stores every week. So I do think that this ... was the perfect fit for ... my life."[10] Others mentioned a sense of being called to positions of important responsibility, to "public influence," or to be "a leader in the world." Several referred to their calling as providing "a platform where [they] can have a certain amount of influence" for faith. They attributed their ascent to God. In the words of one Phoenix executive, "I came to understand that God gave me this platform." Typically, they do not directly link their success with divine sanction. In fact, many spoke disparagingly of this notion; one likened it to a "genie-in-the-bottle-god deal," saying, "That's not really how this stuff works with God." Instead, they see their "platform" as a gift or something entrusted to their care, but in nearly every case, this gift was something that they felt came from God.

They also spoke of their calling as unique. Rick Tompane, a Silicon Valley executive, said, "I can be involved in the lives of my employees at levels most ministers cannot." Tom Morgan, the president and CEO of Hughes Supply, a Fortune 500 company, agreed: "The opportunities I have for ministry in the business world are very different from the opportunity that my pastor has." Morgan and other business leaders believe they can bear witness to their faith and be of greater assistance, both directly and indirectly, to the evangelical community as business executives than they could as ministers. As another business leader told me, "There are plenty of Christians working on Sunday morning.... There is no more Christian hour in the country than from eleven to noon on Sunday mornings. But Tuesday afternoon seemed open."

In nearly every case, evangelical business leaders think of their work as making a difference in the world. This is not altogether surprising, given their positions and the size of the companies they lead. For example, Myron "Mike" Ullman has presided over some of the world's largest retail firms including Macy's, JCPenney, and LVMH Moët Hennessy Louis Vuitton. He talks about his job in this way: "I look at it as 150,000 people that I can reach—maybe not in an evangelical way—but in the way we run the business and the [organizational] culture that we create.... That's exciting to me." But this sentiment is not entirely unique to high-level executives. Nearly all evangelicals believe their work is helping to make the world a better place.[11]

Practically no one spoke about the financial benefits of a calling to business instead of church ministry, but this surely factored into career decisions. David Radcliffe, CEO of the Southern Company in Atlanta, explained his decision to enter the energy business: "I was teaching high school for $325 a month and Georgia Power company offered me $700 a month. It's real simple." Also, a sizable number of former CEOs retired early from their positions of business leadership to found and/or lead faith-based organizations, moving, in their words, from a life oriented around "success" to "significance." Inspired by cable television mogul Bob Buford— who did this and later wrote an account of the transition in a book called *Half Time*—many of these leaders have found it easier to act on their faith convictions while leading an evangelical ministry than while leading a public company.[12]

A calling to business means an acceptance of the capitalist system. Very few questioned the American economic system, and they often linked their ideas about the market to evangelical faith.[13] David Grizzle, an executive with Continental Airlines, said, "I believe that as followers of Jesus, the best thing we can do is let the market work, achieve the most efficient results, and then voluntarily give back to those who came out on the short end of the stick.... To disrupt the market impoverishes everybody." This notion of linking evangelical belief with conservative ideas about the economy has been around for decades, but the growing alliance between American evangelicalism and conservative politics has exacerbated the trend.[14] Business leaders are always quick to qualify their comments favoring capitalism, saying they indeed do want their businesses to succeed, but not for self-aggrandizement. Norm Miller, the CEO of Interstate Batteries, said, "I want to be an instrument of bringing forth much fruit, [but] not for me,...for the Lord." Sherron Watkins, the Enron executive whom *Time* named a Person of the Year in 2002 for blowing the whistle on her company's misdeeds, underscored this idea when we talked after the company's collapse. Over breakfast one Monday morning, she said to me:

> I think the reason we work is to glorify God, and I think the role of business is to create wealth for people to use for God's purposes...through the form of salaries and taxes and charity and philanthropy....Business is what fuels and creates the wealth with which you can either do good or not in the world. So I think that Christians are very, very much called to business.

Some leaders do express a few reservations about capitalism. John Sage, who is regarded by many as a pioneer in the field of social entrepreneurship, believes fair trade businesses like his firm, Pura Vida, should prompt "people to rethink the fundamental tenets of capitalism."[15] He hopes for a system that aligns human interests as "consuming beings" with a "more noble purpose." A fair number of evangelicals agree with Sage's sentiment; 16 percent said the U.S. economic system needs to be replaced by a different system, significantly higher than the 10 percent of the general U.S. population who said so.[16]

So what happens when evangelical workers rise to the top? How do their faith commitments affect their professional commitments? Do careerism and materialism overtake one's concern for deeper human values? Among the most successful business leaders, I found that a tension exists between professional success and spiritual grounding. Dozens of evangelical executives pointed to symptoms of this internal conflict, yet few acknowledged the source of that conflict or the extent to which they themselves contributed to it. Over the course of my interviews, I was struck by how rarely leaders mentioned the many biblical passages that speak against the pursuit of wealth. For example, no one talked about how riches hinder faith, yet Jesus' encounter with the rich young ruler suggested that wealth could, indeed, be an encumbrance to being his disciple. The synoptic gospels were surely hostile to the pursuit of wealth and material gain: Jesus said a camel can pass through the eye of a needle more easily than a rich man can enter the kingdom of God, and elsewhere he declared it impossible to follow both God and Mammon. A handful of business leaders discussed the deleterious effects their careers have had on their families and their own spiritual journeys.[17] Jim Lane, one of the youngest people to be named partner at Goldman Sachs, told me that success can be "very hard on marriage.... Raising five billion dollars and being jetted across the country in a private plane ... is a little bit more fun than changing diapers.... So [professional success and making work your primary source of identity] creates distance, ... it creates issues.... It is very distracting from what's important in life." Many business leaders are defined by their work. It is a mark of personal identity.

A few of them come to grips with this, often dramatically. Don Williams had an epiphany while sprawled on an airport sidewalk. For several years, he had been climbing the corporate ladder at Trammel Crow Company, often working eighty to ninety hours a week and traveling around the world brokering deals. One Friday night, he was changing planes in New York after a whirlwind trip that took him from Dallas to Brazil to Paris to Cairo to Tehran in a matter of days.

> I flew into New York's JFK Airport in the midst of a major snowstorm and found that I had only a few minutes to catch the last flight to Dallas.... I took off on foot toward the Braniff terminal. Running with a suitcase in one hand and a loaded briefcase in the other, I slipped and fell, then slid along my belly and landed spread-eagle and facedown in the snow. At that moment, I asked myself, "What am I doing with my life?" Lying there in the snow, I came to recognize that I was a workaholic, consumed and driven primarily by work and ambition.... I was neglecting not only my wife and five children, but also my spiritual life.... I believe I was called to work, ... [but] what I learned is that if you put [work] in perspective, there's a ... peace ... that comes to you and actually allows you to make better business decisions and better use of your time.... I didn't think about it at the time as an epiphany, but looking back on it, I think it was. In the end this is only business; this isn't your life. This isn't your ultimate destiny, and ... that was a bit of an insight for me.

Williams came to this conclusion at age thirty-six, and afterward he changed his working routine to put the other parts of his life "in balance" with his career and success at the company. Several other evangelical executives made similar decisions about the need to relativize the place of work in their lives. For the vast majority of business leaders I interviewed, though, exceedingly long hours and an intense work ethic are two of the requirements for professional success. While many did speak about "balancing" work with other parts of their lives, few could point to specific practices that reflected this commitment, and my sense is that it is more discussed than done.

One of the most troubling areas for evangelical business leaders is executive compensation. Given the media attention devoted to the subject, I fully expected evangelical business leaders to raise the topic during our conversations. Executive compensation seems like an area where evangelical executives could distinguish themselves from their secular peers. After all, many of the movement's most prominent leaders—including Billy Graham, Bill Bright, and Rick Warren—refuse to accept donors' offers to help purchase luxury vehicles or live in exclusive neighborhoods. And while evangelical business leaders have traditionally received much higher wages than ministers or missionaries, many have believed in economic moderation. Max De Pree, for example, instituted a policy while he was CEO of Herman Miller that capped the income gap between his salary and that of the lowest-paid employee at the firm. While other American CEOs earned hundreds of times the pay of the lowest-paid employee, the ratio at Herman Miller was capped at 20:1. It was a "structural matter" within the firm that "could and should be informed by my faith," De Pree told me.

Excessive executive compensation presents a challenge to the communitarian impulse of evangelical theology, and some business leaders are disturbed by it, referring to pay packages that are "through the roof... [as] morally wrong." Some leaders told me it strikes them as "outrageous," while others said that "the model is broken." On the other hand, one CEO I interviewed was paid more than $20 million the year prior to our conversation.[18] When I raised the subject of executive compensation, he justified the high salary by saying, "It's not even in the same ballpark with athletes and ... stars." He also deflected any critique, saying, "I had very little to do with [the matter]. The board compensation committee would make those decisions ... without any real input from me." Such sentiment strikes some observers as a relatively limited notion of the power executives wield—especially over their personal compensation—and a narrow understanding of the role they can play in managing the privileges they enjoy. Les Csorba, an evangelical who is the partner-in-charge of an executive search firm, acknowledges that his industry has been silent on this matter, "and the reason is because we have an interest. Our fees are tied to the ... annual compensation of the placed candidate. So we've been reluctant to speak out about the abuses because it affects us." All of this has occurred while the inflation-adjusted average hourly earnings for wage and salary workers in the private sector languish, according to Bureau of Labor statistics since 1973.[19] Numerous social observers have decried the widening wage gap in America. Michael Novak, for example, has written, "Business executives are blind to the social destructiveness of current levels of compensation."[20] Excessive compensation erodes social trust; more pernicious for evangelicals, it undermines their ability to frame business as a moral activity, which is critical to expanding evangelical influence in the business sector.

Influence

Despite this, evangelical leaders continue to see business as a moral enterprise because they can use it as an "arena," a "platform," or a "mission field" where they can point out to observers their evangelical commitments. Several said the opportunity for faith-based influence motivated them to perform well in their jobs. While growing up in Germany, Horst Schulze attended a hospitality trade school and apprenticed at a nearby luxury hotel. He says he was always uncomfortable with the exaggerated deference hotel staffers were instructed to give guests. While there, the general manager would say, "Our guests are all very important. They're all very fine people. You cannot be who they are, so never get jealous. . . . That's not what you can be, and that's not what you are." At age fifteen, Schulze wrote an essay for school on his vision for the hospitality industry; the paper's thesis became his mantra: "We are not servants. We are ladies and gentlemen serving ladies and gentlemen." After relocating to the United States, he became a charter member of the Ritz-Carlton Hotel Company, and his conviction about the innate dignity of every human being—from hotel staffer to VIP guest—became part of the corporate culture. Schulze wanted the company to exceed industry expectations since success would provide occasions for him to talk about his faith. Others in the industry would try to learn from Ritz-Carlton, and that would provide Schulze an opportunity to talk about humans as being made in the image of God, about the Golden Rule, and about his evangelical convictions. Under his leadership, Ritz-Carlton was awarded the Malcolm Baldrige National Quality Award twice, and *Hotels* magazine recognized Schulze as "corporate hotelier of the world" in 1991. He is now leading a new luxury chain, Capella Hotels and Resorts, for which he has similar aspirations: Excellence will be "my greatest contribution for my faith because that means people will come and study us to learn how we did it.... [In the process] they will peel down the onion, and at the end, they will see a bunch of Christians praying.... They will see that [we] have values,... and hopefully, everything we do is honoring Christ."

Evangelical business leaders dream big and aspire to financial success, even though some Christian teachings express a preference for the meek and humble. They present their faith as enterprising and industrious: "I don't see that Christ was a patsy. He was ambitious," said Don Soderquist of Wal-Mart. And Intel's senior vice president declared, "I don't believe in papier-mâché, dishrag Christians." Indeed, evangelicals in business refer to ambitious career plans with brazen boldness. John Tyson, who has run the Fortune 500 firm started by his family, told me, "I always thought I'd run a large company.... I just never thought I'd run our family business." They are less comfortable linking their success to divine action. As Bruce Kennedy, once head of Alaska Airlines, said from his home in Seattle, "I don't think God is in the business of prospering businesses." A majority of evangelicals agree: Only 35 percent strongly believe that success in life is determined by religious or spiritual forces. They are more comfortable saying that God wants them to find work that fits their talents (56 percent).[21] Nearly all the people I spoke to said that whatever talents or opportunities they have been given holds them to account, and dozens mentioned a phrase from Luke 12: "From him to whom much is given, much is required."

Relationships in the Workplace

More than half of American evangelicals say their beliefs greatly influence their relationships at work.[22] For several years, an evangelical journal called *Life@Work* explored the intersection of faith and business.[23] It featured hundreds of stories, profiles, and examples of evangelical business leaders, many of whom emphasized human dynamics in the workplace. Feature articles discussed topics like mentoring, developing future leaders, evaluating the work of others, and nurturing relationships with business partners. The journal gave prominence to an idea that several leaders referred to as "covenantal relationships," in which people take an interest in each other's concerns and priorities, even if such matters are only tangentially connected to their business relationship. This creates a better workplace environment. It generates trust among employees, improves retention, generates long-term business relations with vendors, and creates customer loyalty. When I asked how this manifests itself in the workplace, leaders almost always spoke of praying or expressing concern for co-workers. Wayne Huizenga Jr., who runs Huizenga Holdings, an investment and entertainment conglomerate, said, "I pray for our employees . . . almost every day, and the way that I treat our people [is shaped] by my relationship with Christ and by how I'm called to act."

The challenge, of course, arises when executives have to make tough personnel decisions. BellSouth Telecommunications executive Frank Skinner said he never prayed over business deals, but he often prayed about personnel matters: "It should never be easy . . . to fire another employee, and yet there are times when it has to be done. . . . Someone's got to make a decision, and you just pray you're right." Marjorie Dorr, chief strategy officer of WellPoint, spoke about having to dismiss an employee who directly reported to her. The employee was a fellow Christian with whom she had studied the Bible in a small group. Dorr says having to release the employee "broke my heart," but that being a fellow believer doesn't get employees "bonus points": "You don't have to be a Christian to be successful under my leadership and . . . you're not going to be fired if you're not." Indeed, relations with employees can be a difficult issue for executives who have stressed the primacy of relationships in the workplace.

While Bruce Kennedy was leading Alaska Airlines, employee unions decided to strike in what became the longest work stoppage in the history of commercial aviation. For sixty days, Kennedy encountered picketers at airports, his home, and even his church. Picketers put a cross in his lawn at home with a sign asking, "Would Jesus do this?" Kennedy says his family would take lemonade down to the strikers, but he could not bring himself to do that. "It became a very personal thing. . . . They attacked my faith. . . . From their point of view, I was the demon." In the end, management won the battle at Alaska Airlines, but the incident remained a controversial part of Kennedy's tenure at the helm. What one worker frames as an example of responsible stewardship required of all evangelicals, another worker can view as a heartless act of corporate greed.[24]

Prayer

As I talked with business leaders, they often said prayer helped them manage uncertainty, but it also carried a degree of risk. They worried about how others might perceive their praying and the propriety of doing it at work, particularly at publicly traded companies or when it might be witnessed by others whose religious beliefs they did not know. But the more these executives engaged in prayer in these "risky" situations, the less they worried about its consequences. And for many leaders, prayer became a taken-for-granted aspect of their business lives.[25]

Several executives mentioned a leader's need for a "moral compass." For many, prayer in the workplace became a way to reconnect with that moral compass, giving them direction in the face of uncertainty. PepsiCo CEO Steve Reinemund said, "In today's complicated, busy, and challenging life, I don't know how anybody can sort out what's important, what's not important . . . without a grounding and a moral compass, which is based on your faith." Others talked about prayer as a way to deliberate on moral decisions.[26] Michael Volkema of Herman Miller likened the business leader's job to "priestly work" that demands a "moral compass, [for there are] a lot of people who are dependent upon the decisions that [the leader] ultimately makes." Like others, Merrit Quarum, CEO of Qmedtrix, told me his faith shapes his conscience, what he called the "voice in the back of [his] head," directing his decisions. Ann Iverson, who was once one of the highest ranking women in business, said, "I wouldn't make any decision . . . without prayer. When I am sitting in a board meeting now . . . I will ask God to just guide me." She said that these short prayers, often given silently while in a meeting, help her discern right from wrong at a visceral level: "When you're doing the right thing, your heart feels light and good, and when you feel heavy and slimy," things are wrong. In essence, these evangelical business leaders believe prayer enables them to determine what is good, right, and fitting when faced with a challenge in their job. They believe prayer helps them connect with God. The idea, as ConocoPhillips' former CEO Archie Dunham told me, is that "their decisions will maybe be closer to what God would want instead of what man would want."

Only 19 percent of American workers say there are groups that meet regularly at their place of work for prayer or Bible study. And even though evangelicals are significantly more likely to say open expressions of religion would be encouraged at their place of work, only about half of them are actually open about their faith at work.[27] When Norm Miller took the helm of Dallas-based Interstate Batteries, he was concerned that having a too overt Christian ambience might cause his firm to lose customers or employees. Then he came across a passage in the book of Matthew:

It said in essence, "Don't fear, but if you're going to fear, fear him who can do something to you after you're dead." So we [asked God to help us] . . . be perfectly bold and perfectly sensitive [because we did not] want to offend anyone. [We decided that public prayer would be part of the corporate culture.] We would just start the meeting and say, . . . "Heavenly Father, thank you for the day, and for your blessing, everybody getting here. We pray for the food that we are going to eat. . . . Guide and direct our meetings and give everybody safe travel home and that this thing will really help us all, in Christ's name, Amen. Okay, now item number one is . . ." So we just went like that.

The speed with which Miller and his fellow executives offered the prayer was designed to minimize the degree to which it was perceived as an inconvenience, but they also hoped it would happen so quickly that no objection could be raised before they started. Like Miller, Wayne Huizenga Jr. felt that prayer could be an important way of differentiating his company from others, but there was still risk. At the start of a meeting with potential financiers for the Miami Dolphins Huizenga wanted to offer a prayer. His chief financial officer cautioned him that bankers from Israel would be present and might be put off by a public prayer in Jesus' name. In the end, Huizenga prayed in his usual manner, and afterward, a Jewish representative from one of the banks approached him to say how much he appreciated the public expression of Huizenga's faith. "That was one of the first confirmations that I had that it was okay."

Floors of Integration: Building a Corporate Culture

How do firms integrate faith and work? As I observed different businesses, it became obvious that there was remarkable variation among companies. Stephen Graves, one of the founders of the *Life@Work* journal and now a management consultant, referred to these differing degrees of faith–work integration as "floors of integration," which I think is a helpful analogy.[28] As you move up from the ground floor, faith becomes more and more central to the company's mission.

The Ground Floor

When asked how faith impacts his or her work, every executive mentioned some aspect of business ethics—everything from not cheating on expense reports to reporting company misdeeds to government agencies. Ethics is at the ground floor of the integrative task. Most leaders described ethical behavior as straightforward and as the minimum standard to which evangelical business leaders ought to be held. J. McDonald "Don" Williams served at the helm of Trammell Crow, one of the nation's largest commercial real estate firms, from 1977 until 2002. He defined ethical considerations such as honesty and financial transparency as "pretty simple stuff." For him, it was a given that evangelical business leaders would demand that their firms follow strict ethical guidelines; according to him, it is the "least" they can do. Ralph Larsen, who ran Johnson & Johnson for many years, also regards ethical considerations as "fundamental." During our interview he said, "The decisions that I made, the tone that I set, the way that I dealt with employees or treated them were all a reflection of my Christian faith."[29] As the chairman and CEO, Larsen says, "I set the tone and the strategic direction." Sometimes executive decisions are easy, but when they are not, leaders often turn to faith. For example, Larsen struggled to decide whether to allow his firm to enter the emergency contraception business. Even though Johnson & Johnson was the largest birth control producer in the world, Larsen did not want the firm to manufacture the so-called morning-after pill both because of his faith and because "I felt it was bad business. . . . Here we are, the baby company, [so] how can we be producing abortifacients?" Indeed, many executives frame ethical decisions in terms of both their personal faith and their business savvy. Fellow evangelicals agree; 60 percent strongly believe that being ethical pays off economically.[30]

But what about all the evangelicals involved in recent corporate scandals? If so many business leaders think their faith compels them to behave ethically, what accounts for the apparent misdeeds of Bernie Ebbers, once CEO of WorldCom, and Ken Lay, the former head of Enron? Ebbers taught a Sunday school class regularly and was a significant benefactor of many evangelical charities. Yet in 2005, he was sentenced to twenty-five years in prison for his role in orchestrating the biggest corporate fraud in the nation's history. Similarly, Ken Lay was widely known as an evangelical business leader and the son of a Baptist minister. In rare interviews on the subject, Lay alluded to his faith and continued to assert his innocence in the Enron debacle until his death.[31] Other evangelicals who worked with him, like whistle-blower Sherron Watkins, say he and other corporate leaders were "hiding behind their Christianity" for quite some time.

WorldCom and Enron were at the center of two of the largest corporate scandals in history, and their stories undermine any claim that evangelicals are noticeably different in terms of business ethics. But, by the same token, evangelicals have played a significant role in shaping what society regards as "ethical." In this way their influence is often underappreciated. In the wake of Tyco's misdeeds, for example, Eric Pillmore was hired as the firm's senior vice president in charge of corporate governance. Pillmore's work has been featured in *Business Ethics* and the *Harvard Business Review*. Indeed, he is at the leading edge of corporate accountability and transparency, and, according to him, his evangelical faith serves as a "road map" for ethics. And although evangelicals like Pillmore sometimes "clean up" after an ethical explosion, more often they are drawn to companies with already high standards. This was the case for many people, including Ralph Larsen at Johnson & Johnson and Don Williams at Trammell Crow. Leaders who seek to integrate their values into the workplace are naturally attracted to businesses with reputations for high ethical standards.

The Second Floor

On the second floor, business leaders establish internal programs that reflect evangelical sentiments. Two of the most prominent are faith-based affinity groups and corporate chaplaincies. During the 1980s and 1990s, a wave of affinity groups began to meet in workplaces. At Intel, gay and lesbian employees were the first to establish such a group, and evangelical Christians followed their lead: Pat Gelsinger, the firm's chief technology officer at the time, initiated a group for fellow believers. And today, the Intel Christian Bible Network meets regularly for Bible study on the corporate campus. Groups like these exist for all types of employees, from racing car enthusiasts to cancer survivors, but evangelical affinity groups can be found at nearly all the nation's biggest firms.[32] Matthew Rose, head of Forth Worth-based Burlington Northern Santa Fe Corporation, says his firm provides facilities for a weekly Bible study, and employees are allowed to share prayer requests through the company voice mail system. Even though Rose is a fellow evangelical, he says, "I would do that same thing for any religion"— but at this point, only the Christians have asked. Such groups are very important to evangelicalism's rise in corporate America. They create networks of friendship and loyalty that cut across traditional dividing lines like rank and department. They encourage evangelicals to incorporate faith into work. And they provide "safe settings" in which employees can talk about their spiritual lives.

Informal corporate chaplaincy programs have been present in some organizations since the 1950s, but today they are mainstays for firms around the country.[33] The number of corporate chaplains has grown so large that they now have a professional guild, the National Institute of Business and Industrial Chaplains, and groups like Marketplace Ministries supply chaplains to organizations on short- and long-term bases.[34] Corporate chaplains provide counseling services for employees and make hospital and funeral-home visits to workers during times of crisis. They are also known to walk factory floors and to drop in to employees' offices to address spiritual or personal concerns. Many companies justify the expense of these chaplains as part of their corporate wellness program. Some critics say these chaplains are mere pawns, refusing to take up employees' concerns with management, on whom their own employment depends. Yet the growing number of firms that employ corporate chaplains points to the rising legitimacy given to faith in the workplace.

David Weekley in Houston employs workplace chaplains at his home-building business and says this has had a "big impact" on his firm. In the company's 2003 annual report, Weekley wrote, "Of all the things we've done in our employee assistance program . . . nowhere have we gotten more bang for our buck than with Marketplace Ministries. The stories I hear are amazing. I remember a lady in one of our offices telling me how the chaplain showed up two hours after she had been served divorce papers at work. Her comment to me was, 'He saved my life.' " Similarly, Interstate Batteries has employed chaplains since the early 1980s. In addition to counseling with employees, the company's chaplains help CEO Norm Miller manage the company's faith-based philanthropies, which are supported by company profits. Chaplains at his firm also host Bible study and prayer groups. Perhaps most unusual among the firms I studied, they also assist with company-sponsored mission trips, on which employees (who pay a portion of their travel expenses and give up some vacation days) work with orphans or the needy in places like Mexico and Russia.

Like Miller, several other evangelical executives have hired ministers as senior-level consultants. Phil Anschutz hired his Presbyterian pastor to help him with special faith-based projects, and John Tyson has been known to fly a noted evangelical business ethics professor to company headquarters several times a year for consultations. Indeed, there is a niche industry of evangelical consultants who help executives integrate faith into their business responsibilities—a novel form of executive chaplaincy.

Of course, evangelical business leaders hold varying opinions about the propriety of bringing faith into the firm. Ralph Larsen, citing the public nature of Johnson & Johnson and its thousands of shareholders and employees, contends, "I don't . . . have a right to use my position to advocate a particular religious point of view." And these attitudes are not simply a function of firm size and type. Paul Johnson, who owns a private real estate firm based in Birmingham, Michigan, does not believe one should "witness...on the company's time"; instead, workers should remain focused on business matters while at the office. Even though it may require additional resources, many evangelical executives have been willing to add chaplains to the company payroll and set aside space for employees to pray with one another in the workplace. Through a variety of means, faith has become part of the inner workings of companies across the country.

The Third Floor

On the third floor, an evangelical executive seeks not only to shape the organization internally but also to influence its public self-presentation. One of the most striking examples of this is Bruce Kennedy's decision to place cards with printed Bible verses on every meal tray served by Alaska Airlines, working with another Christian in the company's catering department. Kennedy says that the initiative was a "lightning rod"—engendering mostly favorable comments with a smaller number of "extremely hostile comments." On the whole, though, Kennedy was pleased to use his role as CEO to act on his faith. "Our intent is to surprise and delight people.... Certainly there's flack, but [based on the feedback I have gotten] there are thousands, maybe tens of thousands of people who are surprised and delighted by this little piece of paper." For Kennedy, it was a tangible way to differentiate his company from its competitors and, in the process, to express his faith. The ability to take one's personal faith and link it to an entire company is one "benefit," say business leaders, of being a chief executive.[35]

Evangelical business leaders also say faith influences advertising and corporate sponsorships. I interviewed Jockey's CEO, Debra Waller, in the company's Manhattan showroom, which was lined with larger-than-life photos of models in Jockey underwear. I told Waller that I had never conducted an interview surrounded by so much human flesh. She replied, "Well, we have intentionally decided to stay away from the more provocative, sexy type of advertising." When pressed about the extent to which her evangelical faith shapes advertising decisions, Waller, who remains personally involved in approving all of the firm's advertising, pointed out that all Jockey models wear wedding rings in photo shoots involving both men and women, implying that the couple in the ads is married. She also stipulates "a man and a woman can't look like a pretzel. . . . People hugging each other in this situation would be very believable," but the ad must not demonstrate anything more "intimate" than that. Waller thinks that most people in the company know of her faith, either through public comments she has made or by reputation. The firm's public self-presentation, most notably through its decisions on advertising, is something Waller "definitely" regards as "faith-based."

Another business leader told me about a "heated" discussion with his family over his company's use of a particular spokesperson. Over the years, this celebrity had transformed her public persona from that of a relatively mild teenage star into a sexually provocative young woman who wore seductive clothing and was photographed several times in compromising positions. The CEO said his wife and daughter challenged his decision to continue using the star to serve as a spokesperson for the company. In the end, the relationship was terminated by mutual agreement. News of this incident spread throughout the industry, and more than one fellow CEO mentioned it when I asked about the relevance of faith to decision-making, particularly in publicly traded companies. The CEO said his faith convictions were "clearly part of the deliberative process."[36] He then told me, "I think as Christians we do have to ask, 'How are we dealing with those issues on the firing line in a way which is consistent with our faith?'. . . Frankly, that's where a lot of churches don't help laypeople deal with issues [like these], because they're not black and white. . . . Black and white issues are easy; it's the ones that are hard that you [struggle with as a business leader]."

One of the critical issues at the third floor is the effect executive decisions have on lower-level managers. If a middle-level manager perceives a senior executive to be making decisions based on faith convictions, to what extent does that affect deliberations at lower levels? What is the relationship between large-scale executive action and the voluntary actions of individual employees? Ninety-two percent of the executives I interviewed said their colleagues and subordinates know about their evangelical faith. When asked how, they offered dozens of explanations, from comments in the media to faith-based philanthropy and involvement with religious groups. Although not many discussed how their faith might shape lower-level decision-making, a few did. Drew Ladner served as the chief information officer at the U.S. Treasury Department during President George W. Bush's first term. Now a technology executive in the private sector, Ladner believes evangelical business leaders need to think more deeply about how to integrate evangelical faith between the macro and micro levels. The area between individual activism and organizational culture is largely "untilled," says Ladner: "You've got the macro, strategic [type of organizational] change, and you've got the...one-life-at-a-time-kind of change. But in between there's a paucity of understanding of thinking through how...these things connect...for a mid-level manager."

As is the case in the political sphere, evangelical business leaders often make decisions that are in line with their faith commitments but are not *solely explained* by their faith. Jockey's policy of requiring male and female models to wear wedding bands can be explained both by the chief executive's faith-shaped notions of propriety and by the company's image as less risqué than competitors like Victoria's Secret. And the fact that executives frame these as "smart" business decisions demonstrates that the marketplace is still the most important factor in decisions, even if faith plays a role as well. The real significance of the third floor is not sexy underwear models wearing wedding rings but the executive's willingness to publicly link evangelical faith with corporate decision-making. And while people outside the company may not pick up on such nuances, the executive's faith is not likely to be overlooked by employees. A single executive can exert influence that ripples throughout the company.

The Fourth Floor

The most thoroughgoing way in which an evangelical business leader can bring faith to bear on the workplace is by building evangelical ethos into the firm's organizational culture: its values, assumptions, and symbols.[37] Organizational culture not only helps determine who will be the customers, suppliers, and competitors for a particular firm, but it also influences the way in which the firm interacts with those different groups. A "strong" corporate culture can lead to greater productivity, morale, and adaptability. And it can be a source of sustained competitive advantage so long as it is valuable, rare, and not easily imitated.[38]

Rare organizational cultures are few and far between: most firms are strikingly similar. Yet in a given field not all organizations resemble one another. American Airlines and Southwest Airlines present themselves differently, even though the airline industry tends toward conformity.[39] Firms often differentiate themselves through rituals and myths, but organizations can also have extraordinary experiences—a radical change of behavior by the chief executive, for example—that contribute to a distinctive organizational culture.

A strong organizational culture enhances coordination within a firm, improves goal alignment between an organization and its members, and increases employee effort. Strong cultures give work meaning and establish conventions that govern how a firm operates. Perhaps one of the most important elements of strong organizational culture is that it can reduce uncertainty and anxiety among mid-level managers. So how have evangelical business leaders shaped the values, assumptions, and symbols of the firms that they run? Truett Cathy, the founder of Chick-fil-A, started in the restaurant business in 1946. He says he was simply "tired after six days of working," so he chose not to open on Sunday. "That's been the best business decision I've made." He believes it attracts better employees: "They wouldn't work for us if they had to work on Sunday." While Cathy often frames the decision in terms of wanting to rest, there is no mistaking his evangelical convictions, which permeate the organization's culture. Now a $1.2 billion restaurant chain, Chick-fil-A and the Cathy family have donated tens, if not hundreds, of millions of dollars for college scholarships, character-building programs for elementary-school children, foster homes, and a variety of other philanthropic causes. At the heart of this philanthropy is Cathy's desire to serve a "higher calling" through business. The company's official statement of purpose says that the firm exists "to glorify God by being a faithful steward of all that is entrusted to us and to have a positive influence on all who come in contact with Chick-fil-A." Weekly devotional services are held every Monday morning at corporate headquarters, and at their annual meetings the company sponsors a church service for franchise operators who want to attend (and an alternative activity for those who do not). Of course, there have been a few employees who do not like the overtly Christian ethos of Chick-fil-A, but as a private company it avoids some of the pressure felt by evangelical executives at public firms.[40] Like many other founders, Cathy tries to ensure that his faith commitments will continue with the next generation. His son, Dan, has signed a contract promising to run the company in the same manner as his father, and Cathy has also been a personal mentor to several within the company.

At least a dozen employees at Chick-fil-A headquarters were once part of the Sunday school class Cathy has long taught for junior high boys. One executive, Woody Faulk, got to know the Cathy family after his mother died suddenly in a traffic accident. Cathy recounts an early interaction with Faulk: "He told me one Sunday: 'Mr. Cathy, when I grow up, I want to come work for Chick-fil-A. I don't think I want to operate one of those Chick-fil-A units, but I'd like to have a desk and a secretary like you have.'" While attending the University of Georgia, Faulk lived with the Cathy family. Cathy's evangelical influence has continued through Faulk and others who are now part of the company's executive team, and according to Cathy, "Woody now has a beautiful wife and three adorable children, and he has a desk and secretary."

Chick-fil-A has not always had a faith-oriented corporate culture. Sitting in his Atlanta office, Cathy told me that he established the corporate mission statement in 1983 while the firm was in the midst of a significant downturn. Because Chick-fil-A is privately held, the company does not disclose financial information to the same extent as competitors like Burger King and McDonald's. But what financial information is available shows that Chick-fil-A has posted consecutive annual sales increases since it opened its first chain restaurant in 1967. More remarkable in light of the company's culture is that its free-standing restaurants achieve higher sales per unit than McDonald's and Burger King, even though they are closed on Sundays.

Faith-friendly corporate cultures can be found across industries, and some models have been around for quite some time. For example, Marion W. Wade brought his religious convictions to bear when he founded ServiceMaster in 1929 as a moth-proofing company, and he wanted to make sure the company's distinctive culture did not die with him. So far, Wade's guiding vision has remained. In 1973, the company articulated four company objectives: "to honor God in all we do; to help people develop; to pursue excellence; and to grow profitably."[41] In 1981, C. William Pollard, an evangelical who chairs the board of Wheaton College, was elected president. Under Pollard, the firm continued to grow, and by 1985 it had surpassed $1 billion in revenue. Like other evangelical business leaders on the fourth floor, Pollard told me:

> One of the biggest structural questions that I've tried to influence through my leadership [at ServiceMaster] is to have the firm not only make money, not only serve customers, not only provide employment— all of which are important... but also to be moral communities for the development and shaping of human character.... It's so easy to look at people as just... economic animals. But if you step back and say, "No, we're also in the process of shaping and developing human character," then you get into the whole question of what's right, what's wrong... because [through business] you're touching people in all aspects of life.

The firm's name, ServiceMaster, was chosen to remind employees that they are "serving the master," Jesus Christ. The idea of selecting a name that intentionally draws attention to the firm's faith commitment is not uncommon.[42] Paul Klaassen founded Sunrise Assisted Living, choosing the name from a biblical passage that draws a parallel between the sunrise and Jesus as a coming messiah. Of course, organizational rhetoric is just one dimension of corporate culture, but it can be the first one outsiders encounter. The relative dearth of firms that allude to God in organizational mission statements or employ other forms of faith-oriented rhetoric help Chickfil-A and ServiceMaster stand out. Over the course of my research, I encountered a dozen organizations with explicitly religious language in organizational documents—a significant finding given my predominant focus on large firms. Examples include Ken Larson's Slumberland furniture company in Minneapolis and CNL, an Orlando-based real estate investment company founded by evangelical business leader James Seneff.

Several major companies in recent years have witnessed a culture shift as their chief executives have undergone some form of spiritual transformation. While institutional inertia often inhibits a firm's ability to radically readjust, organizational culture can change quickly if the conditions are right.[43] Mac Tools and Tyson Foods are both headed by executives who have become more committed to their evangelical faith since they took the helm. Early in his tenure atop Mac Tools, John Aden had a spiritual renewal, and shortly thereafter he became convinced of the need to transform both his reputation at work and his company's culture:

> For two and a half years I was John Aden one way, and [after my faith transition I] needed to be John Aden the other way. I needed to figure out how to have that conversation in front of people so that, once and for all, we could just kind of give permission to be different.

He decided to introduce six company values that would emphasize respect for one another, high standards of integrity, and a collaborative environment. These values, while not full of what Aden would call "God talk," were important to him because they were in line with "the way Jesus taught us to live" and, in his words, their introduction represented "the first bold thing I did with my faith." Aden credits the values with transforming the corporate culture at Mac Tools: They have given Aden and his executives, many of whom have since experienced spiritual renewals themselves, "permission, in a nonthreatening way, to really talk about treating each other in a different way without having to navigate the minefield of religion." Aden says the company's structure and morale have improved dramatically, and these adjustments have been accompanied by significant increases in profitability. From losing approximately $10 million per year five years ago, Mac Tools now nets $15 to $20 million in profit. While it is impossible to demonstrate a causal link between the firm's organizational culture and its profitability, it is consistent with the idea that strong cultures are good for business.[44]

John Tyson offers a similar account. After experiencing a spiritual transformation well into his career as Tyson's chief executive, he became convinced of the need to articulate corporate values that might produce a "faith-friendly" workplace. With 120,000 employees, Tyson is the world's largest producer of protein products, and the company's leader acknowledges tensions between his hopes for the company and day-to-day reality: "It doesn't say we *are* a faith-friendly company; it says we *strive* to be a faith-friendly company. And we *strive* to honor God; it doesn't say we *do* honor God."[45] Tyson has hired seventy-seven corporate chaplains and, like many other evangelical business leaders, employs an ordained minister as an executive coach who helps him integrate his faith into the corporate culture. Obviously, many ethical questions surround every business. For Tyson, it's things like the large-scale slaughter of animals, capitalist interests, and working conditions for many low-wage, manual labor jobs. Tyson says his coach, David Miller, helps him when he faces an ethical dilemma.

Since Tyson instituted a set of core values, the degree of turnover has diminished dramatically.[46] Tyson has become the largest meat-processing company in the world, generating $26 billion in annual revenues in 2005. The company's growth has accompanied an adjustment of the firm's corporate culture, which corresponded to changes within the executive suite as John Tyson sought to fashion a more faith-friendly firm. Corporate indicators such as market share, price to book the ratio of the value the market places on the company to its book value, and dividend yield point to the strength of Tyson within the industry. Its CEO attributes such strength to the organization's culture, and informal conversations with a few workers I met while visiting the company's headquarters support his assertion.

Some firms attempting fourth-floor approaches exist principally for evangelical purposes. These include banks where workers pray with customers, as well as a host of other companies that exist to make money for evangelistic outreach and social justice.[47] Greg Newman, a San Francisco venture capitalist, refers to these as "businesstries." One for which he provided start-up funds is a candle company in Thailand that employs women recovering from sexual abuse. The company offers these women—many of whom also receive free counseling from evangelical missionaries—job training and steady employment. Newman told me, "I require that the businesses be for-profit. . . . It motivates the workers . . . and then . . . the profits [are channeled] to support some of the ministries and to start [similar] businesses." Newman's venture is part of a new category for business today, the socially responsible firm. Many of these market-driven firms reinvest profits in local communities that produce the commodities sold or donate profits to philanthropic causes. John Sage, a Harvard-trained executive, founded Pura Vida coffee with the intention of creating a corporate culture that "tried hard to integrate and incorporate our . . . beliefs into the fabric of the workplace." Pura Vida holds weekly devotions with workers and closes staff meetings in prayer, but it exists to assist the poor and to prompt conversations about faith. Sage frames the matter this way:

> What we're trying to do here is to create a relationship with a customer through a fairly simple, straightforward business proposition. Try my coffee, and if you like it and think it's fairly priced, then buy it. . . . The hope is [that this leads the customer to ask], 'Why would a company choose to give its profit away?" . . . Then I feel that permission is being given to share [my] faith and to share [my] conviction . . . about Jesus that compels me to do this. . . . I wouldn't have felt as free to share [that] if someone was just standing there on a street corner.

Like other evangelical business leaders, Sage acknowledges that he "doesn't know what to do" with employees who say the firm's explicitly evangelical ethos "makes them feel a little weird." Tensions like these emerged often in my interviews, particularly at private firms that showed high levels of faith–work integration. Executives also expressed concern about potential hypocrisy. One told me about visiting a printing company in Tulsa where the lobby featured a painting of the CEO with Jesus' hand on his shoulder. "That company was full of backbiting and gossip. . . . It seemed as far away from Jesus as it could be." Concerns like these were voiced often, and many leaders cited them as the reason they choose not to further integrate their evangelical commitments into the workplace.[48]

If a firm reflects fourth-floor characteristics of faith integration, it is safe to assume that it also exemplifies first-, second-, and third-floor characteristics. And while some leaders I talked with suggested that fourth-floor integration should be the goal of every evangelical leader, that is not true for most of the people I interviewed. Many factors, including the company's size, its history, and whether it is public or private, influence how an evangelical executive incorporates his or her faith into the workplace. Evangelicals tend to favor at least some measure of integration, but there is no consensus on what that means or how it's done. CEO Paul Klaassen told me, "I... transition back and forth...like the different dials on my radio." Most often, the integrative task reflects a larger process whereby evangelicals try to relate their different identities—as a parent, a businessperson, and/or a Christian—more closely. One *Fortune* 500 CEO said to me, "God really wants you to be who he made you to be in *all* walks of life. So, while you always have [lapsed] moments, my faith started being lived out not just at church but [also in] the way I behaved at home and...at work." Indeed, evangelicals have re-shaped American corporate life, but it started with individual executives trying to make sense of their lives and the jobs they do.

8

Executive Influence

WHILE WAITING TO INTERVIEW real estate developer Paul John-son, I could not help but notice a large wooden sign looming over his desk. It was a verse from Mark 8, "What shall it profit a man if he shall gain the whole world and lose his own soul?" Johnson told me it has hung over his desk for forty-five years. Often when meeting clients or partners in his office, Johnson said he would seat them, then slip out to check on something with his secretary. "Sometimes I really did need to say something to the secretary, but often, I just stepped out to give them a chance to read the sign and think about it for a minute. [It] let people know where [I] stand. . . . It's a declaration without actually shouting from the rooftop." While such a prominent display of evangelical allegiance is rare in the workplaces I visited, nearly three-quarters of the leaders I interviewed had some kind of object in their office that signaled their evangelical leanings. For many, the presence of these objects is intentional and strategic.[1]

Evangelical business leaders have played important roles in American evangelicalism's growing influence. They have provided much of the financial capital for launching new evangelical initiatives and for sustaining long-term organizations. They also have used their executive roles as a platform for their faith. From the factory floor to the corner office, evangelical executives have brought their faith to bear on a range of decisions, at both the corporate and individual levels. The most common way is by personal example.

Going Public

Evangelical business leaders told me they want to live out their faith in attractive, counterintuitive ways that will pique others' curiosity and allow them to talk about their faith. Some of them shared stories of one-on-one evangelism. Far more often, though, they feel that, in the words of one executive, "it's not a particularly good witness...to be so open about your faith in the workplace that you make people uncomfortable." As a result, most have chosen to invoke their faith subtly. When they are explicit, they tend to be away from the workplace. For many, this represents a form of "coming out," and it is the most common way co-workers learn about their faith. None of the executives I interviewed regretted "going public." It's part of the evangelical mandate to spread the good news.

While many business leaders expressed at least some reluctance to talk explicitly about their faith, particularly in the workplace, they wanted opportunities to show that they were "connected to Christ" or that their faith was important to them. In his office overseeing Epcot in the Walt Disney World complex, Brad Rex has placed several objects that he calls "launchers." These items are designed to evoke questions that allow Rex to talk about the important role faith plays in his life. Many executives displayed a Bible, sometimes more than one. I found them on desks, in bookcases, on coffee tables, and even out in the reception area. Quotations from scripture were found in framed artwork, on paperweights, and on placards of various sizes. And while these artifacts were often intended to evoke questions from newcomers, I learned they also served as reminders to the executives themselves. Lou Giuliano placed a plaque in his office that read "Bidden or not bidden, God is present." Giuliano talked about it with me: "Faith has not always been present in my office...because I grew up working in large corporations...and I learned from day one...that you don't talk about religion." But once he was promoted to chief executive at ITT Industries, he felt freer to display such objects, and the plaque reminds Giuliano of his faith commitment every time he looks at it. Clayton Brown, a Chicago business executive, had a nameplate that sat on his desk for many years. What visitors did not know was that on the back of it was inscribed "Perhaps Today," to remind Brown that "the Lord might come any minute, especially today." This sense of immediacy compelled Brown to "be ready" for Jesus' return by living a life of moral rectitude and by sharing his faith with others.

In addition to the Bible, evangelical business leaders displayed books like *Loving Monday, God Is My CEO,* and *Succeeding in Business Without Losing Your Faith.* When I asked if these books really did start conversations, nearly everyone said that, at the least, the books led to questions from visitors, and more than one said it afforded a chance to "share the gospel." Business leaders also shared their faith by what they wore. More than one female executive reported wearing a gold cross as a way to signal her faith. Tami Heim, the president of Borders, was even more creative. At company head-quarters, all employees wear name tags around their necks. Heim's teenage daughter gave her a lanyard to wear with "WWJD" printed on it. Another senior executive asked Heim about the meaning of the letters. Heim told me that the meeting room then turned to a "hush" while her colleagues waited for her response. Heim told the group it stood for "What Would Jesus Do" and explained, "The reason I've been wearing [it] is my daughter really encouraged me that when I'm faced with anything that may be a difficult decision . . . I just need to always think in terms of how would [Jesus] think about the situation." After that comment, there was "dead silence." Heim says the incident even made it into the public chat rooms on the Yahoo! Finance website. She concludes, "It was the first time that I personally ever felt . . . ostracized for my faith." Nonetheless, she does not regret wearing it or having her faith becoming public.

Evangelicals have also promoted their faith in speeches. Often, these opportunities arise away from the office at business schools, fund-raising dinners, and industry events. Typically, faith is not the core of the speech, but it emerges as a subtext. For example, a group of Silicon Valley executives has given, often free of charge, a series of speeches at business schools around the country.[2] One speaker, John Brandon, a technology executive, says they would never ex-plicitly talk about "Christian things. Instead, [we would address] issues of integrity . . . and then . . . let the discussion and the Q&A go however it goes. . . . But almost always people would say, . . . 'Why are you guys here on your own dime?'" That would then open the door for a discussion about their faith and their desire to inspire a new generation of "faithful" business leaders. Subtly slipping matters of faith into a speech as an aside or in the question-and-answer period appeals to these leaders because it spurs dialogue and is not usually off-putting.

Most evangelical business leaders said that they talk about their faith "a lot . . . when asked," but a few also acknowledged that they have been less forthcoming at times. Many even used the phrase "coming out of the closet." Jerry Colangelo, a longtime sports exec-utive in Phoenix, describes it this way: "I was a closet Christian. . . . The first time I came out and gave a personal testimony . . . it was a difficult thing to do." Bruce Kennedy, head of Alaska Airlines, says, "I was in the closet as a Christian, through my senior vice presi-dent years. When I became president . . . I was drawn back to Fairbanks . . . for a function there. . . . [Upon learning that I would be at the meeting, being held at my home church,] they asked me to speak.... I just was pouring sweat because these were Fairbanks people who knew me.... That was really my coming out of the closet." The desire to be public about one's faith is central to evangelicalism. One executive told me, "I'm very pleased that my relationship with Jesus is not...a hidden part of my life." There are many opportunities like this outside the corporate setting, but there are even more within it. Brad Rex, the Epcot executive, talked about the importance of his faith at a company-wide initiative called "Conversations With." The program provides a two-hour open discussion between a Disney executive and other employees. During the question-and-answer session, Rex talked about the fact that he regularly reads the Bible and is involved at his church. Executives at other firms say they have given invocations before meetings or at the ends of important speeches to signal their evangelical convictions. Lou Giuliano of ITT says it is a matter of free expression—"I always say if I was a transvestite Marxist, they would have no trouble giving me a platform"—so he has become more vocal about his faith in company venues. Others, though, might not view the situation the same way, and prayers that are forced upon people are usually not well received. Inserting scriptural references into speeches is less controversial. As Marc Belton of General Mills said when we talked, "Most of the folks really don't know it's a scripture, but the folks who do...love to hear it."

Executives can also do things that subtly show that faith is important to the boss. Bonnie Wurzbacher of Coca-Cola says she attends a company Bible study as a way of signaling her allegiances and encouraging other believers at work: "They need to feel encouraged.... I can't go every Wednesday, but every Wednesday that I'm here, I go." Archie Dunham, who led ConocoPhillips for many years, regularly attended church on Sunday, even while traveling. Invariably, employees at his firm would hear of it: "They would know if I went to church in Dubai or if I went to church in Singapore.... Somehow that kind of information is spread through informal networks throughout the company." Some executives say their faith became known by what they do *not* do. Dale Jones of Halliburton said "there was a lot of joking" at the company about the fact that he did not drink because of evangelical convictions. Over the years, though, as he rose through the executive ranks, his habit became more accepted and his position less controversial.[3] Jerry Miller, another executive in oil and gas, says when he was at Texaco, he was more known for his faith by what he "didn't do... didn't chase women...didn't run around, didn't do a lot of the things that [others] did." One incident stands out from Miller's career. While on a business trip, his colleagues wanted to go to a place

> where the women serve whatever they serve in [their] underwear.... Everybody got out, and my general manager...said, "Come on." I said,... "I don't go in those kind of places, you know that. Go in. I'll sit here in the car, and I'll be fine. I'll get a newspaper."...Well, of course everybody gets mad....Have you ever tried eating with five guys just as mad as a hornet? We got through eating, and they took me back to the hotel and dumped me off. [Then] they went out and did whatever they did.

Though these acts are informal, word spreads through e-mail, jokes, and even, in a couple of cases, skits at company-wide meetings.

Executives also use the media to talk about faith. Business journals and mainstream media outlets often cover the personal lives of prominent business leaders. National news outlets are paying more attention to the intersection of faith and work, and many evangelical business leaders have been interviewed about their religious commitments. Jose Zeilstra of JPMorgan Chase says, "I don't come to work to evangelize [or] to push my faith," but word spread after she was in a 2001 *Fortune* cover story on faith and the workplace. A similar thing happened to Raytheon's Thomas Phillips: "I had been a quiet Christian up until [the publication of Charles Colson's book] *Born Again.* All of a sudden [people at the company] discovered I was [an evangelical. That's when I] came out of the closet.... From that time on, everyone in the company knew I was a born-again Christian." Today, within evangelical business circles there is subtle pressure to speak out. As one leader told me, "Far too many...are timid. They need to be more outspoken about their faith" in order to encourage other evangelical workers to do the same. Of course, many lower-level workers cannot "come out" the way executives do because they are not public figures.

Lifestyle and Faith

More than any other topic, money occupies a central place in the teachings of Jesus. American evangelicals are ambivalent about money, particularly the wealthy evangelicals I interviewed.[4] Over the course of the four gospels, Jesus casts moneychangers out of the temple, tells a rich man to sell all of his possessions, and declares it is easier for a camel to pass through the eye of a needle than for a rich man to enter heaven. Yet He also praises one woman's extravagance and reprimands His disciples for scolding her, declaring that poverty will never be abolished. In some parts of the Bible, the greedy are harshly punished, yet in others they are commended as wise stewards. Riches are sometimes presented as divine gifts, but in other contexts they are encumbrances to one's faith. And many passages of the Bible refer to extravagantly decorated places of worship—from the bejeweled temple built by Solomon to a "New Jerusalem" paved with streets of gold. The Bible exhorts adherents to be diligent with money, but it also admonishes them not to worry about money. Is it any wonder that evangelicals hold contradictory positions on the subject?

A handful of evangelical business leaders see wealth as a resource to benefit society, not the individual. As Curtis McWilliams, an executive in Orlando, said, "God hasn't given us affluence so that we can have a lot of material comfort." In 1998, David Grizzle, a senior executive at Continental Airlines, negotiated a successful deal between Continental and Northwest Airlines. Grizzle received a significant bonus, but he decided to donate it all to charity. That caught the attention of others and inspired several fellow executives to follow suit. In all, Continental executives donated $7 million out of their bonuses from this deal to charitable causes. When I asked Grizzle about the decision, he said that it emerged from a desire to avoid the materialism "trap" that "ensnares" some business leaders: "We live at a significantly lower lifestyle than our income would afford; in fact, sometimes a confusingly lower lifestyle. People don't quite understand why we live in a very small townhouse and drive old cars." Similarly, Ralph Larsen and his wife decided they wanted to live a "very normal, low-key life" as he rose up through the ranks at Johnson & Johnson. They decided not to move to a bigger house or a better neighborhood, even though it meant he would not be able to entertain at home like other CEOs. One day, their eight-year-old son came home from school with an unusual story, which Larsen told me:

> His teacher had given him a copy of *Business Week*, where they had published all the [salaries of CEOs]....The teacher stupidly said, "Garrett, look how much money your dad makes." And he, of course, knew nothing. He [was getting] a dollar a week allowance. He said, "Daddy, she asked me what we did with ... all the money.... I told her we gave most of it away. Don't we?" And I said, "Yes, well, we give a lot of it away." But he was really embarrassed.

I heard numerous stories like this. Several said they feel like outsiders among other executives. In the words of Bruce Kennedy, "I
was an outsider because I don't golf, I don't have a big boat, I don't
go off for the month of August on vacation. The materialistic
things...are a turnoff to me....I'm identified as a Christian, and
[as such] I'm not one of the boys." Most claim they don't miss the
big-ticket items they choose not to purchase but say that the social
isolation does take a significant toll on them.

Joel Manby, who once ran Saab USA, says that today "I drive a
Saturn. I'd rather spend $20,000 and give the $30,000 away than
spend $50,000 on a Saab.... Also, we could afford a second home,
[but] with all these people that...are homeless, I just don't feel right
about that. I'm not saying it's wrong; a lot of people do it, and they
can do what they want, but I'd rather do Habitat for Humanity where
I'm building second homes [rather] than living in one." But within
evangelicalism there is little social pressure to curb materialistic tendencies. At gatherings of wealthy evangelical donors that I attended,
organizers went out of their way to say that they were not the lifestyle
"police" who would enforce standards on others. These gatherings
often included testimonials by people who sought to live a more ascetic lifestyle, but they usually were followed by people who gave the
opposite message.[5] Indeed, evangelical emphasis on the individual
undergirds all discussions about money. One person may, in good
faith, purchase an airplane while another may consider that out of
bounds. At one conference for wealthy evangelical donors, I observed
one of the wealthiest in attendance collecting extra commemorative
gifts left on the tables after the session ended. In response to my observing his action, the donor said, "I can reuse these for the rest of the
year. We can't let them go to waste." That donor is also known to ad-
monish other wealthy evangelicals not to purchase second or third
homes, lest they become "distractions" in their spiritual lives.[6]

More prevalent among the evangelical business elite is the view
that material resources are blessings from God to be enjoyed. Of
course, there are generally accepted norms, and conspicuous consumption is largely frowned upon.[7] But most executives I encountered tend to bracket off their faith from decisions about purchases.
Instead, they focus on faith's implications for production, like hours
worked and career fields, or philanthropy. Evangelical executives
tend to accept the material accoutrements of an affluent lifestyle
without question. As CEO Richard Stearns described his life while
leading Lenox China, "We were living on five acres in a ten-bedroom
house.... We were not interacting with the poor.... You get to this
echelon of business, and you travel to London, Paris, Milan, and

Venice on business. I was a jet-setter, going to black-tie banquets and . . . parties in New York with limousines. . . . That was my life." For many, their generosity justified their wealth. Few talked about income inequality, and when I asked why they have been blessed with more material resources, most were reluctant to answer. As Tom Morgan said, "We're not all going to be blessed equally. I don't know how God makes those decisions."

"Balance" is a term many affluent evangelicals cite as a guiding principle. Jeff Comment, CEO of Helzberg Diamonds, said, "I like to look at everything in life as a balance. . . . There's nothing wrong, in my opinion as a Christian, to be attractively dressed and to have attractive jewelry as long as it's all done in balance." In general, evangelical business leaders justify their wealth by citing "balance" and "philanthropy," saying it compensates for any selfish material-ism they exhibit. But when asked directly, they do not express feelings of guilt or unease about their affluence. It is instead seen as a "gift from God" that they are expected to steward responsibly.[8]

Against this backdrop, those evangelical executives who pursue a more ascetic lifestyle really stand out. They differ not only from their financial peers but also from their fellow evangelicals. This was one of the most powerful demonstrations of evangelical faith I en-countered among business leaders. Though they never trumpeted their frugality, when I asked about it, they showed a passionate com-mitment to financial moderation. While not all of their motivations were faith-oriented, many were. And because this ascetic lifestyle was rare, it was all the more striking.

Many of the activities I've discussed are unique to the world of business executives. Even though they claim to be modeling behav-ior for their employees, few workers would have the chance to talk publicly about their faith to the news media, and few company blogs would chronicle the church attendance of the receptionist. These are unique ways of promulgating the faith. Yet they do demonstrate how the large-scale initiatives discussed in the previous chapter play out at the individual level, as motivated executives look for creative ways to bring their faith into the workplace. These two tributaries have flowed together, creating a wider stream of evangelical influ-ence within the American business sector.

The Fulcrum of Evangelical Influence

Evangelical business leaders have taken active roles as founders, directors, and funders of programs that blend business sensibilities with evangelical fervor. Most of these are outside traditional church settings and operate instead through special-purpose organizations known as parachurches.[9] Their efforts have been so successful that the movement's center of gravity today is not found at the level of the local congregation. Instead, evangelical business leaders, working with entrepreneurial ministers, have organized the movement around a constellation of parachurch organizations with national constituencies and organizational practices that resemble, in many ways, modern corporations.

By 1976, hundreds of parachurch groups existed within the evangelical orbit, and several dozen were headed by movement leaders recognized by the general public. Successful business executives like J. Howard Pew of Sun Oil Company and George Bennett of State Street Investment Corporation provided significant financial support for entities like *Christianity Today*, Wheaton College, and the Billy Graham Evangelistic Association.[10] They also provided institutional leadership for these groups, serving as board members and public advocates. So from the early days of modern American evangelicalism, business leaders found a home in the parachurch. This was a place where business leaders could exert significant influence in ways that matched their lifestyles: short, intensive board meetings over a few days several times a year instead of weekly church board meetings. They also felt more comfortable in the parachurch's corporate environment, where decision-making was quick and centralized compared to the deliberative, democratic process that typified many church boards. Also and perhaps most important, whereas a church board may have included only one major corporate leader among its many members, corporate icons populated many parachurch boards. Within this sector of the evangelical movement, business leaders worked alongside their social and professional peers—something they rarely had the opportunity to do in church settings. This, it turns out, created informal networks of friendship and camaraderie that further strengthened the bond between evangelical executives and these institutions.

As one who has interviewed some of the "first generation" (roughly 1942 to 1976) leaders of the evangelical movement, I notice some important differences between them and the leaders who have emerged in more recent decades. First, many "second generation" leaders feel distant from their own churches and suggest that before the 1970s this gulf was not as wide as it is today. They are not active in the local church but instead focus on the parachurch sector, where active involvement remains. Technology explains some of this. Personal computers and digital technology have connected us in ways that used to be limited to personal, local interactions. As one leader put it to me, "I have deeper relations with fellow board members at [an evangelical ministry] than I do with anyone at my home church. We live in the same world and face the same problems. I relate to nobody at my church in that way." The key, according to him, involves instant communication, even if they meet face-to-face only a few times a year. In fact, jet travel, satellite technology, and the Internet have enabled the parachurch sector to draw national constituencies into closer contact with one another, especially among the movement's leadership. In the aggregate, these developments have fostered deeper ties between evangelical business leaders and the parachurch organizations for which they are directors and financial backers.

Why and how have so many evangelical business leaders come to feel estranged from the local congregations they regularly attend? Many talked about their pastors being completely removed from the working world they inhabit. As Max De Pree told me, "We business types talk a lot about the fact that in the church we get no help at all with our problems,...no sympathy,...no understanding....The pastors know nothing" about life inside a firm. They blame ministers for preaching irrelevant sermons that fail to connect with the challenges faced by business leaders today. Several reported inviting their pastors to their workplaces to help them learn about the working environments of their parishioners. With one exception— nearly forty years ago—not a single pastor had taken them up on their offer. Nationally, only 20 percent of church members report talking about their work with a member of the clergy in the past year.[11] At several gatherings of evangelical pastors and business leaders, I found similar results. Ministers who did seek to address workplace concerns tended to speak in vague generalities about ethics, morality, and the validity of a "calling" to business, while most executives I interviewed wanted straightforward, concrete, and pragmatic counsel. In none of these complaints about the clergy being out of touch did executives acknowledge that they, too, are removed from the concerns of average people. Blind spots like these were common among the executives I interviewed.

Although the general trend among leaders I interviewed is an overall distance from local church life, there are some exceptional cases. For example, evangelical executives praised the workplace ministries in congregations like Menlo Park Presbyterian Church in Silicon Valley and Park Street Church in Boston. Of particular note is the number of business executives involved with the Center for Faith and Work at Redeemer Presbyterian Church in Manhattan, headed by former technology CEO Katherine Leary. When I interviewed Leary, she told me that she hoped that the center would "spin off" various "manifestations" of businesses run by members who wanted to integrate their faith with their work. She said:

> One of my ideas...in our ten-year plan is that we create an incubator...[a] classic venture capitalist–style incubator, and pick two to three ventures a year that we nurture and support and provide, not a lot of financial backing, but a lot of support from within the congregation, in the areas of expertise that they have that can then enable those ventures to go. [These ventures would be separate from the church]....Maybe we'll have a board seat, but what we're doing is we're impacting the culture by helping people think through their venture ideas and being able to launch them soundly....If we could spawn five or ten [businesses or initiatives that would influence] the city we live in, that would be a phenomenal achievement.

Such direct involvement in business activity is rare at the local church level, yet it received nearly unanimous praise from people I interviewed who are familiar with the idea.

Churches have also criticized executives and their firms. Epcot executive Brad Rex said that when the Southern Baptist Convention boycotted Disney, the position of his denomination "set back [his outreach] efforts tremendously" at work, and other executives reported similar problems.[12] More common, though, were tensions between the evangelical executive and a particular pastor. Some leaders I talked to reported feeling "used" by their pastor, claiming that their minister exploited their affiliation with the church as a form of self-affirmation. As one successful CEO saw it, his church affiliation "was a bit of a feather in the church's cap." Others said pastors can be "very judgmental and critical of the business world," which had contributed to "a huge disconnect" between the church and marketplace leaders. When Ralph Larsen was CEO of Johnson & Johnson, his family attended a small church in northern New Jersey. Larsen said his status as an executive made the preacher "very uncomfortable," and one Sunday the sermon seemed particularly directed at Larsen: The pastor "gave a bombastic message on executives who travel on private planes and have big offices and drivers. I was the only [executive] in the church....Everybody understood [it was directed to me]." Such pointed interactions were the exception, but dozens of evangelical business leaders spoke of ongoing tensions with their ministers, and nearly all attributed them to personal insecurity on the part of the pastors or a general inability to lead congregations that included recognized business leaders.

Evangelical executives often had trouble serving in positions of responsibility in a church. James Unruh, who served as the chief executive of Unisys, also served at one time as an elder within his congregation. He has decided he will never serve again. Like other business leaders, the inefficiency of church meetings was too frustrating for Unruh. He said to me, "For most of the people, the biggest event of the month is coming to that meeting.... It's very frustrating to be patient and not to try to run things because that's what you're doing all day in your business." Nearly all the leaders I spoke to mentioned tension or distance between them and their local church.

But there are noteworthy exceptions. Chief among them are places like Chicago's Willow Creek Community Church. Several leaders said they admire the church and its senior pastor, Bill Hybels. "We both come from business backgrounds; we both think in a business way.... We bring that to the Christian community, and Bill has had a tremendous impact on me to bring that gift to the church," said Dick DeVos, a Michigan business leader. Like other megachurches, Willow Creek effuses a corporate professionalism and has followed business models for growth and expansion, something that is attractive to business leaders. With weekly attendance exceeding twenty thousand, Willow Creek has become a cultural phenomenon within the evangelical world, thanks, in part, to its Willow Creek Association (WCA), which links "like-minded, action-oriented churches with each other and with strategic vision, training, and resources." With a network of eleven thousand congregations, the WCA eclipses many denominational bodies in the United States, and with member churches from forty-five countries, its influence reaches around the world.[13]

In 1984, media mogul Bob Buford founded Leadership Network. Disappointed by the poor leadership he observed at the local church level, Buford sought to improve the level of pastoral leadership and organizational innovation in local congregations. Although committed to local church life, Buford's organization is representative of business leaders' preference for parachurch groups, where organizational practices mirror the corporate worlds in which they work. Buford's influence on American evangelicalism is pervasive; fully one in five (20 percent) of the people I interviewed mentioned him as an important influence in their lives. Buford's goal is to transform what he calls the "latent energy" of American Christianity into "active energy." Like other business leaders I met, Buford has little interest in working with pastors of congregations that are of average size and scope; he wants only to "build on the islands of health and strength." In essence, this means he and Leadership Network favor innovative church leaders whose personal styles resemble those of corporate CEOs. When we talked in Dallas, Buford said to me, "I only deal with people who are receptive to what [we're] trying to do, which in our case is to connect innovators to multiply—a lot of people aren't receptive to that." Leadership Network supports local churches by connecting pastors and lay church leaders so they can exchange ideas about local church life. The Leadership Network events I have observed resemble corporate strategy sessions. Even the rhetoric of the organization exhibits a professionalized corporatism: "The DNA of Leadership Network is the diffusion of innovation . . . [to] accelerate the effectiveness of the church by identifying, connecting, and resourcing strategic leaders." Although Buford, echoing the mantra of his mentor Peter Drucker, insists that the church should be less like a business and more like a church focused on its mission, one cannot miss the businesslike ethos of Leadership Network events. Buford and his organization have created a plausibility structure for innovation within the evangelical world that encourages the exploration of new ideas for "doing" church. Many of the practices at megachurches that have attracted attention—from marketing campaigns to creative programming for newcomers—can be traced to the work of Leadership Network. Also, Buford's philanthropic support for the evangelical movement has been substantial. He told me he intended "to reinvest in the work of God's kingdom" with the "exact amount of money" that he made in business, which is estimated to be in the hundreds of millions of dollars.[14]

By Invitation Only

In 1978, Southern Baptist businessman Howard E. Butt Jr. convened the North American Congress of the Laity with former president Gerald Ford as honorary chairman. His goal was to encourage lay leaders to bring their faith to bear on their respective spheres of influence.[15] About ten years later, Butt and his Laity Renewal Foundation hosted a similar gathering, the Laity Lodge Leadership Forum, to which only senior business leaders were invited. It has met regularly ever since and is one of the most exclusive gatherings for evangelical business leaders today. Leaders participate in small-group sessions in which they are asked to explain how they draw on their faith in their jobs. Participants say they come back to each forum because of the high levels of discussion among "interesting people" about "a sense of Christian distinctiveness in the way we exercise our leadership." Typically, a minister addresses the group a couple of times over the multiday conference, and business executives, along with their spouses, participate in large-group presentations and small-group discussions. This is just one of a host of similar groups.[16] At these gatherings, topics range from litigation threats to corporate downsizing to family concerns and executive burnout. Some organizations are targeted toward particular demographic groups like younger professionals, or "emerging leaders."[17] Others are geographically centered. The New Canaan Society, a weekly men's group, meets outside of Manhattan in New Canaan, Connecticut, and Time OUT, an annual conference for men executives, meets in Silicon Valley.[18] Indeed, among most of these groups, women are rarely found, and while organizers say that men-only gatherings encourage openness, many women executives say they limit their access to interpersonal networks. Nearly all of these gatherings are by invitation only, and these invitations come largely through networks of personal friendship, not business dealings or church involvement. Even as specialized parachurch groups have been formed in recent decades, other large parachurch groups have initiated programs for business executives. These are on the rise as well.

One of the earliest large ministries to sponsor such programs was Campus Crusade for Christ. The history of different programs within Campus Crusade is indicative of a wider trend of declining exclusivity. Groups that start out exclusive gradually lower the standards required for admission. For example, Arthur S. DeMoss and his wife, Nancy, sponsored exclusive dinner parties through an arm of Campus Crusade called Executive Ministries. A wealthy couple would host a dinner party at their home or at a private club where they were members. Professional and social peers would be invited. The dinner party would include a talk by a well-known business executive or celebrity sharing his or her evangelical faith. Then, at the end of the evening, participants would be invited to "receive Jesus Christ" and asked to complete a card for follow-up. According to organizational documents, 30 to 40 percent of attendees either made a faith commitment at the dinner or requested more information through the follow-up program. In the 1970s and 1980s, this reached a very exclusive circle of the upper strata. During the late 1990s, though, ministry executives began to realize that they were not reaching the same level of society, so in 2000 they launched a ministry that is now called Impact XXI. Targeted toward the hundred most influential individuals in each of the country's 100 largest cities, the ministry sponsors exclusive events to which evangelical leaders bring a peer who is not an evangelical. These events, according to the ministry's leader, are "things you cannot buy" like visiting a nuclear aircraft carrier in the middle of war games or attending NASCAR training events.[19] During these events, which typically last less than twenty-four hours, Impact XXI will host a "low-key" chapel service and distribute evangelical literature like autographed copies of Rick Warren's *The Purpose-Driven Life*, reflecting what one participant called a "softer sell."

This has been the trajectory of other groups I encountered, such as the First Tuesday Club in Boston. Organized by Raytheon CEO Tom Phillips, it has met, for more than thirty years, on the first Tuesday of every month at the Weston Golf Club in suburban Boston. The group was designed as an evangelical outreach to top civic and business leaders in the area and, according to Phillips, was limited to people of similar economic and organizational "standing." He saw it as a way of fostering an environment of mutual trust and camaraderie. "I kept it with peers.... That was the strategy." Although the group originally focused only on chief executives—"we had a very impressive list in the beginning," says Phillips—it now is directed toward anyone at an executive level. Today, professionals like lawyers, surgeons, and even some ministers participate in the First Tuesday group. Of course, it remains exclusive, and invitations are still difficult to obtain. But in its desire to reach out to younger leaders, it has lowered the bar for admission.

A few groups continue to reach a "very upper slice" of participants. A group of senior executives led by Doug Holladay, a Washington insider and business leader, meets once a month at New York's Links Club for discussion and prayer. About twenty-five individuals are on the invitation list, but only a dozen or so attend regularly. According to participants—none of whom wished to be identified—the group includes devout evangelicals as well as spiritual seekers. As one attendee described the gathering, it is "very low-key," and according to my research, it is the most exclusive regular evangelical fellowship group in the country.

Of similar scope but with a broader reach is the CEO Forum, a parachurch group formed in 1996 as a ministry outreach to chief executives at large firms, generally with annual revenues exceeding $100 million. The CEO Forum is led by Mac McQuiston, who used to raise funds for the evangelical behemoth Focus on the Family.[20]

Now McQuiston spends most of his time organizing biannual, day-long conferences for CEOs and meeting with them, either in person or on the telephone, to discuss spiritual concerns. Many evangelical executives describe McQuiston as a chaplain to the CEO community, and today more than 150 chief executives participate in the CEO Forum. ITT's Lou Giuliano told me, "The forum . . . allowed me to work with my schedule to be engaged in a [spiritual] way that I never had. . . . It introduced me to a whole universe of people and organizations that I have found helpful." Indeed, more than a dozen leaders I interviewed are members of the CEO Forum, and nearly all said this parachurch group had been more important to their personal spiritual journey than their own churches. Participants say that the programs are time "well spent" and that the format of short, intensive seminars followed by monthly conference calls meshes with their schedules and lifestyles. Although the group is now a separate entity, CEO Forum was originally sponsored by Focus on the Family, and several participants said they were uncomfortable with the political overtones of the group. For example, in 2004 members were called by ministry officials and urged to throw their political weight behind the federal marriage amendment. Several people said they did not appreciate this, suggesting the forum had lost a measure of trust it had earned over the years.

No one has adequately explained why these groups have been vital to the movement's rising visibility.[21] The parachurch sector has become the fulcrum of evangelical influence in American society.[22] More than any other group, business executives have been the principal agents of change—as donors, directors, and leaders. Within this sector of the movement, business leaders have found an arena that both matches their ambitious agenda and allows them to contribute in a way that suits their strengths. Over time, this match between institutional needs and what these business leaders can offer has generated significant loyalties. And this sector has become a key portal through which nonevangelical elites have encountered the evangelical world, as evangelical executives introduce their secular peers to initiatives sponsored by the organizations they direct. Over the last thirty years, there has been a flowering of parachurch groups targeted toward business leaders, and I find that the nation's most influential evangelical business leaders—the highest-ranked corporate executives—favor these groups for their own spiritual journeys.[23] This has generated more positive sentiment toward American evangelicalism among pockets of the nation's elite, giving much-needed legitimacy to the wider movement.

Philanthropy as Strategic Investment

Evangelicalism could not be the social movement it is today without the intentional patronage of a number of sympathetic donors and private foundations. However, until recently little has been known about evangelical donors—their motivations, their expectations, and their goals. This is important to explore as evangelicals have prospered financially and have become significantly more active within the business community since the 1970s.[24] Of the 101 business executives interviewed for this study, I was able to obtain data on the annual giving of 84 leaders. I asked a variety of questions regarding their philanthropy, including its beneficiaries and the methods and frequency with which donations are made, as well as their motivation and personal philosophy for philanthropy. I also asked them to provide their total annual giving to evangelical causes, on the condition that such data would not be attributed to them directly.[25] Some were unwilling to specify exact amounts, but most were willing to disclose—at the least—if it was five, six, seven, or eight figures. If I was unable to obtain further information, I used minimum estimates, e.g., $100,000 for a six-figure estimate of annual giving.[26] In addition, I reviewed the tax documents and annual reports of many evangelical organizations, and from that data and interviews conducted with heads of evangelical ministries and pastors, I was able to get a good sense of the annual personal giving of business leaders (not including any corporate philanthropy). The average among them is $1.7 million per year, and in all they contribute over $143 million to various evangelical causes in any given year. The largest annual giving amount I encountered was $15 million, and the smallest amount was $30,000. For evangelicals, philanthropy is an obligation of their faith, and the most common benchmark that guides the amount of their giving is the tithe, a concept from the Old Testament, in which the Hebrew people are instructed to give away 10 percent of their income. It is therefore not surprising that evangelical business leaders associate their philanthropy with tithing. And compared to other sectors of elite society, evangelical leaders appear to be more generous with their wealth.[27] Within the evangelical tradition, philanthropy is seen not only as assistance for the poor but also as a way of enriching one's spiritual life by channeling money away from vices like pride and selfishness. Yet, upon closer examination, it appears that tithing is merely a metaphor. Financial giving for these leaders is not about charity or philanthropy per se. Instead, they regard their charitable giving as "strategic investment." As one evangelical business leader put it, "My philanthropy is not about doing good; it's strategic stewardship."

Observers of evangelical philanthropy note a rising sophistication on the part of many donors. Several now demand measurable benchmarks in exchange for their philanthropic investment. This professionalization of the philanthropic world has occurred in other spheres, as notions of "charity" were replaced by "philanthropy," and eventually "investment." Annual strategic philanthropy conferences have spurred a professionalization of evangelical giving, and almost all of this has developed within the last twenty years. As is the case in other religious traditions, the wealthiest evangelicals give the largest percentage of total dollars: The top 5 percent of all evangelical donors give 51 percent of all charitable dollars given by evangelicals.[28]

Within the evangelical world, a number of organizations and initiatives have been launched to assist donors with their strategic philanthropy. These include conferences such as the Gathering and Generous Giving as well as evangelically oriented community foundations, with donor-advised funds, such as the National Christian Foundation (NCF) of Atlanta.[29] NCF was founded in 1982, and that year its total assets under management were $75,344. It grew slowly in subsequent years, but in the late 1990s the foundation undertook a concerted effort to increase the number of donors channeling their philanthropy through NCF. This also coincided, say informed sources, with a dramatic rise in the number of evangelical families with significant assets to manage due to the financial boom of the 1990s. Between 1999 and 2003, over $58 million was added to the foundation's total assets under management, and it has become one of the nation's largest donor-advised funds—among the top ten U.S. foundations in terms of annual grant distributions. To date, NCF has already distributed $1 billion in grants to various Christian causes. Based on its current projected growth, the foundation expects to be distributing $1 billion annually sometime between 2012 and 2014.[30]

Bob Buford, the founder of Leadership Network, hosted a series of conferences in the 1980s around the subject of strategic or venture philanthropy for evangelicals, and many donors said these were formative to their own philosophies of giving. Dick DeVos of Grand Rapids said, "It was probably the most profound experience in ... reawakening my spiritual energy" on the subject, and many other attendees had similar things to say. Buford himself likened these conferences, where he sought to bring together interested donors and organizations in need of additional funding, to the transcontinental railway: "I'm in the middle [and am] going to drive a golden spike that unites the two." The net result of these meetings and the organizations they have birthed has been the corporatization of evangelical giving. Some, however, are critical of this development, saying it has distanced the donor from the act of giving and the actual people who benefit. Several observers criticize the conferences, which are more like a "country club" than a religious retreat. Often hosted at five-star hotels and resorts, the meetings can involve lavish expenditures in which donors "buy" the opportunity to interact with prominent pastors in a luxurious environment. As one person told me, "It is creating an elite, gated community of the soul."

Drew Ladner, a business leader, says many evangelical executives "use the fact that they've got money and put a spiritual veneer over it." At parachurch gatherings they attend, these executives use religious language "to have...a good time with their wealth [and to] feel better about [spending so much money] on themselves." Having attended some of these meetings, I certainly understand this critique. However, organizers regard these types of gatherings as extensions of, not departures from, the privileged worlds that participants inhabit. Elite philanthropy remains different from the charitable benevolence of average people. While they share the same faith convictions, the different ways they carry out their giving reflect a host of factors, not the least of which is their social position.

Historically, at evangelical churches around the country, the president of the local bank would worship alongside schoolteachers, accountants, and city workers. Now, some of the wealthiest evangelicals prefer parachurch groups to local churches. And because this sector has expanded so significantly in recent years, it is possible for an evangelical business leader to be religiously active for years without interacting with a poor person in a religious setting.[31] Top business leaders can stay among professional peers for their religious lives as well as other parts of their lives.

This stratification has furthered the social isolation of evangelical executives. As Gayle Miller, who presided over Anne Klein II, said, "The executive suite is the loneliest place...because you cannot trust anyone, because you can't take anyone into your confidence." Others say this feeling of isolation—not just at work but at church and in other social settings—contributes to emotional distance for many executives. It's a tough cycle to break because this, in turn, keeps them from knowing about needs in their local community or even their own churches—needs they could address if only they were aware of them. Nearly everyone I interviewed expressed a desire to "make a difference" in the lives of other people. How can they do this if they lose contact with the very neighbors who may need them most? The night before our interview, Dick DeVos met with his small group from church. One couple in the group was struggling financially, while DeVos comes from a family that *Forbes* estimates has a net worth of around $3 billion. He described what he gets from being involved with this young couple:

> Their experiences are very different than ours, . . . but I think through the interaction . . . we are reminded of the reality of life that this couple is struggling with, a reality that we don't confront every day. Through our being there, they're [reminded] that money does not solve your problems, that issues do not go away because you have money. . . . They're merely replaced by other challenges and other responsibilities that become part of your life.

DeVos offered to be of help to the younger couple, and while he would not tell me exactly what that entailed, he noted the importance of his church involvement in keeping him in touch with such struggles. Such local personal involvement with the poor was relatively rare among the executives I interviewed.

The strategic philanthropy of public leaders is important to them principally because of its symbolism. Philanthropy dramatizes commitment, manifesting deeply held notions about humanity, society, and the moral order of the universe. Because of the size of their gifts, evangelical business leaders are prominent actors in the drama of American philanthropy. And within this drama, the character of the steward figures prominently. Whereas most Americans rarely talk about money in terms of stewardship, nearly all the leaders I interviewed view their financial situation through that lens.[32] What precisely that means, of course, varies from person to person. For some, it sanctions their wealth by suggesting that their money is really from God, and they are simply being charged with managing it for a time. For others, being a steward compels them to give away sums of money. As ServiceMaster CEO Bill Pollard said, "My philosophical starting point . . . is . . . God owns everything, including . . . our life and livelihood." The proper response, he feels, is to acknowledge that reality regularly through giving a portion back to God, which usually involves philanthropy to evangelical causes and groups. Scores of wealthy evangelicals said they "cannot outgive God" as they have tried to reduce their net worth through their philanthropy. Wallace Hawley captured this sentiment:

> One of the things I'm wrestling with...is how do I reduce my net
> worth?...I'm not saying how can I spend more; [I mean] giving more.
> [As] they say, "You can't outgive God." It's true. I haven't been able to
> outgive God. [My] net worth is going up, and...I need [it] to go
> the other way and go down. I don't want to stand up there in front of
> the Lord and say, "I gave right on up to the limit of the tax code,"
> because I think he's going to say, "That's funny, I don't remember the
> tax code being in the scripture."

Executives are aware of the symbolism of their philanthropy, and
several said their secular peers know about their giving and regard
it as somewhat "goofy [and] unusual. It makes no sense to [them]."
Yet none expressed a desire to diminish giving, and most have specific, ambitious plans to increase giving in the years ahead.

A related element of philanthropy's symbolic power involves financial scandal, which can be quite damaging. The evangelical movement has been the site of several noteworthy scandals in recent
decades. Among these are ones orchestrated by Jim Bakker with the
PTL Club in the 1980s and Jack Bennett with the Foundation for
New Era Philanthropy in the 1990s. These scandals have significantly eroded public confidence in certain pockets of American
evangelicalism—so much so that several dozen people I interviewed
mentioned them when discussing their attitudes toward money and
giving. This has also contributed to the rise of financial "watchdog"
groups within American evangelicalism.[33]

The symbolic nature of this strategic philanthropy extends even to
how wealthy evangelicals manage their money. Of particular interest is the development of faith-based financial management. At the
rank-and-file level, financial management seminars sponsored by
groups like the Willow Creek Association, Good Sense, and Crown
Financial Ministries have become regular parts of evangelical congregations. Ronald Blue, one of the earliest evangelical financial
planners, now trains other financial planners to help clients integrate their faith with their investing practices through an organization called Christian Financial Planners Network. But faith-inspired
financial planning is not just the province of specialty organizations.
Mary King, a Harvard-educated evangelical, is a financial planner
who specializes in socially responsible investing, avoiding "sin" industries like tobacco and alcohol. Working out of Merrill Lynch's
Beverly Hills office, King advises a select group of clients, most of
whom prefer investments that are not at odds with their faith. Although less than half of evangelicals say their religious beliefs greatly
influence their investing, a number of executives I interviewed

expressed a strong desire to integrate faith into their investing practices.[34] As one executive put it colorfully, "Money is like manure; it's no good unless it's spread around in the right places and it makes things grow."

Evangelical philanthropy has been critical to the prominent role played by business leaders within the movement because much of their giving has been directed toward the parachurch groups that grow the movement.[35] Few leaders mentioned their local church as the principal recipient of their giving. When asked why, most expressed concern over their money "flooding" the local congregation, with its small budget and constituency. Additionally, evangelical business leaders say it is more "exciting" to give to parachurch groups because "they're more entrepreneurial, . . . they're better managed, and they're not spending the majority of their time 'playing church,' which looks trivial and repetitive." There is a long history of evangelical executives giving to the parachurch sector.[36] Wealthy bankers funded Charles Finney's crusading mission in the nineteenth century, and business tycoons like Sid Richardson funded Billy Graham early in his ministry. Today, evangelical philanthropists like Roberta and Howard Ahmanson and Hugh Maclellan support numerous parachurch initiatives. What unites their philanthropic efforts is a desire to initiate change within the evangelical community and the broader American society. When I asked Roberta Ahmanson what she would do if she were able to change the world and the evangelical community, she replied directly: "What we're doing."

CONCLUSION: MOVE-THE-DIAL
CHRISTIANITY

WE HAVE SEEN THAT THE EVANGELICAL MOVEMENT has advanced in so many ways that it now wields power in just about every segment of American society. A movement that was once relegated to the "disadvantaged ranks of the stratification system," evangelicalism has since advanced into much higher circles in a remarkably short time.[1] Evangelical leaders have gained access to powerful social institutions—the U.S. military, large corporations, and many others—and because their religious identities are so important to them, they have brought faith to bear on their leadership, changing the very institutions they lead in the process. How have they done it? And what does it mean, for them and for the country?

The New Evangelical Elite

Two major streams of activity—the *institutional* and the *expressive*—have facilitated evangelicalism's advance. Evangelicals have spent the last thirty years building and strengthening an array of organizations focused on transforming the cultural mainstream. They have generated new ways to talk about the relevance of faith in public life, which has further motivated them to action.

Not only has this buttressed the movement's subculture, but it has also allowed evangelicals from different sectors of society to join together and influence major institutions like Congress and the White House. Over the last thirty years, U.S. presidents have appointed evangelicals to high office. Working at both grassroots and elite levels, evangelicals have formed powerful coalitions around issues as diverse as human trafficking and same-sex marriages. Evangelicals have been active in both parties, increasing their influence across administrations. And evangelicals in government have enlisted the help of fellow believers in other areas like

Hollywood and Wall Street to bring about their vision for a moral society.

Evangelicals have been particularly active in higher education. Within the academy, evangelicals have established networks that link students and scholars as well as professors and people in the pew. As beneficiaries of the Pew Younger Scholars Program and the Harvey Fellows, promising evangelical students have been given an upper hand in gaining admission to major universities. They have also created communities of evangelicals at places like Duke and Stanford, allowing students who share faith convictions to benefit from a supportive environment. By the same token, evangelicals founded and expanded educational initiatives to raise both the intellectual horizons of the larger movement (through journals like *Books & Culture*) and the scholarly possibilities for evangelical academics (through special programs at universities including Yale and the University of Virginia).

At the same time, evangelicals have not forgotten the importance of the arts and entertainment. They have founded institutions and supportive networks within the heart of mainstream culture—Hollywood and Manhattan. Programs like Act One and the International Arts Movement have not only helped newcomers pursue careers in the culture-producing fields, but they have also drawn in seasoned professionals as mentors. At the same time, evangelicals have maintained a robust, creative, and productive subculture with profitable music and publishing industries.

In the world of business, evangelical executives have focused their energies on building corporate cultures amenable to people of faith. To differing degrees—what I referred to as "floors of integration"—these executives have built workplaces where faith is no longer taboo. With President Clinton's 1997 executive order that sanctioned religious expression in the federal workplace, it became acceptable for large publicly held companies to introduce religion at work. This was a pivotal event, for now faith came to work in ways that it previously had only at privately held companies. Evangelicals capitalized on this policy change, and the American workplace has been forever changed. They have formed faith-based groups where evangelicals can pray and study scripture in the workplace. Executives now feel more comfortable incorporating prayer into business activities, such as offering an invocation before a board meeting. Ordained ministers are even on some company payrolls as corporate chaplains, providing counsel through company wellness programs.

Evangelical public leaders have also launched a number of programs for younger leaders. From the Trinity Forum Academy to study programs sponsored by the Council for Christian Colleges and Universities, evangelicals have worked to ensure that their recent gains will continue with the next generation. These programs focus on introducing younger leaders to one another and giving them the professional tools to succeed outside the religious sector. They want young people with faith-shaped vocations not just at First Baptist Church but also at Goldman Sachs, the State Department, and the University of Chicago. Many of these programs are located not in traditional evangelical strongholds but in places of elite cultural influence, which has galvanized evangelical activity in those places while bringing newcomers into the fold as well. All of this institution-building costs money, and evangelical donors have earmarked hundreds of millions of dollars for these ventures. Some of their financial support has come from creative sources like fund-it-yourself-film-making and church-based venture capital. At the same time, a number of evangelical families have become significantly wealthier, with large sums to give away. Evangelicals have professionalized their giving, so that they can now engage in strategic philanthropy, not simply charitable donation. Christian financial planning firms and conferences for high-capacity donors provide the institutional structures that encourage this to happen.

Expressive Symbolism

Expressive elements—language, symbolic action, and creativity—have contributed greatly to evangelical influence by bringing evangelicalism into the public consciousness. In every presidential election since 1976, evangelical language has been an important part of campaign rhetoric. I have argued that evangelicals' voting behavior is best understood as symbolic action. Casting a ballot for a particular candidate is an expressive symbol, a way of saying that one's personal values—embodied in a particular candidate—belong in the public square. Voting for a candidate who shares your evangelical identity becomes an implicit vote for yourself. Evangelical political leaders have effectively incorporated religious rhetoric into their public speech and have framed particular policy issues in moral terms that appeal to evangelical voters. Especially in the Reagan and George W. Bush administrations, evangelicals benefited from high-level presidential appointments, which brought them into the inner chamber of political power, where they now both push for evangelical priorities and serve as symbols of evangelical influence.

Advancing social movements rely on rallying cries and motivating themes, and evangelicals have employed these to great effect. The public leaders I spoke to alluded frequently to scripts from within their tradition (such as the notion of "calling" or the "just war" theory) to frame their activity. These *legitimating narratives,* which often draw on authoritative sources like the Bible, help leaders connect secular work to their religious identities and to justify, in part, their privileged places within secular society. By using shared language—terms like "co-belligerence" and a "cultural mandate"— evangelical leaders call believers to action.[2] This has been critical to evangelical activity on everything from abortion to stem cell research to the environment.

These expressive elements crop up all over the place. Writing in journals like *First Things,* evangelicals have joined with Roman Catholics to do intellectual battle on issues of mutual concern. And the rapprochement with Roman Catholicism has enabled evangelical academics to expand their circle of intellectual influence and to secure much-needed legitimacy for their scholarship outside the evangelical community. The blockbuster success of *The Passion of the Christ* and *The Chronicles of Narnia* demonstrated that creativity born of faith can be profitable. This, in turn, has given evangelicals legitimacy as producers of culture. Indeed, a movement's legitimacy is conveyed through cultural expression. Creative goods—like books and movies—not only convey ideas that secure legitimacy but also serve as symbols for that movement's rising legitimacy.

In corporate life, evangelical executives frame business as a moral activity. They regard their secular work as a "platform" for their faith and an "arena for wider influence." By invoking faith in a company speech or attending Bible study at their firm, evangelical business leaders have given credibility to the idea that religion and work can mix. A few executives have also adopted quasi-ascetic lifestyles, garnering attention from their peers by abstaining from some of the more luxurious perks that come with being a wealthy executive.

Many of the public leaders I interviewed signal their evangelical allegiances in places where speaking directly about it would be taboo. This happens in many ways—from presidential speeches to Bibles placed prominently in an executive's office. This signaling behavior creates special ties between the leader issuing the signal and fellow believers who pick up on it. When explicit reference is not appropriate, evangelicals use signaling to bring faith into the workplace.

Ours is a society where boundaries exist between the sacred and the profane, and many of the leaders I interviewed have breached these boundaries in one way or another.[3] In some cases, this is risky, because it can make others very uncomfortable. Several Hollywood insiders acknowledge that speaking about faith too directly can cause someone to lose favor with casting directors or studio executives. The boundaries are not only external—they are personal. Many leaders spoke about negotiating the demands of their multiple identities as people of faith, successful professionals, and devoted family members.[4] How many hours should they work? How public should they be about their faith? Should they pray at work when others can see? At times, they were quite direct about the "gray areas" they regularly confront. Even when they weren't, I saw them struggling over the right way to invoke their faith in a religiously diverse society. Despite these struggles, many evangelical leaders have been public about their faith and have used their resources—both the institutional and the expressive—to strengthen the evangelical movement.

Networks

American evangelicalism has mobilized its resources to build networks of powerful people. Through political influence, academic respectability, creative inspiration, and financial capital, evangelicals have put significant resources into not only advancing their goals but also building the movement. More money can lead to the establishment of new organizations, which, in turn, can generate sources of political power.[5] These resources build social networks and fuel cultural production, both essential to the movement. Almost all of this activity has begun within elite networks, within webs of interpersonal relations at the highest levels. Evangelicals would not be nearly as influential as they are today without these powerful networks. Leadership expert Michael Useem has argued that within the inner circles of elite influence "acquaintanceship networks are dense, mutual trust and obligation are widespread, and a common sense of identity and culture prevail."[6] That is certainly the case among evangelicals. However, evangelicalism—as a salient, totalizing religious identity—provides a particularly strong bond for networks across sectors. Also, being an evangelical can have an empowering advantage: Fellow believers help each other rise in power.

I found several examples of overlapping networks of evangelical public leaders: Evangelicals in the White House knew evangelicals in Hollywood, and vice versa. They were not simply acquaintances; many times they were collaborators. Collaboration within these prestigious networks has been fundamental to evangelicalism's advance.[7] For example, recall the group of Washington evangelicals mentioned in chapter 2, Faith and Law. Most participants are senior congressional or White House staffers. At one of their gatherings, a participant talked about her interest in the world of fashion and entertainment. Though serving in government, she was interested in "making a difference" through the entertainment world. After that meeting, she and some of her Faith and Law colleagues decided to see what difference they could make as a group. They arranged a breakfast where several high-ranking government officials met with Philip Anschutz, the media executive.[8] After the breakfast meeting, Anschutz agreed to convene a group of business leaders and media "gatekeepers" including the then-chairman of AOL, Steve Case. Out of that meeting, two initiatives were started, one of which involved commissioning a Harvard study to monitor the media's effect on children. This is how evangelical networks get things done.

Some of these networks emerge out of Bible studies and prayer groups. Groups like the Fellowship in Washington provide much-needed social lubrication for leaders who may then collaborate. Through both small fellowship groups (such as the one convened by Edwin Meese when he was in the White House) and larger ministries (like the Trinity Forum), evangelical parachurch groups have created informal networks of influential evangelicals. While no one I interviewed would acknowledge that these ties directly influenced business decisions or political dealings, it would be inconceivable if they did not.[9] Many of these evangelical networks developed from leaders' own social and professional circles. Some started as small gatherings, while others, like the Laity Lodge Leadership Forum, branched off from larger groups. Because professional life in America today is so specialized and differentiated, most professionals rarely interact with leaders in other walks of life. When they do, it happens at a superficial level. By contrast, these evangelical networks have engendered a sense of community, creating bonds of loyalty cemented by shared faith. Evangelical leaders often told me stories of incredible commitment to others within these circles of spiritual friendship. For example, when Value America CEO Tom Morgan's company imploded, putting his personal fortune (including a beloved farm he owned) at great risk, he got a call from Douglas Holladay, a fellow evangelical business leader.[10] Morgan told me: "Doug called me one day and said, 'I just want you to know I'm praying for you through this thing, and I know how hard it is. . . . I know you're concerned about your farm and [that] you may lose it all. . . . I want you to know that's not going to happen. I'll buy it if I have to.'" In the end, that act of friendship was not necessary, but it does show the depth of such friendships that are grounded in faith.

The word "religion" can be traced to a Latin phrase that means "to bind together." In recent decades, evangelical religious identity has facilitated strong ties among public leaders.[11] Because religious identities are connected to moral frameworks, a sense of how things ought to be, this shared evangelical identity has endowed the movement with a seriousness of purpose, an overarching meaning system, and a repertoire of practices—like prayer and fellowship groups— that sustain leaders.

What kinds of institutional structures create and sustain these cross-cutting social networks? Consider the example of World Vision, one of the movement's largest nonprofit organizations.[12] When I attended the World Vision board meeting, I was struck by the number of representatives from different parts of society: government, business, the media, and religion. But I later learned that this was intentional. At every board meeting, there was a spreadsheet detailing the social, religious, and professional profiles of current members and stating that World Vision's board must have representation from four areas of expertise: experience with (1) the poor, (2) financial management, (3) the major donor community in the United States, and (4) the church and ministry world. Other sectors were also included: relief and development, law, education, medicine, human resources, the media, fund-raising, governmental affairs, and senior corporate leadership. World Vision's board meetings, like those of other evangelical institutions, provided opportunities for evangelical public leaders to interact, develop friendships, and collaborate on projects. Indeed, leaders from the evangelical community, the corporate world, the U.S. Agency for International Development, and the Department of State have all been involved with World Vision. The State Department's first ambassador-at-large for international religious freedom, Robert Seiple, assumed the post after stepping down as CEO of World Vision in 1998. His successor, Richard Stearns, came to World Vision after stints as CEO of both Parker Brothers Games and Lenox, the fine china firm. The USAID administrator under President Clinton, Brady Anderson, currently sits on the World Vision board, and the USAID administrator during President George W. Bush's first term, Andrew Natsios, once served as a vice president at World Vision. This overlap of individuals and social sectors also can be found among other evangelical organizations like Prison Fellowship Ministries, Christianity Today International, and Fuller Theological Seminary. Indeed, the parachurch sector is one of the few places where leaders from different sectors regularly interact, and through these organizations they have bridged parts of American society at very high levels. The webs of interpersonal friendship and professional networks have brought evangelical public leaders closer together and, in the process, helped the movement gain influence.[13]

Convening Power

Public leaders wield a particular kind of power, one that comes from their location within these influential networks.[14] Convening power is the ability to bring disparate people together, like introducing a congressional staffer to a senior media executive. It is the ability to set agendas and to coordinate activity. Sociologist Harold Kerbo argues that elite power is the power over social networks, and this certainly proved true among the leaders I studied.[15] Convening power is what that structural strength gives leaders: It enables them to marshal resources, to share information, and to deflect criticism. Elite power is the power to convene, and it is through their privileged positions within various social networks that leaders exercise it, bringing people together and then introducing and recruiting others to join their causes. Persuasion is a far more effective way to exercise power than domination, and convening power relies on convincing others to join.

I have found that the ability of political leaders to convene groups is among their most powerful resources. More than the ability to establish a legislative agenda or to administer a policy through executive action, the power that governmental leaders have to bring groups together is critical to their success. And that convening power rubs off on individual leaders even after they leave office. This is how Bill Clinton has been able to assemble so many high-level participants in the Clinton Global Initiative. The same is true of the World Economic Forum, the Aspen Institute, and other elite gatherings. These meetings create social space for interaction among peers where they can discuss ideas that can then be carried out by the organizations they run. Convening power is a potent resource for a group on the move.

Most striking, though, is that it is not simply the purview of politicians. Cultural icons, professional athletes, celebrated intellectuals, and corporate titans all wield similar influence. Because they serve as nodes of information and points of contact within high-status social networks, leaders wield a form of power that is stronger than one-on-one interaction: the power to mobilize groups and institutions. The number of people who can do this, though, is small, even within elite ranks. Convening power can be used to assemble mass rallies, but it begins with one leader reaching out to his or her small network of friends and associates. Convening power is how leaders in one sector join with other leaders in common cause. As one Hollywood executive told me, "When you get a call from the White House—whether it's the man you voted for or not, you take his call."

Convening power, however, is not enough to accomplish particular goals. For that you need decision-making power. Obviously, bringing parties together is fundamental to decision-making, but overlapping networks, in and of themselves, cannot produce specific outcomes. A leader can bring people together to discuss an issue but cannot make them act. While they may convene, they don't necessarily conspire. I found little support for the conspiracy theorists who think evangelicals are plotting to take over America, but I did find remarkable cohesion that came from a shared religious identity. Talented evangelicals in Hollywood often want the same things as evangelical business executives—namely, for their faith to be seen as a legitimate, and hopefully attractive, way of life for others. And leaders across the country have used their convening power to accomplish this.[16]

The convening power of evangelicals has been so potent because their religious identity is so salient. Because it is a core part of who they are as individuals and as leaders, the bonds between evangelical leaders are uniquely strong. Evangelicalism provides a moral framework through which public leaders make sense of their lives and endow their work with special meaning.[17]

Elastic Orthodoxy

American evangelicalism has the ability to maintain a core set of convictions without being so rigid that it cannot cooperate with others who do not share them. I call this *elastic orthodoxy*, and it has been critical to evangelicalism's success. Evangelicals are committed to shared, fundamental Christian beliefs—orthodoxy—and this keeps the movement cohesive. Sociologist Christian Smith has suggested that commitment to orthodoxy is one of the key explanations for evangelicalism's vitality.[18] Indeed, without strong boundaries and core beliefs, religious movements often fail. Shared beliefs have been of critical importance to evangelicals during their rise to prominence. They shape evangelicals' vision for society and spur them to action. But in order to engage pluralistic society, evangelicals have learned the importance of forming alliances and working with others. This is why the elasticity of their convictions is important. It also is what differentiates them from fundamentalists. Whereas evangelicals and fundamentalists share many of the same beliefs, the two differ in how they act upon these shared convictions: Fundamentalists separate from pluralistic society while evangelicals engage it.

The elasticity of evangelicals' orthodoxy is not a softening of conviction or a blurring of the lines that make Christianity distinctive, as some might think. Certainly that does occur among individuals; people lose their faith all the time. But across the hundreds of people I interviewed within the evangelical world, I did not find widespread apostasy or believers abandoning that which has made evangelicalism distinct. I did find evangelicals working with a variety of different groups, some of other faiths and some of no faith at all. Actually, the strength of evangelicals' religious convictions—and their commitment to engaging others with their faith—has compelled them to work with others. For example, elastic orthodoxy is what led them to lobby with many different groups for the International Religious Freedom Act of 1998 and to build coalitions for the Victims of Trafficking and Violence Protection Act of 2000.

Elastic orthodoxy allows evangelicals to undertake certain projects that might seem hypocritical to others. It requires believers to weigh various options and decide what is most in line with their own moral convictions. On the one hand are the costs of working with people with whom they fundamentally disagree on some matters. On the other is the exhortation that they bring their faith to bear on a range of issues necessitating entanglement with secular society. Evangelicals often disagree with one another because of this. What one believer might consider worth the entanglement, another may not. This was what caused some evangelical leaders to rebuke Pastor Rick Warren in 2006 for inviting the pro-choice Senator Barack Obama to speak at his church for World AIDS Day. Warren's critics—representing eighteen pro-life organizations—wrote to him before the event and said, "If Senator Obama cannot defend [unborn children] the most helpless citizens in our country, he has nothing to say to the AIDS crisis. You cannot fight one evil while justifying another."[19] Warren responded by noting that if he only worked with people he agreed with on everything, he would never work with anyone: "Right wing, left wing. I'm for the whole bird."

Because of evangelicalism's emphasis on individualism—believers are encouraged to take responsibility for their own spiritual growth—there is significant room for disagreement within the movement.

Elastic orthodoxy is how President Carter can campaign for pro-choice Democrats even though he is against abortion. Although they disagree on that subject, Carter finds more consensus than dissent, so he can, in good faith, campaign for such a candidate. Politics demands compromise. It's different, though, when faith becomes enmeshed in decisions about compromise and in forming alliances. It was Francis Schaeffer, decades ago, who vindicated evangelical cooperation with secular co-belligerents. Because American evangelicalism is pandenominational, the movement has a history of reaching across boundaries and finding allies in unusual places. Instead of emphasizing doctrinal differences, modern evangelicals have looked for points of agreement with those who might be brought under the evangelical tent. This has been the movement's strength. What is unique about the current moment is that a large number of evangelicals are now in positions of power that often put them into contact with leaders who do not share their faith.

What Does It Mean?

The rise of American evangelicalism matters not only to the movement itself but to society as a whole. Outside observers might assume that all the evangelical activity in recent decades must have been orchestrated somehow. If no master plan exists, then there must at least be a core group of leaders who coordinate activity, dedicate resources, and launch initiatives. Certainly, there are points of connection between evangelical activists in Washington and American corporate life, or between activity in the entertainment sector and happenings on college campuses. Evangelicals in those different arenas know one another and talk about the meaning of faith in their leadership. The social networks I have discussed in this book link these different leaders in significant ways. Yet too often evangelicals are caricatured in the media by extreme examples. President George W. Bush and Lakewood Church pastor Joel Osteen come from very different worlds. They may share beliefs and may, on occasion, worship together, but they represent two different kinds of evangelical faith.

Cosmopolitan and Populist Evangelicalism

As more evangelicals have entered the elite strata of society, a significant division has emerged within the movement between what

I call "cosmopolitan" and "populist" evangelicalism.[20] Populist evangelicalism depends on mass mobilization and large-scale democratic action. This wing of evangelicalism relies upon a rhetoric of dichotomies (as in "good" and "evil") and appeals to the common-sense concerns of average people. Populist evangelicalism draws sharp divisions between traditional believers (who are "good") and secular activists (who are "bad"). And, capitalizing upon evangelicalism's preference for simplicity and pragmatism, populist evangelicalism typically eschews theological sophistication or complexity in sermons. This is the domain of the PowerPoint sermon and the affect-oriented praise chorus. Populist evangelicalism thrives on the significant size of the evangelical market, and much of Christian publishing, Christian music, and the burgeoning field of Christian film is targeted at populist evangelicals. The Washington for Jesus rally in 1980, the Moral Majority, and the massive mobilization that can come from Focus on the Family's radio programs embody the ideals of populist evangelicalism: a large group (which claims to represent the majority's opinion) mobilized for collective action and directed by movement leaders. These leaders, who are some of the most recognized figures in American evangelicalism—such as James Dobson, Jerry Falwell, and Joel Osteen—are not just heads of evangelical organizations; they are prominent media figures that, at least in part, represent evangelicalism to wider society. Unlike more cosmopolitan public leaders, these movement leaders derive their authority from the evangelical subculture, and the subculture remains their primary point of reference. Indeed, this is one of the structural differences between these two groups: Populist evangelicalism supports a cluster of subcultural institutions. Much of evangelicalism's growth in recent decades—including enrollment gains at evangelical colleges and an expanding market for evangelical publishing and music—has appealed to and been accomplished through the infrastructure of populist evangelicalism.

But many of the leaders I spoke to tried to distance themselves from this part of the evangelical world. People went out of their way to say they had never read *Left Behind* or purchased a painting by Thomas Kinkade. When I asked them directly about this, people offered a range of responses, all of which reflected status concerns. One business leader told me he prefers to read Leo Tolstoy or Dorothy Sayers rather than the "evangelical kitsch" at his local Christian bookstore. Another said she would be attending an art exhibit by Makoto Fujimura instead of a concert by a popular Christian musician, and her tone made clear which of the two she deemed more important. Of course, people mix and match, and one is not necessarily better than the other. What struck me was the extent to which some leaders sought to distinguish themselves from the evangelical subculture.[21]

This is not just a matter of personal taste. Cosmopolitan evangelicals often come from very different backgrounds and have different experiences than their populist counterparts. They travel frequently, are involved in the arts, and live affluent lifestyles. Cosmopolitan evangelicals have greater access to powerful institutions, and the social networks they inhabit are populated by leaders from government, business, and entertainment. As one leader described it, this is "move-the-dial Christianity" in which evangelicals are in a position to use their faith to influence the rest of society. Beyond obvious socioeconomic markers like education and income, these two groups differ from one another religiously as well.[22] Most Americans are born into a religious tradition, and many evangelical adults started off as evangelical children.[23] But a majority of those I interviewed (56 percent) embraced evangelicalism after age seventeen, and over one-quarter were not reared in churchgoing families. What difference does this make? Those who convert to a religious tradition as adults are generally more zealous about their faith.[24] For the most part, the public leaders I interviewed expressed a strong desire to act on their faith, and many liken the process of sharing their faith publicly with "coming out."

Though one might expect cosmopolitan evangelicals to be less fervent than populist evangelicals, I found no evidence of this.[25] The two groups do, however, act on their faith convictions differently. They fund different causes and work through different groups. Cosmopolitan evangelicals frequent exclusive gatherings like the First Tuesday group for business leaders in Boston and the monthly fellowship group that meets at Manhattan's Links Club. These are quiet, invitation-only gatherings of elite social and professional peers. By contrast, populist evangelicals tend toward mass rallies like the stadium events sponsored by the evangelical men's group Promise Keepers. Even in the same field, differences in approach can be dramatic. Take politics, for example. Whereas populist evangelicalism relies on strategies like mobilizing the rank and file to push for legislation, cosmopolitan evangelicalism is more likely to sponsor a year-long internship program for future political leaders. While both hope to result in public policy that reflects evangelical convictions, their strategies could not be further apart. Most efforts within cosmopolitan evangelicalism take longer to achieve but, if successful, could have more lasting results. And whereas converting one's opponent (in religious, political, and social terms) is usually the principal goal of populist evangelicalism, the cosmopolitan brand is more concerned with legitimacy. The leaders I interviewed still want to see their secular peers embrace Christianity, but they tend to see legitimacy as a worthy and more attainable goal. Indeed, for just about everyone I spoke to, legitimacy was a principal concern. As evangelicalism is seen as more legitimate (i.e., "normal" or "acceptable" in elite circles), they believe, it will gain both prestige and prominence and will be embraced by more people. Hence the quest for legitimacy takes on not just social but also religious significance.

Tensions between movement leaders of the evangelical subculture, representing populist evangelicalism, and the public leaders I interviewed, representing cosmopolitan evangelicalism, emerged often. These included colorful exchanges, such as those between Majority Leader Dick Armey and James Dobson.[26] But they also reflect divisions between two segments of the evangelical world. "Cosmopolitan" can connote a more polished, sophisticated, and urbane individual who is both worldly wise and broad-minded.[27] In practice, those I interviewed embody this to varying degrees. They did appear to be more engaged with "the other" than populist evangelicals. While few movement leaders regularly interact at work with nonevangelicals—simply by nature of the hiring practices of their organizations—most public leaders find themselves surrounded by nonevangelicals.

Cosmopolitanism is what enables citizens in a pluralistic society to retain their allegiances to particular identities, such as those based on religion and ethnicity, while also learning from and appreciating those who are different from them. My sense is that cosmopolitan evangelicals hold less sectarian opinions than populist evangelicals. It would be a mistake, however, to equate this with more permissive social values or liberal politics. Divisions along political lines certainly exist, but they do not follow the cosmopolitan/populist divide. And though the public leaders I interviewed may be well traveled and exposed to global developments, theirs is a cosmopolitanism limited by the social world they inhabit. Outside of religious contexts like weekly worship or church-based small groups, most of the public leaders I interviewed inhabit communities, social clubs, and workplace settings that are largely homogeneous. They tend to interact with the same kind of people, whether they are in Los Angeles, London, or Lima. They may indeed travel more frequently and engage different cultures, but most of the time they remain in a world of social, professional, and economic peers. In this way, these cosmopolitan evangelicals are sheltered from the world of economic inequality as much as their secular peers are.[28]

Local church involvement could counter this trend, but these leaders are more active in parachurch groups than in local congregations. This is a troubling development for the movement because local church involvement is the principal way to keep cosmopolitan evangelicals from losing touch with their populist brothers. Dozens of leaders I interviewed talked about their loose church affiliations. In the words of C. Everett Koop, "I never had the time to become part of the workings of a church," or, as Art Linkletter put it, "I've become kind of a floating Christian. . . . I'm not a member of any [particular] church." Many leaders claim more than one church as their "home" congregation, and they often have several affiliations—member at one church, regular attender at another, part of a Bible study at a third congregation, and a financial supporter of another. One senior White House official calls a church in St. Louis his "home church," despite the fact that he has never lived there. He, as well as a Hollywood producer friend, a Nashville country singer, and several other leading evangelicals, flies to St. Louis between four and six times a year for weekend worship services, fellowship with church staff members, and religious contemplation. This does not mean that cosmopolitan evangelicals are not committed to their faith, but it does represent a different kind of religious activism. Instead of devoting large amounts of money to local congregations, most of the leaders I talked with direct the bulk of their donations to parachurch ministries. The development of "strategic philanthropy" has contributed to rising levels of professionalism and financial accountability among parachurch groups, while local congregations maintain a less corporate feel.

Evangelical megachurches are intriguing hybrids. They have the size and scope of a parachurch organization and the organizational mission of a local church.[29] This might explain their attractiveness to several of the leaders I encountered. The size of a megachurch allows it to offer a plethora of specialized ministries headed by professional staff members while its organizational mission remains the same as that of any local church: to minister to the range of spiritual needs of all members. Will megachurches provide a middle ground between the parachurch group and the small congregation? Among cosmopolitan evangelicals, I expect, megachurches will remain popular because they are organizationally similar to the institutions they themselves lead. Further, the leadership acumen of the senior pastor is extremely important to public leaders; most said they cannot worship at a church where they do not respect the senior minister as a leader, and they are most likely to find the kind of pastor they're looking for at a megachurch. One CEO gave his megachurch pastor the highest compliment he could offer—that he "could have been the CEO of a Fortune 10 company."

Parachurch groups and megachurches have risen up alongside cosmopolitan evangelicalism. To the extent that cosmopolitan leaders are active in a local church, it is almost always a megachurch, not a small congregation in their community. The declining importance of small, community-oriented churches for these leaders underscores the divide within American evangelicalism. This division reveals the presence of status and class hierarchies that are grounded in persistent economic divisions.[30] Reflecting this is the fact that not all cosmopolitan evangelicals embrace the term "evangelical" even though they fit the basic criteria.[31] Nearly one in four expressed some hesitation about the term. Often they said they did not want to be identified with particular political positions, but they also wanted to distance themselves from the populist wing of evangelicalism. They object to its separatism, its preference for mobilized action, and its bold confidence in a particular vision for society. By keeping cosmopolitan and populist evangelicals separate, the parachurch sector may actually be exacerbating this division. This distancing mechanism is both the cause and the effect of a declining commitment to a communitarian ethic, to a way of life that cares deeply for one's neighbor—not just around the world but also down the street. Local community churches are among the last remaining places where cosmopolitan evangelicals interact with people who are significantly less affluent. The loss of a communitarian ethic among cosmopolitan evangelicals is especially saddening, for it used to characterize much of American religious life.[32]

What's Missing? Women in Leadership

The gender divide also splits American evangelicalism today. Given evangelicalism's overall conservatism, I was not surprised to find fewer women pastoring local churches. The parachurch sector, though, seemed particularly well suited for female leadership.[33] But in fact, women occupy only 17 percent of all board seats at representative parachurch institutions. In individual organizations, this figure ranged between 10 percent and 31 percent. At secular nonprofit institutions of similar scope and influence, I found that women make up 24 percent of the boards, with different groups ranging from 9 percent to 33 percent.[34] In addition, three secular organizations had a female chief executive as of 2006; none of the evangelical organizations did.[35]

What could explain this? The Bible plays some role. Evangelicals are "people of the Book," and many of those evangelicals who hew to a literalist interpretation of scripture hold patriarchal views. Unlike more liberal religious traditions, evangelicalism makes little room for progressive revelation, whereby divine teachings are gradually revealed to adherents.[36] Hence, gender attitudes follow from larger battles over the sources of religious authority. Scriptures often cited in favor of male headship include passages such as I Corinthians 11 ("The head of a woman is her husband"), Ephesians 5 ("wives also be subject in everything to their husbands"), and I Timothy 2 ("A woman should learn in quietness and full submission.... Do not permit a woman to teach or to have authority over a man; she must be silent"). Many also prefer male pronouns for references to God in the Bible, affirming the traditional interpretation of Trinitarian theology that sees God as Father, Son, and Spirit, and underscoring male headship over the cosmos. In the Genesis account, man is created before woman, which many believe to reflect God's preference for men.[37]

On the other hand, there are several Bible passages that challenge a patriarchal perspective. Galatians 3 says, "There is neither Jew nor Greek, slave nor free, male nor female, for you are all one in Christ Jesus." Women are also prominent in Jesus' ministry; it was women who first bore witness to the resurrection in the gospels of Matthew and Luke. Women also played important roles in the early church, and I Corinthians makes clear that women were praying and prophesying. More recently, evangelicals have founded feminist groups to advance their vision for gender equality, and sociologist Sally Gallagher has shown that though evangelicals pay lip service to male headship in the family, few families actually behave that way.[38] Evangelical women join the American workforce at the same rate as women in the general population. And contrary to claims that evangelical belief contributes to domestic violence, churchgoing evangelicals have the lowest rates of domestic violence of any religious group in the country. Evangelical fathers are more active and expressive with their children and more emotionally engaged with their wives. This has led sociologist Brad Wilcox to conclude that if evangelicals maintain a patriarchy, "theirs is a very soft patriarchy."[39]

Beyond theology, gender inequality arises within evangelicalism through standard social reasons as well.[40] The women I interviewed do not have the same educational credentials as their male counterparts. Only 11 percent of the women I interviewed (compared to 33 percent of the men) attended a highly selective institution for either undergraduate or graduate work. This difference in education between men and women in elite positions is not found in studies of non-evangelicals, suggesting that biases within the movement must be at work. This is significant, since post-secondary education at a major university is virtually required for upward mobility and access to influential positions.[41] Around the country I found that women who rise to the top are still kept outside the inner circle of power among evangelicals. To borrow Gwen Moore's pithy phrase, "women in formal positions of power remain outsiders on the inside." For a movement that wants to continue to advance, evangelicalism has a long way to go in terms of gender relations. The bias against women in leadership is one of the greatest hindrances to evangelicalism's advance.

So what difference will these cleavages make? Will the movement split along socioeconomic lines, as suggested by the differences between populist and cosmopolitan evangelicalism? I doubt it. But resources and attention will increasingly be paid to evangelicalism's cosmopolitan wing. This is the kind of evangelicalism practiced and embraced by politicians, corporate executives, scholars, and artists. These are the evangelicals with capital to invest, and they will pour their resources into initiatives and projects in line with their ideals. This will also increase the respectability of evangelicalism in wider society. American evangelicalism, as it becomes more cosmopolitan, will become more palatable to nonevangelical observers. In addition, many of evangelicalism's most ardent populists are nearing the end of their careers, which could bring about a significant change for the movement. As they get older, generational differences within evangelicalism will increasingly highlight the populist/cosmopolitan divide. But this will not abolish evangelical populism. Populist tendencies will remain and in some quarters will be viewed as a more authentic expression of faith. Leaders whose authority comes from the movement will increasingly prefer populist techniques for mobilizing believers, while public leaders who are evangelicals will continue to gravitate toward cosmopolitan approaches and priorities. For these public leaders, having their faith seen as legitimate—and perhaps attractive—will be enough. Hard-sells for conversion will become the exclusive purview of the populist crowd, which means they will be far more active evangelists. The populist/cosmopolitan division has existed for some time, but the increasing wealth and influence of a small number of powerful evangelicals has exacerbated it in recent years. That trend will continue. Local church involvement will become less important to evangelical spirituality as the cosmopolitan style becomes more accepted within the wider movement.

More women will rise to leaders as cosmopolitan evangelicalism—which mostly favors gender equality—becomes more prominent.

I expect women will assume more leadership on parachurch boards, and capable women (likely from the corporate world) will gradually be tapped to head parachurch organizations. Conservative theology will continue to keep more men on top as pastors at local churches, but those strictures will be loosened for other evangelical institutions, including evangelical colleges, social service organizations, publishing houses, and advocacy groups. The declining importance of the local church and the rise of the parachurch will amplify these gains for women. Evangelicals will continue to refer to male headship, and gender biases will remain. But such talk will increasingly reflect an ideal, not actual practice, as has already been seen in evangelical households. America's leadership is making more room for women, albeit extremely slowly. Evangelicals will do the same, lest they lose touch with the very society they seek to transform.

Speaking more broadly, how has this engagement with society affected American evangelicalism? Is it stronger because of its involvement, or has it weakened to the point where it can be called, in Alan Wolfe's term, "toothless"? Evangelicalism certainly faces formidable challenges, many of which I have discussed. Yet I do not find evidence of eroding evangelical faith. As these leaders have climbed the professional ladder, they have not jettisoned their religious identity. Actually, according to many, the journey has deepened their faith. Yes, the leaders I interviewed fall into the same pits as their secular peers. They are susceptible to materialism and overweening pride. Yet on the whole, they remain very different from other leaders, and the reason is their faith. As evangelicalism has expanded its reach into the fields of politics, the economy, higher education, and the arts, it has adopted some of the conventions of those domains.[42] In the process, the evangelical faith has adapted, not declined. Its elastic orthodoxy allows it to retain its core principles but still change with the times. American evangelicalism is a durable faith.

A New Power Elite

Evangelicals populate elite centers like New York and Los Angeles now more than ever. They can be found at the top of nearly every social institution in America, and their influence can be seen in public policy, commerce, and the media. To determine if evangelicals are "taking over," though, we have to examine the structure of power in this country and whether evangelicals have a decisive edge over other groups in those powerful circles. In general, scholars endorse one of two ways of thinking about power and leadership in a given society. One tradition, which can be traced back to Karl Marx, says there is a single, unified ruling class that dominates society. In the twentieth century, advocates of this perspective—the "monolithic" model—thought social power was held by a small group of leaders who shared backgrounds and experiences. These leaders worked together professionally, sometimes switching positions with one another, and knew each other socially as well. Because they occupied the top positions in society, they were seen as collaborating on decision-making and trying to maintain their privileged positions at whatever cost. Some who favor this perspective think this unified elite is needed for society, but most regard their power as illegitimate because it has been usurped from the people. According to this perspective, power has been passed down from one generation of rulers to the next, usually through a group of families. Gradually, an aristocracy developed. As society continued to evolve and people became more educated, leaders needed to offer an explanation that validated their privileged positions.[43] In the medieval era, one such explanation was the idea that the authority of the king was divinely appointed, which justified his reign. According to this line of thinking, the explanation propounded by the elite helps maintain the status quo, quelling rebellious impulses among the masses.

A second way to look at societal power is to see it as dispersed and held by many different people. In contrast to those who see elite power as cohesive and unified, advocates of this "pluralist" perspective say society is so complicated today that no one group could hold all the powerful positions. In premodern societies, commerce, government, and the arts were directed by a small number of wealthy families, but as those sectors became more independent, the number of people who lead them grew exponentially. Social power is not distributed according to a firm hierarchy, say the pluralists. Instead, it is spread around geographically, in various sectors, and in the hands of many different people and institutions. These different people reach the pinnacle of their respective fields through different paths, which inhibits any sense of cohesion that might result from a shared class sensibility or overlapping authority.[44]

Looking at American evangelicals, I find qualified support for both perspectives. As the pluralist model suggests, power is indeed divided across many different social institutions. Most leaders have spent a majority of their professional lives climbing specific organizational ladders, and rarely does a leader in one sector jump over to lead another. Business leaders do not often come from the world of politics, and academics do not often become entertainers.[45] Also, very few public leaders hold multiple positions of power at the same time. To the extent that evangelical public leaders work together and occupy overlapping positions of responsibility—what C. Wright Mills called "structural coincidence"—it is not in their professional lives but rather in their religious lives.[46]

This, in fact, is the most intriguing thing I found. As Marx and others might have predicted, there are ways in which these public leaders today are united. But it is not principally by social class or shared backgrounds: It is by faith. If American evangelicalism leads to any overlap of people and institutions in the country's elite, it is through parachurch organizations. If evangelical public leaders from different segments of society work together, it is usually in this context as board members at World Vision or as trustees of Fuller Seminary. This, of course, creates special bonds among powerful people, which, no doubt, play a role in their professional lives. But it is through religious institutions, not corporate or professional bodies, that these elites most often overlap today.

In essence, I found an alternative to these two reigning perspectives on societal power in the case of evangelical public leaders. As the monolithic model predicts, there are indeed sources of elite cohesion that can be facilitated by institutional structures like the evangelical nonprofit sector. But like the pluralists, I find society today to be highly differentiated, which makes it difficult for leaders to act in unison. Evangelicalism provides a unique, binding ligament that can, in turn, create additional institutional sources for cohesion. This brings leaders together in a way no other force can. Through this, American evangelicals have built an increasingly powerful movement that unites leaders even in a complex society. Beginning with the Reagan administration, evangelicals came to occupy enough positions of governmental leadership that they represented a distinct segment of the political elite. And because they embraced their evangelical identity, they carried it with them into the professional realm. There have been similar developments in other areas of American culture—in business, the arts, entertainment, and on college campuses. For these public leaders, evangelicalism became part of who they were, both personally and professionally. In this way, faith unifies a segment of the nation's leadership.

Fifty years ago, C. Wright Mills published *The Power Elite*. In it, he argued that the United States was ruled by a small group of political, military, and business leaders. Like most others who studied power at the time, Mills relegated religion to the background. For him, church was just one of many affiliations that these white Protestant males shared with one another. More recently, some have noted how the nation's elite includes a more diverse range of leaders such as women, African Americans, and Latinos.[47] Are evangelicals just another group added to the mix?

The rise of American evangelicalism has coincided with the ascendance of a new power elite. Although the leaders I interviewed—like all leaders when asked—do not see themselves as powerful, they are. Holding what Mills would call a "commanding" position at a major public institution, like the military or a corporation, bestows upon the leader extraordinary influence. As this book has shown, evangelicals are now in those powerful positions. They are not only powerful but wealthy, well educated, and motivated. Through remarkable social networks, they know one another and share a vision for how things ought to be in society. Their faith unites them and provides a broad system of meaning for leadership. But at root, evangelicalism is a reforming movement, which is why evangelicals will never be comfortable with the status quo even within the power elite.

Though evangelical public leaders may be small in number, these faith-inspired leaders are activists, and for at least the next few generations, America's leadership will not be the same. Against those who claimed the elite would be increasingly secularized, evangelicals have shown how faith can not only be part of one's leadership but actually motivate and advance it. Leading a pluralistic society requires people of faith to bridle their zeal, which is why cosmopolitan evangelicals appear more domesticated than their populist kin. But this is not a duller Christianity, just one that is more at home within the establishment.

Does the advent of this new power elite constitute an "Evangelical Establishment"?[48] There are a host of factors standing in the way. First, institutional inertia is often too much for a few leaders to overcome.[49] Also, individual ambition is often an obstacle to achieving shared goals, and, as I have shown, evangelicalism is a movement of big personalities and corresponding egos. In addition, overlapping networks of powerful people are not, in themselves, enough.[50] Though evangelical public leaders have convening power, they do not necessarily have decision-making power. Evangelicals played important roles in policy issues like abortion, foreign relations, and faith-based initiatives, yet I could find little evidence to show that evangelical networks resulted in specific policy outcomes. Decisions at the national level are rarely shaped by individual groups or constellations of networks, no matter how powerful the individuals within those networks. Third, evangelicals are far from dominant among America's leadership. The reason they have received so much attention in recent years is that they represent a prominent, new group entering the elite. But they still comprise only a fraction of the nation's political leadership, and much less in the other sectors examined. Nonetheless, this is a uniquely cohesive and increasingly influential group, and in our segmented society, that is noteworthy.

The growing influence of American evangelicalism, accomplished largely by evangelical public leaders working through their social networks, has brought the movement back into the public square. As evangelicals move beyond the borders of the movement's subculture and into the mainstream, what will happen to evangelicalism? Some suggest that its relationship with the rest of society will become increasingly acrimonious. I have cited several examples of what I call "evangelical triumphalism," whereby movement leaders, in the name of majority rule, sought to impose their vision on society. Empirically, of course, their claim to represent the majority is not true. Even by the most generous accounting, American evangelicals are less than half of the U.S. adult population. Moreover, though evangelicals frequently claim to be marginalized and persecuted, they are curiously insensitive to the possibility that minority groups like Jews or atheists might see their efforts as a crusade for domination. For these groups, the alliance between evangelical fervor and power is a scary prospect that conjures visions of religious zealots ruling the country with intolerant force. Of course, evangelicals do not have to pursue this strategy. The movement's elastic orthodoxy might allow evangelicals to build alliances with even more groups. If the impulse for evangelicalism to become a "counterculture for the common good"—that is, a distinct group that still works for the good of all citizens, not just their own—takes root, the movement will thrive. It can then continue to advance its priorities without becoming the religious crusade its critics fear most. The challenge will be to maintain what one evangelical theologian has called a "soft difference" toward pluralistic society, one in which they can remain open to other people's convictions yet still faithful to their own.[51]

Religious identity is a formative influence in people's lives, and observers since Tocqueville have noted how religion in this country can anchor one's moral obligation to the common good. In an increasingly pluralistic democracy like the United States, we are reminded that enlightened democracy grows from the same root as isolating self-interest. Our best and worst attributes can flow from the same source—the difference is in how those streams are directed. Evangelical public leaders have brought faith convictions to bear in their respective spheres of influence. History will be the judge of whether this contributes to a more enlightened democracy, where engaged citizens use their faith to serve the common good, or whether we have merely witnessed the triumph of another interest group with a distinctive vision for society. What cannot be denied is that these leaders have brought evangelical faith—once confined to the lower ranks of society—into the very halls of power.

APPENDIX

Through semi-structured interviews with 360 leaders as well as archival and ethnographic research, I traced the mechanisms through which evangelicalism rose to prominence in American life. Details about the interviews are below.

Leaders in the Study

Name	Organization or Title	Interview Date	Interview Location
Thomas G. Addington	Cornerstone Consulting	July 27, 2004	Fayetteville, AR
John Aden	Mac Tools	June 14, 2005	Farmington, CT
Roberta and Howard Ahmanson	Fieldstead and Company	April 27, 2004	Newport Beach, CA
David Aikman	Author and journalist; Senior Fellow, Trinity Forum	December 8, 2004	Washington, DC
Chuck Allen	North American Mission Board	September 16, 2005	Osprey Point, MD
Claude A. Allen	Assistant to the President for Domestic Policy; Deputy Secretary, Health and Human Services	December 7, 2004	Washington, DC
J. Brady Anderson	Administrator, United States Agency for International Development	March 27, 2004	Austin, TX
Leith Anderson	National Association of Evangelicals; Wooddale Church	August 23, 2005	Telephone interview
Robert C. Andringa	Council for Christian Colleges and Universities	July 10, 2003	Washington, DC
Victor Anfuso	Christian Copyright Licensing, Inc. (CCLI)	August 19, 2004	Portland, OR
Guy Anthony	Stentor; Intel	May 19, 2004	Brisbane, CA

Name	Organization or Title	Interview Date	Interview Location
Richard K. Armey	Majority Leader, U.S. House of Representatives	February 2, 2005	Washington, DC
William L. Armstrong	U.S. Senator	September 30, 2004	Denver, CO
Ronald Austin	*Mission Impossible; Charlie's Angels; Hawaii Five-O; The Father Dowling Mysteries*	May 14, 2005	El Segundo, CA
Jim Awtrey	CEO, Professional Golfers Association of America	August 13, 2005	Short Hills, NJ
James A. Baker III	Secretary of State; Secretary of Treasury; White House Chief of Staff	November 12, 2004	Houston, TX
Dennis Bakke	AES; Imagine Schools	August 5, 2004	Washington, DC
Stephen Baldwin	Actor	October 1, 2004	Bachelor's Gulch, CO
Jeff Barneson	The United Ministry at Harvard; InterVarsity	August 27, 2004	Telephone interview
Dean Batali	Co-executive producer, *That '70s Show*	September 26, 2004	Glendale, CA
Janet and Lee Batchler	*Batman Forever; Smoke and Mirrors*	May 19, 2005	Beverly Hills, CA
Mariam Bell	The Wilberforce Forum	September 4, 2004	Osprey Point, MD
Marc Belton	General Mills	May 31, 2005	Minneapolis, MN
George Bennett	State Street Investment Corporation	August 29, 2004	Falmouth, MA
Matt Bennett	Christian Union	February 8, 2005	Princeton, NJ
Monty Bennett	Remington Hotel Corporation	October 13, 2004	Dallas, TX
Mark Berner	SDG Resources	July 14, 2004	New York, NY
Brian Bird	Writer and producer	November 8, 2004	Rancho Santa Margarita, CA
Ronald Blue	Christian Financial Professionals Network	February 28, 2005	Atlanta, GA
Edith L. Blumhofer	Institute for the Study of American Evangelicals	October 8, 2004	Wheaton, IL
David Bock	World Bank; I-trax	October 28, 2003	Washington, DC
Pat Boone	Entertainer	April 23, 2004	Los Angeles, CA
Terry Botwick	CBS Entertainment; Thunderpoint Studios	October 3, 2005	Los Angeles, CA
Sandra Bowden	Christians in the Visual Arts	August 29, 2004	Chatham, MA
Jonathan Boyd	Emerging Scholars Network	June 21, 2005	Pentagon City, VA

Name	Organization or Title	Interview Date	Interview Location
William G. "Jerry" Boykin	Deputy Undersecretary of Defense for Intelligence	June 21, 2005	Washington, DC
John Brandon	Apple Computers, Inc.	May 20, 2004	Cupertino, CA
William K. Brehm	SRA International Inc.; Assistant Secretary of Defense	January 13, 2005	Vienna, VA
Frank Brock	Covenant College	May 7, 2003	Chattanooga, TN
Clayton Brown	Clayton Brown & Associates	October 8, 2004	Wheaton, IL
Dan Bryant	Assistant Attorney General	December 10, 2004	Washington, DC
Eric Bryant	Mosaic	May 15, 2005	Pasadena, CA
Bob Buford	Buford Television; The Buford Foundation; Leadership Network	April 12, 2004	Dallas, TX
Phil Burgess	The Clapham Institute	January 21, 2005	Washington, DC
Doug Burleigh	Young Life	September 8, 2004	Gig Harbor, WA
George H. W. Bush	President of the United States	February 9, 2005	Responded via e-mail
Jamie Bush	Boston Fellowship	August 28, 2004	Hingham, MA
Howard Butt	Leadership Laity Forum	February 17, 2005	San Antonio, TX
Gaylen Byker	Calvin College	June 17, 2004	Telephone interview
Tony Campolo	Eastern University	March 3, 2006	Cherry Hill, NJ
Richard G. Capen	U.S. Ambassador to Spain; *Miami Herald*	November 8, 2004	Del Mar, CA
Byron and Laura Carlock	The Carlock Companies; CNL Income Corp.	April 12, 2004	Dallas, TX
Stanley Carlson-Thies	Center for Public Justice	July 26, 2003	Osprey Point, MD
Joel Carpenter	Calvin College	March 26, 2004	Waco, TX
Jimmy Carter	President of the United States	November 16, 2004	Atlanta, GA
Truett Cathy	Chick-fil-A	March 1, 2005	Atlanta, GA
Morris Chapman	Southern Baptist Convention	April 25, 2006	Nashville, TN
William Chatlos	The Chatlos Foundation	November 22, 2004	Longwood, FL
Stephen Clapp	The Juilliard School	January 6, 2005	New York, NY
Corey Cleek	Silicon Valley Fellowship	May 19, 2005	Cupertino, CA
Jerry Colangelo	Arizona Diamondbacks; Phoenix Suns	October 29, 2004	Phoenix, AZ

Name	Organization or Title	Interview Date	Interview Location
Michael Coleman	Integrity Media	September 23, 2004	New York, NY
Francis S. Collins	Director, National Human Genome Research Institute	September 18, 2005	Washington, DC
Timothy C. Collins	The Ripplewood Fund	September 20, 2004	New York, NY
Charles Colson	Prison Fellowship; The Wilberforce Forum	July 17, 2004	Washington, DC
Jeffrey Comment	Helzberg Diamonds	October 23, 2004	Kansas City, MO
Kevin Compton	Kleiner Perkins	August 11, 2005	Palo Alto, CA
Gary Cook	Dallas Baptist University	April 2, 2005	Dallas, TX
Kyle Cooper	Title designer for 52 films	September 26, 2004	Malibu, CA
Karen Covell	Hollywood Prayer Network	November 24, 2003	Hollywood, CA
Michael Cromartie	Ethics and Public Policy Center	July 16, 2003	Washington, DC
Andy Crouch	The Christian Vision Project	January 6, 2004	Princeton, NJ
Les T. Csorba	Special Assistant to the President for Presidential Personnel	February 22, 2005	Houston, TX
Gary Daichendt	Cisco Systems	April 23, 2004	Crystal Cove, CA
John H. Dalton	Secretary of the Navy	July 16, 2004	Washington, DC
David Davenport	Pepperdine University	May 19, 2005	Malibu, CA
Rudy F. deLeon	Deputy Secretary of Defense	January 13, 2005	Washington, DC
Mark DeMoss	The DeMoss Group	February 28, 2005	Laguna Niguel, CA
Max De Pree	Herman Miller	July 9, 2004	Holland, MI
Scott Derrickson	*The Exorcism of Emily Rose*	July 31, 2004	Glendale, CA
Craig Detweiler	Biola University	April 25, 2004	Culver City, CA
Dick De Vos	Alticor/Amway	July 9, 2004	Grand Rapids, MI
Dave Dias	Time Out, InterWest Insurance Services	May 20, 2004	Menlo Park, CA
John J. DiIulio Jr.	Director, Office of Faith-Based and Comm. Initiatives	November 2, 2004	Philadelphia, PA
Mark Dillon	Wheaton College	October 8, 2004	Wheaton, IL
David Dockery	Union University	March 26, 2004	Waco, TX
Marjorie Dorr	Anthem Blue Cross and Blue Shield	April 12, 2005	North Haven, CT
Stephen Douglass	Campus Crusade for Christ	November 22, 2004	Orlando, FL

Name	Organization or Title	Interview Date	Interview Location
Michael Duke	Wal-Mart	March 31, 2005	Bentonville, AR
Ligon Duncan	Alliance of Confessing Evangelicals	April 28, 2005	Jackson, MS
Tony Dungy	Head coach, Indianapolis Colts	June 6, 2006	Indianapolis, IN
Archie Dunham	ConocoPhillips	February 21, 2005	Houston, TX
David Eaton	Arizona Diamondbacks; Phoenix Suns	October 29, 2004	Phoenix, AZ
Don Eberly	Director of Private Assistance for Iraq, State Department; Deputy Director, Office of Faith-Based & Comm. Initiatives	July 15, 2004	McLean, VA
Norm Edwards	Development counselor	September 9, 2004	Seattle, WA
Allan C. Emery	ServiceMaster Hospital Corporation	August 28, 2004	Weymouth, MA
Peter Engel	*Saved by the Bell; Last Comic Standing; Hang Time*	November 15, 2005	Santa Monica, CA
Ted W. Engstrom	World Vision	October 13, 2005	Seattle, WA
William G. Enright	Lake Family Institute for Religion and Giving	October 8, 2003	Indianapolis, IN
David Evans	Electronic Arts	May 20, 2004	Menlo Park, CA
Donald L. Evans	Secretary of Commerce	February 11, 2005	Washington, DC
Bill Ewing	Columbia Pictures	October 3, 2005	Studio City, CA
Steven Feldman	*Sesame Street; Barney and Friends; Politically Incorrect with Bill Maher*	May 17, 2005	Pasadena, CA
Micheal Flaherty	President, Walden Media	February 3, 2005	Washington, DC
Leighton Ford	Leighton Ford Ministries	September 19, 2005	Seattle, WA
Dick Foth	The Fellowship	December 7, 2004	Arlington, VA
Randy Frazee	Willow Creek Community Church	November 7, 2005	Chicago, IL
Abigail Frederick	First Fruit	May 20, 2004	Palo Alto, CA
Steven French	Lifework Leadership	November 23, 2004	Orlando, FL
Robert Fryling	InterVarsity Press	November 12, 2006	Chicago, IL
Makoto Fujimura	Visual Artist; International Arts Movement	August 23, 2004	New York, NY

Name	Organization or Title	Interview Date	Interview Location
George Gallup	Chairman of the Gallup Poll	June 24, 2005	Princeton, NJ
Steve Garber	Evermay; Council for Christian Colleges & Universities	March 18, 2005	Washington, DC
Patrick P. Gelsinger	Intel	October 2, 2004	Bachelor's Gulch, CO
Michael J. Gerson	Assistant to the President for Speechwriting; Assistant to the President for Policy and Strategic Planning	March 17, 2005	Washington, DC
Kathie Lee Gifford	Entertainer	May 23, 2005	New York, NY
Louis Giuliano	ITT Industries	November 18, 2004	White Plains, NY
Brian Godawa	*To End All Wars; The Visitation*	May 17, 2005	Los Angeles, CA
Marcie Gold	*Touched by an Angel*	November 24, 2003	Beverly Hills, CA
Stephen Graves	Cornerstone Consulting	July 29, 2004	Fayetteville, AR
David Grizzle	Continental Airlines	December 31, 2004	Charleston, SC
Duane Grobman	The Mustard Seed Foundation	August 5, 2004	Arlington, VA
Os Guinness	The Augustine Group; The Trinity Forum	July 28, 2003	Tysons Corner, VA
Robert E. Gustafson	The Stony Brook School	November 4, 2003	Princeton, NJ
Ted Haggard	New Life Church; National Assn. of Evangelicals	October 4, 2004	Colorado Springs, CO
Russ Hall	Legacy Ventures	May 19, 2004	Palo Alto, CA
Tony Hall	U.S. Ambassador, Food and Agricultural Organization	February 4, 2005	Washington, DC
Chris Halvorsen	The Fellowship	December 9, 2004	Washington, DC
Michael Hamilton	Pew Evangelical Scholars Program	October 13, 2005	Telephone interview
Pete Hammond	Intervarsity Christian Fellowship	February 18, 2005	San Antonio, TX
John Hamre	Deputy Secretary of Defense; Center for Strategic and International Studies	February 4, 2005	Washington, DC
John Hanford	U.S. Ambassador-at-Large for International Religious Freedom	January 14, 2005	Washington, DC
Alistair Hanna	Alpha	August 23, 2004	New York, NY
Dave Hannah	Impact XXI	November 8, 2004	San Diego, CA

Name	Organization or Title	Interview Date	Interview Location
Sam Haskell III	Worldwide Head of Television, William Morris Agency	November 15, 2005	Los Angeles, CA
Jody Hassett Sanchez	ABC World News Tonight	March 20, 2005	Arlington, VA
Gary Haugen	International Justice Mission	November 22, 2005	Washington, DC
Wallace Hawley	InterWest Partners	August 10, 2005	Menlo Park, CA
Jack Hayford	Church on the Way	March 21, 2005	Telephone interview
Daryl Heald	Generous Giving	July 28, 2005	Chattanooga, TN
Margaret Heckler	Secretary of Health and Human Services	February 6, 2005	Washington, DC
Tami Heim	Borders, Inc.	August 21, 2004	Detroit, MI
Jay F. Hein	Director, Office of Faith-Based and Community Initiatives; Sagamore Institute	November 7, 2003	Indianapolis, IN
Hugh Hewitt	Salem Communications	May 20, 2005	Los Angeles, CA
Alec D. Hill	InterVarsity Christian Fellowship	February 11, 2005	Telephone interview
Donald P. Hodel	Focus on the Family; Secretary of the Interior; Secretary of Energy	October 4, 2004	Colorado Springs, CO
Kirk Hoiberg	CB Richard Ellis	May 20, 2004	San Francisco, CA
Douglas Holladay	Park Avenue Equity Partners	December 9, 2004	Washington, DC
Donald Holt	*Fortune; Newsweek*	October 25, 2004	Wheaton, IL
Philip G. Hubbard	Chicago Research and Trade	October 26, 2004	Northfield, IL
R. Glenn Hubbard	Chair, White House Council of Economic Advisors; Columbia Business School	August 23, 2004	New York, NY
Mike Huckabee	Governor of the State of Arkansas	July 29, 2004	Little Rock, AR
John Huffman	St. Andrew's Presbyterian Church	April 26, 2004	Newport Beach, CA
Karen Hughes	Senior Advisor to the President	January 21, 2005	Washington, DC
Wayne Huizenga Jr.	Miami Dolphins; Huizenga Holdings, Inc.	October 19, 2004	Fort Lauderdale, FL
Asa Hutchinson	Undersecretary of Homeland Security	December 10, 2004	Washington, DC
William Inboden	Senior Director for Strategic Planning, National Security Council	February 4, 2005	Washington, DC

Name	Organization or Title	Interview Date	Interview Location
Chip Ingram	Walk Thru the Bible	June 30, 2004	Telephone interview
Stuart Irby	Stuart C. Irby Company	July 21, 2004	Jackson, MS
Ann Iverson	Laura Ashley; Kay-Bee Toys	June 15, 2005	New York, NY
Peb Jackson	Purpose Driven	September 16, 2004	Osprey Point, MD
Kay Cole James	Director, Office of Personnel Management	September 17, 2004	Washington, DC
David Lyle Jeffrey	Baylor University	March 26, 2004	Waco, TX
Ronald P. Joelson	Prudential Financial Services	December 3, 2004	Newark, NJ
Paul Johnson	Paul Johnson & Company	July 8, 2004	Birmingham, MI
Stephen L. Johnson	Administrator, Environmental Protection Agency	October 25, 2005	Washington, DC
Douglas Johnston	International Center for Religion and Diplomacy	February 11, 2005	Washington, DC
Dale P. Jones	Halliburton	April 12, 2004	Dallas, TX
Jennifer Jukanovich	The Vine	May 28, 2005	Vail, CO
Howard Kazanjian	*JAG; Raiders of the Lost Ark; Star Wars; Return of the Jedi*	November 8, 2004	Pasadena, CA
Kurt Keilhacker	Veritas Forum	October 15, 2004	Telephone interview
Tim Keller	Redeemer Presbyterian Church	May 12, 2005	New York, NY
Jeff Kemp	Families Northwest; Former NFL player	July 16, 2004	Washington, DC
Bruce Kennedy	Alaska Air Group	September 8, 2004	Seattle, WA
Betsy King	LPGA professional golfer	October 29, 2004	Phoenix, AZ
Paul Klaassen	Sunrise Assisted Living	July 15, 2004	McLean, VA
Fritz Kling	Parker Foundation	July 16, 2004	Washington, DC
Todd Komarnicki	*Elf*	April 29, 2004	New York, NY
C. Everett Koop	U.S. Surgeon General	August 27, 2004	Dartmouth, NH
J. David Kuo	Special Assistant to the President	October 28, 2003	Washington, DC
Mark Kuyper	Evangelical Christian Publishers Association	November 6, 2005	Chicago, IL
Linda Lader	Renaissance Institute	April 12, 2005	New Haven, CT
Drew Ladner	Chief Information Officer, U.S. Treasury Department	August 5, 2004	Washington, DC
Jim Lane	New Canaan Society	April 22, 2005	Princeton, NJ

Name	Organization or Title	Interview Date	Interview Location
Steve Largent	Former NFL player	August 4, 2004	Washington, DC
Ralph Larsen	Johnson & Johnson	June 23, 2004	Wyckoff, NJ
Kenneth R. Larson	Slumberland	June 1, 2005	St. Paul, MN
Steven Law	Deputy Secretary of Labor	January 14, 2005	Washington, DC
Katherine Leary	Redeemer Presbyterian Church	July 14, 2004	New York, NY
David Leitch	Deputy Counsel to the President	December 6, 2004	Washington, DC
David LeShana	Seattle Pacific University; George Fox University	August 19, 2004	Lake Oswego, OR
Lauren Libby	Navigators	April 4, 2005	Colorado Springs, CO
Keith Lindner	AFG/Chiquita	June 9, 2004	Cincinnati, OH
Art Linkletter	*People Are Funny; House Party; Kids Say the Darndest Things*	May 19, 2005	Beverly Hills, CA
Duane Litfin	Wheaton College	October 8, 2004	Wheaton, IL
Erik Lokkesmoe	Brewing Culture	September 5, 2004	Osprey Point, MD
Brad Lomenick	Life@Work	September 16, 2004	Osprey Point, MD
Terry Looper	Texon	February 17, 2005	Houston, TX
Nancy Lopez	LPGA professional golfer	August 25, 2004	Kutztown, PA
Lindy Lowry	*Outreach* Magazine	March 8, 2005	Vista, CA
Luis Lugo	Pew Forum on Religion and Public Life	January 13, 2005	Washington, DC
Gabe Lyons	Relevate	September 16, 2005	Osprey Point, MD
Allan MacArthur	Halftime	April 16, 2004	Atlanta, GA
Hugh O. Maclellan	Maclellan Foundation	October 1, 2004	Bachelor's Gulch, CO
Pat MacMillan	TEAM Resources	November 16, 2004	Atlanta, GA
David and Karen Mahan	Rivendell	August 26, 2004	New Haven, CT
Theodore Roosevelt Malloch	The Roosevelt Group; World Economic Summit	February 3, 2005	Washington, DC
Joel Manby	Saab USA; Herschend Family Entertainment	February 28, 2005	Norcross, GA
Lynne Marian	Outreach, Inc.	March 8, 2005	Vista, CA
Mike Marker	Christian Business Men's Committee	June 9, 2004	Telephone interview
Thomas McCallie	The Maclellan Foundation	February 3, 2005	Washington, DC

Name	Organization or Title	Interview Date	Interview Location
Alonzo McDonald	Deputy White House Chief of Staff; McKinsey & Company; The Trinity Forum	July 8, 2004	Birmingham, MI
Steve McEveety	*The Passion of the Christ*; Icon Productions	September 5, 2004	Osprey Point, MD
David McFadzean	*Home Improvement; Roseanne*	September 27, 2004	Pasadena, CA
Robert "Bud" McFarlane	National Security Advisor	December 8, 2004	Washington, DC
Joel McHale	*Talk Soup; The Soup*	November 8, 2004	Los Angeles, CA
Mac McQuiston	CEO Forum	April 4, 2005	Colorado Springs, CO
Curtis McWilliams	CNL Restaurant Properties	November 23, 2004	Orlando, FL
Edwin Meese III	U.S. Attorney General and Counselor to the President	September 14, 2004	Washington, DC
Jim Mellado	Willow Creek Association	June 18, 2004	Telephone interview
Marilee Melvin	Wheaton College	May 25, 2004	Wheaton, IL
Eric Metaxas	Socrates in the City	September 7, 2004	New York, NY
Mike Metzger	The Clapham Institute; The Trinity Forum	January 21, 2005	Washington, DC
David Miller	Yale Center on Faith and Culture	July 28, 2004	Springdale, AR
Gayle Miller	Anne Klein II	July 31, 2004	Hollywood, CA
Jerry Miller	Texaco; The Cove, Billy Graham Evangelistic Association	March 15, 2004	Asheville, NC
Norm Miller	Interstate Batteries	October 14, 2004	Dallas, TX
Billy Mitchell	Carter & Associates	April 15, 2004	Atlanta, GA
Jack Modesett	Christian Stewardship Association	November 12, 2004	Houston, TX
Thomas I. Morgan	Hughes Supply Company	November 22, 2004	Orlando, FL
Allen Morris	The Allen Morris Company	October 19, 2004	Coral Gables, FL
Malcolm Morris	Stewart Title and Stewart Information Services	November 12, 2004	Houston, TX
Richard Mouw	Fuller Theological Seminary	May 27, 2003	Pasadena, CA
Edmund C. Moy	Director, U.S. Mint; Special Assistant to the President, Office of Presidential Personnel; White House Christian Fellowship	July 16, 2004	Washington, DC

Name	Organization or Title	Interview Date	Interview Location
Ken Myers	*Mars Hill Audio Journal*	September 23, 2005	Telephone interview
John Naber	President, U.S. Olympic Alumni Association; Olympic swimmer	May 18, 2004	Pasadena, CA
Chuck Neder	Presbyterians for Renewal	May 7, 2003	Chattanooga, TN
Larry Nelson	Champions Tour professional golfer	July 8, 2004	Dearborn, MI
Paul D. Nelson	Evangelical Council for Financial Accountability	August 1, 2003	Washington, DC
Paul E. Nelson	Crowell Trust	April 4, 2005	Colorado Springs, CO
Steven R. Nelson	Executive Director, MBA Program Harvard Business School	August 27, 2004	Cambridge, MA
Greg Newman	C2B Technology; Macromedia	May 19, 2004	Burlingame, CA
Armand Nicholi	Harvard Medical School	August 27, 2004	Concord, MA
Barbara Nicolosi	Act One	September 27, 2004	Los Angeles, CA
Mark Noll	Wheaton College	March 18, 2005	Washington, DC
Peter Ochs	Fieldstone Communities; First Fruit	April 26, 2004	Newport Beach, CA
Richard Ohman	Colonial Penn Life Insurance; The Augustine Group; The Trinity Forum	August 26, 2004	Hancock, NH
John Ortberg	Menlo Park Presbyterian Church; Willow Creek Community Church	May 16, 2005	Pasadena, CA
Cary Paine	Stewardship Foundation	September 10, 2004	Seattle, WA
Kevin Palau	Luis Palau Association	October 2, 2004	Bachelor's Gulch, CO
Luis Palau	Luis Palau Association	October 6, 2006	Houston, TX
Earl Palmer	University Presbyterian Church	October 14, 2003	Princeton, NJ
Roger Parrott	Belhaven College; Lausanne Committee	December 21, 2004	Jackson, MS
Jon Passavant	Celebrity fashion model	February 20, 2006	New York, NY
Rena Pederson	*Dallas Morning News*	November 13, 2004	Dallas, TX
Wayne Pederson	MissionAmerica Coalition; Moody Broadcasting Network	October 2, 2003	Philadelphia, PA
Gordon Pennington	Tommy Hilfiger	September 7, 2004	New York, NY

Name	Organization or Title	Interview Date	Interview Location
Ken Perez	Omnicell	May 20, 2004	Mountain View, CA
Thomas L. Phillips	Raytheon	August 30, 2004	Boston, MA
Tim Philpot	Christian Business Men's Committee	June 11, 2004	Lexington, KY
Eric Pillmore	Tyco	May 10, 2005	Princeton, NJ
William M. Pinson	Baptist General Convention of Texas	January 2, 2005	Dallas, TX
Larry W. Poland	Mastermedia International	May 18, 2005	Los Angeles, CA
C. William Pollard	ServiceMaster	May 24, 2004	Wheaton, IL
Donald E. Powell	Chairman, Federal Deposit Insurance Corporation	February 19, 2006	Washington, DC
Barbara Priddy	The Fellowship	December 8, 2004	Washington, DC
William Pugh	Athletes in Action	June 9, 2004	Xenia, OH
Merrit Quarum	Qmedtrix	July 31, 2004	Calabasas, CA
David Radcliffe	The Southern Company	April 15, 2004	Atlanta, GA
Tom Randall	World Harvest Ministries	July 8, 2004	Dearborn, MI
Michael Regan	TranzAct Technologies; Vision and Values Conference	October 7, 2004	Chicago, IL
Steven S. Reinemund	PepsiCo	November 13, 2004	Dallas, TX
Brad Rex	Epcot; Walt Disney Company	November 23, 2004	Orlando, FL
Herbert Reynolds	Baylor University	March 26, 2004	Responded via e-mail
Mercer Reynolds	U.S. Ambassador to Switzerland and Lichtenstein	June 9, 2004	Cincinnati, OH
James H. Richardson	Alexandria Real Estate Services	May 19, 2004	Palo Alto, CA
Paul D. Robbins	Christianity Today International	May 6, 2004	Wheaton, IL
M. G. "Pat" Robertson	CBN; Regent University	October 24, 2003	Virginia Beach, VA
David Robinson	NBA professional basketball player	October 1, 2004	Bachelor's Gulch, CO
Joyce Robinson	Marie Walsh Sharpe Foundation	October 4, 2004	Colorado Springs, CO
Mark Rodgers	Faith & Law	September 5, 2004	Osprey Point, MD
Matthew K. Rose	Burlington Northern Santa Fe	January 3, 2005	Dallas, TX
Daniel Russ	Center for Christian Studies, Gordon College; Trinity Christian Academy	August 28, 2004	Boston, MA

Name	Organization or Title	Interview Date	Interview Location
Joseph F. "Skip" Ryan	Park Cities Presbyterian Church	April 5, 2004	Dallas, TX
Denny Rydberg	Young Life	April 4, 2005	Colorado Springs, CO
John Sage	Pura Vida Coffee	September 10, 2004	Seattle, WA
David Sampson	Deputy Secretary of Commerce	December 6, 2004	Washington, DC
Rick and Soozie Schneider	The Rivendell Institute	August 26, 2004	New Haven, CT
Thom and Joani Schultz	Group	February 7, 2005	Loveland, CO
Horst Schulze	Ritz-Carlton	March 1, 2005	Atlanta, GA
Robert Seiple	World Vision; Institute for Global Engagement; U.S. Ambassador-at-Large for International Religious Freedom	November 2, 2004	St. David's, PA
George Selden	Christian Embassy	March 20, 2005	Arlington, VA
Dal Shealy	Fellowship of Christian Athletes	December 1, 2004	Telephone interview
John Shepherd	*Bobby Jones: Stroke of Genius*	May 19, 2004	Los Angeles, CA
Ronald J. Sider	Evangelicals for Social Action	December 31, 2005	Charleston, SC
Fred Sievert	New York Life	September 21, 2004	New York, NY
Al Sikes	Chairman, Federal Communications Commission	July 14, 2004	New York, NY
Karl Singer	AON Insurance; Ryan Insurance Group	April 12, 2004	Dallas, TX
Paul Singer	Target	May 31, 2005	Minneapolis, MN
Frank Skinner	BellSouth Telecommunications	February 25, 2005	Atlanta, GA
James Skillen	Center for Public Justice	July 16, 2003	Washington, DC
Robert Sloan	Baylor University	April 18, 2005	Waco, TX
Kevin Small	INJOY; The Marcus Buckingham Company	September 16, 2005	Osprey Point, MD
Brad Smith	Bakke Graduate University Leadership Network	March 24, 2004	Dallas, TX
Fred Smith Jr.	The Gathering	April 5, 2004	Dallas, TX
Fred Smith Sr.	Fred Smith Associates	November 26, 2003	Dallas, TX
Ray Smith	Kirell Energy Systems	May 22, 2004	El Camino Real, CA
Stan Smith	Professional tennis player	September 7, 2004	New York, NY
Donald Soderquist	Wal-Mart	July 28, 2004	Rogers, AR

Name	Organization or Title	Interview Date	Interview Location
Gearl Spicer	First Baptist Church, Atlanta	July 29, 2005	Atlanta, GA
Nancy Stafford	*Matlock; St. Elsewhere*	November 9, 2004	Marina del Rey, CA
Kenneth W. Starr	Solicitor General; Independent Counsel on Whitewater; Pepperdine Law School	May 19, 2005	Malibu, CA
Richard Stearns	World Vision; Lenox; Parker Brothers	September 9, 2004	Bellevue, WA
Thomas W. Steipp	Symmetricom	August 11, 2005	San Jose, CA
Chuck Stetson	National Bible Association	July 14, 2004	Washington, DC
Cris Stevens	Women's Professional Golf Fellowship	June 16, 2004	Atlantic City, NJ
Michelle Suh	Hollywood Connect	May 24, 2005	Telephone interview
Julie Sulc	Pew Charitable Trusts	September 11, 2003	Philadelphia, PA
Thomas A. Tarrants III	C. S. Lewis Institute	March 18, 2005	Washington, DC
John M. Templeton Jr.	John Templeton Foundation	April 15, 2005	Philadelphia, PA
Douglas TenNapel	*Catscratch*; Nickelodeon	September 27, 2004	Burbank, CA
John Terrill	InterVarsity Professional Schools Ministries	September 13, 2005	Telephone interview
Cal Thomas	Syndicated columnist; *After Hours with Cal Thomas*	June 23, 2005	Washington, DC
Roger Thompson	Regal Books	November 7, 2005	Chicago, IL
Michael Timmis	Talon LLC	August 20, 2004	Gross Pointe Farms, MI
Richard Tompane	Gemfire	October 31, 2003	Los Altos, CA
Michael Tremain	Blue Sky Ministries	September 16, 2005	Osprey Point, MD
John Tyson	Tyson Foods	July 27, 2004	Springdale, AR
Myron Ullman	JCPenney; LVMH Moët Hennessy Louis Vuitton; Macy's	October 6, 2004	New York, NY
James Unruh	Unisys	October 28, 2004	Scottsdale, AZ
Rollin Van Broekhoven	Judge; Department of Defense	December 7, 2004	Washington, DC
Daniel Vestal	Cooperative Baptist Fellowship	April 19, 2005	Waco, TX
Phil Vischer	*VeggieTales*	November 12, 2005	Wheaton, IL

Name	Organization or Title	Interview Date	Interview Location
Michael Volkema	Herman Miller	November 17, 2004	New York, NY
Ken Wales	*Amazing Grace; Christy*	November 23, 2003	Santa Monica, CA
Jon Wallace	Azusa Pacific University	November 4, 2004	Los Angeles, CA
Debra Waller	Jockey	March 22, 2005	New York, NY
Jim Wallis	*Sojourners;* Call to Renewal	December 31, 2005	Charleston, SC
Rusty Walter	Walter Oil	February 17, 2005	Houston, TX
Kurt Warner	NFL professional football player	June 2, 2005	Phoenix, AZ
Michael Warren	*Happy Days; Family Matters; Step by Step*	April 26, 2004	West Lake Village, CA
Sherron Watkins	Enron	February 21, 2005	Houston, TX
James Watt	Secretary of the Interior	October 28, 2004	Wickenburg, AZ
Greg Waybright	Trinity International University	October 1, 2004	Vail, CO
B.J. Weber	New York Fellowship	September 20, 2004	New York, NY
David Weekley	David Weekley Homes	November 12, 2004	Houston, TX
Peter Wehner	Deputy Assistant to the President and Director of Strategic Initiatives	August 4, 2004	Washington, DC
Luder Whitlock	Excelsis; The Trinity Forum	November 22, 2004	Orlando, FL
Bill Wichterman	Faith & Law	October 28, 2003	Washington, DC
J. McDonald "Don" Williams	Trammell Crow	July 25, 2005	Dallas, TX
Martha Williamson	*Touched by an Angel*	April 23, 2004	San Marino, CA
David Wills	National Christian Foundation	February 11, 2005	Washington, DC
John A. Wilson	*Books & Culture*	October 27, 2004	Phoenix, AZ
Ralph Winter	*X-Men; Planet of the Apes; The Fantastic Four*	April 25, 2004	Glendale, CA
Gregory Wolfe	*Image: A Journal of the Arts & Religion*	September 9, 2004	Seattle, WA
Kathy Wills Wright	Deputy Director, USA Freedom Corps; Special Assistant to the President	July 16, 2004	Washington, DC
Bonnie Wurzbacher	Coca-Cola	November 16, 2004	Atlanta, GA

Name	Organization or Title	Interview Date	Interview Location
Paul Wylie	Olympic and professional ice skater	August 30, 2004	Hyannis, MA
Michael Yang	mySimon.com; Become.com	October 11, 2004	Monterey, CA
David Young	Oxford Analytica	April 22 and 23, 2005	Princeton, NJ
Jose Zeilstra	JPMorgan Chase	September 9, 2004	New York, NY

Note: N = 360; because of space constraints, listed positions and organizations are not exhaustive, but they do reflect at least one major leadership position held by the study participant or organization(s) he or she led.

Regarding organizations listed, the individual serves or has served as a firm executive, most often as president, chairman, or chief executive officer. For cultural leaders, I identify a few—certainly not all—of their recognized cultural goods.

Research Methods

Data for this book are based on three primary sources: interviews (N = 360), organizational archives, and ethnographic observations. Participants for this study were selected using a two-stage method of sample selection. First, I identified the nation's largest organizations within American evangelicalism. Using a variety of connections, I interviewed 157 leaders of evangelically oriented institutions. At the end of these interviews, I asked participants to identify public leaders whose Christian faith was an important aspect of their life. Many then helped me request an interview with the public leaders they recommended. This technique, which I call the "leapfrog" method for informant selection, granted me unusual access to leaders in government, business, and culture (N = 203) without the usual impediments of secretarial gatekeepers or organizational barriers. Indeed, this methodological innovation, coupled with the traditional "snowball" method for informant selection, created an unusually large number of high-ranking, willing participants.[1]

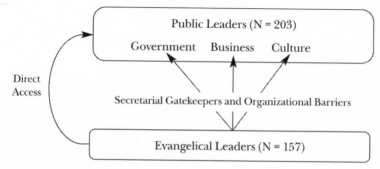

Figure 1. Informant Universe and "Leapfrog" Method of Sample Selection

Commensurate with other leadership studies that have identified a range of institutional sectors, I did not limit the areas of influence when soliciting recommendations from the study's early participants.[2] Evangelical institutional leaders were able to recommend anyone they regarded as holding a position of public influence at some time between 1976 and 2006 whom they also regarded as serious about his or her faith. Those recommendations coalesced along three substantive areas: government, business, and a broad area I call "culture." (This includes the entertainment sector—television, film, and professional athletics—the visual and performing arts, the media, philanthropy, and the nonprofit sector.) Because the interviews were conducted mostly on the record for direct attribution, I was uncertain how to analyze the comments of currently elected politicians whose constituents could learn of their comments and thereby influence what the official might say.[3] Hence, I did not interview anyone in currently elected office, which is why there are no current members of Congress—certainly an institution of public influence—among this study's participants. With the possible exceptions of Congress and the Supreme Court, this study includes leaders from every domain of public influence examined in previous investigations.[4]

Interviews with public leaders ranged in length from thirty-five minutes to more than four hours, but the average interview lasted sixty-three minutes. These interviews were digitally recorded and then professionally transcribed. A research associate checked the accuracy of the transcripts and sent copies of them to those participants (13 percent) who requested the opportunity to review (and possibly edit) their remarks for accuracy. The cleaned interview transcripts were then coded along forty-six variables for various demographic and religious categories. This book is based on quantitative and qualitative analyses drawn from the interview data, which totaled more than five thousand pages of material in all.[5]

Interview Guide

Religious Identity

1. First, say someone were to sit beside you on the airplane or have a few minutes to visit with you. They turn to you and say, "I hear you are a person of faith." How would you describe your faith to someone who does not know you?
2. Do you call yourself an evangelical? Why or why not?
3. What makes someone an evangelical?
4. Take a few minutes to describe your faith journey. Did you have a "conversion" experience? Is that important to you?
5. How do you nourish your spiritual faith?
6. What types of churches have you been affiliated with? Are you currently a member of a church? If so, what is it and where? How frequently do you attend? What denomination is this?
7. How would you describe the congregation theologically? Are most people fairly conservative or fairly liberal?
8. Do you attend services at another church regularly? If so, which one(s)?
9. Is church involvement important to your spiritual life, or not?
10. How about people outside your faith community (neighbors, co-workers)? Do you talk about your religious beliefs with them?
11. Are there certain people you encounter with whom you'd prefer not to discuss your faith? Why or why not?
12. Can you give me a story or an example of how you have sought to "live out" your faith?

Personal Background: Family and Career

1. Briefly, I'd like to know something about your family. Where did you grow up? Where did you go to school (and when)? What did your parents do for a living?
2. Have you done better economically than your parents?
3. Take a few minutes to trace your professional journey from your days as a student to now.
4. What do you consider to be your "gifts" and talents?
5. In politics, do you favor one party over another? If so, which one? Why?

Let me ask some basic demographic questions for bookkeeping purposes.

Demographics (if not previously revealed)
1. Are you married or single? Do you have children?
2. Can you tell me your age?
3. Are you involved in particular evangelical projects, ministries, or initiatives?

Faith, Beliefs, and the Workplace
1. When you think about how you spend your time, would you say you feel "called" to the work you do or have done? What does this mean to you?
2. Who have been mentors to you? Who has shaped this sense of calling?
3. What books have you read that have been particularly meaningful in this area of your life? Are there certain authors that you read regularly? Who are they? What do you like about them?
4. Are you involved in any faith-based small groups? If so, who are the types of people involved in these?
5. Do you have a group of friends to whom you regularly turn during hard times? What would be an example of a "hard time" that you've faced?
6. When you think about your interactions at work, how many people do you have regular contact with in the workplace in a typical week? Of those, how many do you think know that you are a person of faith? How would they know?
7. Can you give me an example of how your faith has helped or sustained you as a professional? How about an example of where your faith challenged you in your professional responsibilities?
8. Are you ambitious? Is that a virtue or a vice for you as a person of faith?

Faith and Society
1. Some people of faith believe that American society is entering a state of serious, desperate crisis, that it is beginning to fall apart at the seams. What do you think about this? Do you share this concern?
2. Should people of faith be involved in society to try to exert a religious influence? Why or why not?
3. Are there certain Christian groups or people who you think are particularly effective in influencing society? What do they do to accomplish this?
4. Do you think the evangelical branch of American Christianity is growing in America today, or not? Is this a good thing?
5. Do you think evangelicals have become more "worldly" in the last twenty-five to thirty years? What does that mean?
6. Do you think evangelicalism has changed since, say, Jimmy Carter's election? How so?

Power, Status, and Wealth
I'm talking to people about big issues—things like influence and personal philanthropy—to see how they relate to their religious lives, if at all.
1. Do you think of yourself as powerful or as wielding influence? Why or why not? In what ways do you influence others (probe for power and influence within evangelicalism and to a wider audience)?
2. How many employees work under you?
3. Have you ever had an incident where a co-worker or a neighbor questioned your faith because of some decision you made or were facing? Can you give me an example?

Affiliations and Involvements
1. Are you involved in particular faith-based projects, ministries, or initiatives?
2. Have you served on the boards of any faith-based organizations? If so, can you tell me a little bit about them? Tell me the story of how you got involved.
3. (If involved as a board member) How long have you served on this (these) board(s)? Who are some of the other people that serve on these boards? How well do you know them?

4. What types of organizations and ministries do you support financially?
5. Do you have a family foundation? If so, how did that come about?
6. Over the last thirty years, what organizations have you financially supported the most?
7. If you had to total all of your financial giving over the last three to five years, how much have you given away per year, on average, to faith-related causes? To all causes?
8. In return for your financial investment, have you played a role in shaping that organization? If so, how?
9. Are there certain programs or products that you have personally endorsed over the last thirty years? What are these, and how did you come to endorsing them?

[Add specific questions for each informant based on his/her biographical background and position of influence.]

I am interviewing many of the nation's top leaders who are people of faith—people who, like you, have held leadership positions in society (government, business, and culture) who would also seek to be faithful to their religious and spiritual convictions. Can you recommend some other people whom I should include in this study?

Profile of Leaders

In all, 47 percent of this study's informants come from the business elite, 29 percent from the cultural and entertainment elite, and 24 percent from the governmental elite.[6] Among the public leaders interviewed, women represent 10 percent of all participants. Women comprise the largest segment of the culture sector, representing 17 percent of all participants. Among governmental informants, they represent 9 percent and among the business leaders, 6 percent of the total number of study participants.

Education remains an important determinant of institutional leadership.[7] One in three leaders (33 percent) attended a very selective university for undergraduate or graduate education.[8] Among those attending very selective institutions, a plurality (11 percent of study participants) earned a degree from Harvard. The institution whose graduates formed the second highest category is Wheaton College, an evangelical institution in suburban Chicago. Fifteen participants received a degree from Wheaton. Other institutions with more than five graduates represented in this study include Oxford (7), Stanford (7), Columbia (6), University of Pennsylvania (6), University of Southern California (6), University of Texas (6), Cornell (5), Princeton (5), U.S. Naval Academy (5), University of Virginia (5), and Yale (5).

Geographical diversity within American evangelicalism has been of recent interest to scholars in the field, so that was one of the main forms of diversity I sought in the research design.[9] Excepting a few cases with unusual circumstances, all interviews were conducted in person, in the location of the interviewee's primary residence. Study participants come from all four regions of the country: the Northeast (34 percent), the South (29 percent), the Midwest (10 percent), and the West (27 percent).[10] Not all interviews took place in the region of the country where the leader lives as some interviews took place at board meetings, conferences, and retreats around the country. Because some leaders hold multiple residences or, in a few cases, work in a region different from where they live, study participants are classified by the region where they spent most of their time at the time of the interview.

Regarding leaders' religious lives, practically all (92 percent) say their co-workers and friends know about their faith commitments, and a variety of answers was given as to how. These include episodes where the leader has had direct conversations about spiritual topics with others (reported by 73 percent of informants) and public speeches in which the leader has alluded to his or her faith or evangelical involvements, as well as media accounts and personal scheduling decisions regarding religious involvement that are made public. Another interesting result of this study relates to religious leadership. The principal way in which study participants provide some form of leadership within evangelicalism is not through local church involvement but rather service on the board of a faith-based nonprofit organization. Nearly three in four (72 percent) currently serve as a board member on one of these organizations.

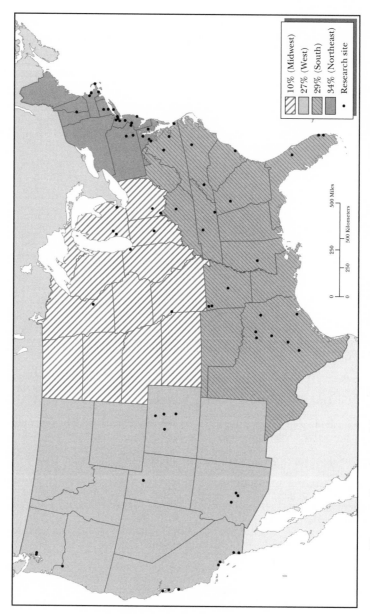

Figure 2. Locations of Interviews and Regional Representation Among Study Participants

10% (Midwest)
27% (West)
29% (South)
34% (Northeast)
• Research site

500 Miles
500 Kilometers
0   250   500
0   250

Younger public leaders are less likely to talk about their faith with others (40 percent), whereas among the study's oldest participants (over age sixty-five), the percentage is more than double (84 percent). A large number (80 percent) over age sixty-five have spent their entire lives in the church, and they are less likely than the other age categories to report changing churches or denominations. Finally, older study participants are the age group least likely to say they feel a sense of spiritual calling to the work that they do (44 percent). By contrast, a majority of public leaders (59 percent) say they believe their professional lives represent, at least in some way, a "calling" they have received from God.

The people who serve in positions of public responsibility appear to get more serious about faith considerations well into their careers. This may reflect their upbringing and background; after all, 29 percent of them did not come from families that attended church, which is nearly double the percentage in the general population.[11] In essence, the background of those who rise to prominent positions is not as religiously oriented as that of the general population. Alternatively, the frequency with which public leaders report significant spiritual decisions as adults may reflect their desire to engage religion as a way of handling the challenges that come with powerful positions. From the White House to the corner office at Enron, the halls of power are places of remarkable evangelical ferment. The embrace of faith that has come later in life for most informants has energized them to act on their evangelical sensibilities.

Two final items are worthy of attention. First, a sizable number of evangelical public leaders expressed hesitancy in using the term "evangelical" to refer to their own religious identities. Nearly one in four (23 percent) expressed such a concern, which is curious since everyone in this study exemplifies evangelical convictions and sensibilities, and many of them currently serve on the boards of avowedly evangelical institutions. Most are not bothered by the religious connotations of being "evangelical." Instead, those who eschew the term prefer not to be identified with particular elements of the movement, most notably conservative politics and the evangelical subculture. The second item to note is the optimism of this group. Only around one in five (22 percent) expressed concern that America was in a moral freefall. While nearly all raised particular items of concern, such as the prevalence of corporate scandals or adultery among the evangelical faithful, most believed that America's current problems could be addressed. And importantly, they believe that evangelicalism can be part of the solution.

NOTES

Introduction

1. Linker (2006) articulates the desire of many secular and progressive observers that every citizen in a liberal democracy accept the "liberal bargain" requiring believers to give up their "ambition to political rule in the name of faith" in exchange for the benefits of a pluralistic, free society. Linker misses, however, the extent to which salient identities—such as those formed by religion—can have such a profound influence on adherents' lives that they cannot conceive of active citizenship apart from their moral convictions, which are conditioned by their faith.
2. Four traditions are particularly important to evangelicalism: Calvinism, Pietism-Methodism, Anabaptism, and Holiness-Pentecostalism. American evangelicalism shares with Calvinism a preference for asceticism and discipline; this is part of the reforming impulse within the tradition, which was carried to American soil by the Puritans and the Pietists of the seventeenth century. Pietism stressed an experiential spirituality, individual piety, and vigorous Christian practice. German Pietism was the forerunner to the Methodist movement that John Wesley popularized after having his heart "strangely warmed" while attending a Moravian meeting in London. Wesley, along with his younger brother Charles and a group of fellow students at Oxford, had begun a "holy club" known for its methodical spiritual disciplines like prayer and Bible reading. The blending of devotional piety and experiential spirituality became important aspects of that segment of Protestantism that came to be associated with evangelicalism. A related religious stream of American evangelicalism can be traced back to the Anabaptists, who stressed the importance of personal conversion for the devout Christian. Oriented toward social activism, Anabaptists were not reticent to speak prophetically to the governing authorities on matters with which they disagreed. Each of these traditions—Calvinism, Pietism-Methodism, and Anabaptism—emerged in a European context. In its own way, each sought to recover a purer, more authentic form of Christianity. The fourth tributary of contemporary evangelicalism began in a uniquely American context. The Holiness-Pentecostal tradition began in New York City in 1836 out of a gathering called the Tuesday Meeting for the Promotion of Holiness. Nineteenth-century preachers D. L. Moody and Charles Finney advocated the holiness tradition, and, as they traveled the country, they stoked the fires of American revivalism that had been prominent in the First and Second Great Awakenings. Together, these four traditions underlie the contemporary evangelical mosaic.
3. Noll (2001) and Marsden (1991). Most studies employ one of three methods to define the evangelical population. The most common method involves denominational affiliation; individuals affiliated with evangelical denominations are considered evangelicals (Smith 1987; Greeley 1972; Glock and Stark 1965). According to measures that rely on denominational affiliation, approximately 25 percent of the U.S. population should be classified as "evangelical." However, this approach has been criticized as crude and imprecise, so a second perspective defines evangelicals by self-descriptions. Surveys sponsored by polling organizations like Gallup have

followed this model, suggesting that the percentage of Americans classified as evangelical is between 36 percent and 47 percent of the adult population (Gallup and Lindsay 1999). Gallup's definition allows non-Protestants to be considered "evangelical" if they respond affirmatively to the question of "Would you describe yourself as a 'born-again' or evangelical Christan?" Examining Gallup data that is aggregated for all religious surveys between 1992 and 1998 (N = 24,871), I find that more than half of Protestants (54 percent) label themselves as born-again or evangelical Christians, and sizable segments among other religious traditions use the same self-identifications, including 31 percent of those in the Orthodox tradition, 21 percent among Catholics, and even 7 percent among Jews. It is possible that this segment represents those Americans who refer to themselves as "Jews for Jesus." Other studies have affirmed the merits of the self-identification method for defining evangelicals but prefer to place additional qualifications on the term. Screening respondents to include only Protestants and those who either attend church at least two or three times per month or who regard religion as "extremely important" in their lives, Smith (2000, 1998) found that only 7 percent of the U.S. adult population is evangelical according to those parameters. The third way to define evangelicals involves measurements of belief. Hunter (1983), using survey measurements about interpretations of scripture and beliefs about Jesus, identified 22 percent of the adult population as evangelical. Similarly, Barna (1994, 1992, 1991, 1990) uses an elaborate set of belief affirmations to identify evangelicals. Barna differentiated between born-again, which he estimates around 40 percent of the adult population, and evangelical, which he says comprises only 7 percent of American adults. In sum, depending on how one defines the population, evangelicals make up between 7 percent and 47 percent of the U.S. adult population—a staggering difference that, as I explore elsewhere (Hackett and Lindsay 2004), can greatly influence the demographic profile of evangelicalism that emerges.

4. Smith (2000); Kellstedt et al. (1996); Martin (1990); Bebbington (1989); Wald, Owen, and Hill (1989). The usefulness of the term "evangelical" has been challenged recently, and many within the movement dislike the term because of its theological and analytical fuzziness (Hart 2004; Noll 2001; Woodberry and Smith 1998; Dayton and Johnson 1991). "Evangelism" and "evangelicalism" are derived from the Greek word for "good news," which is also etymologically related to "gospel." As the phrase connotes, evangelicals have been particularly interested in *verbally* communicating their religious convictions as a means of sharing this "good news" or "gospel" about Jesus Christ. This is a cardinal attribute of these theological conservatives within American Christianity, and therefore "evangelical" is an appropriate name.

5. Regarding the "personal relationship with Jesus," I agree with Hunter (1983) that a dramatic born-again experience or a gradual unfolding of this relationship between the believer and God is equally appropriate for an evangelical. What differentiates an evangelical from, say, a mainline Protestant is the centrality of a *personal* relationship with God, stressing the individualism, relationalism, and devotional piety of evangelicalism.

6. Within the literature on religious identity, three vital themes emerge: coherence and contingency; institutionalized patterns and improvised construction; and the management of public and private selves. First, social scientists have noted the multiplicity of personal identities that can be found within a single individual, some of which may conflict with one another (Thumma 1991; Hewitt 1989). We may have one identity at work and another at home, and between those identities there will be varying degrees of coherence and contingency. Second, the extent to which identity is institutionalized or constructed alludes to an ongoing discussion about the place of structure and agency within human action. Social constructionism suggests that we may improvise our identity, but even that rests on larger cultural scripts (Berger and Luckmann 1966). We cannot separate ourselves from the institutionalized narratives and social symbols at will, for, in part, we construct them as much as we are constrained by them. A third element of identity refers to impression management (Goffman 1967, 1959). In social interaction, people put on a "show" for each other, stage-managing the identities that others see. This, in turn, suggests the presence of at least two selves: one publicly available and one enacted in nonpublic settings. All three currents inform my analysis in this book on evangelical religious identity.

7. This element has spurred scholars to study relations between evangelicalism and gender (Griffith 1997), political activism (Smith 2000; Marsden 1991), and race relations (Emerson 2006; Emerson and Smith 2000), among others. Much of this literature has considered these relations from a grassroots, rank-and-file level (Webber 2002; Smith 1998; Shibley 1996; Dayton and Johnson 1991; Marsden 1991; Hunter 1987, 1983). Very little attention has been devoted to the role of leaders within these connections. Studies that have considered elite evangelicalism have looked primarily at texts written by the movement's leaders (Gallagher 2003; Bartkowski 2001; Ellison and Sherkat 1993).

8. I recognize that evangelicalism, as a pan-denominational movement, has no single, coherent evangelical theology; it is probably more accurate to refer to evangelical theologies. However, this is a teaching common to the various traditions that fall within the spectrum of American evangelicalism.

9. Young (2002).

10. Evangelicals' robust understanding of sin also informs this impulse to make the world better. It conditions ideas about authority, which can be seen in parenting relations, schooling, and other social interactions. According to them, the Christian gospel both redeems believers from this sinful world and provides a guideline for their ongoing relations with that world (Ellison and Sherkat 1993).

11. I focus on the *social dimensions* of contemporary American evangelicalism, paying lesser attention to it as a theological or religious *tradition,* even as I acknowledge the salience of this dimension for many adherents. As a sociologist, I will invariably attend to different issues than a theologian examining evangelicalism would consider. The advantage of framing American evangelicalism as a movement is that it enables the researcher to explore ways that it has crossed traditional denominational divides, allowing, for example, Roman Catholics to express their affinity with evangelicalism. Because this is such a salient point, I deal with evangelicalism as a movement instead of a religious tradition.

    Tilly (2004) argues that social movements entail a sustained campaign for a particular set of objectives. According to him, participants must demonstrate worthiness, unity, numbers, and commitments to secure legitimacy and cohesion. For an excellent overview of morality and its structural order that humans engage in constructing meaning, see Wuthnow (1987).

12. On the robust sector of evangelical special-purpose organizations, see Schmalzbauer (2003); Balmer (2000a); Burtchaell (1998); and Marsden (1991). Regarding the place of organizations in movement mobilization, see Bowers, Ochs, and Jenson (1993). This has been shown to be particularly true within the realm of religion. See Wood (1999) and Patillo-McCoy (1998).

    Institutional elements of evangelical activity include the founding of new organizations, the distribution of resources and particular social networks that facilitate this process, and patterned modes of action that evangelical leaders and their organizations exemplify. The expressive component of evangelicalism's advance considers the language and the symbolic acts that point to deeper meaning systems for evangelicals. As Douglas (1970, 1966) has suggested, meaning and moral order are embedded in symbol systems, so in the forthcoming chapters I examine specific symbols and how leaders frame their significance. Confirmatory narratives, or modes of discourse that provide confirmation for a particular course of action, will also emerge as we trace evangelical activity in different social sectors.

13. Regarding evangelicalism's "advance," I use the term as a way of discussing the movement's forward momentum. In this case, it entails an extension into different sectors of society—politics and the world of business, for example—as well as the introduction of evangelicalism into society's upper strata. I do not mean to imply by the term that there is a normative ideal for evangelicalism, one that it has somehow reached in its most recent transformation. In this regard, I view the various stages of American evangelicalism discussed in this chapter as categorically, not ordinally, different.

14. For "religious establishment," see Marsden (2006: 6). On evangelical activity regarding temperance, see Young (2002) and Krout (1925); regarding women's suffrage, see Kirkley (1990); and abolition, see Goen (1985). Of course, there were significant differences among evangelicals in the North and the South on the issue of slavery.

15. The term "fundamentalist" comes from a theological booklet series published between 1910 and 1915 called "The Fundamentals: A Testimony to the Truth" that explicated conservative Protestant theology.

    On the Great Reversal, see Regnerus and Smith (1998); Moberg (1977). This pessimism was fueled by a theological perspective of American fundamentalism called "premillennialist dispensationalism." According to this belief, in a cosmic sequence ordained by God, society would degenerate into a state of complete moral and civil decay, the nadir of which would result in the second coming of Jesus Christ to establish a good and just earthly realm. This stood in stark contrast to a postmillennialist dispensationalism, popular among progressive and liberal Protestants who advocated a "social gospel" whereby society would continue to improve, the apex of which would result in the second coming of Jesus Christ.

16. Of course, religious identities are located in wider contexts. These are ongoing storylines of which one's own narrative is just one scene in a larger tale. Religious institutions and faith communities provide the "grammar" for the stories adherents tell, supplying public narratives and "stock characters" from which they can draw to craft their own accounts (Ammerman 2003).

17. This had been the case with intellectuals like Benjamin Warfield at Princeton Seminary. Neo-evangelical leaders esteemed Warfield, and he represented a model for their vision.

18. This act was in direct opposition to ardent fundamentalists like Carl McIntire, whose own organization, the American Council of Christian Churches (formed in 1941), did not admit any churches or denominations already aligned with the Federal Council of Churches.

19. The publication was originally titled *The Post-American: Voice of the People's Christian Coalition,* a title it held from 1971 until 1975. It was then renamed *Sojourners* and is still published today.

20. Martin (1996: 147).

21. Representative of this transition of leadership and its wider implications is Howard Lindsell's 1977 book, *Battle for the Bible.* Biblical inerrancy—the idea that the Bible is literally true and without any error—had been a core conviction that the neo-evangelicals and their fundamentalist forebears shared. Lindsell, as a professor at Fuller Seminary and then editor and publisher of *Christianity Today,* was at the core of the leadership cohort behind neo-evangelicalism from the 1940s through the 1970s. Convinced that anything short of a doctrine of biblical inerrancy would lead to apostasy, Lindsell in his 1977 publication laid down the gauntlet that subscribing to inerrancy was a requirement to being an evangelical. Although his book eventually led to an evangelical council that met on the subject (the International Council of Biblical Inerrancy), the council's statement did not forge any lasting consensus. Evangelicals since have included those who do and do not subscribe to biblical inerrancy, but it is no longer a defining boundary for the movement. Indeed, the inability of Lindsell's impassioned plea to generate consensus in 1977 points to the wider leadership transition within the movement that took place around that time.

22. Empirical studies often explore the extent to which leaders are united by social background and worldview (Domhoff 2006; Dye 2002; Baltzell 1958; Mills 1956) or are fragmented and specialized (Keller 1963; Mannheim 1940). I endeavor to determine whether shared religious conviction surpasses other markers of elite status like education and professional recognition. Another motif involves leaders' modes of differentiation—that is, ways of distinguishing oneself from others (Lamont 1992; Bourdieu 1984)—so it is important to consider the extent to which evangelical public leaders employ frames for social differentiation. This book explores these ideas.

    I refer to "public" instead of "national" leaders (and "public leadership"), even though this is a book about evangelicalism in a single country. In an era of multinational corporations and media icons that reach audiences around the globe, "public leaders" is a more appropriate designation for those business and entertainment leaders in this study. Moreover, the social dimensions explored in this study, while occurring in the particularistic context of contemporary America, are applicable to other national contexts.

23. I conducted all of the interviews myself, avoiding the bias of multiple interviewers, and almost all interviews were conducted in person.

24. Major evangelical organizations represented in the study include informants associated with the Billy Graham Evangelistic Association, the Christian Broadcasting Network, Christianity Today International, the Evangelical Council for Financial Accountability, Campus Crusade for Christ, Focus on the Family, the Fellowship, Fuller Theological Seminary, Half Time, International Justice Mission, InterVarsity Christian Fellowship, Leadership Network, the North American Mission Board, the Trinity Forum, the Vine, Wheaton College, the Willow Creek Association, World Vision, Young Life, and Youth for Christ, among others.

   I supplemented interview data with ethnographic observations and archival research at 110 evangelical institutions. These included observing board meetings of the following groups: Christianity Today International, Evangelicals and Catholics Together, the Evangelical Council for Financial Accountability, Fuller Theological Seminary, InterVarsity Christian Fellowship, Prison Fellowship Ministries, Wheaton College, the Willow Creek Association, and World Vision.

   I also observed numerous meetings and conferences for different evangelical constituents including those for evangelical donors (the Gathering and Generous Giving) as well as young and emerging leaders (Act One, Civitas by the Center for Public Justice, Axiom Conversation, and the Vine). Archival and ethnographic research was also conducted on groups who shared particular areas of mutual interest or affiliation such as the White House Christian Fellowship, Faith and Law's annual retreat, and the Legacy Group in politics; the summer institute of the Harvey Fellows program, Emerging Scholars Network, Christian Union's Ivy League Congress, and Christian Leadership Ministries' academic conference for faculty in higher education; Socrates in the City, the PGA and LPGA weekly fellowship services on tour, and International Arts Movement in the culture/entertainment realm; and Time OUT for business leaders.

25. Because this study examines the influence of public leaders between 1976 and 2006, leaders did not have to be occupying their position at the time of the interview (as was the case with former presidents Carter and Bush). However, a majority (63 percent) were in their position of public responsibility at the time of the interview.

26. An exhaustive list of all *Fortune* 500 companies was compiled from 1976 to 2006 using Standard & Poor's Compustat data. Up until the early 1990s, Fortune compiled five separate lists for the different industrial sectors, each listing one hundred top firms. In the aggregate, the total number of firms exceeded five hundred in these cases, but applying today's methodology to previous years, they are all considered Fortune 500 firms.

27. I agree with others who deem black Protestantism to be different in kind from American evangelicalism (Steensland et al. 2000). In nearly every case, the people of color who are in this study (African American, Asian American, and Hispanics) attend mostly white congregations and affiliate with evangelical groups that serve mostly a white constituency.

28. I oversampled to include as many women as possible. On a few occasions when soliciting potential leaders to be interviewed for the project, I asked early participants specifically to recommend potential female leaders. However, I did not change the study's standard of occupying a position of public influence in order to find women. The women in this study have held positions equivalent with the project's male participants. On a few occasions, I interviewed married partners who share responsibility for an organization; in those cases, the women held senior enough positions to participate without their husbands, but since both were willing to participate, I interviewed them both.

   Regarding the difference between the number of women leaders and women in the workforce, this study confirms the conclusions of others who have examined the role of gender at the top of the social strata (Dolan 2001; Moore 1988; Epstein and Coser 1980). Fifteen percent of congressional representatives are women as of 2005 (data from the Center for American Women in Politics), and 16 percent of U.S. corporate officers are women. Women represent 46 percent of the U.S. labor force, according to the Women's Bureau at the U.S. Department of Labor. According to the C200 Business Leadership Index, women represent 30 percent of the MBA student bodies at elite business schools.

29. When speaking off the record, several women mentioned that their churches offer little support for female executives.

30. Barna (2003). He writes, "We discovered that the probability of someone embracing Jesus as his or her Savior was 32 percent for those between the ages of 5 and 12; 4 percent for those in the 13-to-18 age range; and 6 percent for people 19 or older" (34).

31. Collins (1998) examines how social networks and the relationships that constitute them distributed prestige and scholarly recognition among three world philosophies.

Chapter 1. Presidents and Politics

1. Others noted many years ago (Peterson 1979; Fiorina 1976) that voting, like all cultural phenomena, has a distinctly expressive dimension within pluralistic democracy. People enact certain cultural rituals as a way of expressing norms and beliefs that they hold dear.

2. On distance, see Smith (2000, 1998).

   Greeley and Hout (2006) find that income affects voting patterns in presidential elections for all denominations, but it affects the votes of conservative Protestants almost 50 percent more than it does others' votes. And the impact of family income on voting increased more than the differences among religion did from 1970 to 2000. Despite these economic differences, still more than half of poor conservative Protestants voted Republican in the 1992, 1996, and 2000 elections; evangelicals continue to cast their votes more according to candidates' positions on moral issues than on economic issues. Thomas Frank in *What's the Matter with Kansas* (2004) argued that the Republican Party united business and blue-collar voters in a conservative alliance. According to Frank, Republicans successfully persuaded the poor and working class to vote against their economic interests in favor of conservative social issues. In a subsequent essay, Bartels (2005) challenged Frank's argument and, by inference, the implication of Greeley and Hout's research about the voting practices of the poor. This points to the complicated work required of analysts who seek to separate economic from cultural issues in predicting voting behavior and the sometimes contradictory picture that emerges from different empirical investigations.

3. Several studies have explored the rise of evangelical political influence, largely addressing the topic as a social movement (Marsden 2006; Diamond 1995; Lienesch 1982). Most of this literature presents evangelicals as political outsiders seeking to bring about their vision for America through grassroots civic engagement (Smith 2000; Rozell and Wilcox 1995) or sometimes militant force (Kaplan 2004; Cox 1995; Hunter 1991; Conway and Siegelman 1984). Others have documented the role of evangelicals as a powerful voting bloc, especially within the Republican Party in recent decades (Green 2005; Regnerus, Sikkink, and Smith 1999; Oldfield 1996; Kellstedt et al. 1994).

4. "Movement leaders" refers to those individuals who served in a leadership position within the evangelical movement, typically heading a prominent evangelical organization. Following Keller (1963), I differentiate between leaders over a *segment* of society (like evangelicalism) and public leaders who occupy positions of societal influence. Billy Graham, as head of the Billy Graham Evangelistic Association and a prominent evangelist, is a movement leader whose authority arose from his position within a segment of American life (namely, the evangelical movement). By contrast, President Jimmy Carter, an evangelical like Graham, held a position that did not depend upon the evangelical movement for authority; his was based on societal influence.

5. Robertson failed the bar exam, so he decided not to pursue a career in law. Around the same time, Robertson had a personal religious experience and shortly thereafter enrolled in New York Theological Seminary where he earned a master of divinity degree in 1959.

6. Transcript from "Jimmy Carter" documentary in the *American Experience* series, Public Broadcasting System. See http://www.pbs.org/wgbh/amex/carter/filmmore/fd .html for complete transcript.

7. Established in 1973, the Trilateral Commission is a private organization that began at the encouragement of David Rockefeller, Henry Kissinger, and Zbigniew Brzezinksi. The approximately three hundred members include private citizens and world leaders from Japan, North America, and Europe.

8. Evangelicals were not opposed to racial desegregation per se, but they vehemently opposed governmental involvement in the internal affairs of religious institutions (Emerson and Smith 2000). For more on the evangelical sensibility regarding this perceived "attack" on their faith, see Martin (1996).

9. Also, President Carter was the first American president to issue public statements in support of gay rights. His White House hosted the first official visit by a gay rights organization, and his administration allowed a group of gay veterans to participate in an official ceremony at the Vietnam War Memorial. Actions like these shocked conservative evangelicals.

10. Led by evangelist James Robison, the lineup of speakers clearly leaned to the right on the political spectrum. It came as no surprise, then, when President Carter and Independent candidate John Anderson declined an invitation to address the group.

11. Representative of Reagan's tacit identification with evangelicals was his description of communism as an "evil empire." Indeed, the "evil empire" speech was one of Reagan's most memorable addresses, and it was delivered at the Annual Convention of the National Association of Evangelicals on March 8, 1983, in Orlando, Florida. Reagan's selection of the NAE venue points to his mastery of the symbolic gesture that has been crucial to rising evangelical political influence.

12. Practically all movement leaders, including Pat Robertson, Jerry Falwell, and James Robison, backed Reagan's candidacy, but not all evangelical voters agreed (Woodberry and Smith 1998; Manza and Brooks 1997; Woodberry and Brink 1996). The tide would turn by 1984, at which time nearly all rank-and-file members followed movement leaders in backing Reagan and moving squarely inside the Republican fold.

13. Comments to the U.S. Chamber of Commerce, September 21, 1983.

14. William Patrick Clark served for the fourteen months between the two.

15. It is interesting to see how the term "pro-life" became synonymous with a political position against abortion. The term has not been closely identified, for example, with opposition to capital punishment. In 1995, Pope John Paul II issued the encyclical *Evangelium Vitae*, which means "Gospel of Life." There, he speaks of a "culture of life" that encompasses a range of issues around the sanctity of human life. Here, the Catholic Church officially began to link opposition to abortion with an opposition to capital punishment. See Luker (1984) on the emergence of a rhetoric of "pro-life."

16. Dobson, a former faculty member at the University of Southern California School of Medicine, founded Focus on the Family in 1977. Previously, he had gained national attention with the publication of his 1970 best-selling book, *Dare to Discipline*. The book, relying on both his evangelical background as the son and grandson of Nazarene preachers and his experience as a psychologist, encouraged parents to exert greater authority over their children's lives. Bucking the prevailing thought at the time, Dobson advocated the use of corporal punishment and stronger boundaries for children. With this start, Dobson began speaking to groups around the country about the book, offering advice on parenting and family issues. Eventually, Dobson's interest in the American family took him into the world of politics. He and other movement leaders were very pleased with the 1980 Republican platform that had dropped support for the ERA and advocated a constitutional amendment outlawing abortion.

17. Dobson also helped launch the Family Research Council, a political advocacy operation designed to advance evangelical positions on marriage and the family, in 1982.

18. Senior-level evangelicals in the Bush administration were Vice President Quayle, whose placement on the Bush ticket in 1988 surprised many; Elizabeth Dole, secretary of labor; Jack Kemp, secretary of housing and urban development; and Al Sikes, chairman of the Federal Communications Commission. All these individuals were known for their evangelical faith.

19. Decisions like who is allowed to address delegates at the national party conventions—and, important in an era of limited network television coverage of the conventions, at what time they address the delegates—are strategically symbolic gestures.

Evangelicals I interviewed noted, for instance, when pro-life Democrat Governor Robert Casey of Pennsylvania was denied the chance to address the 1992 Democratic National Convention. They also noted (some with great chagrin because of their loyalty to conservative Republican ideology) the prominence of moderate Republicans who addressed the 2004 Republican National Convention.

20. Hunter (1991).
21. Data from the National Survey of Religion and Politics conducted at the University of Akron in the spring of 1992 confirm this. At that time, 43 percent of evangelicals gave a high evaluation of Bush's job in office, compared to only 38 percent of mainline Protestants and only 35 percent of Roman Catholics.
22. Ironically, Clinton actually received a lower percentage of evangelical votes than Dukakis did in 1988 (Kellstedt et al. 1994).
23. This was particularly effective with swing voting blocs like Roman Catholics in 1992.
24. Goldstein (1997); Hunt (1997).
25. Kengor (2004) finds a statistically significant difference between these two figures.
26. Kengor (2004) cites explicitly partisan statements by President Clinton such as identifying New York's Democratic governor Mario Cuomo as a "prophet" and instructing worshippers to vote. At Shiloh Baptist Church in October 2000, President Clinton said, "I am pleading with you.... I have done everything I know to do.... [But] you have to show.... Make sure nobody takes a pass on November seventh." In addition to black churches, President Clinton spoke between 1993 and 2000 at twenty-one different churches from a variety of religious traditions, including evangelical congregations like the Willow Creek Community Church.
27. According to a knowledgeable source, "It wasn't that Clinton said, 'I hate this stuff, let's get rid of it.' But among the people that President Clinton hired, it was a badge of dishonor to be a part of that. [So Christians after the first two years] didn't have an official Bible study, but they met informally and infrequently in people's offices."
28. Reich (2004: 40).
29. The Clinton administration also did not have a close relationship with the only other Democrat—and fellow evangelical—to occupy the White House in recent memory. President Carter reports he received the worst treatment since leaving office from the Clinton administration, while the elder Bush administration treated him the best (Hallow 2005).
30. Pastor of Grace Chapel in Massachusetts, McDonald admitted to an adulterous affair in 1987. In addition, the Reverend Philip Wogaman, pastor of Foundry United Methodist Church in Washington, which the Clintons attended, was part of the group that provided spiritual counsel for the president.
31. According to Seiple, the group included a variety of evangelical leaders such as Fuller Theological Seminary president Richard Mouw and *Christianity Today* columnist and popular writer Philip Yancey.
32. At his final public event, held in New York City in June 2005, Graham came the closest to endorsing a candidate for president since he seated Richard Nixon in the VIP section at his 1968 crusade in Pittsburgh. Graham declared, "I told President Clinton that when he left office, he should be an evangelist because he has all the right gifts for it, and he should leave his wife to run the country."
33. David Kuo, a former member of the Bush White House, has suggested that this is only in appearance. In reality, says Kuo, White House staffers refer to evangelical leaders as "crazies" and "nuts" (Kuo 2006: 229–30). I interviewed Kuo as he was leaving the White House in 2003. At that time, he gave no indication of such behavior, even as I pressed him for tensions between politics and evangelical faith. Based on the interviews and observations I conducted in and around the Bush White House, I think such name-calling likely did occur among junior staff members. Among senior staffers and those within the president's inner circle, I found displeasure or unease with aspects of the evangelical movement, but never to the point that Kuo suggests.
34. In fact, Richard Mouw, an evangelical philosopher at Calvin College, told *Newsweek* in 1984 that President Reagan, despite his rhetoric, did not even show the "marks" of an evangelical—namely "personal spirituality, a solid grasp of Christian doctrine,

or desire to help the poor" (Woodward 1984). However, Reagan did use his bully pulpit to address religious gatherings. No president has spoken to more religious meetings while in office than Reagan. Five addresses to the National Religious Broadcasters and two addresses to the National Association of Evangelicals are among these (Smith 2006).

35. It is interesting that Bush has publicly identified his conversion to evangelical Christianity only with Graham. A year earlier, he had met with Arthur Blessitt, an evangelist who dragged a twelve-foot cross around the world, at the Holidome restaurant at a West Texas Holiday Inn. David Aikman, whose book *A Man of Faith* (2004) chronicles the spiritual journey of George W. Bush, says both events happened. Blessitt claims that their conversation ended with the two men holding hands and praying for Bush's salvation. The president's identifying his conversion with Graham and not Blessitt reflects the extent to which affiliation with certain pockets of evangelicalism can be more important than others. Regardless, by 1985, the younger Bush left behind his wilder days as a West Texas oilman and pursued the disciplined life familiar to many American evangelicals. Encounters with these two evangelists and a small group of evangelical men (including Don Evans, who would become secretary of commerce) transformed his life, according to many people I interviewed close to the president. Regarding Bush's comment about Jesus as his favorite political philosopher, made while visiting Iowa in 1999, it is surprising that other candidates have not received as much attention for similar comments. In December 2003, presidential candidate Dick Gephardt made a much more explicit link between partisan politics and religious faith. Speaking to a group of Democratic voters in Iowa, Gephardt said, "He [Jesus] was a Democrat, I think."

36. Some have claimed (McGarvey 2004; Sullivan 2004) that George W. Bush attends church significantly less than President Clinton did while in Washington. A careful review of the president's weekly schedule, as released by the White House Press Office, for several administrations reveals that the weekly digest of the president's schedule rarely contains references to church attendance, aside from religious holiday services (like Easter services attended in a military chapel) or highly unusual events (as in the first White House church service conducted in 1969 at the start of the Nixon administration). Therefore, I find little support, according to the weekly compilation of presidential documents, that President Clinton attended church more often than President George W. Bush. However, people I interviewed have said that while at Camp David, President Bush uses the chapel more frequently than President Clinton did during his trips to the presidential retreat. By the same token, informed observers say President Bush attends church relatively infrequently while staying at his ranch in Crawford, Texas.

37. In nearly all of these references, the president goes out of his way to identify the enemies of "darkness" as terrorists and rogue regimes, not Muslims in general. In fact, Bush has made more positive statements on Islam and Muslims than any other U.S. president and was the first sitting president to visit a mosque. This may be the result of the sincerity of his own faith (Bush has distanced himself from fellow evangelicals who have described Muslims in offensive ways), or it could be a politically smart move. Perhaps Bush's religious conviction causes him to show greater sensitivity to people of other faiths; observers believe President Carter effectively brokered the Camp David Peace Accords because he shared with Sadat and Begin sincere religious belief, albeit in different traditions. Most likely, though, Bush's positive statements on Islam are the result of his desire to maintain good relations with moderate Muslim states in the wake of the attacks of September 11, 2001. Speaking on the White House lawn on September 16, 2001, the president referred to a "crusade" against terrorism, drawing widespread ire and bewilderment from Muslim leaders around the world. He never used the term publicly again.

38. On rhetorical tradition, see Meacham (2006). See also Shogan (2006). Neuhaus quoted in Cooperman (2004).

39. As will be discussed later, evangelical Protestants and some Roman Catholics prefer the formulation of Lewis' "mere Christianity" for its commitment to traditional orthodoxy without the symbolic boundaries that exist among religious traditions today. By eschewing the term "evangelical" in favor of "mere Christian," President Bush employs a discourse that is not immediately off-putting to those who may not

see themselves as co-religionists with evangelical Protestants (such as mainline Protestants and Roman Catholics).

40. The fact that two of the most prominent evangelicals appointed by President Bush, Karen Hughes and Condoleezza Rice, are women reflects that Bush's brand of evangelicalism is not entirely conservative.

41. However, an important faction of the Bush administration, including Vice President Cheney, Deputy White House Chief of Staff Karl Rove, and former secretary of defense Donald Rumsfeld, has little religious kinship with the president's evangelical faith.

42. Frum (2003: 3–4). Lefkowitz quoted in Cooperman (2004).

43. Officials of the Jewish faith in the Bush White House have included the following: Elliott Abrams (deputy national security adviser), Joshua Bolten (chief of staff), Michael Chertoff (secretary of homeland security), Ari Fleischer (White House press secretary), Blake Gottesman (personal aide to the president), I. Lewis Libby (chief of staff to the vice president), Ken Mehlman (White House political director), and Paul Wolfowitz (deputy secretary of defense).

44. In this context, "liberal evangelicals" and "progressive evangelicals" are synonyms, but they are employed by different camps, conservatives and liberals, respectively. Rhetorical strategies such as these are reflected in other evangelical contexts like the designation between "fundamentalists" and "conservatives" within the Southern Baptist Convention over the last twenty-five years. With regard to the legacy of progressive evangelicals, see Ribuffo (1980).

45. The ad appearing in the *Grand Rapids Press* on May 21, 2005, said in part, "We, the undersigned, respect your office, and we join the college in welcoming you to our campus. Like you, we recognize the importance of religious commitment in American political life. We seek open and honest dialogue about the Christian faith and how it is best expressed in the political sphere. While recognizing God as sovereign over individuals and institutions alike, we understand that no single political position should be identified with God's will, and we are conscious that this applies to our own views as well as those of others. At the same time we see conflicts between our understanding of what Christians are called to do and many of the policies of your administration." Some faculty and students also wore stickers to commencement that declared "God Is Not a Democrat or a Republican."

46. The term arose from various items John Green, a political scientist at the University of Akron, and Steve Waldman, editor of Beliefnet.com, have published on www.beliefnet.com.

47. On the political diversity of American evangelicals, see McGarvey (2004). Regarding the number of evangelicals who do not identify with the Religious Right, see Smith (2000).

48. I am not sure how "authentic" is defined by Strider, but the context in which he mentioned the term suggests the group is for members who are interested in the relation between religion and politics out of both spiritual and political concern.

49. The consulting firm is Common Good Strategies, founded by Eric Sapp and Mara Vanderslice in Washington, D.C. Faithful Democrats is chaired by Tennessee politician Roy Herron and social justice advocate Revered Romal J. Tune.

50. See www.sojo.net for the best explication of this argument.

51. As Mary Douglas has argued (1970), morals are powerful forces because they affirm or violate "natural symbols." In society, these natural symbols are represented by mores and taboos with reference to the human body.

52. In their classic text, Peter Berger and Thomas Luckmann (1966) examine the process by which subjective meaning becomes part of everyday life. Language, they argued, is the key symbol system through which social reality is constructed; through it, subjective meaning systems become internalized and then taken for granted, which is the most powerful way meaning systems (like evangelical belief) become embedded in society. More recent work (Wuthnow 1987; Swidler 2000) has argued that social scientific data cannot be directly mapped to subjective meaning; interview transcripts do not convey meaning per se, but they provide discourses about meaning that, in themselves, are worthy of examination. Early writings within the sociology of religion, such as those of Durkheim and Weber, dedicated much energy to analyzing the meaning systems and religious motivations behind rituals, beliefs,

and symbols. However, today scholars study religious phenomena by attending more carefully to the ways in which adherents live out their religion (Hall 1997) and the various ways believers talk about their spiritual lives (Griffith 1997). It is in this spirit that I seek to make sense of leaders' discourse on meaning and purpose.

53. Carter's book *Palestine: Peace, Not Apartheid* (2006) raised concerns among fellow evangelists as well as members of the Jewish community because he links Israeli policy with South Africa's history of racial apartheid.

54. Holifield (1976) suggested three major influences on Carter's ideology: his evangelical beliefs, the Christian realism of Reinhold Niebuhr, and Baptist notions of the separation of church and state.

55. Address to Congressional subcommittee on apartheid, December 4, 1984 (Washington, D.C.).

56. I do not mean to imply that Baker's comments were given for instrumental purposes. Data from this study cannot assess issues like these; however, it is striking that by 1990 an Episcopalian like Baker would use evangelical rhetoric in much the same way it might have been used by a Southern Baptist like Jimmy Carter in the 1970s. Indeed, Baker's comments and the wide reception they received after the National Prayer Breakfast suggest the increasing "publicness" of the evangelical movement that occurred between the 1970s and the 1990s.

57. Unlike Roman Catholicism, which has a more structured approach to spiritual practices (namely through the Church's seven sacraments), evangelical spirituality encourages improvisation, and the robust sector of evangelical publishing and conferences (Hendershot 2004; Willmer, Schmidt, and Smith 1998) provides multiple venues through which adherents can learn of different ways to pray, study scripture, and act on their faith convictions through various spiritual practices. By the same token, evangelical spirituality features a sentiment of straightforwardness and simplicity. Unlike mainline Protestantism, with its regard for theological sophistication, evangelicalism prefers activism over contemplation, enthusiastic expressiveness over quiet resolve. As a result, evangelical adherents are encouraged by their churches and fellow believers to express their spirituality regularly and unabashedly. All of these have contributed to more visible expressions of evangelical faith by public leaders.

58. In 1988, McFarlane pleaded guilty to withholding information from Congress, was sentenced to two years' probation and a fine, but was pardoned on Christmas Eve in 1992 by President George H.W. Bush. Today, he serves as chairman of Energy & Communications Solutions LLC in Washington.

59. Officially founded in 1944, the organization has changed names several times in intervening years and is now known as the International Foundation, or informally as "the Fellowship." The first National Prayer Breakfast included dignitaries from Congress, the Pentagon, and around the world and was hosted by hotel magnate Conrad Hilton at his Mayflower Hotel in downtown Washington.

60. Van Biema et al. (2005).

61. The "quiet diplomacy" remark was made by President Bush at the 1990 National Prayer Breakfast.

62. I identified about ten different religious groups that reach an elite constituency, but none of those organizations is mentioned nearly as often as the Fellowship.

63. I find less support for the Fellowship's involvement in domestic issues, and because of the group's nonpartisan nature, they never take positions on contentious political issues.

64. Obviously, closer elections and the need to persuade moderate voters have also contributed to greater partisanship, yet observers say the lack of social interaction among members of Congress and their families is one of the most underappreciated contributing factors. Every leader who raised this point with me mentioned the Fellowship as countering this trend.

65. Elsewhere, I write at length (Lindsay 2006) about critiques of this powerful group, some of which my research supports. However, in this section, I am focusing my comments on how the Fellowship has contributed toward elite cohesion.

66. It is not coincidental that the photograph of Doug Coe in *Time*'s "25 Most Influential Evangelicals" issue featured Coe shaking hands with the elder President Bush. See van Biema et al. (2005).

Chapter 2. Allies and Enemies

1. It also helps that Gifford is a celebrity, although she, like other leaders I interviewed, downplayed the benefits of location within the structure of social networks that come with celebrity status.
2. As governor of California, remember, Reagan had liberalized abortion policies.
3. In 1981, the Court upheld a Utah parental notification law, but in 1983, it struck down Ohio requirements for hospital-only procedures after the first trimester and mandatory waiting periods before the procedure is performed.
4. Not coincidentally, the book was produced by an evangelical publishing house, ThomasNelson.
5. Pro-choice groups refer to the policy as the "gag rule."
6. Clinton also reversed Reagan-era restrictions on abortion including Title X regulations banning abortion referral by federal employees and the ban on military hospitals performing abortions.
7. Reagan Supreme Court appointees Sandra Day O'Connor and Anthony Kennedy reaffirmed the validity of a woman's right to abortion under *Roe v. Wade* in *Planned Parenthood v. Casey*.
8. Evangelical rhetoric regarding abortion has effectively reified their position through specific policies while maintaining symbolic boundaries—that is, conceptual distinctions used to categorize ideas (Lamont and Molnar 2002)—that identify God with a pro-life position and the opposite side with pro-choice.
9. The Defense of Marriage Act defines "marriage" and "spouse" for purposes of federal law. The legislation was in response to a decision by the Hawaii State Supreme Court declaring that the prohibition against marriage for same-sex couples could be unconstitutional and that such a prohibition could only be upheld for a "compelling reason." The federal legislation was aimed at curbing the likelihood that other states would be required to recognize a same-sex union under the Full Faith and Credit Clause of the U.S. Constitution.
10. Hertzke (2004).
11. As others have shown (Jacobs 1996; Griswold 1983), movement leaders can promulgate confirmatory, or legitimating, narratives as a way of validating involvement in cultural change (in this case, an evangelical discourse favoring religious liberty legitimated movement activism in foreign affairs). Other scholarship has shown that the way groups talk about themselves and their identity often grounds collective mobilization (Hart 1992). Social movements must capitalize upon this identity discourse in order to bring about societal change (Wuthnow 1989).
12. The legislation stipulated that a country found to be an egregious transgressor of religious freedom could be designated as a "country of particular concern" based on the report's findings. This "name and shame" factor, insiders tell me, has been effective at achieving quick results from countries that want amicable relations with the U.S. government.
13. Smith (2006) makes this point by noting the salience of human rights in Carter's foreign policy and the ways in which faith compelled him to act in the Panama Canal treaties and the Camp David Accords, among other diplomatic efforts while in office.
14. Nonetheless, there were many prominent Clinton appointees who did not share the president's evangelical proclivities (such as Robert Reich, previously cited). Notwithstanding a few appointments, the Clinton administration was not as friendly to evangelical leaders as other administrations had been.
15. Appointments like these demonstrate the small network of influential evangelicals involved with international aid and religious freedom. Seiple moved from World Vision to the State Department when named the first ambassador-at-large for international religious freedom. Anderson, who serves on the executive committee of World Vision's board of directors, presided over USAID from 1999 until early 2002. He was succeeded by Andrew S. Natsios, who previously had served as a vice president of World Vision from 1993 until 1998. Seiple's successor, John V. Hanford III, has theological training from the evangelical seminary Gordon-Conwell, but for ten years prior to his appointment at the State Department he served as a congressional fellow in international religious freedom.

16. The "social gospel" refers to a religio-political orientation, popular in the late nineteenth and early twentieth centuries in the United States, whereby people of faith advocated liberal social programs, often sponsored by the government with additional support from civil society, as a means of bearing witness to the "good news" (hence the term "gospel") of their faith. One of the principal proponents of the social gospel was liberal Protestant theologian Walter Rauschenbusch. The social gospel movement was one of the key elements to the union of left-of-center political orientation and mainline Protestantism in twentieth-century American religious life.

17. I should note that none of the evangelicals I interviewed ever mentioned the fact that many evangelical denominations in the antebellum South opposed the abolitionist movement.

18. Wilberforce has become an increasingly popular figure for the evangelical movement. Charles Colson launched an organization in 1991 called the Wilberforce Forum that is dedicated to public issues and cultural concerns similar to Wilberforce's vision for Victorian England, and Walden Media released a film in 2007 about the parliamentarian, *Amazing Grace.*

19. PEACE stands for a fivefold objective of planting churches, equipping leaders, assisting the poor, caring for the sick, and educating the next generation.

20. Lawson (2003).

21. Of course, it should be noted that Bush's policy is more amenable to conservative evangelicals, in part, because it focuses on arresting mother-to-child transmission of AIDS in Africa and the Caribbean. It does not address more contentious issues like issuing free condoms or clean needles to at-risk populations in the United States. But as this example shows, certain well-placed advisors can play a critical role in shaping an administration's policy. It also reveals the way in which U.S. presidents can advance particular policies more easily on the international front than at home.

22. On the high esteem in which Stott is held by evangelicals worldwide, see Brooks (2004).

23. Executive Order, the White House, January 29, 2001.

24. Research by Chaves (1999) shows that faith-based initiatives and the "charitable choice" provisions of 1996 welfare reform were likewise supported not by rank-and-file evangelicals but by evangelical elites.

25. People I interviewed who held leadership positions at grant-making agencies insist they did not exert pressure on grant panels to award evangelical groups federal money. Based on interviews with leaders at these various evangelical groups, I conclude that the number of grant applications that have been rejected by federal agencies where evangelicals have held positions of leadership suggests that this has, in fact, been the case. Also, grant rejections and approvals, most of which required panel review, occurred during both the Clinton and the Bush administrations. This further supports these assertions of no bias.

26. The phrase alludes to an evangelical hymn by Lewis E. Jones entitled "Power in the Blood." The referent of the "power, wonder-working power" in the hymn is the redeeming work of Jesus Christ, which evangelicals believe happened in his death and resurrection.

27. Phillips (2006); Kaplan (2004). This is often referred to as dispensational theology and is the theological scaffolding for the apocalyptic-thriller series *Left Behind*, co-authored by Tim LaHaye and Jerry Jenkins.

28. David Aikman, whom I interviewed and who has had the best access to examine President Bush's religious faith, concurs.

29. While I have focused largely on activity within the executive branch, corollary research in other parts of the federal government suggests similar developments have likely happened in places like the U.S. Congress (Guth and Kellstedt 1999).

30. Nettl (1967). In examining American political life, several scholars have documented the grassroots political mobilization of evangelicals (Harding 2001; Smith 2000), yet few of them have attended to the task of exploring the interaction between evangelical movement leaders (like Jerry Falwell and James Dobson) and those who actually occupied positions of political power. Surprising differences of opinion emerged as I talked with leaders from both camps. Moreover, studies that rely on national survey data or single case studies are unable to discern the

historical and comparative elements that have contributed to the ways in which populist campaigns (like the Moral Majority) have been woven into the fabric of the American political establishment. They also miss pockets of the evangelical movement that strongly disagree with these tactics.

31. Hoffer ([1951] 2002).

32. Of course, it should be noted that not all evangelicals shared these sentiments then, and certainly do not today. Black evangelicals, for example, do not long for a return to colonial or antebellum America, and few of them think of this era of American history as particularly "Christian." See Emerson and Smith (2000).

33. This patriotism is part of why William Randolph Hearst liked the group and eventually telegrammed the editors at his newspapers to "puff Graham," an act that catapulted Billy Graham to celebrity status in midcentury America. Graham began his preaching career through Youth for Christ (YFC), and Ted Engstrom, who later headed World Vision and Zondervan Publishing House, was an early leader within YFC.

34. In other contexts, such as Great Britain, evangelicals are often at the other end of the political spectrum, advocating liberal and sometimes socialist political positions.

35. Marsden (2006).

36. The phrase "Free Congress" originated from the desire of conservatives like Wey-rich to "free" or rid Congress of increasing liberal influence. This mission no longer applies to the foundation, but the group still exists, and the name has not changed.

37. Charles Colson, one of the president's closest advisors, was asked to develop a list of "rich people with strong religious interest to be invited to the White House for church services" (Martin 1996: 98).

38. Curiously, many who have occupied this position since the Reagan administration have been particularly focused on the evangelical community; notable liaisons include Mariam Bell (Reagan), Doug Wead (George H. W. Bush), Flo McAfee, with help from Linda Lader (Clinton), and Timothy Goeglein (George W. Bush).

39. Schaeffer (1982) was influenced by Rousas John Rushdoony, an ultra-conservative Presbyterian. Born into an Armenian immigrant family and educated at Berkeley, Rushdoony held a postmillennial eschatology that believed Jesus would return once the church had claimed "dominion" over all the earth. His philosophy, called Reconstructionism (or Theonomy or Dominionism) advocated the establishment of a theocratic state based on Mosaic civil law, which included about six hundred statutes. Rushdoony's ideas are expounded in his 1973 *Institutes of Biblical Law,* an eight-hundred-page tome. A few observers (Clarkson 1997) have overstated the influence of Rushdoony's Reconstructionism, suggesting that everyone from Jack Hayford to Marvin Olasky to Howard Ahmanson embraces his radical views. For a more nuanced analysis of Rushdoony's influence on Schaeffer, see Diamond (1995).

40. Prior to their meeting, Carter had been tangentially involved with political strife occurring within the Southern Baptist Convention (SBC). Like several other denominations, the SBC sponsored seminaries whose faculty members included some liberal theologians. In the post–World War II era, ideas from liberal institutions like Union Theological Seminary in New York surfaced at places like Southern Baptist seminaries, as Union Seminary doctoral graduates joined the ranks of various faculties. As Nancy Ammerman (1990) details, the theological ethos at these seminaries was quite different from that of most Southern Baptist churches; young seminarians were often shocked to hear their professors' ideas about Jesus, miracles, and the authority of the Bible. During seminary, many of these students who held more conservative theological positions (like the current head of the convention, Morris Chapman) decided they would "do something about this" when they graduated. In 1979, at the annual Southern Baptist Convention, held that year in Houston's Astrodome, these conservative pastors took decisive action. Working in cooperation with lay leaders like Judge Paul Pressler, the conservative faction began a takeover of the Southern Baptist Convention, electing Memphis pastor Adrian Rogers to the SBC presidency. Using a political strategy of issues-based campaigning around the concept of biblical inerrancy (a conviction that says the Bible is word-for-word, literally true), the conservative faction won the presidency of the SBC every year thereafter. Its first political victory was the election of Rogers in 1979, and the Oval Office meeting between

Carter and Rogers and his wife happened shortly after he assumed the SBC presidency.

41. Such divisions between an elected official and his or her administration have been more common in recent decades during Democratic rather than Republican administrations, a point to which we will return later.

42. Wilcox (1996).

43. During that part of the campaign, David Broder of the *Washington Post* wrote, "It's a healthy phenomenon, in the eyes of this secular reporter-critic, and not the menace some see. The clerics sometimes speak uncomfortable truths to the mighty" (Silk 2005).

44. The Values Action Team includes representatives from Focus on the Family, the Family Research Council, the Eagle Forum, the Traditional Values Coalition, and Concerned Women for America, among others. Insiders report that these Thursday gatherings, which began in 1998, discuss issues like Supreme Court nominees, policies on the family, and the execution of a pro-life agenda. The Arlington Group—named for its original meeting spot in northern Virginia—is composed of roughly seventy-five members who meet regularly for off-the-record brainstorming sessions on conservative policies and media messages. With Paul Weyrich as the main convener of the Arlington Group, breakfasts that it sponsors for lawmakers are often called "Weyrich breakfasts" inside the Washington Beltway. Regarding the long tenure of groups like these, remember that Weyrich, at the encouragement of Mike Valerio (a mentor for many conservative leaders), organized a group in 1977 called the Free Congress Foundation. This was a coalition for chief architects of the Religious Right in the 1970s. Weyrich served as president of the Free Congress Research and Education Foundation from 1977 to 2002 and has served as chairman and CEO since then. The Arlington Group represents the next generation of evangelical political coalitions. African-American pastors like the Reverend Bill Owens and Bishop Keith Butler now participate, reflecting the wider tent of evangelical political activism.

45. Gilgoff (2007) chronicles the various accomplishments of Dobson and his organization. Many of the people I interviewed agreed with Gilgoff's assessment of Dobson's influence in the late 1970s and 1980s, but they did not share his conclusion that Dobson had "unmatched political influence in the evangelical world" (xiii), especially in recent years

46. This has been the case in previous societies, as Padgett and Ansell (1993) noted of Renaissance Italy.

47. See www.policycounsel.org for more information.

48. Allen (2006).

49. Every attendee, including children, must participate in the program in some way.

50. Indeed, at the 2006 Renaissance Weekend in Charleston, one of the main speakers related a story with the punch line "Don't buy a house from a born-again Christian." The crowd roared with laughter. Later, a couple of evangelical attendees suggested in an off-the-record conversation with me that Renaissance leaders would never allow another group to be so characterized. This episode reveals the tension between evangelicals and non-evangelicals at left-of-center gatherings, a particularly intriguing tension given the evangelical faith of Linda LeSourd Lader, who runs Renaissance Weekend.

51. For the quote, see Huntington (2000: xiv). Harrison (2006) addresses this notion more fully.

52. For example, the group championed a campaign called Healthy Media, Healthy Children.

53. Others have shown that salient identities like gender (Moore 1988) and race (Smith 1981) can produce important forms of elite cohesion and unity within the corridors of power. And because of the deeply binding nature a shared religious identity can produce, the emergence of evangelicalism as a form of elite unity is extremely important, one that has not been examined fully until now. Also, while I have focused in this line of research largely on the executive branch, other examinations have indicated similar levels of salient evangelical identity for many on Capitol Hill (Guth and Kellstedt 1999; Benson and Williams 1982). Guth and Kellstedt (1999) have shown that evangelicals are among the most religiously active of all major religious groups represented among members of Congress; in fact,

86 percent of them exhibit "strong" religious involvement. This large degree of religious activity and conservative religious tradition, in turn, has yielded powerful results in terms of loyalty to the GOP. They find that evangelical members are "consistently more conservative than their political, demographic, regional, and district characteristics would predict" (Guth and Kellstedt 1999: 11).

54. Indeed, Jerry Falwell endorsed Vice President Bush during the 1988 Republican primary season, and other movement leaders supported Jack Kemp and Robert Dole over Robertson.

55. Christian Reconstructionism is a religious philosophy that advocates the establishment of a theocratic state based on Mosaic civil law; see note 39 above. On the other hand, apocalyptic premillennialism, which is reflected in works like the *Left Behind* series, posits the end of the world will come about by a complete deterioration of the moral order. This order will be destroyed in the eschaton—the final days of the world—and Jesus will come back and restore a thousand-year reign.

56. Comment by William H. McBeath, executive director, American Public Health Association, Washington, D.C.

57. At the time, the nomination for surgeon general did not require congressional approval, but the 64-year-old Koop exceeded the age limit for the office by a hundred days.

58. Letter from Phyllis Schlafly and Paul Weyrich regarding the 1987 "Salute to the Surgeon General" dinner.

59. Recent scholarship has demonstrated the importance of differentiating white evangelicalism from black Protestantism (Steensland et al. 2000). Black Protestantism is different in kind from American evangelicalism, and my focus is on the latter. Hence, in this study, the few African Americans who were interviewed mostly attend churches or are involved in ministries more traditionally associated with white evangelicalism. Nevertheless, racial divisions are salient for any discussion relating to the connection between religion and politics.

60. Emerson and Smith (2000: 170).

61. Christerson, Edwards, and Emerson (2005); Yancey (1996); Perkins and Tarrants (1994); Washington and Kehrein (1993).

62. Martin (1996: 44). A counterexample can be found in a 1958 sermon by Jerry Falwell entitled "Segregation and Integration: Which?" In the sermon, Falwell suggested that racial integration would lead to the destruction of the white race. In 1965, Falwell preached another sermon, "Ministers and Marches," that condemned the activism of Dr. Martin Luther King Jr. In subsequent years, Falwell repudiated both sermons.

63. James had served as assistant secretary of health and human services under President George H. W. Bush as well as a senior fellow at the Heritage Foundation prior to her appointment at OPM.

64. It is interesting also to note how little the African American leaders that I interviewed talked about matters of racial inequality. Indeed, they are part of a social context in which racial division is not often raised as an issue of great social concern among evangelicals. This reflects the individualistic ethic within the movement (Smith 1998; Hunter 1983) over a concern for transforming social structures, which has been more closely associated with other religious traditions like liberation theology in Latin America, or even black Protestantism in this country through religious leaders like Jesse Jackson or the Reverend Al Sharpton.

65. Evangelicals have helped fund programs at the Heritage Foundation, the Family Research Council, the Center for Public Justice, the Ethics and Public Policy Center, and the Institute for Global Engagement, among others. O'Connor (2001) has shown how powerful this can be for mobilizing ideas; she concludes that conservatives have done a notably effective job in using think tanks to establish the intellectual foundations for policies that they favor.

66. Subsequently, Sider and Knippers (who died in early 2005) co-edited a volume, *Toward an Evangelical Public Policy* (2005), that articulated the core convictions of the original document and then expanded on its implications through essays written by various voices within the evangelical community.

67. Reflecting this sentiment, President Bill Clinton spoke positively of the two elements working together: "conservatism, which, at its very best, draws lines that should not be crossed, and progressivism, which, at its very best, breaks down [lines] that are

no longer needed or should never have been erected in the first place" (Public statement, November 18, 2004, Little Rock, Arkansas).

68. Green's research (2005) shows that Bush captured a "decisive advantage in a very tight election" (3), by capturing the votes in 2004 of all kinds of churchgoers including those who only attend on a monthly basis—a group that is closely divided between Republicans and Democrats.

69. Colson (1994).

70. See Hackett and Lindsay (2004) as well as Gallup and Lindsay (1999).

71. Smith (2000).

72. On the triumph of an organized minority, see Mosca ([1896] 1939), who has argued that power resides in the ability of a group to organize.

Like other groups, evangelicals appeared more united on their ascent to political power. A closer examination, such as ours in this chapter, reveals the presence of several different movements that existed within, but there appears to be more outspoken divergence of opinion on political matters today than was the case in the 1970s, 1980s, or 1990s.

73. Indeed, numerous governmental leaders talked about regular, tense meetings where movement leaders charged Republican leaders with "not delivering" what they promised in exchange for political support. Jim Dobson's public support for a third-party candidate instead of Bob Dole, who he felt was "soft" on abortion, in 1996 is representative of this ongoing tension between conservative evangelical leaders and conservative politicians.

Chapter 3. Knowledge to Change the World

1. Harper (1905: 34).

2. Schmalzbauer (2005), Smith (2003), and Roberts and Turner (2000) have argued that secularism is, in fact, a form of sectarianism: a movement with identifiable leaders, resources, and collective objectives.

3. Evangelicals have also been very interested in education at the primary and secondary levels. For information about the complicated relationship between evangelicals and education, see Beyerlein (2004), Smith and Sikkink (2000), Sikkink (1999), Darnell and Sherkat (1997), Wagner (1990), and Peshkin (1986). However, this section focuses on developments in higher education because this level of education has been particularly hostile to American evangelicals since the 1940s; indeed, *The Williamsburg Charter Survey on Religion and Public Life*, published in 1988, found that "nearly one out of three academics (34 percent) said that evangelicals are 'a threat to democracy.'" Additionally, this section focuses on higher education because of the interest that leaders I interviewed expressed in issues surrounding knowledge production and university life—a topic that has been largely unexamined thus far.

4. See Marsden (1991) and Noll (1983).

5. See Carpenter (1997) and Marsden (1991).

6. Several works have previously demonstrated the differences between American fundamentalism and American evangelicalism. See Wolfe (2003), Smith (1998), and Marsden (1991).

7. Henry earned two doctorates, one from Northern Baptist Theological Seminary in theology and one from Boston University in philosophy.

8. As Wuthnow (1993, 1988) shows, the education gap between evangelicals and the general population that was pronounced during the 1950s diminished to negligible differences by the 1980s.

9. For the lingering Protestant influence on American university life, see Karabel (2005), Cherry, DeBerg, and Porterfield (2001), Burtchaell (1998), and Baltzell (1964). For more on the secularization of university life, see Burtchaell (1998), Sloan (1994), and Thalheimer (1973).

10. Marsden (1994: 33). See also Berger (1967) for similar conclusions.

11. See Sommerville (2006: 13). Sommerville points to many forms that this "hermeneutic stage" has taken, but one exemplar is the argument of MacIntyre (1990, 1988) that human rationality is not a single, shared tradition but actually reflects

different traditions, such as those that emerged from Aristotle, Augustine, and Scottish Common-Sense. On the de-privatization of religion, see Casanova (1994).

12. On evangelicals at major universities, see Goodstein and Kirkpatrick (2005), Swidey (2003), and Schmalzbauer (2003).

Regarding demographic trends, I found that the percentage of evangelicals with a college degree in 1976 was 9 percent; by 2004, it had more than doubled and was at 21 percent. Over the same span of time, college degree attainment increased 72 percent among Jews, 54 percent among mainline Protestants, 49 percent among black Protestants, and 49 percent among the general population. This confirms earlier research, like that of Hendricks (1977), who found the educational gap has narrowed considerably among evangelicals.

13. See Swidey (2003). Mark Noll, a historian who held a visiting appointment at Harvard, also told me that there are more "self-consciously Christian scholars" who are faculty members at Harvard than there have been in decades.

14. The influx of Asian Americans, African Americans, and students from across the country is changing the student population on Ivy League campuses. These campuses have witnessed dramatic increases among the Asian American student population. Examining the American Council on Education National Statistics in 1982 and 2006 (as released by the American Council on Education; no editions were printed between 1973 and 1982), we see that the percentage of Asian Americans at Ivy League campuses hovered around 3 percent in the early 1980s and now ranges from 13 percent to 19 percent of the student body. At Harvard, the number of Asian American students increased sixfold. See also Zhou and Gatewood (2000). For more information on Asian Americans' relationship with evangelicalism, see Ecklund (2006), Kim (2004), and Busto (1999). Asian Americans have also become a sizable percentage of the wider evangelical student population. At the most recent Urbana conference, sponsored by InterVarsity Christian Fellowship in 2003, one-quarter of attendees were Asian American (data archives provided to the author by InterVarsity Christian Fellowship). Also, between 1989 and 1999, the Asian American membership in InterVarsity Christian Fellowship nationwide rose 84 percent, compared to an overall membership increase of only 31 percent (Ch'ien 2000).

15. Data are based on Kim's research (2004) and organizational archives obtained by the author on campus ministry groups at Ivy League campuses. These figures are even more striking considering that only 1 percent of American evangelicals are Asian American (Wuthnow 2005). Asian American evangelicals are greatly overrepresented among Ivy League evangelical campus groups, given their small numbers among the general U.S. population and among the American evangelical population.

16. On participation and fervency, see Brooks (2001). On the American Dream, see Wuthnow (1996).

17. Hout, Greeley, and Wilde (2001).

18. "Fitz-Randolph Gate": John DiIulio, "God and Man at Yale Revisited: The Coming Religious Revival at Elite Universities," Princeton University, April 9, 2003. Gomes quoted in Swidey (2003). On unintended consequences, see Swidey (2003).

19. On the rise of individual scholars and their research agendas, see Schmalzbauer (2003) and Sloan (1994). On the rise in prestige accorded to evangelical institutions and their students, see Riley (2005), Bramadat (2000), and Turner (1999).

20. For "largely poor," see Weisskopf (1993). For "intellectual disaster," see Noll (1994). For "dead last," see Wolfe (2000: 56).

21. Applicants must sign the Lausanne Covenant, which is a faith statement first drafted in 1974 by the International Congress on World Evangelization in Lausanne, Switzerland. The evangelical pastor John Stott was one of the document's principal drafters.

22. Goodstein and Kirkpatrick (2005).

23. Wheaton's conference on the Bible was timely. It followed on the heels of Harold Lindsell's 1977 book, *The Battle for the Bible*, in which Lindsell, a leader in the early days of the modern evangelical movement, insisted on a literalist interpretation of scripture. Incidentally, Lindsell was also a trustee of Wheaton at the time.

24. See http://www.consultation.rhodes.edu.

25. See http://www.ptev.org/history.

26. Data from the Foundation Center on grants for religious causes between 1999 and 2003 show that Lilly contributed more than $305 million (in 2003 dollars). The

Arthur S. DeMoss Foundation contributed approximately $94 million, the Pew Charitable Trusts gave $70 million, the Koch Foundation gave $48 million, and the Richard and Helen DeVos Foundation contributed $45 million. For more information, see Wuthnow and Lindsay (2006). Although much of Lilly's philanthropy to religious colleges and universities has been directed toward mainline Protestant institutions, a number of evangelical schools have benefited as well. These include Azusa Pacific, Baylor, Calvin, Pepperdine, and Samford.

27. This is taken from multiple interviews with knowledgeable sources both inside and outside the organization.

28. Details on the religious philanthropy of Lilly and Pew come from multiple sources, including interviews with program officers, grant recipients, organizational documents, tax records, and secondary sources.

29. See Kroll and Cornejo (2003) for a complete evaluation of Pew's philanthropy to evangelical causes. Quotes are from Turner (1999) and Wolfe (2000), respectively.

30. Institutions within the Council for Christian Colleges and Universities are almost all four-year liberal arts colleges institutionally committed to Christianity that preferentially hire faculty members who are co-religionists and that seek to provide a Christian ethos across the university campus. Founded in 1976 with thirty-eight members, the Council has grown to 105 members in North America and seventy affiliate institutions in twenty-four countries. See www.cccu.org and Riley (2005) for more information.

31. Every other Monday, these seven individuals—the president, the treasurer, and five fellows—meet to review reports, allocate resources, and administer university policy. It is known as the oldest self-perpetuating body in the Western Hemisphere, and despite its long-term presence on campus, most Harvard insiders know little about its members or their proceedings. The official title of the group is President and Fellows of Harvard College.

32. "Christian Academe vs. Christians in Academe," address by Kenneth G. Elzinga, Abilene Christian University, September 2005.

33. George's academic appointment is among Princeton's most prestigious. Woodrow Wilson originally held the McCormick Professorship of Jurisprudence.

34. Golden (2006).

35. Although employment law prohibits Harvard from directly inquiring about a candidate's religious affiliation, it is conventional for named chairs of particular religious traditions to be held by an adherent of that faith. McDonald's family has also established a distinguished professorship at Emory, where he is also an alumnus. The gift supports a visiting scholar to explore "the comparative study of Jesus and His impact on culture."

36. George (2004).

37. Information about this transaction is based on interviews with several knowledgeable sources (all of whom wished to remain off the record) conducted in 2005 and 2006. The King's College remains in New York, located inside the Empire State Building.

38. The annual NACUBO Endowment Study (NES), the largest and longest-running voluntary survey of higher education institutions and their foundations about their endowment holdings, showed the market value of Baylor's endowment assets at $672,341,000 in FY 2004. Baylor's fiscal year ends May 31. At the end of December 2004, the fund stood at $750 million, a high-water mark for the university.

39. In 2005, Baylor president Robert Sloan resigned amid faculty discontent with his leadership (and, observers claim, Baylor 2012 as well). Shortly thereafter, Interim President Bill Underwood fired Baylor provost David Lyle Jeffrey. With Sloan and Jeffrey, the principal architects of Baylor 2012, removed from office, several people I interviewed doubt the success of Baylor 2012. In early 2006, Baylor alumnus and seasoned university president John Lilley was named Baylor's president. To date, he has expressed continuing enthusiasm for Baylor 2012.

40. For an example of this news coverage, see Rosin (2005b). Another newsworthy event happened at Patrick Henry in 2005. That year, four faculty members resigned to protest the school's handling of a dispute with a faculty colleague in relation to the institution's biblical worldview policy, which they believe inhibited academic freedom. Tensions such as these have emerged at other evangelical institutions and will be explored later.

41. Several studies on evangelicals and higher education have been conducted in recent years (Burtchaell 1998; Hughes and Adrian 1997; Hunter 1987), but few have paid attention to the flexible structure of networks that unite scholars and students across institutional contexts. Tracing the development of three world philosophies—the Western, Indian, and Asian—Collins (1998) demonstrates how social networks and the "emotional energy" that radiates out from those networks generate intellectual advances. He found that once overlapping networks of intellectuals and ideas were formed, newcomers sustained and deepened the relevance of these networks, making it more difficult for rival factions to overturn their ideas or the privileged place those ideas occupied. And because newcomers continued to be drawn to these established networks, they remained dynamic, changing entities even as they grew more established. He writes, "Intellectual groups, master–pupil chains, and contemporaneous rivalries together make up a structured field of forces within which intellectual activity takes place" (7). Disavowing the notion that academic reputation is secured by an individual's brilliance, Collins claims the key to scholarly recognition is secured through hierarchical, structured intellectual networks.

42. This observation was confirmed with data from organizational archives from various campus groups; larger organizations like Campus Crusade for Christ require detailed, regular reports of participation in various programs, thereby increasing the accuracy of these head counts. Information was provided to the author by Christian Union, an evangelical ministry to the Ivy League, which has provided organizational and financial support to a variety of the campus groups on the eight Ivy campuses.

43. Officially, Harvard does not permit any national student groups to organize chapters on campus. This policy applies not only to religious groups but also to political, social, and service clubs ranging from the Young Democrats to national fraternities. As a result, Harvard does not technically have a chapter of Campus Crusade for Christ, but there is a group of students that draws upon the resources (personnel, programming, finances) of the national organization of Campus Crusade for Christ, and that is the group I am referring to in this section.

44. According to the chairman of the board of Veritas Forums, the organization desires to host campus-wide events only at top liberal arts schools and the top one hundred Research I institutions as measured by the Carnegie Classification of Institutions of Higher Education.

45. Quotes on this interaction are from McDowell (2001).

46. Goodstein and Kirkpatrick (2005).

47. Stuntz (2004).

48. 2004 survey on white evangelicals in the United States conducted for *Religion and Ethics Newsweekly* (N = 1,610).

Chapter 4. Life of the Mind

1. See Binder (2005: 24). Although the battle over intelligent design is frequently framed in terms of children and their education (by both sides), I agree with Binder's argument that it is more about "cultural legitimacy." She writes, "Symbolic inclusion, not religious imperialism, [seems] to be the ultimate goal of most of the creationists I studied, if not because of their ideological commitments, then at least because of their understanding of pragmatics in a nation where government is constitutionally separated from church" (37).

2. Hunter's books include *Culture Wars* (1991) and *The Death of Character* (2000). His research center at Virginia is called the Institute for Advanced Studies in Culture. Research centers that address issues important to people of faith can be found at other, large universities such as the University of Colorado and the University of Florida.

3. See Schmalzbauer (2005, 2003).

4. Examples include Christians in Political Science, Christian Sociological Society, Christians in the Visual Arts, and the Association of Christian Economists.

5. For example, consider the collaborative work in political science among the "gang of four" scholars (John Green, James Guth, Lyman Kellstedt, and Corwin Smidt) or the contributions in American history by Edith Blumhofer, Joel Carpenter, Nathan Hatch, George Marsden, Mark Noll, and Harry Stout as detailed in Schmalz-bauer (2003).
6. See Noll (2004).
7. Westminster Confession of 1647.
8. Lindsell (1949: 219).
9. On developments within Roman Catholicism, see Shea (2004).
10. Machen [1923] (1999: 52).
11. See Mohler (2003); Hunter (1991).
12. See Sproul (1995: 44). Shortly after the release of the ECT statement, a group called the Alliance of Confessing Evangelicals published "The Cambridge Decla-ration," which expressed concern over evangelicalism's apparent theological con-fusion. As conveyed in the ECT document, it was not clear to this group why the sixteenth-century Reformation occurred and what rapprochement with Roman Catholics could mean in terms of abandoning classical Protestant dogma. Pastors and theologians from the Reformed wing of the evangelical movement (largely Presbyterian) were among the most ardent detractors of the ECT project, in-cluding Sproul.
13. Graham's meeting with the pope was related to me by David Aikman, who learned of it when interviewing Graham in 1990 for *Time*. For "lessening of suspicion," see McGrath (1994: 28).
14. See Noll and Nystrom (2005) for this line of thinking. Of course, others, who focus more on relations in the past than in the present, come to different conclusions. See Shea (2004) as an example.
15. See Kroll and Cornejo (2003) for a full overview of the results of Pew's philan-thropy.
16. Not all evangelical institutions have followed this trajectory. Wheaton College, for example, still does not hire Roman Catholics as faculty members, and when a current Wheaton faculty member sought to convert to Catholicism but remain on the faculty, Wheaton's president, Duane Litfin, issued a statement on August 1, 2004, reasserting Wheaton's position that a person could not in good conscience affirm Catholic teaching and Wheaton's faith statement, which is required of all faculty members.
17. A notable exception is those evangelical scholars who rely on Dutch Reformed the-ology as inspiration for scholarly pursuits. Scholars at places like Calvin and those who are members of Reformed traditions (such as Presbyterians) have drawn on their own evangelical traditions much more robustly for their intellectual pursuits.
18. Schmalzbauer (2003).
19. For example, the Madison Program sponsored a conference on "Faith and the Challenges of Secularism" in 2003. The event was co-sponsored by the University Center for Human Values at Princeton University, the Center for Research on Religion and Urban Civil Society at the University of Pennsylvania, and the Prov-idence Forum, demonstrating the extent to which alliances can be created among elite institutions. This conference featured several evangelical speakers including Oxford's Alister McGrath, Harvard's Armand Nicholi, and John DiIluio of the University of Pennsylvania.
20. This approach has been more prominent in disciplines like American history and philosophy; it is striking that this "religious way of knowing" has been far less prevalent among both camps in fields like environmental science and women's studies. The implication, of course, is that certain disciplines have been more con-ducive to this religious hermeneutic. Certainly, prevailing philosophical outlooks (including conservative and liberal perspectives) are part of this arrangement.
21. As opposed to hiding one's religious convictions. Alvin Plantinga, an evangelical who served as president of the American Philosophical Association's Central Di-vision, delivered a speech in 1982 at Notre Dame in which he urged believers to be more "transparent about their religious commitments." See Schmalzbauer and Mahoney, unpublished manuscript. Also, evangelical–Catholic unity is not limited to higher education; they share similar convictions on public education. See Sik-kink (1999).

22. Hofstadter's conclusions echoed earlier sentiments as seen in O'Dea (1958), Weigel (1957), and Ellis (1955). On their obsolescence, see Greeley (1990, 1977).
23. Rigney and Hoffman (1993: 221).
24. Schmalzbauer (2003: 31). Wuthnow (1996) refers to this as "bilingual sophistication."
25. The evaluation study was conducted by Rhys Williams and Eugene Lowe. Today, Pew no longer funds scholarly activities of evangelicals. Not surprisingly, many academics I interviewed expressed dismay over this significant loss in research funding.
26. Wolfe (1996).
27. Social status is an important aspect of the study of stratification, and I employ Weber's ([1946] 1991) use of the term as a way of discerning signs of prestige and high esteem within this particular group.
28. See www.ttf.org for more information.
29. The reticence to consume alcohol among previous generations of evangelicals has nearly disappeared among the leaders in this study, especially among those under age fifty.
30. Asma (2004).
31. On evangelicals and the Bible, see Marsden (1991) and Ammerman (1987).
32. It was launched as a publication of Christianity Today International in September 1995. See http://www.christianitytoday.com/books/features/info.html.
33. *First Things* is published by the Institute on Religion and Public Life, an "interreligious, nonpartisan research and education institute whose purpose is to advance a religiously informed public philosophy for the ordering of society."
34. See www.cslewisinstitute.org for more information.
35. As in many large social movements, within evangelicalism there is a wide range of opinion on what constitutes priorities for evangelicals in the public square, and there is no consensus on most contentious issues such as abortion, stem cell research, or the death penalty. These programs, however, all seek to raise the possibility that their participants will be taken more seriously by secular opponents, and familiarity with various perspectives on pressing moral issues is one way program organizers hope to achieve that aim.
36. Woodard (2005).
37. See Schaeffer (1976).
38. Noah Riner, Student Body President's Convocation Address, September 20, 2005, Dartmouth College, Hanover, New Hampshire. Praise could be found in articles such as "Convocation Conviction" by Mark Bergin in *World,* October 8, 2005. Critical commentary could also be found, such as "Too Much...Too Fast" by Mike Metzger, the Clapham Institute, November 1, 2005 (www.claphaminstitute.org/commentaries).
39. For AAUP, see McConnell (1990). For Phi Beta Kappa, see Marsden (1993).
40. Ecklund (2005).
41. The figures fluctuate based on how "evangelical" is defined (Hackett and Lindsay 2004). See also Ecklund and Park (2006).
42. General population figures from Greeley and Hout (2006). Gross and Simmons (2006) also found that 37 percent of professors at elite institutions are atheists or agnostics, a figure considerably higher than for professors at places like community colleges. Significant differences appeared in their study between academics at the most and least prestigious institutions in higher education. Their overall finding matches Ecklund's (2005) conclusions.
43. Hurlbert and Rosenfeld (1992); Long, Allison, and McGinnis (1979).
44. Wolfe (2000).
45. As will be noted later, some notable megachurches—such as Redeemer Presbyterian Church in New York City, Willow Creek Community Church in Chicago, and Menlo Park Presbyterian Church in San Francisco—do not follow this model of lower levels of interest in the life of the mind, but they are exceptions to the overall trend among evangelical megachurches. Data are based on observations at more than seventy megachurches around the country.
46. Tamney and Johnson (1997).
47. Data from the General Social Survey from 1976 to 2004 reveal an increase of 133 percent in the number of evangelicals earning a bachelor's degree, which is more than double the rate of growth among the general population.

48. Massengill (2006); Darnell and Sherkat (1997).
49. See Chopp (2002), Roberts and Turner (2000), Burtchaell (1998), Zerubavel (1995), and Marsden (1994) for a synthesis of contemporary developments in higher education and responses by religious institutions to them.
50. Kirp (2003).
51. Bellah et al. (1985). However, as will be noted later, evangelicalism is not perceived as supportive of a communitarian ethic. The possibility that evangelical—or, more generally, conservative Christian—theology could provide a framework for talking about communitarian ideals does not necessarily indicate its probability. Significantly more work within the evangelical community would have to occur on this front in order for such a thing to occur. It is notable, however, how often social movements that emphasize communitarian ideals rely on the moral vocabulary provided by particular communities of faith.
52. Fish (2005).
53. See Binder (2005) for similar observations about evangelicalism's quest for cultural legitimacy. Hollinger (2002) is among those who favor less religion in the academy.
54. See Noll (2004).

Chapter 5. From Protest to Patronage

1. Incidentally, Kazantzakis was nearly excommunicated by his own faith tradition, the Greek Orthodox Church, when the book was first published in 1955. Various Christ figures appear throughout Kazantzakis' work, including *The Greek Passion* and *The Saviors of God: Spiritual Exercises.*
2. Medved (1993); Poland (1988). Originally, Paramount Pictures was going to produce Scorsese's film, but early calls of protest by the religious community caused that studio eventually to pass on the project.
3. Tertullian, a church leader in the second century, condemned the "immodesty of the theater" and the "atrocities of the arena." The historical record suggests that Christians did, indeed, stay away. See Spickard and Cragg (1994).
4. Among other things, the code prohibited the depiction of brothels or nudity and governed how movies could portray religious subjects and people of faith.
5. Even though the National Association of Evangelicals was formed as an alternative to the National Council of Churches (NCC), evangelicals informally relied on the NCC's Protestant Film Commission to represent their opinions in Hollywood. NAE's affiliate, the National Religious Broadcasters (NRB), was more principally charged with helping to foster "electronic media access for the Gospel." NRB's more recent interest in Hollywood reflects wider trends within the evangelical movement than this chapter explores. See www.nrb.org.

   The Roman Catholic Legion of Decency was formed in 1934; in the 1960s and 1970s, its duties were gradually replaced by what is now called the United States Conference of Catholic Bishops' Office for Film and Broadcasting.

   Burstyn v. Wilson (1952) was a decisive turn in the battle over film censorship. In that case, the Court decided that motion pictures were protected by the First Amendment, thus overturning an earlier decision (*Mutual Film Corp v. Industrial Commission,* 1915) that had said the exhibition of moving pictures was a business and therefore did not have free speech protection like the press.
6. The American Family Association was founded in 1977 as the National Federation for Decency and renamed in 1987.
7. For more information on religious groups invoking the "outsider" frame, see Moore (1986).
8. Austin (2005: 94).
9. See Mattingly (2006). Christian Smith (2004) made a similar observation: "I received a phone message from a journalist from a major Dallas newspaper who wanted to talk to me about a story he was writing about 'Episcopals,' about how the controversy over the 2003 General Convention's approval of the homosexual bishop Gene Robinson, would affect 'Episcopals.' What an embarrassment. How

do I break the news to him that there are no 'Episcopals'? Actually, they are called Episcopalians. Of greater concern, I wonder how this journalist is going to write an informed and informing story in a few days about such an important and complex matter when he doesn't even know enough in starting to call his subjects by their right name."

10. Data from the Arts and Religion Survey directed by Robert Wuthnow (2003) of Princeton's Center for the Study of Religion (N = 1,530). Based on one of the last surveys conducted by Gallup that involved in-home interviews, these data offer unique insights into the breadth of respondents' opinions on religion and the arts. The study shows that 63 percent of evangelicals think the arts are materialistic, compared to 44 percent of mainline Protestants and 46 percent of Roman Catholics. Thirty percent of evangelicals say that artists dishonor God, compared to only 19 percent of mainline Protestants and Roman Catholics. Additionally, 34 percent say that artists have "no respect for churches," while only 26 percent of mainline Protestants and 23 percent of Roman Catholics agree. Nearly half (49 percent) have heard a sermon on the dangers of contemporary art and music, while only 13 percent of mainline Protestants and 23 percent of Roman Catholics have heard similar messages at church.

11. Adorno ([1970] 1997, [1949] 2003) was particularly interested in the role of cultural production in manipulating populations. Like Marx ([1845] 1978), Adorno argued that ideology-producing systems (such as the media) could thwart the revolutionary propensities of the masses and maintain the dominating position of those who control those institutions of ideological production.

12. Hangen (2002).

13. Stewart Hoover has extensively explored the relations between media consumption, production, and religion. See Hoover (2006, 1988) and Hoover and Clark (2002).

    Subcultures are best defined not simply by their symbols and audiences but by the broader framework of values, attitudes, behavior, and lifestyles of a particular group within a larger collectivity. The earliest research on subculture was conducted by Frederic Thrasher ([1927] 1963), who explored the traditions of delinquent gangs in urban Chicago, although the exact term "subculture" did not appear in this early work. Subcultures often apply to deviant or oppositional groups who, for whatever reason, disagree with the dominant culture or values of society. Often subcultures provide adherents with a sense of shared identity and common cause, be it age (Bernard 1961), social class (Miller and Riessman 1961), gang involvement (Patrick 1973; Yablonsky 1959), or others. Additionally, scholars debate the category of "subculture" and the varying ways in which it is defined and operationalized in social scientific research. See Fine and Kleinman (1979). Religious groups have been studied as subcultures, including the Amish (Kraybill 1989), Mormons (Mauss 1994), and Orthodox Jews (Davidman 1993). Several scholars have explored American evangelicalism as a distinct subculture (Balmer 2000a; Schmalzbauer 1993; Watt 1991), but it is Christian Smith and his colleagues (1998) who consider the movement's subculture as vital to American evangelicalism. Evangelical subcultural production is most apparent in the music and publishing industries, where they have been producing goods since the earliest days of modern American evangelicalism in the 1940s (Fisher 2003, 1998). There are no Christian theaters or distribution companies, which has hindered evangelical efforts to establish separate channels of cultural production through film.

14. For varying estimates of the evangelical population, see Hackett and Lindsay (2004). As the introduction noted, researchers define "evangelical" in different ways, which results in vastly different estimates of the total evangelical population. Regarding the religious market, consider that Salem Communications, a Christian radio company with 104 stations, is the third largest radio conglomerate in the nation's top twenty-five markets, behind media giants Clear Channel and Infinity Broadcasting. Subcultural institutions like Salem often provide a mechanism by which cultural goods gain wider acceptance.

15. This ranking is based on the industry standard of not adjusting highest-grossing films for ticket price inflation. If one adjusts for inflation, *The Passion* is the fifty-fifth highest-grossing film domestically ($392 million in 2006 dollars). According to this measure, *The Ten Commandments* is the fifth highest-grossing film of all time in the United States ($862 million) behind *Gone with the Wind* ($1.3 billion),

Star Wars ($1.2 billion), *The Sound of Music* ($937 million), and *E.T.: The Extra-Terrestrial* ($933 million).

16. Many recent works including those by Griffith (2004) and Hendershot (2004) demonstrate the ongoing salience of subcultural identity for elements of American evangelicalism.

17. Advertising slogan for one of the nation's most successful Christian radio stations, KLTY in Dallas–Fort Worth.

18. Joseph (2002) contends that many groups that are Christian, such as Creed or U2, are not counted within this ambiguous category. If they and other groups were "counted," the percentage of Christian music's market share would be significantly higher.

19. Hollywood leaders expressed similar sentiments about a program recently launched at Biola University under the direction of Hollywood insider Craig Detweiler.

20. Lokkesmoe (2006); Morefield quoted in Houpt (2005).

21. Multiple leaders I interviewed reported displeasure with Baehr; according to them, he has a habit of referring to himself as "the only Christian in Hollywood" at various gatherings around the country.

22. Lewerenz and Nicolosi (2005).

23. 60 *Minutes*, CBS News, July 4, 2004.

24. Balmer (2000b).

25. This resonates with Bourdieu's work (1984) on ways certain groups seek to distinguish themselves from lower-brow tastes and activities.

26. See Crouch (2007) for more on the theological motivation for cultural production. Examples of evangelical institutions providing support include programs at Azusa Pacific University; Baylor University; Calvin College; the Council for Christian Colleges and Universities; Full Sail: School of Film, Art, Design, Music & Media Production; Fuller Theological Seminary; Gordon College; Regent University; Seattle Pacific University; Wheaton College; and the World Journalism Institute.

27. Although the Family Channel was not explicitly an evangelical network, it certainly fell within a similarly circumscribed sphere of influence that was in a similar position of opposition to the cultural mainstream as the more narrowly defined evangelical subculture.

28. John Shepherd, Ken Wales, and Michael Warren perfected their craft at the Billy Graham Evangelistic Association, and all three attributed success in Hollywood to their time at BGEA.

29. Unlike Schmalzbauer (2003), I found leaders going back and forth between the mainstream and the evangelical subculture, traversing the boundaries throughout their careers.

30. From personal correspondence with Gabriel Rossman and Nicole Esparza, who have collected data on Hollywood actors, writers, and directors, I determined the relatively small role played by evangelicals within the larger entertainment world. Among directors with active careers between 2000 and 2005, Rossman and Esparza count 1,091 directors who have received screen credits for four or more English-language, nonpornographic films, thereby demonstrating a track record of some success in Hollywood. Within that category, no more than 5 percent could be considered conservative Christians, and among those, many would not necessarily be considered "evangelical." Using the same data, Rossman and Esparza identify approximately 17,500 actors (both union and nonunion) who were working during that time period and had been cast in four or more films over their lifetime. Based on my research, I estimate the number of evangelical actors in that category to be between 3 percent and 5 percent, although no informed source in Hollywood was able to speak definitively on the subject. Regardless, nearly every observer acknowledges the relatively small proportion evangelicals currently occupy among Hollywood's elite.

31. Wolfe (2003: 3).

32. Pierre Bourdieu (1977) first defined cultural capital as endowments like cultural and linguistic competence that enable certain students to succeed in the educational system. In his later work (1984), Bourdieu expanded the notion of cultural capital by associating it with educational qualifications, specific tastes, and manners of lifestyle associated with the dominant class of a given society.

33. Keller's phrase "a counterculture for the common good" became the foundational element of a year-long series of articles and columns sponsored by the leading

publication of the evangelical subculture, *Christianity Today*. This editorial decision by the magazine's publisher reflects the ways in which the evangelical subculture is changing.

34. See www.gracehillmedia.com.

35. Wolfe (2003: 206).

36. Examples of evangelical media initiatives include World Wide Films, sponsored by the Billy Graham Evangelistic Association, which produced and distributed films with explicitly evangelistic messages. Also, Campus Crusade for Christ sponsored a group called Associates in Media during the 1980s that was designed to evangelize among Hollywood media personnel. Regarding the popularity of *The Jesus Film*, the 5.4 billion figure includes individuals who have seen the movie more than once. Accurate estimates on the number of *different* individuals who have seen the movie are impossible to calculate because the film is often shown in stadiums and meeting halls before large crowds. Regardless, it is certainly among one of the most watched films in the world.

37. *Mars Hill Audio Journal* is one of the cultural products cited by informants around the country as particularly effective in raising evangelicals' intellectual horizons. With approximately nine thousand subscribers to the bimonthly audio journal, Myers and his staff review books, music, and other media forms while also conducting NPR-like interviews (Myers used to work at National Public Radio) with writers and thinkers of interest to their mostly evangelical audience.

38. The Reformed wing of American evangelicalism, which includes Presbyterian churches like Winter's, embraces the doctrine of "common grace," which says God bestows favor on all people—not just Christian believers—so that their lives and the fruit of their labor can bear witness to God's character. Common grace is not a means for eternal salvation, but it endows all humans, regardless of their religious belief, with the prospect of demonstrating a portion of God's nature. This, in turn, leads to a much higher view of all humans, not just those who believe. Many evangelical megachurches embrace Reformed theology and are particularly prominent in centers of elite cultural production. These include Bel Air Presbyterian and Hollywood Presbyterian in Los Angeles, Menlo Park Presbyterian in Silicon Valley, National and Fourth Presbyterian in Washington, and Redeemer Presbyterian and Fifth Avenue Presbyterian in New York. Pastors and theologians along the West Coast—especially at churches like First Presbyterian of Hollywood, First Presbyterian in Berkeley, and University Presbyterian in Seattle, as well as institutions like Fuller Seminary in Pasadena—have promulgated biblical and theological warrants for evangelical engagement in mainstream outlets.

39. The former is the mission of Brewing Culture, a group founded in 1977 and reorganized in 2002. See www.brewingculture.org. The latter is the aim of the International Arts Movement, founded in 1991. See www.iamny.org.

40. I adopt the conventional use of "Hollywood" as a synonym for the Los Angeles–area entertainment industry; it is not strictly a geographical term but one describing a loose group of professional cultural workers who work in various segments of entertainment including television, film, and music (Gamson 1995).

41. The reference comes from an ancient Chinese proverb that was popularized in the United States by Adlai Stevenson. In a 1962 address to the United Nations General Assembly, Stevenson described Eleanor Roosevelt by saying, "She would rather light candles than curse the darkness, and her glow has warmed the world."

42. Information in this section comes from a variety of sources, including correspondence with Beltz and Anschutz's office, in-depth interviews with Flaherty, Ken Wales, and others working on projects backed by Anschutz, and comments made by other Hollywood informants. I also had the opportunity to hear Anschutz and his associates speak on the relationship between faith and the entertainment world at a small gathering at the Four Seasons Hotel in Beverly Hills in the fall of 2004. Perhaps most helpful for my research, during that event I sat down with Anschutz and had an off-the-record conversation with him over lunch.

43. Like C. S. Lewis, Wilberforce enjoys iconic status within the evangelical orbit: If evangelicals had saints, Lewis and Wilberforce would be among them. Of the leaders I interviewed, almost 40 percent explicitly mentioned either Lewis or Wilberforce as a personal inspiration.

Wales began his career as a child actor; he played Betty's boyfriend in *Father Knows Best* and later received a gift of $5,000 from Walt Disney, who was one of his mentors, to attend film school at the University of Southern California.

44. Colorado Springs, Colorado, is home to more than one hundred evangelical para-church organizations including Focus on the Family, the Navigators, and New Life Church, which was pastored by Ted Haggard—head of the National Association of Evangelicals from 2003 to 2006.

Chapter 6. A Cultural Revolution

1. Wuthnow (2001).
2. Belz (2005).
3. For more on the religious imagination, see Wuthnow (2003), Greeley (2000), Green (1989), and Miles (1985).
4. Analysis revealed no correlation between those who prayed to win and the sport they competed in, their religious background, their gender, or their career trajectory up to the time of the interview.
5. Data from Wuthnow's (2003) Arts and Religion Survey show that 73 percent of evangelicals feel close to God from any music or art, which is higher than mainline Protestants (65 percent) and Roman Catholics (54 percent). Perhaps most surprising, evangelicals are much more likely to say music is important to their spiritual lives (81 percent) compared to mainline Protestants (72 percent) or Roman Catholics (61 percent).
6. See http://www.fpch.org/mission.htm.
7. This is no different from other minority groups.
8. For other works on evangelicalism's individualistic emphasis, see Wolfe (2003), Emerson and Smith (2000), Smith (1998), and Griffith (1997). The interview transcripts also reveal some interest in social structures and collective-level agency, but almost all of those comments quickly moved into the realm of abstraction. All the concrete examples that I counted from the transcripts referred to individual-level agency: what the informant did or could do in his professional arena, family, or circle of influence. The motif of individualism, which emerges throughout many interviews, is most often pronounced when informants answered questions about "making a difference in the world" or "acting on their faith commitments." This resonates with others' findings on evangelicalism. See Emerson and Smith (2000), Smith (1998), and Griffith (1997).
9. A few groups, such as Campus Crusade's Associates in Media, have died or evolved into other organizations (one of the ministry's founders now runs another, similar organization called MasterMedia), but these are rare exceptions to an overall healthy and expanding sector.
10. For IAM's mission, see www.iamny.org. IAM is actually representative of several organizations founded over the last thirty years that bridge the artistic and evangelical worlds. These include Christians in the Visual Arts (1977), Christian Performing Artists' Fellowship (1979), and Christians in Theater Arts (1989), among others.
11. It should be noted that when most informants referred to secular peers not feeling threatened by them or their faith, the reference was at the individual, not the collective, level.
12. These include, in order of organizational purpose mentioned in the text: Hollywood Connect, Actors Co-Op, Inter-Mission, Damah Film Festival, and the Brehm Center for Worship, Theology, and the Arts at Fuller Seminary.
13. Henrietta Mears had a profound influence on many of the first-generation leaders of modern American evangelism. These included Billy Graham and Bill Bright, who founded Campus Crusade for Christ at the University of California, Los Angeles in 1951. Today, other large fellowships for Hollywood professionals include ones at Bel Air Presbyterian Church, Ronald Reagan's home church, and the Bridge Entertainment Fellowship, sponsored by Lake Avenue Church in Pasadena.

14. As has been the case in previous studies, gender inequality remains strong within the culture-producing industries. See Bielby and Bielby (1996).

15. Griffith (2004) details the ambivalence with which evangelicals and other people of faith regard the body: It can both advance and inhibit salvation. She argues that the evangelical subculture idolizes slim, white bodies, the achievement of which symbolizes divine favor. Yet evangelicals maintain strictures regarding extramarital sex and are reticent to reveal too much of their bodies, suggesting the continuing salience of norms of modesty and propriety even as definitions of those concepts change for movement adherents.

16. Williams (1991) has explored the place of gender in different occupational sectors and finds analogous results in other fields.

17. Campus Crusade for Christ's sponsorship of Associates in Media is representative of this class of organization.

18. Interview with Terry Mattingly on *Religion and Ethics Newsweekly,* episode 913, PBS, November 25, 2005.

19. Survey conducted by the George H. Gallup International Institute under a grant from William Moss, September 1994.

20. See www.ksg.harvard.edu/leadership/usnews for full results from the study.

21. More often, professional sports teams have chaplains that lead prayer times and studies of scripture away from the playing field; Robinson's active role, as a player and a team leader, in both initiating and leading the regular prayer time was unusual. For "exclusive form," see Krattenmaker (2006).

22. Mike Nawrocki co-founded Big Idea Productions with Phil Vischer and is the voice of several Veggie characters.

23. Bono and McCormick (2006: 303).

24. Some refer to evangelical tactics like signaling as "stealthy" (see Powell 2002), but signaling is a common part of public life. See Turner (1986) and Meyer (1979). On Caviezel, see S. Smith (2004).

25. "Do They See Jesus in Me?" is a song by Joy Williams; "I Can See Jesus in You" is a song by Twila Paris.

26. The context of this quote suggests that the informant, speaking without attribution in this part of the interview, was not hoping that more gay and lesbian entertainers would self-identify, or "come out," as evangelical. Instead, he desires for evangelicals in Hollywood to self-identify with their religious identity. This is the kind of "coming out" he hopes will happen more in the future.

27. It is interesting to note the strong opposition voiced by some evangelical leaders to the gay actor Chad Allen's portrayal of Nate and Steve Saint in *The End of the Spear* (2006), yet the lack of opposition to gay actor Ian Charleson's portrayal of Eric Liddell in *Chariots of Fire* (1981). This paradox is not lost on movement leaders. As Marvin Olasky, editor of the evangelical *World* magazine, states, "Because God has placed us in a modern Babylon rather than ancient Israel, I'm not troubled by the presence of gay actors in movies with theistic themes. . . . Few people urged Christians to boycott . . . films [like *Chariots of Fire*] that wonderfully communicated truths about Christian conscience and divine providence" (Olasky 2006).

28. See "Eye on the Media" reports at www.glaad.org. The earliest treatment of the subject on television occurred in a 1971 episode of *All in the Family*; the sitcom would explore homosexuality again in a 1977 episode. The first extended treatment on television appeared in a 1972 TV movie called *That Certain Summer* in which a son discovers his divorced father is living with another man. Beginning in 1977, Jodie Dallas on *Soap* (played by Billy Crystal) was the first recurring gay character on a major television network show. ABC/Disney canceled *Ellen* in 1998; with many speculating this was related to the lead character's coming out openly.

29. Lichter, Lichter, and Rothman (1991: 12), as well as Newcomb and Alley (1983) and even earlier research by Cantor (1971).

30. Survey data from the National Opinion Research Corporation (1982). With regard to positive portrayals on primetime television, I found that media creators regularly invite feedback from the gay and lesbian community on scripts addressing gay themes. The Gay Media Task Force was created by the National Gay Task Force in 1972 to serve as a resource organization for network television programming as it addressed gay issues. Also, see www.glaad.org/media for information about the annual GLAAD Media Awards, which regularly recognize creators for their "fair, accu-

rate, and inclusive representations" of gays and lesbians and the "issues that affect their lives."

31. For national figures on religious service attendance, see Gallup and Lindsay (1999). Lichter, Lichter, and Rothman (1991) stress that personal attitudes and demographic background factors are among *several* components that influence media content. They find only a "rough correspondence" between these two elements. Noting the biases of social desirability and low self-reflexivity in survey and interview responses, they acknowledge that many members of the Hollywood creative community do not recognize the extent to which their creations are influenced by their own personal stories and convictions. This does not, however, change their conclusion that these factors are critical to understanding creative content.

32. Nicolosi related the incident to others as well; see Rosin (2005c).

Chapter 7. Faith-Friendly Firms

1. For this chapter, work is defined as gainful employment.

2. For Jesus as a "founder," see Barton (1924: iv).

   The Roman Catholic Church began to advocate for an empowered laity, both inside and outside the institutional church, starting with Vatican II. The *Dogmatic Constitution on the Church* included a chapter on the laity, and the Vatican also issued the *Decree on the Apostolate of the Lay People*.

   Regarding the faith-at-work movement, Miller (2006) finds that this most recent development in the commercial sector benefited from the mobilization that occurred around earlier religious movements such as the social gospel movement of the early twentieth century and the ecumenical and lay ministry movement from the 1940s until the 1970s. He also notes that the faith-at-work movement is more amenable to corporate managers and the professional class than worker-centered theological movements like Christian socialism and liberation theology.

3. For more on "quest spirituality," see Roof (1999). Also, Wuthnow (1998) refers to this shift in the religious sphere as a move from a "spirituality of dwelling" to a "spirituality of seeking." Since the 1990s, the literature on faith and work has multiplied. Scholars have examined the subject at the level of rank-and-file workers (Wuthnow 1994) and as a social movement (Miller 2006). Major media outlets have devoted growing attention to the convergence of religion and business (Gunther 2001; Conlin 1999). Today, a vast prescriptive literature deals with faith-and-work integration, most of which has been geared toward those in business leadership. *The Marketplace Annotated Bibliography: A Christian Guide to Books on Work* (2002) gives overviews of seven hundred texts on the subject. And some of the most popular titles within this genre include *God Is My CEO* (2001), *Loving Monday* (1998), *The Soul of a Firm* (1996), *Half Time* (1995), *Jesus CEO* (1995), and *Roaring Lambs* (1993). Nearly all of these are written from an evangelical faith perspective, but they tend to appeal to a broader audience. At the same time these books have been written, there have also been studies of the business elite. Most rely on a relatively small number of executive informants—not surprising given the challenge of securing elite informants, but this makes it difficult to trace collective action among a cohort of leaders, and almost none has considered the role of religion (Morrill 1995; Jackall 1988; Kotter 1983; Mintzberg 1973; Carlson 1951). There have, of course, been a few studies with a large number of informants. Theoretical and empirical contributions on organizational life, while also not focused on the role of religion, have certainly added to our knowledge of institutions and the place of managerial behavior within those institutional contexts (Powell and DiMaggio 1991; Hannan and Freeman 1989; Kanter 1977). One study, did, however, interview a large cohort of business leaders about their evangelical faith (Nash 1994), and in several ways, this study expands upon Nash's work; instead of focusing on issues internal to the lives of elite informants, however, this chapter traces how this sample of nationwide business executives has acted on their faith and catapulted the evangelical movement to prominence. By placing their actions within the context of evangelical public leaders, we can see the unique role

business leaders have played in implementing movement priorities in recent decades. Like Nash, I recognize that personal rationalizations may not match reality when examining the actions of business leaders. However, the discourse, models, and norms invoked in these accounts are instructive even if the empirical reality differs in some ways—which will be discussed later.

4. "Guidelines on Religious Exercise and Religious Expression in the Federal Workplace," issued by the White House Office of the Press Secretary, August 14, 1997.

5. Subsequent research (Hicks 2003; Nash and McLennan 2001; Mitroff and Denton 1999) reveals several important findings in the wake of the 1997 federal guidelines. Generally speaking, Americans are more approving of broad-based discussions on "spirituality" than they are of conversations about sectarian "religion." Spirituality is tethered to a notion of individual agency in which the worker who seeks to live an integrated life crafts for himself norms and practices that govern the conventions of that integration. Instead of a following standard rubric, the individual creates an improvised, personal style that varies according to his or her context. Hicks notes that the highly personalized nature of this phenomenon has caused some observers to focus exclusively on the integrative work done by corporate leaders. Moreover, the increasing religious diversity among workers has introduced a range of challenges that face corporate leaders seeking to integrate faith in the workplace.

6. Friedland and Alford (1991) identify several institutional domains, each with its own "logic of action" emphasizing different bases of evaluation and the predominance of different action-orientations in various contexts: cognitive in the marketplace, affective in the family, evaluative in religion. They contend that society comprises several different institutional orders, each with a central logic (while also acknowledging the lack of coherence due to some cultural bricolage). Conflict occurs when institutional orders contradict one another.

7. For more on the encroachment of business on the faith arena, see Budde and Brimlow (2002). The prominence of business credentials over theological credentials among many executives at evangelical organizations is evident in the education of Mellado and Douglass: Neither has a seminary degree. And among ministry leaders, Douglass said to me, while "an MBA from Harvard would be uncommon . . . an MBA would not be uncommon."

8. This idea emerges from a "theology of vocation" in the Protestant tradition that was first articulated by church reformer Martin Luther (Wingren 1957; Luther [1519] 1915). According to this line of thinking, not only the clergy but also lay leaders are "called" to serve God through their professional vocations; it does not matter whether—to use Luther's language—one is a priest, a cobbler, or some other profession, so long as he works "for the glory of God."

9. "Economic and Spiritual State of the Union Survey," conducted by the Gallup Organization for the Spiritual Enterprise Institute, 2006. Here are the full results.

	Percentage of U.S. Adult Population (μ Americans)	Percentage of U.S. Evangelical Adult Population (μ Evangelicals)	Probability $\mu A = \mu E$
The U.S. economic system is basically OK.	46%	42%	
The U.S. economic system is in need of some fundamental changes.	34	30	
The U.S. economic system needs to be replaced by a different system.	10	16	*
My work is helping to make the world a better place.**	82	87	
Being ethical will pay off economically.†	51	60	*

	Percentage of U.S. Adult Population (μ Americans)	Percentage of U.S. Evangelical Adult Population (μ Evangelicals)	Probability μA = μE
An open expression of religion (invoking God or saying a prayer before a meeting) would be encouraged at my place of work.**	32	51	*
There are groups in my workplace that meet for prayer or Bible study.**	19	25	
Success in life is pretty much determined by religious or spiritual forces in our lives.†	22	35	*
God wants us to find work that best suits our individual talents.†	47	56	*
My religious or spiritual beliefs have a great deal of effect on how I invest my money.	22	39	*
My religious or spiritual beliefs have a great deal of effect on my relationships at work.**	35	52	*
My religious or spiritual beliefs have a great deal of effect on the field of work I chose.	30	40	*

* p < .05
**Asked only of those currently working.
†Percentage that "completely agree" with this statement.

10. In the context surrounding these comments, Duke suggests that his love for working with people in a business setting is one of the main reasons he feels "called" to this line of work. The size and scope of Wal-Mart are appealing because, he says, it has opened up more opportunities for him to work with a larger group of people, and like many other executives, he likes the chance he has to influence a large number of people. Of course, Wal-Mart has come under close scrutiny for some of its business practices that are deleterious to the communities it serves and the workers it employs. See Goetz and Swaminathan (2006).

11. In the Economic and Spiritual State of the Union Survey, 87 percent of evangelicals said their work helps make the world a better place. This was significantly higher than the figure among the general public (82 percent).

12. Because of the public disclosures and the tacit norms associated with stock ownership, executives at public firms are more constrained in what they can do. This has obvious implications on the extent to which an executive can bring his faith commitments to bear on the workplace.

13. Unlike evangelicals in Great Britain, who are far more left of center on economic concerns and sometimes favor a form of Christian socialism (Davie 1994), American evangelicals—and especially the movement's leadership—are largely political, social, and economic conservatives.

14. Oil magnate J. Howard Pew and his friends established the Christian Freedom Foundation in the wake of World War II to promote "Christian Economics," which was a synthesis of evangelical belief, conservative politics, and market-based economic theory.

15. With regard to leaders' reservations about capitalism, consider this comment from Michael Volkema, the CEO of Herman Miller. During our interview, he said, "I can find recognition for a few institutions—government, family, the church, but I have [not] yet been able to find scriptural authority for a corporation." With regard to

social entrepreneurship and particular kinds of firms, fair trade companies ensure minimum production standards, ethical purchasing practices (including bans on child and slave labor), safe workplace environments, adherence to the U.N. charter of human rights, and a fair price to cover the cost of production and the conservation of the communities and environment in which the good was produced. In the United States and in Europe, there is a fair trade certification system to assist consumers who wish to purchase products that meet these standards. It usually involves protection for workers in the second and third worlds.

16. Economic and Spiritual State of the Union Survey, 2006. Differences are statistically significant at the 5 percent confidence level.

17. As others have shown, America's business leaders have blurred the boundaries between the professional self and the personal self (Jackall 1988) to such an extent that it is difficult for many to distinguish between the two. This has contributed to a decline of personal leisure time (Schor 1991) and a "workaholism" that is pervasive.

18. It should be noted that this figure in no way represents the most egregious examples of excessive executive compensation. In 2005, Yahoo CEO Terry Semel was paid $230 million, ten times the figure of the CEO I mention in this section. Nonetheless, the total compensation packages for Fortune 500 companies grew 54 percent over the previous year, and as a group their total compensation equaled $5.1 billion, which is considerably higher than the $3.3 billion total figure in fiscal year 2003.

19. Analysis conducted by the Economic Policy Institute in 2003 shows the hourly wage earnings in the tenth percentile in 1973 was $6.55 (in 2003 dollars); in 2003 it was $7.00, an increase of only 6 percent over 30 years. As recently as 1999, that figure was $6.67, an increase of only 1 percent in 26 years.

20. Novak (1996: 11).

21. "Economic and Spiritual State of the Union Survey," 2006.

22. "Economic and Spiritual State of the Union Survey," 2006. This is significantly higher than that of the general population (35 percent).

23. The journal ceased publication because of lack of funding. There is a long history of journals targeted toward evangelicals who are in business. Samuel Shoemaker published a magazine called *Faith at Work* starting in 1927. At its peak, the magazine had a circulation of 120,000. Other magazines in this genre include *FaithWorks* and *The Christian Businessman*, both of which are no longer in print. I conducted a content analysis of *Life@Work* because many business leaders in this study subscribed to the journal, and several of them were also interviewed for feature profiles that appeared in one of the magazine's issues over the five years it was in print.

24. Not only do interactions like these dramatize symbolic boundaries, but they can actually create social distinctions, as John Mohr has argued (1994). The moral order that undergirds evangelical activity in business entails ongoing boundary negotiation. The borders are often challenged and open to amendment. For example, even as business leaders have sought to redraw the dividing line between so-called sacred and secular realms, employing terms like "calling" and "mission field" to describe the professional arena, there remain elements of the market that are at odds with evangelical expression. These emerge in the context of personnel decisions, labor disputes, and financial prosperity. Just as organizations rely on myths and symbols to create a sense of order and stability (Meyer and Rowan 1977), evangelical business leaders engage in rituals, or patterned social practices, as a way of maintaining a moral order within the workplace as boundaries are challenged and ambiguity persists. While rituals can, at times, exaggerate uncertainty in a situation (Swidler 2000), they typically make ambiguity or uncertainty more tolerable for the person. Patterned social practices are engaged to reduce the uneasiness of ambiguity. And among the business leaders I interviewed, prayer emerged as the most common practice that helped them maintain a moral dimension within the commercial sphere.

25. The expressive dimension of prayer enables people to articulate their own relationship to a moral order. As Griffith (1997) has shown, prayer can be particularly empowering for believers facing direct challenge or confounding uncertainty.

26. Sometimes, leaders said, they would do "most of the talking" in their prayers, and other times, they were really "listening" for divine guidance. Although none claimed to "hear from God" when listening for an answer, the process of centering through

quiet reflection was part of the deliberative process that they credited for being able to reach a decision after a few moments in prayer.

27. "Economic and Spiritual State of the Union Survey," 2006. This figure among evangelicals is noticeably higher than among the general population (51 percent compared to 32 percent).

28. Several evangelical business leaders told me that "how you integrate your faith into your work" is the wrong matter to pursue. Instead, they prefer to consider, as one put it, "how do you integrate your work up into your faith?" In the words of former Herman Miller CEO Max De Pree, "[A good evangelical doesn't] try to integrate your faith into your work. You've got to get the hierarchy established properly." Miller (2006) suggests that the quest among executives to integrate faith and work falls into one of four areas: evangelization (talking about one's faith with others), ethics, experiential (connecting a sense of spiritual meaning to one's professional life), and enrichment (spiritual practices like prayer "enriching" the workplace setting).

29. Larsen assumed the CEO position after Johnson & Johnson's decision to recall all Tylenol capsules in 1982, but he says the ethical culture of the firm permeated the entire organization, based in large part on the company's "credo" written by founder Robert Wood Johnson in the 1940s.

30. Economic and Spiritual State of the Union Survey, 2006. This is significantly higher than that of the general population (51 percent).

31. Seay and Bryan (2002).

32. Coca-Cola is an interesting example, for the company decided to establish affinity groups after settling a $192 million racial discrimination suit brought by black employees. A Coca-Cola spokeswoman told the *New York Times* that the Christian affinity group is "almost an underground group" (Shorto 2004), but during my research, I learned of multiple executives who regularly attend this gathering of employees at the company's Atlanta headquarters.

33. RJR Nabisco (formerly R. J. Reynolds Tobacco Company) began employing full-time chaplains in 1949 (Budde and Brimlow 2002).

34. Founded in 1984 by retired military chaplain Gil Stricklin, Marketplace Ministries has placed more than a thousand chaplains at companies across the country. See www.marketplaceministries.com for more information.

35. A number of leaders acknowledged that they have an easier time bringing their faith to bear on their work now as chief executives than they did when working in junior positions. As a Wal-Mart executive stated, "In a junior position, if the person above you is not [a fellow person of faith], it can become...difficult to [bring faith] into that environment." Likewise, a Cisco senior executive said bringing his faith to bear in the workplace became easier as he moved up the corporate ladder: "It got easy because I was in command."

36. He also said the insistence of his wife and daughter "kept up the heat."

37. Organizational studies have done much to advance our knowledge of corporate culture. For example, see Sorenson (2002), Denison (1996), Hatch (1993), Kotter and Heskett (1992), Ouchi and Wilkins (1985), Schein (1985, 1984, 1983), and Pfeffer (1981). Most studies of organizational culture have focused on the role of executives and senior management, and a few have relied on interview data to assess the salience and strength of corporate culture within specific firms (Kotter and Heskett 1992; Denison 1990). Nearly all of these studies have noted how organizational culture can be employed as a form of social control (Kunda 1992; Miles 1987; Kilman et al. 1985; Bendix 1956). While I am not in a position to assess the strength of various corporate cultures at firms in multiple industries, it is instructive to hear the accounts given by evangelical business leaders on their role in shaping the ethos that they believe permeates their firm. This, in turn, reveals another way in which evangelicals have sought to influence American society since 1976.

38. Barney (1986).

39. On homogeneity within institutional fields, see DiMaggio and Powell (1983). For ways in which organizations substantively differentiate themselves, see Lindsay (2005), and for an example of differentiation within conformity-oriented fields like commercial aviation, see Deephouse (1999).

40. One terminated employee, Aziz Latif, claims that while training to become a franchise operator, he was fired because of his Muslim faith. The dismissal occurred in 2000, six years after Latif had begun working at Chick-fil-A. In an interview with

Fortune Small Business, Latif's lawyer claimed, "Latif lost his job after he did not participate in a prayer to Jesus Christ." The suit contended, "Religion should not be brought into the workplace. What does glorifying God have to do with making chicken?" When questioned about Latif's lawsuit, Cathy responded that no one is required to pray and that religious concerns were not why Latif was fired. However, Cathy does acknowledge that he seeks to run his company based on biblical precepts, and for that, he offers no apology.

41. In 2005, the board of directors modified this objective to "excel with customers." This represents the first amendment to the company's objectives in over thirty years.

42. Several accounts in the New Testament link Jesus to the character of "a master."

43. Dyer (1985).

44. Additional analysis reveals the strength of Mac Tools within its industry. Comparing the performance of its parent company (Stanley Works) with peer organizations Black & Decker, Danaher (Matco Tools), Snap-on, and Riviera Tool Company, Stanley Works is an industry leader as of 2006, with strong net profit margins, robust stock price to free cash flow, and healthy price to earnings. Stanley's return on earnings is not as strong as Black & Decker's (19 percent compared to 36 percent as of late 2006), but its dividend yield is stronger than other firms' in the industry, and industry analysts I consulted with praise Stanley (and specifically Mac Tools) for its efficient management and healthy corporate culture. The firm's turnaround to profitability since Aden introduced the six new corporate values is commensurate with the positive appraisal of many analysts in recent years.

45. Tyson, like other evangelical CEOs I interviewed, has been criticized at times for his compensation package when other workers' salaries were being cut. Eric Schlosser (2004) wrote in the *Nation,* "At a time when the company was demanding wage and benefit cuts from impoverished meatpacking workers, John Tyson's annual compensation nearly tripled [to $20.9 million]. During an interview . . . Tyson outlined his personal theory of labor management, . . . [citing the importance of] a moral anchor. Tyson said, 'You have to serve the people that work for you . . . and in effect become a servant to the people that work for you.' He said it with a straight face." Schlosser's tone resonates with many of the critiques leveled against Christian CEOs who appear hypocritical when accepting large pay packages. Many evangelical executives I interviewed are aware of these criticisms but disagree with them in various ways.

46. Structural changes like rotating workers every thirty minutes on the job have coincided with a drop in the annual turnover rate from about 100 percent a decade ago to 30 percent today. This, Tyson says, is in line with the company's core values that esteem "creating value" for employees and being "respectful" of each other at the company.

47. Shorto (2004).

48. Also, a study where primary data comes from chief executives invariably will miss the gap between executive intent and actual implementation. Nevertheless, rhetorical shifts at companies in different industries discussed in this section still signal significant changes within American corporate life.

Chapter 8. Executive Influence

1. As Gagliardi (1990) has reminded us, artifacts like office arrangements, photographs, and even coffee table books in the reception lobby can become pathways by which the analyst discerns more fully organizational life and modes of self-expression within bureaucratic corporate life.

2. The group includes Gary Daichendt of Cisco Systems, venture capitalists Eff Martin and Wallace Hawley, Michael Yang of mySimon.com, and Guy Anthony of Stentor, among others.

3. Part of this, no doubt, came from his senior position within the firm; by the time he was Halliburton's president and then chairman, no one was going to question his actions. However, Jones also believed the oil and gas industry was not very amen-

able to evangelicals or their mores thirty years ago. As he said, "It was a rough crowd for the most part." Today, there are several industry executives who are considered "outstanding" Christians, according to Jones.

4. Eskridge and Noll (2000) discuss average evangelicals' ambivalence on the subject.

5. It is hard for an outside observer to assess fully the extent to which informants lived a more ascetic lifestyle than their peers, especially since not all interviews were conducted in informants' homes. However, I was able to verify the details of those individuals mentioned in the previous paragraph, either by direct observation or by further investigation.

6. This contrasts with the guilt felt by informants in other studies of business leaders (Nash 1994), even among those I interviewed who are remarkably frugal.

7. Unlike for other executives (Jackall 1988), perks like first-class travel and vacation homes were not primary motivators for the people I interviewed, regardless of their approach to material goods. They do, however, share with other executives a lifestyle centered around their work, an orientation that gives their life meaning and shapes their daily routines.

8. It is interesting to note the number of high-end luxury goods companies that have been headed by evangelicals, further buttressing the notion that evangelicals do not feel conflicted about purchasing luxury items. The following firms have been headed by an evangelical included in this study: Helzberg Diamonds, Lenox, LVMH Moët Hennessy Louis Vuitton, and Ritz-Carlton.

The concept of "balance" emerged throughout interviews, not only in reference to money issues but also surrounding work-life issues like allocating time and priorities. Nash and Stevenson (2004) have suggested "balancing" multiple priorities like work, family, and personal life and doing "just enough" in different areas of life is what contributes to a "successful life." Although no one referred to this work, a similar message appeared across interviews. Matthew Rose framed the matter as a "three-legged stool of family, faith, and career. [If] one of those legs gets out of whack or gets out of equilibrium, [the stool] won't work." Countering this general trend, though, a few leaders I interviewed felt that "balance" is not a biblical ideal that evangelicals should pursue. As Les Csorba asked, "Is that biblical? Is 'balance' a good word [to describe] the Apostle Paul? . . . No, I don't think so."

9. Wuthnow (1988).

10. The Protestant and Catholic traditions have long recognized the legitimacy of two forms of religious organization: modalities and sodalities. Anchored by geographical function, a modality is a permanent, localized religious structure that serves a range of constituents. The traditional church parish exemplifies a religious modality, serving young and old alike. By contrast, a sodality focuses on particular religious functions and is not tethered to geography in the same way. Examples include medieval Catholic orders and Protestant missionary agencies. Sodalities serve more specialized functions than modalities. During the Reformation, Luther tried to eradicate sodalities from the church, but by the time of William Carey in the nineteenth century, Protestants had rediscovered the tactical benefits of sodalities, finding them helpful in accomplishing goals that were larger than could be undertaken by a single congregation. These groups continued to burgeon in Victorian England and following the Second Great Awakening in America. Evangelical sodalities like Youth for Christ and the Navigators predated the modern evangelical era in the United States, and in the movement's early decades (1940s to 1970s), sodalities like Campus Crusade for Christ and the Billy Graham Evangelistic Association grew financially and in influence. On evangelical parachurch groups, see Hambrick-Stowe (2000).

11. National data from Wuthnow (1994). Also, Nash and McLennan (2001) found that few religious institutions provided the kind of support that church members wanted in terms of bridging their faith commitments to their daily work, a finding that appeared in earlier studies as well (Mitroff and Denton 1999). Theologians like Volf (1991) bemoan the dearth of constructive, practical theology on topics pertaining to work and workplace concerns.

12. Rex pointed out that his home congregation, First Baptist Church of Windermere, did not support the denomination's decision to boycott Disney over corporate policy of medical benefits for same-sex partners of employees and so-called annual Gay Days at Disney theme parks.

13. This model of American churches studying business patterns for church growth and internal strategies has been around for quite some time. The *Journal of Church Management* began in 1923, and a number of related books date from the 1920s and 1930s. Examples include *Business Methods for the Clergy* (1923) and *The Practical and Profitable in Church Administration* (1930). For more information on the Willow Creek Association, see www.willowcreek.com. Interestingly, the association was founded in a secular setting with the aim of bringing managerial acumen to bear on the church and its leadership. Jim Mellado, founding and current president of WCA, was an Olympic athlete in the 1988 Seoul Olympics who went to business school after returning to the States. While pursuing an MBA at Harvard, he wrote a case study for Harvard Business School about Willow Creek Community Church. Bill Hybels, pastor of the church at the time, heard about Mellado's case study—which is still used today at Harvard—and eventually hired him to found and develop the WCA as an organization that would offer the types of services many churches said they wanted. These services included leadership training and development outside of existing avenues like denominational bodies. Today, the Willow Creek Association hosts numerous meetings for evangelical leaders throughout the year, often inviting prominent evangelicals and secular elites to address conference participants. As mentioned in chapter 1, President Bill Clinton spoke to its Leadership Summit during his term in office. Since 1992, the organization has featured hundreds of speakers at various conferences that bridge elite and evangelical arenas in domains like professional athletics, business management, and American political life.

14. The rise of American megachurches and many of their accoutrements, such as concert-quality music in worship services, professional set designs, and stadium seating in church sanctuaries, can be traced to the work of Leadership Network. Buford's organization and similar ventures have imbued evangelical initiatives with a discourse that is consonant with secular notions of management and leadership, helping legitimate the movement to a wider audience.

    Buford says his professional journey from running a cable company for nearly forty years to becoming a leader in the social sector has accompanied a personal transition, one he describes as a transition from seeking "success to significance." Although his book *Half Time* is more autobiography than prescription, many readers surmised that Buford divorced his professional life (when pursuing success) from a life of faith. My interview with him suggests that this is not the case, but a dozen or so leaders I talked with cited his journey as a counterexample to what they were seeking to do, namely, wed evangelical conviction to professional competence. As one said, "The underlying assumption [of Buford's argument] was that . . . you don't really find significance until you walk away from [a successful career] and throw yourself into ministry. To me, that feels flawed. It's . . . binary. . . . You're either in the business to make money, or you're in the business to steward it and give it away for social or ministerial purposes. [According to this mindset] somehow you can't possibly be about both simultaneously. I disagree with that."
    See www.leadnet.org for more information.

15. Nearly twenty years prior to the Congress of the Laity in 1978, Butt and Billy Graham had organized the Layman's Leadership Institute for business leaders, a gathering where business leaders could discuss the relation between their faith and leadership concerns. However, the 1978 Congress was the largest event and signaled a more concerted effort on the part of Butt and his foundation to reach out to business executives.

16. These include the C12 Group, the Center for FaithWalk Leadership, the Pinnacle Forum, the Christian Entrepreneurs Organization, and the Vision and Values Forum of the Young Presidents' Organization, among others.

17. These include the Silicon Valley Fellowship, Priority Associates, and Lifework Leadership. Lifework Leadership was originally founded as the Greater Orlando Leadership Foundation in Orlando, Florida. GOLF was birthed out of the Trinity Forum, a parachurch group mentioned earlier, and was designed to be a local organization to complement the national focus of Trinity Forum. Today, Lifework Leadership is launching similar groups in other places. It is now under the leadership of Steven French.

18. Founded in 1994 by Goldman Sachs partner Jim Lane, New Canaan Society now has chapters around the country, although each maintains a local constituency.

Local chapters can now be found in Menlo Park, California; Dallas, Texas; and Sydney, Australia, among other places.

19. Regarding Impact XXI events on military carriers, I learned that many senior leaders in government and business visit military installations as part of an intentional outreach by the Pentagon. I was told by multiple sources, both inside and outside the military, that the invitation for Impact XXI participants to observe military exercises deals less with the evangelical proclivities of Pentagon decision-makers and the ministry's evangelical outreach and more with the senior level of participants invited to Impact XXI events.

20. At both Focus on the Family and Campus Crusade for Christ, the parent organizations where these ministry leaders once raised funds, the leaders of CEO Forum and Impact XXI, respectively, have distanced themselves from fund-raising for the larger group. In fact, in 2005, the CEO Forum incorporated as a separate group. However, it is not coincidental that the heads of these ministries spent a great deal of time with major donors. As will be seen shortly, philanthropy is a critical link between senior business executives and the parachurch sector within the evangelical movement.

21. A few have discussed the presence of these parachurch groups within American evangelicalism, yet no one has attended to the critical role played by business leaders in shaping this sector of the evangelical world. See Willmer, Schmidt, and Smith (1998), Smith (1998), and Hunter (1983). By the same token, others such as Vogel (1996), Useem (1984), and Domhoff (1975) have shown that a variety of formal and informal social networks exist among the business elite and have existed for quite some time. From the Young Presidents' Organization to the Committee of 200 to the Business Roundtable, various organizations have provided social space in which business executives have networked professionally, established personal friendships, and worked to achieve mutual objectives. However, there is a *genus* of business organizations that has been largely overlooked by those who study the business elite—namely, ones within the realm of religion.

22. Bruno Latour (1988) refers to Louis Pasteur's laboratory as the "fulcrum" by which he transformed medicine and, more generally, French society. Working through the preexisting hygienist movement of the early nineteenth century, Pasteur was able to frame his work in such a way that it continually addressed societal concerns. Pasteur was a skilled researcher, so the laboratory was a conducive environment that allowed him to maximize his strengths and garner the attention of leading officials in government and science. Latour argues that Pasteur's ability to capitalize on a particular institutional environment generated trust and respect for him and his theories. His genius, according to Latour, derives not so much from the *content* of his scientific discoveries but from his ability to capitalize upon the *environment* where his strengths displayed best. Lamont (1987) offers a similar argument regarding the reception of Jacques Derrida's work: Derrida capitalized upon the structural environment that best enabled his work to gain intellectual legitimacy. By examining how this took place in two different cultural contexts (France and the United States), Lamont shows the critical role that institutional and social conditions can play in the diffusion of ideas. Like Latour and Lamont, I argue that institutional environment is a critical factor in determining the success of a movement or an idea. This has clearly been the case for the parachurch sector within modern American evangelicalism.

23. Groups for evangelical business leaders have been around for decades. The Gideons—founded in 1899 for "commercial travelers"—is the nation's oldest Christian businessmen's association. Its focus on business travelers is what precipitated its most recognized activity, placing Bibles in hotel rooms as a "silent witness." Another group dating back several decades is the Christian Business Men's Committee (CBMC), founded in 1937 as a nascent national network drawn from gatherings of Christian businessmen in cities around the country. Today, CBMC is headquartered in Chattanooga, Tennessee, and now includes more than fifty thousand members in over seventy countries. Other groups include the Full Gospel Business Men's Fellowship International and the Fellowship of Companies for Christ International. Several evangelical groups targeted toward business leaders have been established since 1976. These include Search Ministries and a ministry called Marketplace under the auspices of InterVarsity Christian Fellowship.

Pete Hammond has been one of the most active ministry entrepreneurs in this area and has worked for InterVarsity since 1979.

24. Until now, no one has examined the ways in which major evangelical donors talk about their philanthropy or the initiatives they support. The subject of religious philanthropy has been explored elsewhere (Eskridge and Noll 2000; Chaves and Miller 1999; Hodgkinson 1990; Wood and Houghland 1990; Wuthnow and Hodgkinson 1990), and the place of religious sentiment in studies of elite philanthropy has also been touched upon (Ostrower 1995; Odendahl 1990; Zweigenhaft and Domhoff 1982). But none of these relied upon primary data from the devout donors themselves.

    For more on evangelicals' rising fortunes and business activity, see Murphy (2006), Woodberry and Smith (1998), and Green et al. (1996).

25. More than one leader expressed disbelief that, in the end, they disclosed this information. One said, "I haven't even told my parents what you now know."

26. Supplemental research was conducted on the foundations and trusts through which nearly half (49 percent) of the study's informants channel at least a portion of their philanthropy. This data is available by public release of the charitable foundation's tax records (available online via www.guidestar.org) as well as from annual reports published by many private foundations. Not all donations are channeled through these private foundations, so estimates derived from these sources are conservative estimates.

27. Ostrower (1995).

28. On professionalization, see Himmelstein (1997) and Smith (1994).

    Analysis from General Social Survey data (1998) shows that among those who identify as Christian and report giving money away annually, the top income category (over $90,000) report giving 5.7 percent of their annual household income, which is noticeably higher than other income categories (such as 3.1 percent among those with household incomes between $30,000 and $39,999 and 3.6 percent for those between $40,000 and $59,999). This is vastly different from the general giving population (without regard to religious affiliation), where those with annual household income between $75,000 and $99,000 report giving only 2.7 percent of their annual income, and those earning over $100,000 report giving only 2.7 percent of their annual household income.

29. The Gathering was founded in 1985 in Arlington, Virginia, and is now headquartered in Tyler, Texas. Approximately four hundred Christian donors attend this annual meeting, whose purpose is to help family foundations and individual donors learn the fundamentals of "strategic philanthropy." Participating foundations and individuals—almost entirely evangelical—distribute at least $200,000 annually to Christian ministries and programs. Many in attendance give away millions each year to various evangelical causes. On the other hand, Generous Giving was launched in 2000 under the auspices of the Maclellan Foundation of Chattanooga, Tennessee. It hosts an annual conference to spur a "renewed, Spirit-led commitment to generosity among Christians." For more information, see www.generousgiving.org.

30. Organizational documents and background information provided by David Wills, president of the National Christian Foundation, through correspondence with the author in 2006.

31. In the past, economic stratification tended to exist at the denominational level, with wealthy business owners being Episcopalian or Presbyterian while working classes flocked to Baptist, Pentecostal, and other "low" (both liturgically and socioeconomically) churches (Niebuhr 1929). Invariably, this influenced the degree of economic homogeneity within local congregations, but at least the upper and middle classes could be found in the same congregations. In contrast, what we have witnessed within the last twenty years signals a deepening divide within the movement along economic lines. It is now possible for an evangelical executive to participate in worship regularly, attend Bible studies, and serve in a leadership capacity beyond the context of a local congregation, which inhibits the executive's likelihood of interacting with the poor in a religious context.

32. Wuthnow (1994) reports the relative obscurity of "stewardship" in average Americans' discourse about giving.

33. The largest of these is the Evangelical Council for Financial Accountability (ECFA), with more than 1,100 member organizations and a combined member income of

approximately $14 billion. ECFA members are required to submit audited financial statements, IRS 990 forms, and other financial information. In addition, the ECFA conducts on-site field reviews of member organizations and publicizes information for prospective donors. See www.ecfa.org for more information.

34. In the Economic and Spiritual State of the Union Survey (2006), 39 percent of evangelicals said their religious beliefs greatly influence their investing.

35. Some observers, such as David Barrett at the World Evangelization Research Center, estimate that giving to parachurches has now surpassed giving to traditional churches within the evangelical world. Comments delivered on "The Present and Future of Religious Giving," Philanthropy Roundtable Panel, October 29, 1999, Naples, Florida.

36. Examples include the support of wealthy merchants in establishing the Society for the Promotion of Christian Knowledge (1698) and the YMCA, which in 1905 became the first religious agency to employ a capital campaign with a specific monetary goal and competition among teams of fund-raising volunteers (Cutlim 1965).

Conclusion

1. Wuthnow (1995).

2. The notion of a "cultural commission" or "mandate" dates back to the writings of Francis Shaeffer and has been popularized through the writings of Richard Mouw and Charles Colson. It suggests that all Christians (including evangelicals) are to care for the world and engage society because of a command in Genesis. This has legitimated evangelical engagement in multiple spheres of cultural influence, particularly culture-producing industries like film, television, the arts, and academic scholarship.

3. Douglas (1970, 1966) discusses the importance of boundary maintenance and its relevance to modern life.

4. Although they did not use such language to describe small-group gatherings, most fellowship groups I observed for these leaders centered around the challenges of being a faithful evangelical, an accomplished professional, an engaged family member, and a virtuous person—all at the same time.

5. Zald and Denton (1963) show how the acquisition of one set of resources can help acquire additional resources for a social movement.

6. Useem (1984: 63). Clawson and Neustadtl (1989) have also documented the centripetal force of inner circle power.

7. Collins (1998) showed how affiliation with prestigious networks permits individuals and their ideas to gain widespread acceptance.

8. It is important to say that the "difference" advocated by these evangelical leaders in government was not a sectarian aim; as they related the story, it largely involved concern over the effect of mainstream media on children. Obviously, though, views on what was deemed "appropriate" content for the media were born of evangelical conviction. This was not a religious aim per se, but the moral conviction that something ought to be done and the drawing of boundaries between "acceptable" and "unacceptable" content were most certainly shaped by evangelical norms. I also sense that these leaders had deeper levels of conviction on the matter because of their faith.

9. Discerning exactly what role those spiritual kinships play requires careful decision-making analysis on specific matters in particular contexts. While important for particular policy outcomes, that is not the purpose of this book.

10. The story of this implosion at Morgan's firm, the Internet company Value America, is detailed in *Dot Bomb* by J. David Kuo (2003).

11. In premodern societies, *individuals* exerted power in multiple social arenas like the Medici family in Renaissance Italy. Padgett and Ansell (1993) have argued that Cosimo the Elder's multiple identities enabled him to take advantage of network disjunctures among the area's elite. In other words, he and his interpersonal network were particularly powerful because of their ability to span institutional and interpersonal boundaries, whereby they served as nodes of introduction and in-

formation within multiple elite networks. Since then, it has been the *social worlds* of society's elite that have provided sources of cohesion (Baltzell 1958, 1964; Domhoff 2006, 1975). Social settings like boarding schools and debutante societies provided contexts that facilitated close relationships among leaders. For a religious identity to be providing similar cohesion today—in the midst of institutional differentiation in the professional sphere—is a noteworthy development.

12. In 2005, World Vision had annual revenues of $905 million, contributed from more than 5 million donors and volunteers. As a Christian relief and development organization, World Vision's programs reached more than 100 million people in nearly a hundred countries in 2005. I observed the World Vision, United States, board in September 2005 after having previously interviewed the CEO and five board members.

13. I agree with Mills (1956), Keller (1963), and Dye (2002) that power inheres in vital, national institutions. By bridging personnel at these important institutions, evangelicalism has built an infrastructure for long-term influence.

14. Since Max Weber ([1946] 1991), some scholars have equated power with domination, the probability that a person can carry out his or her own will, despite resistance. Legitimated power, in Weber's formulation, is authority. Antonio Gramsci ([1947] 1994) subsequently argued that the dominant class uses ideology, or worldview, to support its authoritative positions over the dominated classes. Through both political and ideological means, the ruling class relies on hegemony to secure the consent of the dominated classes for this arrangement, which obviously is not always in the best interest of the masses. While this notion of a ruling class has persisted (Domhoff 2006), some sociologists have articulated a view of power that does not focus on domination and manipulation to the exclusion of feedback mechanisms between "subjects" and "rulers." Steven Lukes, in his original text, *Power: A Radical View* (1974), argued that power involved both observable decision-making and informal influences like persuasion and manipulation. But it also included nonobservable phenomena such as the shaping of preferences. More recently, though, Lukes has published a second edition to the text (2005) whereby he repudiates his earlier notion of power that equated it with domination. My notion of convening power is based on a transactional view of power that, like Foucault (2000), treats power as something that works *through* people, rather than directly *on* them.

15. Kerbo (1993).

16. I imagine this type of cohesion and convening power can be found in overlapping networks of other influential groups. Shared identities organized around things like gender, race, and sexual orientation likely have analogous networks. And while I cannot comment on those specifically, I hope this examination of American evangelicalism and the powerful role of overlapping networks will spur similar investigations of other groups.

17. It is surprising that previous examinations of cohesion among leaders have not considered the binding power that a salient religious identity can provide. As stated in the introduction, some studies—like Mayo, Nohria, and Singleton (2006), Baltzell (1964), and Keller (1963)—have examined religious *affiliation,* but they have not distinguished between *affiliation* and *identity.* Cadge and Davidman (2006) have shown that religious adherents blend different parts of their lives creatively together in their own narratives of religious identity, a finding of particular relevance among those leaders I interviewed who embraced an evangelical faith later in life.

18. Smith's (1998) subcultural theory of religious vitality underscores how increasing religious pluralism has actually strengthened, not weakened, the evangelical movement in recent decades. Building on his work, I believe this tension between deeply held belief and engagement with wider society has contributed to the movement's advance.

19. Signatures on the letter, which was leaked to the press, included Phyllis Schlafly of the Eagle Forum and Tim Wildmon of the American Family Association.

20. By cosmopolitan evangelicalism, I borrow from Merton's notion of "cosmopolitan" (1957, 1946) which distinguishes between those who are oriented toward an internal community ("locals") and those oriented toward wider society outside that community ("cosmopolitans"). Merton was interested in exploring how certain people

influence others in a given community, differentiating between "local influentials" and "cosmopolitan influentials." For both, the local community is important, but the two interact with that community differently and carry out distinct roles. At root is orientation, as Gouldner (1957) demonstrated in his study of academic communities. His study expanded on Merton's work. In it, cosmopolitans were those members of the university whose primary orientation was toward their disciplinary guild or profession; their reference group involved colleagues around the world with whom they shared professional and intellectual interests. Locals, by contrast, were university members whose first loyalty resided in the local institution. They were often legendary figures on campus, well known in the local community but less involved with the guild or in collaborating with colleagues at other institutions. While I build upon all of these notions of "cosmopolitan," I find the category of "locals" found in Merton and Gouldner less applicable to elite levels today. "Local" seems less relevant as a comparison to "cosmopolitan" in an era of instant communication networks, mass transportation, frequent relocation, and declining civic involvement. Instead of the category of "local," I prefer "populist evangelicalism," building on previous work in political science (Kazin 1995; Canovan 1981).

21. Bourdieu's (1984) informants in his study of aesthetic taste showed similar status concerns. I recognize that my presence as a researcher from a major university may have influenced the self-presentation of some leaders, but over the three years of my research, I encountered the distancing mechanism mentioned above many times before the other individual knew my own background or experience. This frequently occurred while observing conferences or board meetings where evangelical public leaders were in attendance. Sullivan (2004) describes similar experiences.

22. The concept of "cosmopolitanism" has been applied by others to the religious domain. Roof (1978) found cosmopolitans in his study of Episcopalians; they had higher levels of education, lived in larger cities, and were less involved in local religious life. "Locals," on the other hand, exhibited higher degrees of religious orthodoxy and were more likely to have ideologies shaped by particularistic, "close-to-home" values and norms. Heilman and Cohen (1989) also discussed the presence of "cosmopolitans" in their study of Orthodox Judaism and, like Roof, found cosmopolitans to have the least traditional religious orientation among the groups studied.

23. Smith (2005); Hout, Greeley, and Wilde (2001).

24. Hoffer ([1951] 2002).

25. In this way, "cosmopolitanism" as used here is different from the term's use in Heilman and Cohen (1989) or Roof (1978), who found lower levels of religious commitment among their "cosmopolitans."

26. Tensions between a religious subculture and co-religionists who occupy positions of societal influence have appeared in other contexts. Greeley (1989) referred to feelings of "envy" on the part of Catholic clergy toward Catholic artists, politicians, and executives and concluded that "the ecclesiastical institution does not know what to do with this elite" (429).

27. Appiah (2006) frames cosmopolitanism in terms of intentional interaction with the other. Civil engagement with people different from ourselves is the goal he advocates.

28. Hunter and Yates (2002).

29. A megachurch is a congregation that averages two thousand people or more attending weekly worship services.

30. This resonates with Greeley and Hout (2006).

31. I define these as (1) holding a particular regard for the Bible, (2) embracing a personal relationship with God through a "conversion" to Jesus Christ, and (3) seeking to lead others on a similar spiritual journey (Kellstedt et al. 1996; Bebbington 1989).

32. Bellah et al. (1985); Tocqueville ([1834] 2000).

33. Conservative evangelical denominations like the Presbyterian Church in America and the Southern Baptist Convention have particularly few female pastors.

There is a history of women occupying influential roles in the parachurch context. For instance, several missionary programs emerged out of these special-purpose organizations; women were very active in these programs, often serving as leaders (Robert 1996). In addition, previous work has shown that the "parachurch" sector is more open to diversity, in terms of both organizational mission and constituencies served (Willmer and Schmidt 1998). Hence, I would expect this sector to demonstrate similar openness to diversity in terms of leadership.

34. Neither the list of evangelical institutions, nor this comparison category, was drawn randomly. I examined the board composition at fifteen large, influential evangelical nonprofit organizations. These are Baylor University, the Billy Graham Evangelistic Association, Campus Crusade for Christ, Christianity Today International, Evangelical Council for Financial Accountability, Evangelicals and Catholics Together, Focus on the Family, Fuller Theological Seminary, InterVarsity Christian Fellowship, Prison Fellowship Ministries, Trinity Forum, Wheaton College, Willow Creek Association, World Vision, and Young Life. For comparison, I selected secular organizations of significant scope and influence within the nonprofit sector by talking with several experts in the field (both those inside and outside the evangelical world). Although a few of the organizations in the comparison group have either evangelical roots or religious missions, none of them exists primarily for evangelical constituents, which is different from the group of evangelical institutions. I also consulted *Forbes'* annual list of the two hundred largest U.S. charities when drawing this comparison group; gender-exclusive organizations like the Girl Scouts of America are omitted from the comparison in order to avoid intentional gender bias in board recruitment and selection. Organizations examined are the American Cancer Society, American Heart Association, American National Red Cross, Big Brothers Big Sisters of America, Boys and Girls Clubs of America, Harvard University Board of Overseers, Mayo Foundation, Public Broadcasting Service, Smithsonian Institution, Special Olympics, Stanford University, Salvation Army, United Way, Yale University Corporation, and YMCA of the USA. Analysis is based on the most recent board lists available (typically 2005 or 2006), which are based on annual reports, tax documents, and/or personal observations of board deliberations by me. For both the evangelical and comparison groups, I exclude ex officio members from the analyses. Specific institutions referenced are Wheaton College, where 10 percent of the board are women, InterVarsity Christian Fellowship (31 percent), Harvard's Board of Overseers (33 percent), and Boys and Girls Clubs of America (9 percent).

35. It is interesting that no parachurch organization excludes women altogether. Even the Executive Committee of the Southern Baptist Convention (SBC), a denomination that has issued some of the most conservative statements on women in leadership, has several female members (seven as of 2006, constituting 9 percent of the total board). Similar trends are found at other SBC entities, including its International Mission Board and its North American Mission Board. It seems unlikely, therefore, that theology, even in conservative circles, bars women from holding governance positions on evangelical boards.

36. Bah'ai World Faith, on the other hand, endorses progressive revelation: "As the human race has developed through time we have gradually understood more clearly the world around us. During our progress God has sent us Messengers whose Messages were according to our understanding in the time during which we lived." See www.bci.org/konabahais/intro.htm for more information.

37. Some further cite the Garden of Eden account in Genesis 3, in which the woman eats the forbidden fruit before the man, as support for a male-dominated culture (Henry 1957).

38. Gallagher (2003). She discovered that an overwhelming majority of evangelical families affirm that husbands should be the head of the home (90 percent) while also saying that marriage should be an equal partnership between husband and wife (87 percent). Moreover, 78 percent affirm both claims. Hence, evangelical attitudes around responses to gender are complex and, at times, contradictory. Historian Pamela Cochran (2005) details the intriguing history of two large feminist bodies within modern American evangelicalism: the Evangelical Women's Caucus (EWC) and Christians for Biblical Equality (CBE). These groups—and especially CBE, which benefited from the support of evangelical leaders like Ron Sider, John Stott, and Bill Hybels—promulgated feminist ideas within a largely conservative theology that affirmed the authority of the Bible. Over time, these ideas influenced the behavior of evangelicals, even if they did not change doctrinal statements within the movement.

39. Wilcox (2004). This research buttresses earlier studies that found similar results (Brinkerhoff, Grandin, and Lupri 1992; Ferguson et al. 1986; Strauss, Gelles, and Steinmetz 1980). Pollock and Steele (1968) first argued that "strong, rigid, authoritarian fundamentalist types of belief" tended to be more abusive to children, although subsequent studies have not always supported this assertion (Neufeld 1979; Herrenkohl 1978; Smith, Hanson, and Noble 1974). Scanzoni (1988), however, continued to argue that patriarchal dogma, such as that of conservative evangelicals, has "fostered and excused family violence" (137). More recently, Cokie Roberts and Steve Roberts suggested that notions of male headship in marriage "can clearly lead to abuse, both physical and emotional" (Roberts and Roberts 1998).

    For "soft patriarchy," see Wilcox (2004: 191). Although research has confirmed that conservative religion is often joined to sexism in one form or another (Peek, Lowe, and Williams 1991), American evangelicalism has spawned feminism as well. For instance, Griffith (1997) demonstrated how the largest evangelical women's organization in the world provides a crucible through which evangelical women achieve a surprising degree of power, autonomy, and personal liberation—even when affirming traditional evangelical dogma.

40. Over the years, conservative evangelicals have mounted significant opposition to feminist-friendly groups like CBE. In 1987, Minneapolis pastor John Piper and Wayne Grudem, a professor at Trinity Evangelical Divinity School, founded the Council on Biblical Manhood and Womanhood to oppose efforts promoting biblical feminism. Also, politically oriented groups like the Moral Majority and Concerned Women for America have mobilized conservative evangelicals against feminist ideals in the public square. These include resistance initiatives against the Equal Rights Amendment and universal childcare (Lindner 1996). Bill Gothard's marriage and family seminars, which were much more prominent in the 1970s and 1980s, advocate a hierarchical chain of command for families, churches, and even civic life—with only men in positions of authority. There have also been a number of evangelical programs and organizations targeted toward only men or only women, further exacerbating the notion of separate spheres along gender lines. Promise Keepers, founded in 1990 by University of Colorado football coach Bill McCartney, is a popular men's group that many have regarded as legitimating sexism and hegemony (Donovan 1998). Men-only spiritual retreats, especially among business leaders, exclude women co-religionists from the opportunity to fellowship with professional peers and widen the gap between men and women within evangelicalism.

41. See Borrelli (1997), Martin (1989), and Fisher (1987). Incidentally, other educational outcomes—college-graduate rates, percentage with advanced degrees—do not differ dramatically between the men and the women I interviewed. It is the percentages with degrees from highly selective universities where gender differences appear most dramatic. Dye's examination (2002) of the structure of institutional power in the United States reveals that 54 percent of the nation's corporate leaders and 42 percent of the governmental leaders today graduated from one of twelve highly selective universities. Access to elite education is a strong predictor for securing positions of public influence, and since they have been a minority within the nation's elite, this is even more critical for women.

42. Stout (1988) argues that social practices are embodied in institutions, which necessarily trade heavily in external goods like money, power, and status.

43. In *The German Ideology*, Marx argued that the capitalist class controlled not just the economic sphere but also the political and ideological spheres to such an extent that "the ideas of the ruling class are in every epoch the ruling ideas" ([1845] 1978: 172). Marx argued that economic power unites a ruling group of capitalists, permitting their domination over the abject masses. The goal for society, according to Marx's view, was to overthrow the dominating class and to distribute power among the people.

    In *The Ruling Class*, Mosca ([1896] 1939) agreed with Marx that there are two classes: those who rule and those who are ruled. But he believed that social power was not united in the hands of capitalists; rather it resided with a society's political leadership. With regard to specific arguments, this monolithic tradition says a cohesive unity among leaders emerges from shared decision-making (Mills 1956; Hunter 1953), shared backgrounds and experiences (Baltzell 1964, 1958), shared institutional positions (Domhoff 2006; Useem 1984), or a shared social milieu (Bourdieu 1984; Domhoff 1975).

In the middle of the twentieth century, Mills (1956) called on his fellow intellectuals to challenge the legitimacy of the governmental-business-military "power elite" that ruled his day. Mills went on to say that "mass society is the obverse of the power elite; as power has been concentrated at the top, the mass has been denuded of it" (1956: 19). Mills identified two sources of elite unity: structural coincidence (business leaders and military leaders at the top of one another's sectors) and social similarity. All of the decisions that Mills explored in *The Power Elite* related to violence, and his reference to societal elites as "command posts" reflected this fascination with the military complex following World War II. However, it is surprising that Mills relegated Congress to the "middle level" of the power structure and that he ignored the role of political parties, associations, the judicial system, the arts, entertainment, and media sectors, among others. Throughout Mills' book there is also a curious lack of definitional elaboration of power; only twice does he mention the term, the first time taking Weber's definition, and then at the end declaring that "the ultimate kind of power is violence" (1956: 171). Despite these shortcomings, Mills' work is a classic work that provides a scheme for analyzing social power, even if it does not provide an empirical study per se.

Building on the work of Marx, Gramsci ([1947] 1994) suggested that leaders maintained control not simply through violence or coercion but also through a hegemonic culture in which a legitimating ideology led the dominated masses to identify their own good with the good of their rulers. Mosca ([1896] 1939) also had written about a legitimating narrative decades earlier; according to him, every leading group had to justify itself by means of a "political formula" that made their positions of power and privilege more palatable to the masses. Althusser ([1969] 1977) expanded Gramsci's notion of hegemony and identified a series of ideological state apparatuses such as religion, education, the legal system, communications, and trade unions, among others. These apparatuses promulgate ideology that legitimates the power held by society's leaders. This ideology is so acute and powerful, Althusser claimed, because it is taken for granted. These structures, therefore, can be viewed as agents of repression.

44. Robert A. Dahl (1961) first made the pluralist argument at the local level. He studied decision-making in New Haven, Connecticut, and refuted Floyd Hunter's (1953) assertion that business leaders dominated decision-making in Atlanta. Shortly thereafter, Suzanne Keller (1963) was the first to challenge the monolithic model with data on leaders at the societal level. In her work, Keller differentiated between strategic elites and a ruling class; she concluded that the two differed in their manner of recruitment, their internal organization, and their degree of specialization. Accordingly, the notion of a single pyramid capped by a ruling class had given way with modern society to a number of parallel pyramids, each capped by an elite. Subsequent works have shown empirical differences between economic and political power in post–World War II France (Aron 1950) and contemporary America (Lerner, Nagai, and Rothman 1996; Vogel 1996), supporting the pluralist interpretation of contemporary power structures.

In Dye's most recent analysis of the structure of America's leadership cohort (2002), he identified close to six thousand individuals who wield significant influence in nearly a dozen different fields. His analysis showed that only a small percentage of public leaders (15 percent) occupied more than one influential position at the same time. While there is a concentration of the nation's resources in a relatively small number of institutions, the individuals who lead those institutions reach such heights by upward mobility and by demonstrating their capability within those institutions, not through class cohesion or overlapping institutional structures.

45. One class of counterexamples that did emerge in this study, however, relates to the focus of Mills' study (1956). It was not uncommon for a Pentagon official (usually a civilian officer) to serve subsequently as a business executive in the related defense industry or as head of a nonprofit organization specializing in military matters. For example, Deputy Secretary of Defense Rudy de Leon now serves as the head of Boeing's Washington office, out of which most of Boeing's defense contracts are handled. Also, Deputy Secretary of Defense John Hamre now heads the

Center for Strategic and International Studies, a Washington-based nonprofit organization focused on global security issues.

46. Useem (1984) and Dye (2002) have noted the persistence of an "inner circle" of leaders in contemporary America. Useem defines the "inner circle" as those business leaders who serve as directors of several large corporations (in diverse industry sectors) while also, in some cases, heading their own firms. These inner-circle members tend to be active members of major business associations (like the Business Roundtable) and government advisory boards (like the Council on Foreign Relations) as well. Dye also suggested the persistence of interlocking directorates as a source of inner-circle power whereby individuals are in a unique position to communicate and coordinate the activities of multiple organizations because of their structural location on multiple boards. Perhaps one of the reasons these individuals did not emerge in this present study relates to Useem's finding that "inner circle" members tended to be socially and politically more liberal and reflected higher degrees of class consciousness. Those are not traits commonly found among evangelical public leaders.

Indeed, just as others have concluded (Dye 2002; Lerner, Nagai, and Rothman 1996; Putnam 1976; Keller 1963), the various sectors explored reflect differing recruitment mechanisms for leaders, and the individuals who reach the top of these institutional sectors spend relatively little time interacting with leaders of other sectors in their professional duties. And while there are a few parachurch organizations that create bonds across institutional sectors, most groups that minister to an elite constituency stay within a single domain.

47. Hutchison's edited volume (1989) chronicles the declining influence of mainline Protestantism in American public life over the twentieth century, and like this book, considers the role of religion in government, higher education, media, and business. Likewise, Mayo, Nohria, and Singleton (2006) explore the way that religious affiliation (not necessarily religious identity) facilitated elite power during the early decades of the twentieth century. On diversity, see Zweigenhaft and Domhoff (2006).

48. Baltzell (1964) used the term "establishment" to refer to a traditional aristocracy that ruled American society with legitimate authority. This he compared to a caste, which is an upper class that protects its privileged position without contributing to public leadership. Echoing Tocqueville's concern in *The Old Regime and the Revolution* (1856), Baltzell was concerned that America's WASP establishment (the "Protestant Establishment") was denigrating into a caste, much like the "old regime" in Tocqueville's native pre-Revolutionary France.

49. To take just one example, consider the literature on university presidencies that has uniformly concluded the persisting, inhibiting effect of institutional inertia, even as presidents have sought to achieve certain outcomes. For comments from the presidents themselves, see Brodie and Banner (2005), Bok (2004) and Bowen and Shapiro (1998).

50. In other words, cohesion is not the same as collusion. Every empirical analyst studying a cohort of national leaders must distinguish between these two. While both rely upon a shared attraction that results in a united, consistent whole, collusion entails a secretive pact among actors, often connoting sinister intentions.

51. Volf (1994).

Appendix

1. The snowball method has been used in a number of projects involving elite informants (Schmalzbauer 2003; Kadushin 1995; Barton, Denitch, and Kadushin 1973). According to this method, public leader informants are asked at the end of each interview to identify other, similarly stationed leaders who share their religious commitments; this method is both appropriate and useful for the present study. The leapfrog method, however, represents a methodological innovation by engaging nonparticipants who are well qualified (through both information and network advantages) to help identify potential informants while minimizing the

bias of limited interpersonal networks and shared personal identities that typically encumber the snowball method by itself. Of course, the leapfrog method relies upon interpersonal networks as well, but the breadth of these networks is much wider. In this particular study, for instance, informants were selected from 157 more organizational networks than would have been the case if I relied solely on the snowball method. Also, because the leapfrog method begins with organizations as the unit of analysis, instead of individuals, informants are more likely to represent diverse social locations (geographically, institutionally, and demographically) than is often the case in studies that employ only the snowball method.

2. Dye (2002); Putnam (1976); Keller (1963); Mannheim (1940).

3. Informants did have the option of speaking, at times, off the record. However, the majority of the interview was on the record.

4. The one exception to interviewing currently elected officials was an interview with Governor Mike Huckabee (R-AR) conducted in July 2004. I finally decided not to interview currently elected officials in September 2004, after the Huckabee interview. As a result, I used the data collected from that interview as background information and for quantitative analysis, but I did not rely on it for further empirical investigation.

5. All generalizations are based on a dominant pattern across the interviews where a particular issue was discussed; because these were not highly structured interviews, not all topics were covered in every single interview. However, when I quote from a particular interview, it represents a theme common to multiple interviews; I do not discuss findings that are not general. Informants had the option of responding to certain questions off the record, in which case no direct attribution would be given. In those instances, no identifying information is provided. I present additional, nonattributed information from conversations conducted with informants before or after the formal interview. In those cases, I rely on copious notes and subsequent communication with the leaders to assure accuracy and the tone with which the comments were made. On several occasions when participants relayed negative appraisals of a particular group or entity, they requested that information be reported off the record. I was able to persuade a few of them to change their minds on this issue, but most often those efforts were unsuccessful.

6. In a few instances, an informant served in more than one area of public influence. Alonzo McDonald, for instance, served as both Deputy White House Chief of Staff and managing partner of McKinsey & Company. In those cases, the informant is listed under only one category (government, in this case).

7. Karabel (2005); Dye (2002); Cookson and Persell (1985); Baltzell (1964); Keller (1963).

8. The following institutions are coded "highly selective": the eight Ivy League campuses (Brown, Columbia, Cornell, Dartmouth, Harvard, University of Pennsylvania, Princeton, and Yale), the University of Chicago, Duke University, Oxford University, and Stanford University.

9. Smith, Sikkink, and Bailey (1998); Shibley (1996, 1991).

10. States comprising the Northeast are ME, NH, VT, MA, RI, CT, NY, NJ, PA, MD, DE, and the District of Columbia. States comprising the South are VA, WV, NC, SC, GA, FL, AL, MS, TN, KY, AR, LA, TX, and OK. States comprising the Midwest are OH, MI, IN, IL, MO, WI, MN, ND, SD, NE, KS, IA, and MT. States comprising the West are ID, WY, CO, UT, AZ, NM, NV, CA, OR, WA, AL, and HI.

11. Fourteen percent; see Gallup and Lindsay (1999).

REFERENCES

Adorno, Theodor. [1949] 2003. *Philosophy of Modern Music*. Trans. Anne G. Mitchell and Wesley V. Blomster. New York: Continuum.

———. [1970] 1997. *Aesthetic Theory*. Ed. Gretel Adorno and Rolf Tiedermann. Minneapolis: University of Minnesota Press.

Aikman, David. 2004. *A Man of Faith: The Spiritual Journey of George W. Bush*. Nashville, TN: W Publishing Group.

Allen, Mike. 2006. "Courting a New Coalition." *Time*. August 7.

Althusser, Louis. [1969] 1977. "Ideology and Ideological State Apparatuses: Notes Toward an Investigation." In *Lenin and Philosophy and Other Essays*. London: New Left Books.

Ammerman, Nancy Tatom. 1987. *Bible Believers: Fundamentalists in the Modern World*. New Brunswick: Rutgers University Press.

———. 1990. *Baptist Battles: Social Change and Religious Conflict in the Southern Baptist Convention*. New Brunswick: Rutgers University Press.

———. 2003. "Religious Identities and Religious Institutions" in *The Handbook of the Sociology of Religion*, ed. Michele Dilon. New York: Cambridge University Press.

Appiah, Anthony. 2006. *Cosmopolitanism: Ethics in a World of Strangers*. New York: Norton.

Aron, Raymond. 1950. "Social Structure and Ruling Class." *British Journal of Sociology* 1, no. 1:1–16, no. 2:126–43.

Asma, Stephen. 2004. "A Review of PBS's *The Question of God*." *Chronicle Review*. September 12.

Austin, Ron. 2005. "Christians in Hollywood: A Treatment." *Image* 43:94–100.

Balmer, Randall, 2000a. *Mine Eyes Have Seen the Glory: A Journey into the Evangelical Subculture in America*. New York: Oxford University Press.

———. 2000b. "The Kinkade Crusade." *Christianity Today*. December 4.

Baltzell, E. Digby. 1958. *Philadelphia Gentlemen: The Making of a National Upper Class*. New York: Free Press.

———. 1964. *The Protestant Establishment: Aristocracy and Caste in America*. New York: Random House.

Barna, George. 1990. *The Frog in the Kettle: What Christians Need to Know About Life in the Year 2000*. Ventura, CA: Regal Books.

———. 1991. *User Friendly Churches: What Christians Need to Know About the Churches People Love to Go To*. Ventura, CA: Regal Books.

———. 1992. *The Power of Vision: How You Can Capture and Apply God's Vision for Your Ministry*. Ventura, CA: Regal Books.

———. 1994. *Virtual America: What Every Church Leader Needs to Know About Ministering in an Age of Spiritual and Technological Revolution*. Ventura, CA: Regal Books.

———. 2003. *Transforming Children into Spiritual Champions*. Ventura, CA: Regal Books.

Barney, Jay B. 1986. "Organizational Culture: Can It Be a Source of Sustained Competitive Advantage?" *Academy of Management Review* 11:656–65.

Bartels, Larry M. 2005. "What's the Matter with *What's the Matter with Kansas?*" Presentation at the annual meeting of the American Political Science Association, Washington, September 1–4, 2005.

Bartkowski, John P. 2001. *Remaking the Godly Marriage: Gender Negotiation in Evangelical Families*. New Brunswick: Rutgers University Press.

Barton, Allen H., Bogdan Denitch, and Charles Kadushin. 1973. "Determinants of Leadership Attitudes in a Socialist Study." In *Opinion-Making Elites in Yugoslavia*. New York: Praeger.

Barton, Bruce. 1924. *The Man Nobody Knows*. Indianapolis: Bobbs-Merrill.

Bebbington, David. 1989. *Evangelicalism in Modern Britain: A History from the 1730s to the 1980s*. London: Unwin Hyman.

Bellah, Robert, Richard Madsen, William M. Sullivan, Ann Swidler, and Steven M. Tipton. 1985. *Habits of the Heart: Individualism and Commitment in American Life*. Berkeley: University of California Press.

Belmonte, Kevin. 2002. *Hero for Humanity: A Biography of William Wilberforce*. Colorado Springs, CO: NavPress.

Belz, Mindy. 2005. "Daniel of the Year: Makoto Fujimura." *World*. December 17.

Bendix, Reinhard. 1956. *Work and Authority in Industry*. New York: Wiley.

Benson, Peter, and Dorothy Williams. 1982. *Religion on Capitol Hill: Myth and Realities*. San Francisco: Harper & Row.

Berger, Peter L. 1967. *The Sacred Canopy: Elements of a Sociological Theory of Religion*. Garden City, NY: Doubleday.

Berger, Peter L., and Thomas Luckmann. 1966. *The Social Construction of Reality*. Garden City, NY: Doubleday.

Bernard, Jessie. 1961. "Teen-Age Culture: An Overview." *Annals of the American Academy of Political and Social Science* 338:1–12.

Beyerlein, Kraig. 2004. "Specifying the Impact of Conservative Protestantism on Educational Attainment." *Journal for the Scientific Study of Religion* 43:505–18.

Bielby, Denise D., and William T. Bielby. 1996. "Women and Men in Film: Gender Inequality Among Writers in a Culture Industry." *Gender & Society* 10, no. 3:248–70.

Binder, Amy. 2005. "Gathering Intelligence on 'Intelligent Design': Where Did It Come From, Where Is It Going, and How Do (and Should) Educators, Scientists, Non-Profit Organizations, and the Media Manage It?" Presented at the Center for Arts and Cultural Policy and Studies, Princeton University, November 17.

Bok, Derek. 2004. *Universities in the Marketplace: The Commercialization of Higher Education*. Princeton: Princeton University Press.

Bolce, Louis, and Gerald De Maio. 2002. "Our Secularist Democratic Party." *Public Interest*. Fall.

Bono and McCormick, Neil, eds. 2006. *U2 by U2: Bono, the Edge, Adam Clayton, Larry Mullen Jr.* New York: Harper Entertainment.

Borrelli, Mary Anne. 1997. "Campaign Promises, Transition Dilemmas: Cabinet Building and Executive Representation." In *The Other Elites: Women, Politics, and Power in the Executive Branch*, ed. Mary Anne Borrelli and Janet M. Martin. Boulder, CO: Lynne Rienner.

Bourdieu, Pierre. 1977. *Reproduction in Education, Society, and Culture*. Trans. Richard Nice. Beverly Hills, CA: Sage Publications.

———. 1984. *Distinction: A Social Critique of the Judgment of Taste*. Trans. Richard Nice. Cambridge: Harvard University Press.

Bowen, William G., and Harold T. Shapiro, eds. 1998. *Universities and Their Leadership*. Princeton: Princeton University Press.

Bowers, John W., Donovan J. Ochs, and Richard J. Jenson. 1993. *The Rhetoric of Agitation and Control*. 2nd ed. Prospect Heights, IL: Waveland.

Bramadat, Paul A. 2000. *The Church on the World's Turf: An Evangelical Christian Group at a Secular University*. New York: Oxford University Press.

Brinkerhoff, Merlin B., Elaine Grandin, and Eugen Lupri. 1992. "Religious Involvement and Spousal Violence: The Canadian Case." *Journal for the Scientific Study of Religion* 31:15–31.

Brodie, Keith H., and Leslie Banner. 2005. *The Research University Presidency in the Late Twentieth Century*. Westport, CT: Praeger.

Brooks, David. 2001. "The Organization Kid." *Atlantic Monthly*. April.

———. 2004. "Who Is John Stott?" *New York Times*. November 30.

Budde, Michael L., and Robert W. Brimlow. 2002. *Christianity Incorporated: How Big Business Is Buying the Church*. Grand Rapids, MI: Brazos Press.

Burtchaell, James Tunstead. 1998. *The Dying of the Light*. Grand Rapids, MI: Eerdmans.

Busto, Rudy V. 1999. "The Gospel According to the Model Minority? Hazarding an Interpretation of Asian American Evangelical College Students." In *New Spiritual Homes; Religion and Asian Americans,* ed. David Yoo. Honolulu: University of Hawaii Press.

Butler, Jon. 1991. "Born-Again America? A Critique of the New 'Evangelical Thesis' in Recent American Historigraphy." Unpublished paper, Organization of American Historians, Spring. Cited in Harry Stout and Robert Taylor, "Studies of Religion in American Society," in *New Directions in American Religious History,* ed. Harry Stout and D. G. Hart. New York: Oxford University Press.

Cadge, Wendy, and Lynn Davidman. 2006. "Ascription, Choice, and the Construction of Religious Identities in the Contemporary United States." *Journal for the Scientific Study of Religion* 45:23–38.

Canovan, Margaret. 1981. *Populism.* New York: Harcourt Brace Jovanovich.

Cantor, Muriel. 1971. *The Hollywood TV Producer.* New York: Basic Books.

Carlson, Sune. 1951. *Executive Behavior: A Study of the Work Load and the Working Methods of Managing Directors.* Stockholm: Strombergs.

Carpenter, Joel. 1997. *Revive Us Again: The Reawakening of American Fundamentalism.* New York: Oxford University Press.

Casanova, Jose. 1994. *Public Religions in the Modern World.* Chicago: University of Chicago Press.

Chaves, Mark. 1999. "Religious Congregations and Welfare Reform: Who Will Take Advantage of 'Charitable Choice'?" *American Sociological Review* 64:836–46.

Chaves, Mark, and Sharon L. Miller, eds. 1999. *Financing American Religion.* Walnut Creek, CA: Altamira Press.

Cherry, Conrad, Betty A. DeBerg, and Amanda Porterfield. 2001. *Religion on Campus.* Chapel Hill: University of North Carolina Press.

Ch'ien, Evelyn. 2000. "Evangels on Campus: Asian American College Students Are Making the Grade with God." *A. Magazine.* April/May.

Chopp, Rebecca. 2002. "Beyond the Founding Fratricidal Conflict: A Tale of Three Cities." *Journal of the American Academy of Religion* 70:461–74.

Christerson, Brad, Korie L. Edwards, and Michael O. Emerson. 2005. *Against All Odds: The Struggle for Racial Integration in Religious Organizations.* New York: New York University Press.

Clarkson, Frederick. 1997. *Eternal Hostility: The Struggle Between Theocracy and Democracy.* Monroe, ME: Common Courage Press.

Clawson, Dan, and Alan Neustadtl. 1989. "Interlocks, PACs, and Corporate Conservatism." *American Journal of Sociology* 94:779–93.

Cochran, Pamela D. H. 2005. *Evangelical Feminism: A History.* New York: New York University Press.

Collins, Randall. 1998. *The Sociology of Philosophies: A Global Theory of Intellectual Change.* Cambridge: Belknap Press of Harvard University Press.

Colson, Charles. 1994. "Christians in Politics: Being Salt or Being Suckers." *Rutherford.* March.

Conlin, Michelle. 1999. "Religion in the Workplace: The Growing Presence of Spirituality in Corporate America." *Business Week.* October 25.

Conway, Flo, and Jim Siegelman. 1984. *Holy Terror: The Fundamentalist War on America's Freedoms in Religion, Politics, and Our Private Lives.* New York: Dell.

Cookson, Peter W., and Caroline Hodges Persell. 1985. *Preparing for Power: America's Elite Boarding Schools.* New York: Basic Books.

Cooperman, Alan. 2004. "Openly Religious, to a Point." *Washington Post.* September 15.

Cox, Harvey. 1995. "The Warring Visions of the Religious Right." *Atlantic Monthly.* November.

Crouch, Andy. 2007. *Culture Makers.* Downers Grove, IL: IVP Press.

Cutlim, Scott M. 1965. *Fund-Raising in the United States: Its Role in American Philanthropy.* New Brunswick: Rutgers University Press

Dahl, Robert A. 1961. *Who Governs? Democracy and Power in an American City.* New Haven: Yale University Press.

Darnell, Alfred, and Darren E. Sherkat. 1997. "The Impact of Protestant Fundamentalism on Educational Attainment." *American Sociological Review* 62:306–15.

Davidman, Lynn. 1993. *Tradition in a Rootless World: Women Turn to Orthodox Judaism.* Berkeley: University of California Press.

Davie, Grace. 1994. *Religion in Britain Since 1945: Believing Without Belonging*. Oxford: Blackwell.

Dayton, Donald W., and Robert K. Johnson, eds. 1991. *The Variety of American Evangelicalism*. Knoxville: University of Tennessee Press.

Deephouse, David L. 1999. "To Be Different, or to Be the Same? It's a Question (and Theory) of Strategic Balance." *Strategic Management Journal* 20:147–66.

Denison, Daniel R. 1990. *Corporate Culture and Organizational Effectiveness*. New York: Wiley.

———. 1996. "What Is the Difference Between Organizational Culture and Organizational Climate? A Native's Point of View on a Decade of Paradigm Wars." *Academy of Management Review* 21:619–54.

Diamond, Sara. 1995. *Roads to Dominion: Right-Wing Movements and Political Power in the United States*. New York: Guilford Press.

DiMaggio, Paul, and Walter W. Powell. 1983. "The Iron Cage Revisited: Institutional Isomorphism and Collective Rationality in Organizational Fields." *American Sociological Review* 48:147–60.

———. 1991. "Introduction." In *The New Institutionalism in Organizational Analysis*. Chicago: University of Chicago Press.

Dolan, Julie. 2001. "Political Appointees in the United States: Does Gender Make a Difference? *PS: Political Science and Politics* 34, no. 2:213–16.

Domhoff, G. William. 1975. *The Bohemian Grove and Other Retreats: A Study in Ruling-Class Cohesiveness*. New York: Harper Torchbooks.

———. 2006. *Who Rules America Now? Power, Politics, and Social Change*. New York: McGraw-Hill. 5th edition.

Donovan, Brian, 1998. "Political Consequences of Private Authority: Promise Keepers and the Transformation of Hegemonic Masculinity." *Theory and Society* 27, no. 6: 817–43.

Douglas, Mary. 1966. *Purity and Danger*. London: Routledge and Kegan Paul.

———. 1970. *Natural Symbols: Explorations in Cosmology*. London: Barrie & Rockliff the Cresset.

Dye, Thomas R. 2002, *Who Is Running America? The Bush Restoration*. 7th ed. Upper Saddle River, NJ: Prentice Hall.

Dyer, W. Gibb, Jr. 1985. "The Cycle of Cultural Evolution in Organizations." In *Gaining Control of the Corporate Culture*, ed. Ralph H. Kilman et al. San Francisco: Jossey-Bass.

Ecklund, Elaine Howard, 2005. "Irreconcilable Conflict? How Scientists Understand the Relationship Between Religion and Science," Sociology Department Workshop, Princeton University, November 28.

———. 2006. *Korean American Evangelicals: New Models for Civic Life*. New York: Oxford University Press.

Ecklund, Elaine Howard, and Jerry Park, 2006. "Predicting Conflict Between Religion and Science Among Academic Scientists." Working Paper, Department of Sociology, Rice University.

Ellis, John Tracey. 1955. "American Catholics and the Intellectual Life." *Thought* 30: 351–88.

Ellison, Christopher G., and Darren E. Sherkat. 1993. "Conservative Protestantism and Support for Corporal Punishment." *American Sociological Review* 58:131–44.

Emerson, Michael O. 2006. *People of the Dream: Multiracial Congregations in the United States*. Princeton: Princeton University Press.

Emerson, Michael O., and Christian Smith. 2000. *Divided by Faith: Evangelical Religion and the Problem of Race in America*. New York: Oxford University Press.

Epstein, Cynthia Fuchs, and Rose Laub Coser. 1980. *Access to Power: Cross-National Studies of Women and Elites*. London: Allen & Unwin.

Eskridge, Larry, and Mark A. Noll. 2000. *More Money, More Ministry: Money and Evangelicals in Recent North American History*. Grand Rapids, MI: Eerdmans.

Ferguson, David M., L. John Horwood, Kathryn L. Kershaw, and Frederick T. Shannon. 1986. "Factors Associated with Reports of Wife Assault in New Zealand." *Journal of Marriage and the Family* 48:407–12.

Fine, Gary Alan, and Sherryl Kleinman. 1979. "Rethinking Subculture: An Interactionist Analysis." *American Journal of Sociology* 85, no. 1:1–20.

Fiorina, Morris P. 1976. "The Voting Decision: Instrumental and Expressive Aspects." *Journal of Politics* 38, no. 2:390–413.

Fish, Stanley. 2005. "One University, Under God?" *Chronicle of Higher Education.* January 7.

Fisher, Allan. 1998. "Evangelical-Christian Publishing: Where It's Been and Where It's Going." *Publishing Research Quarterly* 14:3–11.

———. 2003. "Five Surprising Years for Evangelical-Christian Publishing: 1998 to 2002." *Publishing Research Quarterly* 19:20–36.

Fisher, Linda L., 1987. "Fifty Years of Presidential Appointments." In *The In and Outers: Presidential Appointees and Transient Government in Washington,* ed. C. Calvin Mackenzie. Baltimore: Johns Hopkins University Press.

Foucault, Michel. 2000. *Power.* Ed. James D. Faubion. Trans. Robert Hurley. New York: New Press.

Frank, Thomas, 2004. *What's the Matter with Kansas? How Conservatives Won the Heart of America.* New York: Metropolitan Books.

Friedland, Roger, and Robert R. Alford. 1991. "Bringing Society Back In: Symbols, Practices, and Institutional Contradictions." In *The New Institutionalism in Organizational Analysis,* ed. Walter W. Powell and Paul J. DiMaggio. Chicago: University of Chicago Press.

Frum, David. 2003. *The Right Man: The Surprise Presidency of George W. Bush.* New York: Random House.

Gagliardi, Pasquale. 1990. *Symbols and Artifacts: Views of the Corporate Landscape.* Hawthorne, NY: Walter de Gruyter.

Gallagher, Sally K. 2003. *Evangelical Identity and Gendered Family Life.* New Brunswick: Rutgers University Press.

Gallup, George H., and D. Michael Lindsay. 1999. *Surveying the Religious Landscape: Trends in U.S. Beliefs.* Harrisburg, PA: Morehouse.

Gamson, Joshua. 1995. "Stopping the Spin and Becoming a Prop: Fieldwork on Hollywood Elites." In *Studying Elites Using Qualitative Methods,* ed. Rosanna Hertz and Jonathan B. Imber. Thousand Oaks, CA: Sage.

George, Timothy. 2004. "Inventing Evangelicalism: No One Was More Pivotal to the Emerging Movement than Carl F. H. Henry." *Christianity Today.* March.

Gilgoff, Dan. 2007. *The Jesus Machine: How James Doloson, Focus on the Family, and Evangelical America Are Winning the Culture War.* New York: St. Martin's Press.

Glock, Charles Y., and Rodney Stark. 1965. *Religion and Society in Tension.* Chicago: Rand McNally.

Goen, C.C. 1985. *Broken Churches, Broken Nation: Denominational Schisms and the Coming of the American Civil War.* Macon, GA: Mercer University Press.

Goetz, Stephan J., and Hema Swaminathan. 2006 "Wal-Mart and County-Wide Poverty." *Social Science Quarterly* 87:211–27.

Goffman, Erving. 1959. *The Presentation of Self in Everyday Life.* New York: Doubleday.

———. 1967. *Interaction Ritual: Essays on Face-to-Face Behavior.* New York: Doubleday.

Golden, Daniel. 2006. "In Religious Studies, Universities Bend to Views of the Faithful." *Wall Street Journal.* April 6.

Goldstein, Amy. 1997. "Part of, but Apart from, It All." *Washington Post.* January 20.

Goodstein, Laurie, and David D. Kirkpatrick. 2005. "On a Christian Mission to the Top." *New York Times.* May 22.

Gouldner, Alvin G. 1957. "Cosmopolitans and Locals: Toward an Analysis of Latent Social Roles." *Administrative Science Quarterly* 2:281–306.

Gramsci, Antonio. [1947] 1994. *Letters from Prison.* Ed. Frank Rosengarten. Trans. Ray Rosenthal. New York: Columbia University Press.

Greeley, Andrew, 1972. *The Denominational Society.* Glenview, IL: Scott Foresman.

———. 1977. *The American Catholic.* New York: Basic Books.

———. 1989. "Is There an American Catholic Elite?" *America.* May 6.

———. 1990. *The Catholic Myth.* New York: Scribner.

———. 2000. *The Catholic Imagination.* Berkeley: University of California Press.

Greeley, Andrew, and Michael Hout. 2006. *The Facts About Conservative Christians.* Chicago: University of Chicago Press.

Green, Garrett. 1989. *Imagining God: Theology and the Religious Imagination.* San Francisco: Harper & Row.

Green, John C. 2005. "Religion Gap Swings New Ways." *Religion in the News* 7, no. 3:2–3.

Green, John C., James L. Guth, Corwin E. Smidt, and Lyman A. Kellstedt. 1996. *Religion and the Culture Wars: Dispatches from the Front.* Lanham, MD: Rowman & Littlefield.

Griffith, R. Marie. 1997. *God's Daughters: Evangelical Women and the Power of Submission.* Berkeley: University of California Press.

———. 2004. *Born Again Bodies: Flesh and Spirit in American Christianity.* Berkeley: University of California Press.

Griswold, Wendy. 1983. "The Devil's Techniques: Cultural Legitimation and Social Change." *American Sociological Review* 48, no. 5:668–80.

Gross, Niel, and Solon J. Simmons. 2006. "How Religious Are America's College and University Professors." In *The Post Secular University,* ed. Douglas Jacobsen. New York: Oxford University Press.

Gunther, Marc. 2001. "God and Business: The Surprising Quest for Spiritual Renewal in the Workplace." *Fortune.* July 9.

Guth, James L., and Lyman A. Kellstedt. 1999. "Religion on Capitol Hill: The Case of the House of Representatives in the 105th Congress." Presented at the Annual Meeting of the Society for the Scientific Study of Religion, Boston, November 5–7.

Hackett, Conrad, and D. Michael Lindsay. 2004. "Measuring Evangelicalism: Consequences of Different Operationalization Strategies." Presented at the Annual Meeting of the Society for the Scientific Study of Religion, Kansas City, MO, October 21–24.

Hall, David. 1997. *Lived Religion in America.* Princeton: Princeton University Press.

Hallow, Ralph Z. 2005. "Carter Condemns Abortion Culture." *Washington Times.* November 4.

Hambrick-Stowe, Charles E. 2000. " 'Sanctified Business': Historical Perspectives on Financing Revivals of Religion." In *More Money, More Ministry: Money and Evangelicals in Recent North American History,* ed. Larry Eskridge and Mark A. Noll, 2000. Grand Rapids, MI: Eerdmans.

Hangen, Tona J. 2002. *Redeeming the Dial: Radio, Religion, and Popular Culture in America.* Chapel Hill: University of North Carolina Press.

Hannan, Michael T., and John Freeman. 1989. *Organizational Ecology.* Cambridge: Harvard University Press.

Harding, Susan Friend. 2001. *The Book of Jerry Falwell: Fundamentalist Language and Politics.* Princeton: Princeton University Press.

Harper, William Rainey. 1905. "The University and Democracy." In *The Trend in Higher Education.* Chicago: University of Chicago Press.

Harrison, Lawrence E. 2006. *The Central Liberal Truth: How Politics Can Change a Culture and Save It from Itself.* New York: Oxford University Press.

Hart, D. G. 2004. *Deconstructing Evangelicalism: Conservative Protestantism in the Age of Billy Graham.* Grand Rapids, MI: Baker Book House.

Hart, Janet. 1992. "Cracking the Code: Narrative and Political Mobilization in the Greek Resistance." *Social Science History* 16, no. 4:631–68.

Hatch, Mary Jo. 1993. "The Dynamics of Organizational Culture." *Academy of Management Review* 18:657–93.

Heilman, Samuel C., and Steven M. Cohen. 1989. *Cosmopolitans and Parochials: Modern Orthodox Jews in America.* Chicago: University of Chicago Press.

Hendershot, Heather. 2004. *Shaking the World for Jesus: Media and Conservative Evangelical Culture.* Chicago: University of Chicago Press.

Hendricks, John Stephen. 1977. "Religious and Political Fundamentalism: The Links between Alienation and Ideology." Ph.D. dissertation, University of Michigan.

Henry, Carl F. H., 1947. *The Uneasy Conscience of Modern Fundamentalism.* Grand Rapids, MI: Eerdmans.

———. 1957. *Evangelical Responsibility in Contemporary Theology.* Grand Rapids, MI: Eerdmans.

Herrenkohl, Ellen C. 1978. "Parallels in the Process of Achieving Personal Growth by Abusing Parents through Participation in Group Therapy Programs in Religious Groups." *Family Coordinator* 27:279–82.

Hertzke, Allen D. 2004. *Freeing God's Children: The Unlikely Alliance for Global Human Rights.* Lanham, MD: Rowman & Littlefield.

Hewitt, John P. 1989. *Dilemmas of the American Self.* Philadelphia: Temple University Press.

Hicks, Douglas A. 2003. *Religion and the Workplace: Pluralism, Spirituality, Leadership.* New York: Cambridge University Press.

Himmelstein, Jerome L. 1997. *Looking Good and Doing Good: Corporate Philanthropy and Corporate Power.* Bloomington: Indiana University Press.

Hodgkinson, Virginia A. 1990. *Giving and Volunteering in the United States.* Washington: Independent Sector.

Hoffer, Eric. [1951] 2002. *The True Believer: Thoughts on the Nature of Mass Movements.* New York: Harper Perennial Modern Classics.

Hofstadter, Richard. 1963. *Anti-Intellectualism in America.* New York: Knopf.

Holifield, E. Brooks. 1976. "The Three Strands of Jimmy Carter's Religion." *New Republic.* June 5.

Hollinger, David. 2002. "Enough Already: Universities Do Not Need More Christianity." In *Religion, Scholarship, and Higher Education: Perspectives, Models, and Future Prospects,* ed. Andrea Sterk. Notre Dame: University of Notre Dame Press.

Hoover, Stewart M. 1988. *Mass Media Religion: The Social Sources of the Electronic Church.* Newbury Park, CA: Sage.

———. 2006. *Religion in the Media Age.* New York: Routledge.

Hoover, Stewart M., and Lynn Schofield Clark. 2002. *Practicing Religion in the Age of the Media: Explorations in Media, Religion, and Culture.* New York: Columbia University Press.

Houpt, Simon. 2005. "Offspring of Mel Gibson's *Passion.*" *Globe and Mail.* September 8.

Hout, Michael, Andrew Greeley, and Melissa J. Wilde. 2001. "The Demographic Imperative in Religious Change in the United States." *American Journal of Sociology* 107:468–500.

Howard, Victor B. 1996. *The Evangelical War against Slavery and Caste: The Life and Times of John G. Fee.* Selinsgrove, PA: Susquehanna University Press.

Hughes, Richard T., and William B. Adrian. 1997. *Models for Christian Higher Education.* Grand Rapids, MI: Eerdmans.

Hunt, Terence, 1997. "Inaugural II Marks Renewal of Democracy." Associated Press news release. January 20.

Hunter, Floyd. 1953. *Community Power Structure: A Study of Decision Makers.* Chapel Hill: University of North Carolina Press.

Hunter, James Davison. 1983. *American Evangelicalism: Conservative Religion and the Quandary of Moderntiy.* New Brunswick: Rutgers University Press.

———. 1987. *Evangelicalism: The Coming Generation.* Chicago: University of Chicago Press.

———. 1991. *Culture Wars: The Struggle to Define America.* New York: Basic Books.

———. 2000. *The Death of Character: Moral Education in an Age Without Good or Evil.* New York: Basic Books.

Hunter, James Davison, and Joshua Yates. 2002. "In the Vanguard of Globalization: The World of the American Globalizers." In *Many Globalizations: Cultural Diversity in the Contemporary World,* ed. Peter L. Berger and Samuel P. Huntington. Oxford: Oxford University Press.

Huntington, Samuel P. 2000. "Cultures Count." In *Culture Matters: How Values Shape Human Progress,* ed. Lawrence E. Harrison and Samuel P. Huntington. New York: Basic Books.

Hurlbert, Jeanne S., and Rachel A. Rosenfeld. 1992. "Getting a Good Job: Rank and Institutional Prestige in Academic Psychologists' Careers." *Sociology of Education* 65:188–207.

Hutchison, William R., ed. 1989. *Between the Times: The Travail of the Protestant Establishment in America, 1900–1960.* New York: Cambridge University Press.

Jackall, Robert. 1988. *Moral Mazes: The World of Corporate Managers.* New York: Oxford University Press.

Jacobs, Ronald N. 1996. "Civil Society and Crisis: Culture, Discourse, and the Rodney King Beating." *American Journal of Sociology* 101:1238–72.

Joseph, Mark, 2002. "Is There Really a Christian Music Boom?" *Christianity Today* online. February 1.

Kadushin, Charles. 1995. "Friendship Among the French Financial Elite." *American Sociological Review* 60:202–21.

Kanter, Rosabeth Moss. 1977. *Men and Women of the Corporation.* New York: Basic Books.

Kaplan, Esther. 2004. *With God on Their Side.* New York: New Press.

Karabel, Jerome. 2005. *The Chosen: The Hidden History of Admission and Exclusion at Harvard, Yale, and Princeton.* Boston: Houghton Mifflin.

Kazin, Michael. 1995. *The Populist Persuasion: An American History.* New York: Basic Books.

Keller, Suzanne. 1963. *Beyond the Ruling Class: Strategic Elites in Modern Society*. New York: Random House.

Kellstedt, Lyman A., John C. Green, James L. Guth, and Corwin E. Smidt. 1994. "Religious Voting Blocs in the 1992 Election: The Year of the Evangelical?" *Sociology of Religion* 55, no. 3:307–26.

———. 1996. "Grasping the Essentials: The Social Embodiment of Religion and Social Behavior." In *Religion and the Culture Wars: Dispatches from the Front*, ed. John C. Green, James L. Guth, Corwin E. Smidt, and Lyman A. Kellstedt. Lanham, MD: Rowman & Littlefield.

Kengor, Paul. 2004. "Talking About God: Clinton vs. Bush." Posted on www.newsmax .com. September 4.

Kerbo, Harold R. 1993. "Upper Class Power." In *Power in Modern Societies*, ed. Marvin E. Olsen and Martin N. Marger. Boulder, CO: Westview Press.

Kilman, Ralph H., Mary J. Saxton, and Roy Sherpa, eds. 1985. *Gaining Control of the Corporate Culture*. San Francisco: Jossey-Bass.

Kim, Rebecca Y. 2004. "Second-Generation Korean American Evangelicals: Ethnic, Multiethnic, or White Campus Ministries?" *Sociology of Religion* 65:19–34.

Kirkley, Evelyn A. 1990. " 'This Work Is God's Cause': Religion in the Southern Woman Suffrage Movement, 1880–1920." *Church History* 59:507–22.

Kirp, David L. 2003. *Shakespeare, Einstein, and the Bottom Line: The Marketing of Higher Education*. Cambridge: Harvard University Press.

Kotter, John. 1983. *The General Managers*. New York: Free Press.

Kotter, John P., and James L. Heskett. 1992. *Corporate Culture and Performance*. New York: Free Press.

Krattenmaker, Tom. 2006. "Reggie's (Whole) Story." *USA Today*. July 30.

Kraybill, Donald B. 1989. *The Riddle of Amish Culture*. Baltimore: Johns Hopkins University Press.

Kroll, Janet L., and Rebecca A. Cornejo. 2003. "Onward Christian Soldiers." *In Trust*. May.

Krout, John Allen. 1925. *The Origins of Prohibition*. New York: Knopf.

Kunda, Gideon. 1992. *Engineering Culture: Control and Commitment in a High-Tech Corporation*. Philadelphia: Temple University Press.

Kuo, David. 2006. *Tempting Faith: An Inside Story of Political Seduction*. New York: Free Press.

Lamont, Michele. 1987. "How to Become a Dominant French Philosopher: The Case of Jacques Derrida." *American Journal of Sociology* 93:584–622.

———. 1992. *Money, Morals, and Manners: The Culture of the French and the American Upper-Middle Class*. Chicago: University of Chicago Press.

Lamont, Michele, and Virag Molnar. 2002. "The Study of Boundaries in the Social Sciences." *Annual Review of Sociology* 28:167–95.

Latour, Bruno. 1988. *The Pasteurization of France*. Cambridge: Harvard University Press.

Lawson, Guy. 2003. "George W. Bush's Personal Jesus." *Gentlemen's Quarterly*. September.

Layman, Geoffrey. 2001. *The Great Divide : Religious and Cultural Conflict in American Party Politics*. New York: Columbia University Press.

Lemann, Nicholas. 1999. *The Big Test: The Secret History of the American Meritocracy*. New York: Farrar Straus Giroux.

Lerner, Robert, Althea K. Nagai, and Stanley Rothman. 1996. *American Elites*. New Haven: Yale University Press.

Lewerenz, Spencer, and Barbara Nicolosi, eds. 2005. *Behind the Screen: Hollywood Insiders on Faith, Film, and Culture*. Grand Rapids, MI: Baker Books.

Lewis, C. S. 1960. *Mere Christianity*. New York: Macmillan.

Lichter, S. Robert, Linda S. Lichter, and Stanley Rothman. 1991. *Watching America*. New York: Prentice Hall.

Lienesch, Michael. 1982. "Right-Wing Religion: Christian Conservatism as a Political Movement." *Political Science Quarterly* 97:403–25.

Lindner, Eileen W. 1996. "Ecumenical and Interdenominational: Private and Public Approaches to Family Issues." in *Faith Traditions and the Family*. Ed. Phyllis D. Airhart and Margaret Lamberts Bendroth. Louisville, KY: Westminster John Knox Press.

Lindsay, D. Michael. 2005. "Liminality: A New Form of Organizational Differentiation." Paper presented at Northwestern University Culture and Society Workshop, May 5.

————. 2006. "Is the National Prayer Breakfast Surrounded by a 'Christian Mafia'? Religious Publicity and Secrecy Within the Corridors of Power." *Journal of the American Academy of Religion* 74, no. 2:390–419.

Lindsell, Harold. 1949. *An Evangelical Theology of Missions*. Grand Rapids, MI: Zondervan.

Linker, Damon. 2006. *The Theocons: Secular American Under Siege*. New York: Doubleday.

Lokkesmoe, Eric. 2006. "10 Mistakes Conservatives Make in Art and Entertainment." Books & Entertainment column, www.townhall.com. February 7.

Long, J. Scott, Paul D. Allison, and Robert McGinnis. 1979. "Entrance into the Academic Career." *American Sociological Review* 44:816–30.

Luker, Kristin. 1984. *Abortion and the Politics of Motherhood*. Berkeley: University of California Press.

Lukes, Steven. 2005. *Power: A Radical View*. 2nd ed. New York: Palgrave.

Luther, Martin. [1519] 1915. "Treatise on Good Works." In *Works of Martin Luther*, vol. 1. Trans. C. M. Jacobs. Philadelphia: A. J. Holman. Volume I.

Machen, J. Gresham. 1999 [1923]. *Christianity and Liberalism*. Grand Rapids, MI: Eerdmans.

MacIntyre, Alasdair C. 1988. *Whose Justice? Which Rationality?* Notre Dame: University of Notre Dame Press.

————. 1990. *First Principle, Final Ends, and Contemporary Philosophical Issues*. Milwaukee: Marquette University Press.

Mannheim, Karl. 1940. *Man and Society in an Age of Reconstruction: Studies in Modern Social Structure*. New York: Harcourt, Brace & World.

Manza, Jeff, and Clem Brooks. 1997. "The Religious Factor in US Presidential Elections, 1960–1992." *American Journal of Sociology* 103:38–81.

Marsden, George. 1991. *Fundamentalism and Evangelicalism*. Grand Rapids, MI: Eerdmans.

————. 1993. "The Ambiguities of Academic Freedom." *Church History* 62, no. 2:221–36.

————. 1994. *The Soul of the American University: From Protestant Establishment to Established Nonbelief*. New York: Oxford University Press.

————. 2006. *Fundamentalism and American Culture*. 2nd ed. New York: Oxford University Press.

Martin, David. 1990. *Tongues of Fire: The Explosion of Protestantism in Latin America*. Oxford: Blackwell.

Martin, Janet M. 1989. "The Recruitment of Women to Cabinet and Subcabinet Posts." *Western Political Quarterly* 42, no. 1:161–72.

Martin, William C. 1996. *With God on Our Side: The Rise of the Religious Right in America*. New York: Broadway Books.

Marx, Karl. [1845] 1978. "The German Ideology." In *The Marx-Engels Reader*, ed. Robert C. Tucker. 2nd ed. New York: Norton.

Massengill, Rebekah Peeples. 2006. "The Unevenness of Modernity: Educational Attainment and Cohort Change Among Conservative Protestants." Presented at the Center for the Study of Religion, Princeton University, March 15.

Mattingly, Terry. 2005. *Pop Goes Religion: Faith in Popular Culture*. Gen. ed. Mark Joseph. Nashville, TN: W Pub. Group.

————. 2006. "The Media, God, and Gaffes." *USA Today* editorial. June 25.

Mauss, Armand L. 1994. *The Angel and the Beehive: The Mormon Struggle with Assimilation*. Chicago: University of Illinois Press.

Mayo, Anthony J., Nitin Nohria, and Laura G. Singleton. 2006. *Paths to Power: How Insiders and Outsiders Shaped American Business Leadership*. Boston: Harvard Business School Press.

McConnell, Michael W. 1990. "Academic Freedom in Religious Colleges and Universities." *Law and Contemporary Problems* 53:308–10.

McDowell, Josh. 1979. *Evidence That Demands a Verdict: Historical Evidences for the Christian Faith*. Nashville, TN: Thomas Nelson.

McDowell, Wendy. 2001. "Baylor University Delegation Pays a Visit." *News and Events*. Harvard Divinity School. April.

McGarvey, Ayelish. 2004. "Reaching to the Choir." *American Prospect*. April.

McGrath, Alister E. 1994. "Do We Still Need the Reformation?" *Christianity Today*. December 12.

McKivigan, John R. 1984. *The War Against Proslavery Religion: Abolitionism and the Northern Churches, 1830–1865*. Ithaca: Cornell University Press.

Meacham, Jon. 2006. *American Gospel: God, the Founding Fathers, and the Making of a Nation.* New York: Random House.

Medved, Michael. 1993. *Hollywood v. America.* New York: HarperCollins.

Merton, Robert K. 1957. *Social Theory and Social Structure.* Glencoe, IL: Free Press.

Merton, Robert King, with Marjorie Fiske and Alberta Curtis. 1946. *Mass Persuasion: The Social Psychology of a War Bond Drive.* New York: Harper.

Meyer, John W., and Brian Rowan. 1977. "Institutional Organizations: Formal Structure as Myth and Ceremony." *American Journal of Sociology* 83:929–84.

Meyer, Marshall W. 1979. "Organizational Structure as Signaling." *Pacific Sociological Review* 22, no. 4:481–500.

Miles, Margaret R. 1985. *Image as Insight: Visual Understanding in Western Christianity and Secular Culture.* Boston: Beacon Press.

Miles, Robert H. 1987. *Managing the Corporate Social Environment: A Grounded Theory.* Englewood Cliffs, NJ: Prentice Hall.

Miller, David. 2006. *God at Work.* New York: Oxford University Press.

Miller, S. M., and Frank Riessman. 1961. "The Working Class Subculture: A New View." *Social Problems* 9:86–97.

Mills, C. Wright. 1956. *The Power Elite.* New York: Oxford University Press.

Mintzberg, Henry. 1973. *The Nature of Managerial Work.* New York: Harper & Row.

Mitroff, Ian, and Elizabeth Denton. 1999. *A Spiritual Audit of Corporate America: A Hard Look at Spirituality, Religion, and Values in the Workplace.* San Francisco: Jossey-Bass.

Moberg, David O. 1977. *The Great Reversal.* Philadelphia: Lippincott.

Mohler, R. Albert, Jr. 2003. "Standing Together, Standing Apart: Cultural Co-belligerence Without Theological Compromise." *Touchstone.* July/August.

Mohr, John W. 1994. "Soldiers, Mothers, Tramps and Others: Discourse Roles in the 1907 Charity Directory." *Poetics* 22:327–58.

Moore, Gwen. 1988. "Women in Elite Positions: Insiders or Outsiders?" *Sociological Forum* 3, no. 4:566–85.

Moore, R. Laurence. 1986. *Religious Outsiders and the Making of Americans.* New York: Oxford University Press.

Morrill, Calvin. 1995. *The Executive Way: Conflict Management in Corporations.* Chicago: University of Chicago Press.

Mosca, Gaetano. [1896] 1939. *The Ruling Class.* Trans. Hannah D. Kahn. New York: McGraw-Hill.

Murphy, Richard McGill. 2006. "Jesus Inc.: What Does It Take to Serve God and Mammon?" *Fortune Small Business.* February 1.

Nash, Laura L. 1994. *Believers in Business.* Nashville, TN: Thomas Nelson.

Nash, Laura, and Scotty McLennan. 2001. *Church on Sunday, Work on Monday: The Challenge of Fusing Christian Values with Business Life.* San Francisco: Jossey-Bass.

Nash, Laura, and Howard Stevenson. 2004. *Just Enough: Tools for Creating Success in Your Work and Life.* New York: Wiley.

Nettl, J. P. 1967. *Political Mobilization: A Sociological Analysis of Methods and Concepts.* New York: Basic Books.

Neufeld, Kathryn. 1979. "Child-rearing, Religion, and Abusive Parents." *Religious Education* 74:234–44.

Newcomb, Horace, and Robert E. Alley. 1983. *The Producer's Medium: Conversations with Creators of American TV.* New York: Oxford University Press.

Niebuhr, H. Richard. 1929. *The Social Sources of Denominationalism.* New York: Henry Holt.

Noll, Mark A. 1983. *The Princeton Theology, 1812–1921: Scripture, Science, Theological Method from Archibald Alexander to Benjamin Breckinridge Warfield.* Grand Rapids, MI: Baker Book House.

———. 1994. *The Scandal of the Evangelical Mind.* Grand Rapids, MI: Eerdmans.

———. 2001. *American Evangelical Christianity: An Introduction.* Oxford; Malden, MA.: Blackwell.

———. 2004. "The Evangelical Mind Today." *First Things* 146. October.

Noll, Mark, and Carolyn Nystrom. 2005. *Is the Reformation Over?* Grand Rapids, MI: Baker Books.

Novak, Michael. 1996. *Business as a Calling.* New York: Free Press.

O'Connor, Alice. 2001. *Poverty Knowledge: Social Science, Social Policy, and the Poor in Twentieth-Century U.S. History.* Princeton: Princeton University Press.

O'Dea, Thomas F. 1958. *American Catholic Dilemma.* New York: Sheed & Ward.

Odendahl, Teresa. 1990. *Charity Begins at Home: Generosity and Self-Interest Among the Philanthropic Elite*. New York: Basic Books.

Olasky, Marvin. 2006. "Tighter Lips? Raining on Spear's Parade." *World*. February 18.

Oldfield, Duane. 1996. *The Right and the Righteous: The Christian Right Confronts the Republican Party*. Lanham, MD: Rowman & Littlefield.

Ostrower, Francie. 1995. *Why the Wealthy Give: The Culture of Elite Philanthropy*. Princeton: Princeton University Press.

Ouchi, William G., and Alan L. Wilkins. 1985. "Organizational Culture." *Annual Review of Sociology* 11:457–83.

Padgett, John F., and Christopher K. Ansell. 1993. "Robust Action and the Rise of the Medici, 1400–1434." *American Journal of Sociology* 98:1259–319.

Pareto, Vilfredo. [1901] 1968. *The Rise and Fall of Elites*. New York: Bedminster Press.

Parsons, Talcott. 1963. "On the Concept of Political Power." *Proceedings of the American Philosophical Society* 107:232–62.

Patillo-McCoy, Mary, 1998. "Church Culture as a Strategy of Action in the Black Community." *American Sociological Review* 63:767–84.

Patrick, James. 1973. *A Glasgow Gang Observed*. London: Methuen.

Peek, Charles W., George D. Lowe, and L. Susan Williams, 1991. "Gender and God's Word: Another Look at Religious Fundamentalism and Sexism." *Social Forces* 69, no. 4:1205–21.

Perkins, John, and Thomas Tarrants III. 1994. *He's My Brother: Former Racial Foes Offer Strategy for Reconciliation*. Grand Rapids, MI: Chosen Books.

Peshkin, Alan. 1986. *God's Choice: The Total World of a Fundamentalist Christian School*. Chicago: University of Chicago Press.

Peterson, Richard A. 1979. "Revitalizing the Culture Concept." *Annual Review of Sociology* 5:137–66.

Pfeffer, Jeffrey. 1981. "Management as Symbolic Action: The Creation and Maintenance of Organizational Paradigms." In *Research in Organizational Behavior*, vol. 3, ed. L. Cummings and B. Staw. Greenwich, CT: JAI Press.

Phillips, Kevin. 2006. *American Theocracy: The Perils and Politics of Radical Religion, Oil, and Borrowed Money in the 21st Century*. New York: Viking.

Poland, Larry W. 1988. *The Last Temptation of Hollywood*. Redlands, CA: MasterMedia.

Pollock, C. B., and B. F. Steele. 1968. "A Psychiatric Study of Parents Who Abuse Infants and Small Children." In *The Battered Child*, ed. C. Henry Kempe and Ray E. Helfer. Chicago: University of Chicago Press.

Powell, Mark Allan. 2002. *Encyclopedia of Contemporary Christian Music*. Peabody, MA: Hendrickson.

Powell, Walter W., and Paul J. DiMaggio, eds. 1991. *The New Institutionalism in Organizational Analysis*. Chicago: University of Chicago Press.

Putnam, Robert D. 1976. *The Comparative Study of Political Elites*. Englewood Cliffs, NJ: Prentice Hall.

Regnerus, Mark D, and Christian Smith. 1998. "Selective Deprivatization Among American Religious Traditions: The Reversal of the Great Reversal." *Social Forces* 76:1347–72.

Regnerus, Mark, David Sikkink, and Christian Smith, 1999. "Voting with the Christian Right: Contextual and Individual Patterns of Electoral Influence." *Social Forces* 77:1375–401.

Reich, Robert. 2004. "The Last Word." *American Prospect*. July.

Ribuffo, Leo P. 1980. "Liberals and That Old-Time Religion." *Nation*. November 29.

Rigney, Daniel, and Thomas J. Hoffman. 1993. "Is American Catholicism Anti-Intellectual?" *Journal for the Scientific Study of Religion* 32:211–22.

Riley, Naomi Schaefer. 2005. *God on the Quad: How Religious Colleges and the Missionary Generation Are Changing America*. New York: St. Martin's Press.

Robert, Dana L. 1996. *American Women in Mission: A Social History of Their Thought and Practice*. Macon, GA: Mercer University Press.

Roberts, Cokie, and Steven V. Roberts. 1998. "Southern Baptists Have a Distorted View of the Family." *Denver Rocky Mountain News*. June 21.

Roberts, Jon, and James Turner. 2000. *The Sacred and Secular University*. Princeton: Princeton University Press.

Roof, Wade Clark. 1978. *Community and Commitment: Religious Plausibility in a Liberal Protestant Church*. New York: Elsevier.

———. 1999. *Spiritual Marketplace: Baby Boomers and the Remaking of American Religion.* Princeton: Princeton University Press.

Rosin, Hanna. 2005a. "Right with God: Evangelical Conservatives Find a Spiritual Home on the Hill." *Washington Post.* March 6.

———. 2005b. "God and Country: A College That Trains Young Christians to Be Politicians." *New Yorker.* June 27.

———. 2005c. "Can Jesus Save Hollywood?" *Atlantic Monthly.* December.

Rost, Joseph. 1991. *Leadership for the Twenty-First Century.* Westport, CT: Praeger.

Rozell, Mark, and Clyde Wilcox. 1995. *God at the Grassroots.* Lanham, MD: Rowman & Littlefield.

Scanzoni, Letha Dawson. 1988. "Contemporary Challenges for Religion and Family from a Protestant Woman's Point of View." In *The Religion and Family Connection: Social Sciences Perspectives,* ed. Darwin L. Thomas. Provo: Brigham Young University Press.

Schaeffer, Francis. 1976. *How Should We Then Live? The Rise and Decline of Western Thought and Culture.* Westwood, NJ: F. H. Revell.

———. 1982. *The Complete Works of Francis A. Schaeffer: A Christian Worldview.* Westchester, IL: Crossways Books.

Schein, Edgar. 1983. "The Role of the Founder in Creating Organizational Culture." *Organizational Dynamics* 23:13–28.

———. 1984. "Coming to a New Awareness of Organizational Culture." *Sloan Management Review* 25:3–16.

———. 1985. *Organizational Culture and Leadership.* San Francisco: Jossey-Bass.

Schlosser, Eric. 2004. "Tyson's Moral Anchor." *Nation.* July 12.

Schmalzbauer, John. 1993. "Evangelicals in the New Class: Class Versus Subcultural Predictors of Ideology." *Journal for the Scientific Study of Religion* 32:330–42.

———. 2003. *People of Faith: Religious Conviction in American Journalism and Higher Education.* Ithaca: Cornell University Press.

———. 2005. "Religion and Knowledge in the Post-Secular Academy." Presented at the Annual Meeting of the Association for the Sociology of Religion, Philadelphia, August 14.

Schmalzbauer, John, and Kathleen Mahoney. *The Post-Secular Academy: The Return of Religion in American Higher Education.* Unpublished manuscript.

Schor, Juliet B. 1991. *The Overworked American: The Unexpected Decline of Leisure.* New York: Basic Books.

Seay, Chris, and Chris Bryan. 2002. *The Tao of Enron: Spiritual Lessons from a Fortune 500 Fallout.* Colorado Springs, CO: NavPress.

Shea, William M. 2004. *The Lion and the Lamb: Evangelicals and Catholics in America.* New York: Oxford University Press.

Shibley, Mark A. 1991. "The Southernization of American Religion: Testing a Hypothesis." *Sociological Analysis* 52:159–74.

———. 1996. *Resurgent Evangelicalism in the United States: Mapping Cultural Change Since 1970.* Columbia: University of South Carolina Press.

Shogan, Colleen J. 2006. *The Moral Rhetoric of American Presidents.* College Station: Texas A&M University Press.

Shorto, Russell. 2004. "With God at Our Desks." *New York Times Magazine.* October 31.

Sider, Ronald J. and Diane Knippers, eds. 2005. *Toward an Evangelical Public Policy : Political Strategies for the Health of the Nation.* Grand Rapids, MI: Baker Books.

Sikkink, David. 1999. "The Social Sources of Alienation from Public Schools." *Social Forces* 78:51–86.

Silk, Mark. 2005. "Our New Religious Politics." *Religion in the News* 7. Winter.

Sloan, Douglas. 1994. *Faith and Knowledge: Mainline Protestantism and American Higher Education.* Louisville, KY: Westminster John Knox Press.

Smith, Christian. 2000. *Christian America? What Evangelicals Really Want.* Berkeley: University of California Press.

———. 2004. "Religiously Ignorant Journalists." *Books & Culture.* January/February.

Smith, Christian, with Melinda Lundquist Denton. 2005. *Soul Searching: The Religious and Spiritual Lives of American Teenagers.* New York: Oxford University Press.

Smith, Christian, with Michael Emerson, Sally Gallagher, Paul Kennedy, and David Sikkink. 1998. *American Evangelicalism: Embattled and Thriving.* Chicago: University of Chicago Press.

Smith, Christian, and David Sikkink. 2000. "Evangelicals on Education." In *Christian America? What Evangelicals Really Want.* Berkeley: University of California Press.

———. 2003. "Social Predictors of Retention in and Switching from the Religious Faith of Family of Origin: Another Look Using Religious Tradition Self-Identification." *Review of Religious Research* 45:188–206.

Smith, Christian, David Sikkink, and Jason Bailey. 1998. "Devotion in Dixie and Beyond: A Test of the 'Shibley Thesis' on the Effects of Regional Origin and Migration on Individual Religiosity." *Journal for the Scientific Study of Religion* 37:494–506.

Smith, Craig. 1994. "The New Corporate Philanthropy." *Harvard Business Review* 72, no. 3:105–16.

Smith, Gary Scott. 2006. *Faith and the Presidency.* New York: Oxford University Press.

Smith, Robert C. 1981. "The Black Congressional Delegation." *Western Political Quarterly* 34, no. 2:203–21.

Smith, Sean. 2004. "You Want Me to Play Jesus?" *Newsweek.* February 16.

Smith, Selwyn M., Ruth Hanson, and Sheila Noble. 1974. "Social Aspects of the Battered Baby Syndrome." *British Journal of Psychiatry* 125:568–82.

Smith, Tom W., 1987. "Classifying Protestant Denominations." GSS Methodological Report 43.

Sommerville, C. John. 2006. *The Decline of the Secular University.* New York: Oxford University Press.

Sorenson, Jesper B. 2002. "The Strength of Corporate Culture and the Reliability of Firm Performance." *Administrative Science Quarterly* 47:70–91.

Spickard, Paul R., and Kevin M. Cragg. 1994. *God's Peoples: A Social History of Christians.* Grand Rapids, MI: Baker Books.

Sproul, R. C. 1995. *Faith Alone: The Evangelical Doctrine of Justification.* Grand Rapids, MI: Baker Books.

Steensland, Brian, Jerry Z. Park, Mark D. Regnerus, Lynn D. Robinson, W. Bradford Wilcox, and Robert D. Woodberry. 2000. "The Measure of American Religion: Toward Improving the State of the Art." *Social Forces* 79:291–318.

Stout, Jeffrey. 1988. *Ethics After Babel.* Boston: Beacon Press.

Strauss, Murray, R. J. Gelles, and Susan K. Steinmetz. 1980. *Behind Closed Doors: Violence in the American Family.* New York: Anchor Books.

Stuntz, William J. 2004. "Faculty Clubs and Church Pews." *Tech Central Station.* November 29.

Sullivan, Amy. 2004. "Why W. Doesn't Go to Church: Empty Pew." *National Review Online.* October 11.

Swidey, Neil. 2003. "God on the Quad." *Boston Globe.* November 30.

Swidler, Ann. 2000. *Talk of Love: How Americans Use Their Culture.* Chicago: University of Chicago Press.

Tamney, Joseph B., and Stephen D. Johnson. 1997. "Christianity and Public Book Banning." *Review of Religious Research* Volume 38: 263–71.

Thalheimer, Fred. 1973. "Religiosity and Secularization in the Academic Professions." *Sociology of Education* 46:183–202.

Thrasher, Frederick. [1927] 1963. *The Gang.* Chicago: University of Chicago Press.

Thumma, Scott. 1991. "Negotiating a Religious Identity." *Sociological Analysis* 52: 333–47.

Tilly, Charles. 2004. *Social Movements, 1768–2004.* Boulder, CO: Paradigm.

Tocqueville, Alexis de. 1834 [2000]. *Democracy in America.* Trans. and annotated by Stephen D. Grant. Indianapolis: Hackett.

Trueblood, Elton. 1949. *The Common Ventures of Life: Marriage, Birth, Work, and Death.* New York: Harper & Brothers.

Turner, James. 1999. "Something to Be Reckoned With: The Evangelical Mind Reawakens." *Commonweal.* January 15.

Turner, Jonathan H. 1986. "The Mechanics of Social Interaction: Toward a Composite Model of Signaling and Interpreting." *Sociological Theory* 4, no. 1:95–105.

Useem, Michael. 1984. *The Inner Circle: Large Corporations and the Rise of Business Political Activity in the U.S. and the U.K.* New York: Oxford University Press.

Van Biema, David, Cathy Booth-Thomas, Massimo Calabresi, John F. Dickerson, John Cloud, Rebecca Winters, and Sonja Steptoe. 2005. "The 25 Most Influential Evangelicals in America." *Time.* February 7.

Vogel, David. 1996. *Kindred Strangers: The Uneasy Relationship Between Politics and Business in America.* Princeton: Princeton University Press.

Volf, Miroslav. 1991. *Work in the Spirit: Toward a Theology of Work.* Eugene, OR: Wipf and Stock.

———. 1994. "Soft Difference: Theological Reflections on the Relation Between Church and Culture in I Peter." *Ex Auditu* 10:15–30.

Wagner, Melinda Bollar. 1990. *God's Schools: Choice and Compromise in American Society.* New Brunswick: Rutgers University Press.

Wald, K. D., D. E. Owen, and S. S. Hill. 1989. "Evangelical Politics and Status Issues." *Journal for the Scientific Study of Religion* 28:1–16.

Washington, Raleigh, and Glen Kehrein. 1993. *Breaking Down Walls: A Model for Reconciliation in an Age of Racial Strife.* Chicago: Moody Press.

Watt, David Harrington. 1991. *A Transforming Faith: Explorations of Twentieth-Century American Evangelicalism.* New Brunswick: Rutgers University Press.

Webber, Robert E. 2002. *The Younger Evangelicals: Facing the Challenges of the New World.* Grand Rapids, MI: Baker Books.

Weber, Max. [1946] 1991. *Max Weber: Essays in Sociology.* Ed. Hans H. Gerth and C. Wright Mills. London: Routledge.

Weigel, Gustave. 1957. "American Catholic Intellectualism: A Theologian's Reflections." *Review of Politics* 19:275–307.

Weisskopf, Michael. 1993. "Energized by Pulpit or Passion, the Public Is Calling." *Washington Post.* February 1.

Wilcox, Clyde. 1996. *Onward Christian Soldiers: The Religious Right in American Politics.* Boulder, CO: Westview Press.

Wilcox, W. Bradford. 2004. *Soft Patriarchs, New Men: How Christianity Shapes Fathers and Husbands.* Chicago: University of Chicago Press.

Williams, Christine L. 1991. *Gender Differences at Work: Women and Men in Nontraditional Occupations.* Berkeley: University of California Press.

Willmer, Wesley K., and J. David Schmidt with Martyn Smith. 1998. *The Prospering Parachurch: Enlarging the Boundaries of God's Kingdom.* San Francisco: Jossey-Bass.

Wingren, Gustaf. 1957. *Luther on Vocation.* Trans. Carl C. Rasmussen. Philadelphia: Muhlenberg Press.

Wolfe, Alan. 1996. "Religion and American Higher Education: Rethinking a National Dilemma." *Current.* July.

———. 2000. "The Opening of the Evangelical Mind." *Atlantic Monthly.* October.

———. 2003. *The Transformation of American Religion: How We Actually Live Our Faith.* New York: Free Press.

Wood, James R., and James G. Houghland Jr. 1990. "The Role of Religion in Philanthropy." In *Critical Issues in American Philanthropy,* ed. John Van Til et al. San Francisco: Jossey-Bass.

Wood, Richard L. 1999. "Religious Culture and Political Action." *Sociological Theory* 17:307–32.

Woodard, Joe. 2005. "Solving the Secular Paradox: How Can Christianity Influence World Culture?" *Calgary Herald.* June 19.

Woodberry, Robert D., and Paul Brink. 1996. "Evangelicals and Politics: Surveying a Contemporary Mason-Dixon Line." Presented at Annual Meeting of American Sociological Association, New York City, August.

Woodberry, Robert D., and Christian S. Smith. 1998. "Fundamentalism et al.: Conservative Protestants in America." *Annual Review of Sociology* 24:25–56.

Woodward, Kenneth, with Elizabeth Bailey. 1984. "Who's a Good Christian?" *Newsweek.* August 6.

Wuthnow, Robert. 1987. *Meaning and Moral Order: Explorations in Cultural Analysis.* Berkeley: University of California Press.

———. 1988. *The Restructuring of American Religion.* Princeton: Princeton University Press.

———. 1989. *Communities of Discourse.* Cambridge: Harvard University Press.

———. 1993. *Acts of Compassion: Caring for Others and Helping Ourselves.* Princeton: Princeton University Press.

———. 1994. *God and Mammon in America.* New York: Macmillan.

———. 1995. *Christianity in the Twenty-First Century: Reflections on the Challenges Ahead.* New York: Oxford University Press.

———. 1996. *Poor Richard's Principle: Recovering the American Dream Through the Moral Dimensions of Work, Business, and Money.* Princeton: Princeton University Press.

———. 1998. *After Heaven: Spirituality in America Since the 1950s.* Berkeley: University of California Press.

———. 2001. *Creative Spirituality: The Way of the Artist.* Berkeley: University of California Press.

———. 2003. *All in Sync: How Music and Art Are Revitalizing American Religion.* Berkeley: University of California Press.

———. 2005. *America and the Challenges of Religious Diversity.* Princeton: Princeton University Press.

Wuthnow, Robert, and Virginia A. Hodgkinson, eds. 1990. *Faith and Philanthropy in America.* San Francisco: Jossey-Bass.

Wuthnow, Robert, and D. Michael Lindsay. 2006. "The Role of Foundations in American Religion." Working Paper, Center for the Study of Religion, Princeton University.

Wyatt-Brown, Bertram. 1969. *Lewis Tappan and the Evangelical War Against Slavery.* Cleveland: Press of Case Western University.

Yablonsky, Lewis. 1959. "The Delinquent Gang as a Near Group." *Social Problems* 7: 108–17.

Yancey, George. 1996. *Beyond Black and White: Reflections on Racial Reconciliation.* Grand Rapids, MI: Baker Books.

Young, Michael P. 2002. "Confessional Protest: The Religious Birth of U.S. National Social Movements." *American Sociological Review* 67:660–88.

Zald, Mayer N., and Patricia Denton. 1963. "From Evangelism to General Service: The Transformation of the YMCA." *Administrative Science Quarterly* 8:214–34.

Zerubavel, Eviatar. 1995. "The Rigid, the Fuzzy, and the Flexible: Notes on the Mental Sculpting of Academic Identity." *Social Research* 62:1093–107.

Zhou, Min, and James V. Gatewood. 2000. *Contemporary Asian America: A Multidisciplinary Reader.* New York: New York University Press.

Zweigenhaft, Richard L., and G. William Domhoff. 1982. *Jews in the Protestant Establishment.* New York: Praeger.

———. 2006. *Diversity in the Power Elite: How It Happened, Why It Matters.* Lanham, MD: Rowman & Littlefield.

INDEX